James Shannon

James Shannon

The Journey of an Irish family (AD812–1886)
from slavery and serfdom to socialism

Peter Ford Mason

James Shannon (Mason), master pit sinker (photograph c 1880)

First published in 2015 on behalf of the author by
Scotforth Books (www.scotforthbooks.com)

ISBN   978-1-909817-23-4

Typesetting and design by Carnegie Book Production, Lancaster.

Printed in the UK by Jellyfish Solutions

Dedicated to my wife Philomena
and to the Irish people who struggled so long to regain Independence

Contents

Acknowledgements   ix

Historical Maps and Shannon Family Trees   x

Introduction   1

1: 812–1815 Ireland Invasion, Plantation and Penal Slavery   3

2: 1815 Emigration to Scotland   42

3: 1815–1829 Scotland Combinations and Emancipation   58

4: 1830–1833 North East England – Cholera and Reform   84

5: 1834–1836 Pauperism, Poor Laws and Workhouses   107

6: 1837–1840 Chartism and Corn Laws   120

7: 1841–1844 Child Labour and The Great Strike   137

8: 1845–1848 Railway Mania and the Irish Famine   157

9: 1849–1853 The Great Exhibition after the Great Hunger   171

10: 1854–1859 Crimean War and Darwinism   189

11: 1860–1866 American Civil War, Fenians and Franchise   206

12: 1867–1873 New Reform and Trade Unions   220

13: 1874–1879 The Great Depression and Irish Land War   240

14: 1880–1886 Socialism, Irish Agitation and Home Rule   251

Conclusion: Starvation and Slavery to Social Justice   273

Appendix A Change from Shannon to Mason   286

Appendix B Connection between James Storey Reed, Mary Ann Hall
and James Mason   288

Bibliography   290

Index   297

Acknowledgements

Ancestry.co.uk
National Archives
National Museums Liverpool
The Kintyre Antiquarian and Natural History Society
British Library Newspapers
National Galleries
Enniskillen Library
Ewart Library Dumfries
Wirral Library Services
Scottish Record Office
Northumberland Record Office
Durham County Record Office
Beamish Museum, Co. Durham
Illustrated London News
Tyne & Wear Archives
South Tyneside Resource Centre
People's History Museum, Salford
National Mining Museum, Wakefield
Museum of Lead Mining, Wanlockhead
The Coalmining History Resources Centre
Arigna Mining Centre, Roscommon, Ireland
Institute of Mining and Mechanical Engineers, Newcastle
Tate Gallery Publications
Getty Images
Bridgeman Images

I wish to thank my family who through the years have helped me on this journey of discovery, with special thanks to my twin brother, Paul Ford Mason.

NORTH BRITAIN 812–1066

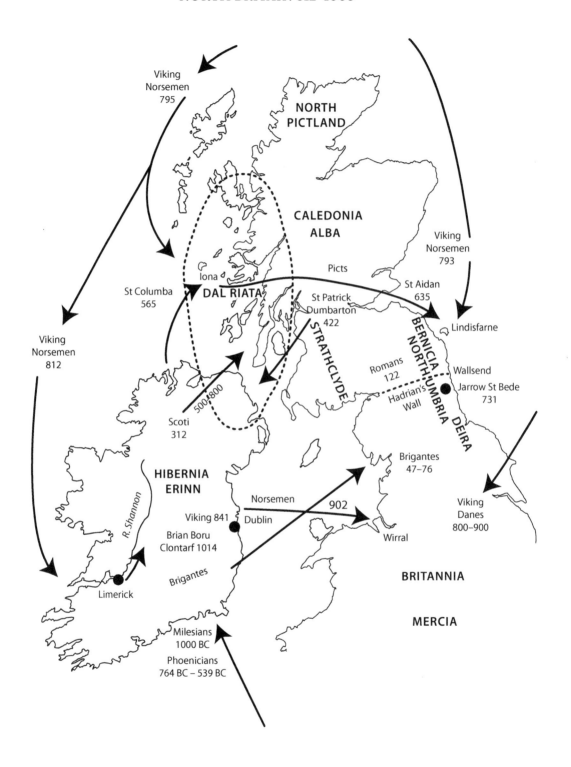

Viking
Norsemen
795

NORTH
PICTLAND

CALEDONIA
ALBA

Viking
Norsemen
793

Picts

Iona

St Columba
565

DAL RIATA

St Patrick
Dumbarton
422

St Aidan
635

Lindisfarne

STRATHCLYDE

BERNICIA
NORTHUMBRIA
DEIRA

Romans
122

Wallsend

Viking
Norsemen
812

500–800

Hadrian's
Wall

Jarrow St Bede
731

Scoti
312

Brigantes
47–76

HIBERNIA
ERINN

Viking
Danes
800–900

R. Shannon

Viking 841

Norsemen
Dublin

902

Brian Boru
Clontarf 1014

Wirral

Brigantes

BRITANNIA

Limerick

MERCIA

Milesians
1000 BC

Phoenicians
764 BC – 539 BC

NORTH BRITAIN 1066–1815

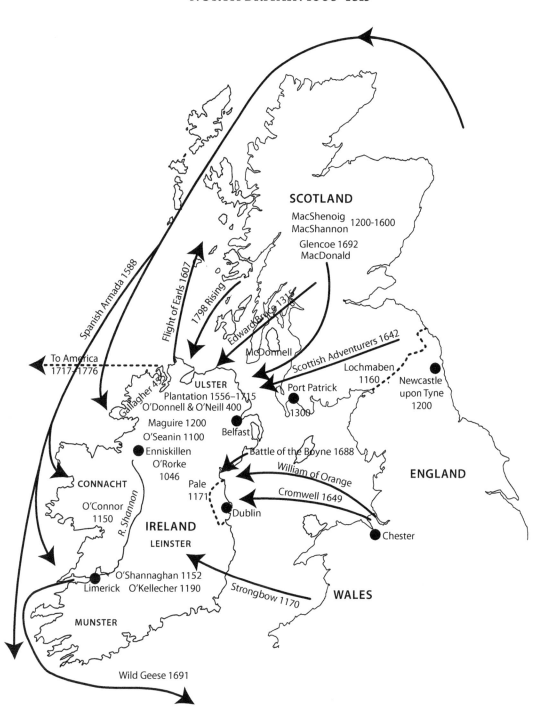

SCOTLAND

MacShenoig
MacShannon 1200-1600

Glencoe 1692
MacDonald

Spanish Armada 1588

Flight of Earls 1607

1798 Rising

Edward Bruce 1316

McDonnell

Scottish Adventurers 1642

Lochmaben
1160

Newcastle
upon Tyne
1200

To America
1717-1776

Gallagher 430

ULSTER
Plantation 1556–1715
O'Donnell & O'Neill 400

Port Patrick

1300

Maguire 1200
O'Seanin 1100

Belfast

Enniskillen
O'Rorke
1046

Battle of the Boyne 1688

William of Orange

ENGLAND

CONNACHT

O'Connor
1150

R. Shannon

Pale
1171

Dublin

Cromwell 1649

IRELAND

LEINSTER

O'Shannaghan 1152
Limerick O'Kellecher 1190

Strongbow 1170

WALES

Chester

MUNSTER

Wild Geese 1691

SHANNON JOURNEY 812–1829

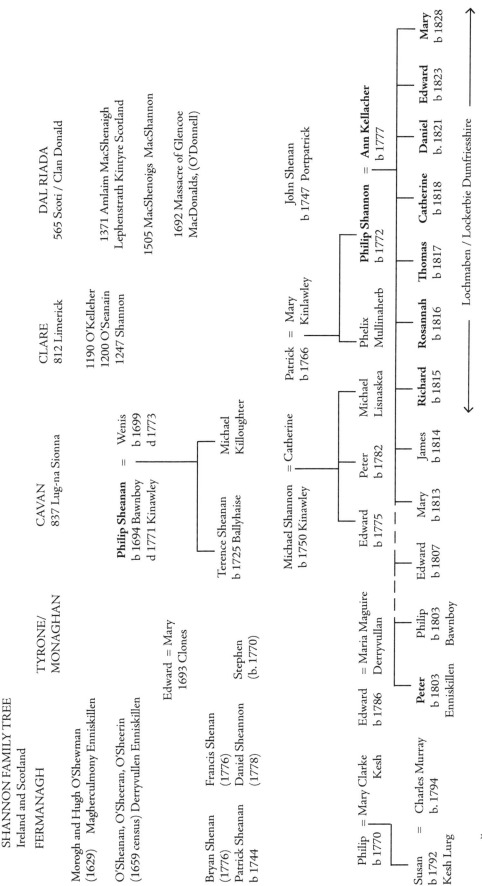

SHANNON FAMILY TREE
Ireland and Scotland

FERMANAGH

TYRONE/ MONAGHAN

CAVAN
837 Lug-na Sionna

CLARE
812 Limerick

DAL RIADA
565 Scoti / Clan Donald

Morogh and Hugh O'Shewman
(1629)   Magherculmony Enniskillen

1190 O'Kelleher
1200 O'Seanain
1247 Shannon

1371 Amlaim MacShenaigh
Lephenstrath Kintyre Scotland

O'Sheanan, O'Sheeran, O'Sheerin
(1659 census) Derryvullen Enniskillen

1505 MacShenoigs MacShannon

1692 Massacre of Glencoe
MacDonalds, (O'Donnell)

Edward = Mary
1693 Clones

Philip Sheanan = Wenis
b 1694 Bawnboy   b 1699
d 1771 Kinawley   d 1773

John Shenan
b 1747 Portpatrick

Terence Sheanan   Michael
b 1725 Ballyhaise   Killoughter

Francis Shenan
(1776)

Bryan Shenan
(1776)

Patrick Sheanan   Daniel Sheannon   Stephen
b 1744   (1778)   (b. 1770)

Michael Shannon = Catherine
b 1750 Kinawley

Patrick = Mary
b 1766   Kinlawley

Philip Shannon = **Ann Kellacher**
b 1772   b 1777

Phelix
Mullinaherb

Edward   Mary   Peter   Michael   Richard   Rosannah   Thomas   Catherine   Daniel   Edward   Mary
b 1775   b 1813   b 1782   Lisnaskea b 1815   b 1816   b 1817   b 1818   b. 1821   b 1823   b 1828

Edward   Philip
b 1807   b 1803

Peter   Edward   = Maria Maguire
b 1803   b 1786   Derryvullan
Enniskillen Bawnboy

Philip = Mary Clarke
b 1770   Kesh

Susan = Charles Murray
b 1792   b. 1794
Kesh Lurg

Lochmaben / Lockerbie Dumfriesshire

xiii

SHANNON FAMILY TREE
Scotland (Lochmaben / Lockerbie)

Thomas Shannon/Shenan

Philip Shannon/Shenan = **Ann (Agnes) Kellegher**
b 1772   b 1781
m
d 1849   d 1854

Peter = **Isabella Gallagher**	**Richard** = Ann Fenwick	**Rossanah** = William Fenwick	**Thomas** = Elizabeth Walker	**Ralph** = Catherine Reed	Daniel	Edward = Jane Donaldson	Mary
b 1779 / b 1807	b 1815 / b 1811	b 1816 / b 1811	b 1817 / b 1793	b 1816 / b 1819	b. 1821	b 1825 / b 1834	b 1828
m 1832	m 1837	m 1836	m 1834	m 1839		m 1860	d (1864)
d 1837	d 1881	d (1846)	d 1869	d 1850		d 1880	

SHANNON FAMILY TREE
Newcastle upon Tyne Northumberland

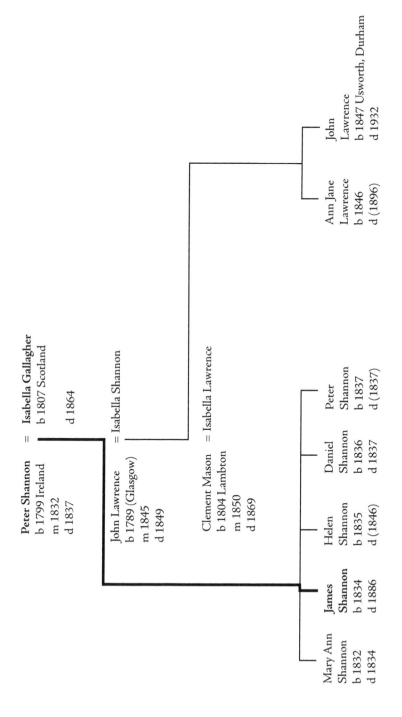

Peter Shannon = Isabella Gallagher
b 1799 Ireland   b 1807 Scotland
m 1832
d 1837   d 1864

John Lawrence = Isabella Shannon
b 1789 (Glasgow)
m 1845
d 1849

Clement Mason = Isabella Lawrence
b 1804 Lambton
m 1850
d 1869

Mary Ann   James   Helen   Daniel   Peter
Shannon   Shannon   Shannon   Shannon   Shannon
b 1832   b 1834   b 1835   b 1836   b 1837
d 1834   d 1886   d (1846)   d 1837   d (1837)

Ann Jane   John
Lawrence   Lawrence
b 1846   b 1847 Usworth, Durham
d (1896)   d 1932

SHANNON FAMILY TREE
County Durham

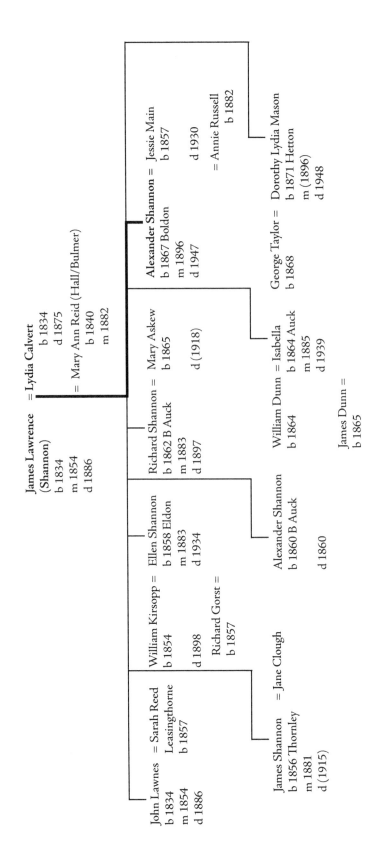

SHANNON FAMILY TREE
Reed / Mason connection

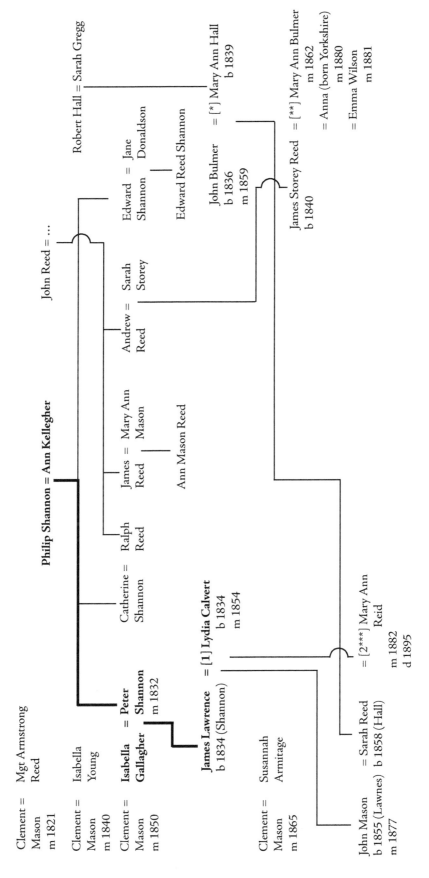

PIT SINKING BY JAMES MASON

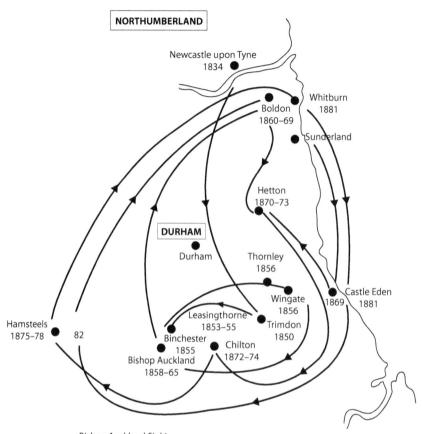

NORTHUMBERLAND

Newcastle upon Tyne
1834

Boldon
1860–69

Whitburn
1881

Sunderland

Hetton
1870–73

DURHAM

Durham

Thornley
1856

Wingate
1856

Castle Eden
1869   1881

Hamsteels
1875–78   82

Leasingthorne
1853–55

Trimdon
1850

Binchester
1855

Chilton
1872–74

Bishop Auckland
1858–65

Bishop Auckland Sinkings

1858 Page Bank (New Brancepath)
1860 St Andrews Aukland
1861 Copy Crooks St Andrews
1862 Old Pit Eldon
1863 Auckland Park (Black Boy)
1864 Eldon (Harry Pit)
1865 Cassop

Introduction

It is appropriate that derived from my father's family name, **Shannon or Shenan**, is the word Shanachie (in Old Irish, Seánchai), meaning an Irish storyteller/historian. The Irish tradition of story-telling is said to have been inherited from the Vikings who invaded Ireland in the ninth century when it was a centre of learning in a mainly barbaric world.

The Abuse of Power and Search for Social Justice

Since early times men have searched for greater power than nature provided, to secure and improve their existence. The use of tools such as levers and wheels was the first significant advance towards the evolution of engines of power. Rulers and Governments have used mining to obtain metals and fuel to fund their wars and trade, and the means of exercising control over their subjects. In order retain and expand their authority, some countries have applied their power beyond their national boundaries, leading to colonisation, religious implantation, slavery and exploitation.

Working people have always been subject to the will of their masters, mainly accepting the limitations of their feudal life apart from occasional revolts and uprisings. During later centuries, they were forced into the serfdom of mills, factories and mines. Most industrial owners tolerated the use of child labour. When miners fought for better conditions by means of strikes, owners brought in blackleg labour and vindictively ordered the eviction of miners with their wives and young children from their homes, even when those evicted were suffering from fever and without alternative shelter. Irish landlords had evicted their tenants in a similar manner. Collectively, as workers' numbers increased, especially in urban areas, this eventually gave them the power to win democratic freedoms and rights, and in the case of Ireland, also their independence. The Irish and the mining communities have always been outcasts so they had nothing to lose through revolutionary action.

Over seven centuries, English authorities have been guilty of the grievous abuse of power in their enslavement of the Irish people and the theft of their land, culminating in the Great Famine when the Irish poor were considered worthless and left to starve. Only a few years later Britain glorified in her tainted achievements at the Great Exhibition.

The English Government and their agents spoke openly of their plans for extermination of the Irish. There has been little gratitude shown for the gifts freely given to Britain by those early Irish missionaries, and later by the Irish workers during the Industrial Revolution.

This book sets out the historical journey of the family of the author's great grandfather, James Shannon. The journey started with the Vikings moving up the River Shannon from south-west to north-west Ireland. Two hundred years ago the Shannons travelled to south-west Scotland, finally ending in north-east England. During this journey they experienced the domination of an alien power determined to destroy the Gaelic people's way of life and religion. Forced to leave their homeland, Irish emigrants across the world have fought for better conditions and have made a major contribution towards a fairer and more just society.

CHAPTER 1

812 to 1817, Ireland – Invasion, Plantation and Penal Slavery

(The Shannons in Ireland, a thousand years up to Waterloo)

'I believe neither in idols nor demons. I put my trust in my own strength and soul'. The ancient crest was a pickaxe with the motto 'Either I will find a way or make one'.

(A Norseman's famous speech recorded by Samuel Smiles)

' ….. condemned with severity this invasion against an inoffensive nation [Ireland] who had always been friendly to the English ..'

(Venerable Bede 684)

'to Hell or to Connacht …. crossing of the Shannon'

(Cromwell's campaign of retribution 1650)

'People crushed by law have no hopes but from power. If laws are their enemies, they will be enemies to laws; and those who have much to hope and nothing to lose will always be dangerous, more or less'

(Burke's letter to Charles James Fox 1777)

Origins of the Shannons in Ireland

George Macaulay Trevelyan, a historian of Whig tradition, believing that God sent the [Great] 'Famine', noted that 'Ireland was cut adrift from England before the piercing of the Dover Straits by the sea, and is, for that reason, poorer in mammals, plants and reptiles'. He also noted that the mountains of England, Wales and Scotland stopped the Saxons overrunning into Ireland. History has been governed by geography, and within Ireland the River Shannon has played a dominant part, as the longest river in the British Isles. Both the Vikings and Cromwell invaded Ireland by means of this natural artery, which also provided a major line of separation and refuge.

At least 500 years before the Romans came to Britain, the Phoenicians had invaded Cornwall to exploit its tin mines. Later the Phoenicians colonised Ireland then rich in minerals, and introduced laws, customs, and knowledge, with a high level of civilisation shown by metal-working and weaving. Irish annalists considered that the Irish Celts were descended from the Scythians who were an ancient Iranic people known as horse-riding nomadic pastoralists. They had been expelled from the Red Sea area, and after settling in Spain, arrived in

Erinn, the name given to Ireland by this Milesian race, practising druidism. With command of the River Shannon in 1000BC, they drove the indigenous tribes Firbolgs and Tuatha dé Danann north into Connaught, and thereby gained overall control of Ireland.

Ireland, known as Hibernia by the Romans, was never formally part of the Roman empire, although Ptolemy, a Greco-Eygptian geographer, had drawn up an accurate map of the River Shannon (Senu) and associated lakes. However, the Romans directed by their military engineers were more attracted to the lead mines and other mineral wealth in England, and decided to leave Ireland well alone.

The beginnings of the Shannon family name may have arisen from Viking invaders reaching the mouth of the River Shannon near Limerick in the year 812; these invaders gradually made their way up to the river's source (Lug-na-Sionna or Shannon Pot) in County Cavan close to the borders with counties Fermanagh, Donegal, Leitrim, Tyrone and Monaghan. The largest groupings of Shannon and derived names now congregate in two locations, around the mouth and the source of the River Shannon.

From Irish mythology, the meaning of the River Shannon (anglicised from Abhainne na Sionainn), was given as the 'wise river', and the Shannon was said to be one of the seven rivers of knowledge. It was believed that Sionann was goddess of the river, and the drowning of a goddess in a river represented the dissolving of her divine power into the water which gave life to the land. Thus Shannon became the name of a person noted for possessing great wisdom, or an elderly person, and thus someone who has gained from life's experience. 'Wherever there is water, there is life'.

Shannon (O Seánain) was an old Tirkennedy family reaching prominence in Fermanagh before the Maguire era started in the thirteenth century. The cognate MacGiolla Seánain, became anglicized as Gilshenan or Gilsenan. The census of 1659 gave O'Sheanan and O'Sionain as two of the principal Irish names in the district of Enniskillen in County Fermanagh and Clones in County Tyrone. By the end of the eighteenth century, the Shannons were practically all in Lurg, a barony in north Fermanagh.

Shannon and its synonym Shananhan (in Irish, O' Seánachain) were also found in County Clare and Belfast. O'Shanahan was a Dalcassian sept and descendent of St Senan, a sixth century abbot-bishop who settled on Scattery Island in the Shannon estuary, part of the Norse kingdom of Limerick; he had connections with Brian Buro, the High King of Ireland.

Another sept of the Shannons, like the Stuarts, was descended from the Dalriadan race, originally from the Hebrides Islands, and the Irish Scoti clan. Their area of dominance was in north-west Scotland and east Ulster. Their derivative names, MacShannon or MacShenoig, have their roots as hereditary harpers to the greatest clan of Scotland, Clan

Donald of the Western Isles. In the Annals of Ulster was recorded the name 'Amlaim MacShenaigh, an accomplished emperor of melody' who died of plague in Tuaim-da-ghulann (Kintyre) in 1371. The Irish have always been renowned for their musical talent, with links back to Egypt. Many bards travelled the country as wandering singers, persecuted by the English, who saw them as the main bearers of the national, anti-English tradition.

In Antrim it is said the name Mac an tSionaigh was later changed to Shannon by Protestants, and by Catholics to Fox. Thus the word 'shenanigan' originates from the Irish sionnachuighim meaning 'I play the fox'. The Shannons would need all their cunning and resilience to survive the trials ahead.

Early Links between Ireland, Scotland and Northumberland

There has existed a continuing exchange between the missionaries of Ireland and the kings of Northumberland. Records show that an Irish prince visited Agricola, the Roman Governor of Britain in AD78, before returning to seize power in Ireland. To 'separate the Romans from the barbarians', Hadrian built in AD122 a defensive wall from Wallsend to Bowness-on-Solway. In the last half of the fourth century, as Britain was under attack from raiding northern bands of Picti and Brigantes, the wild Irish tribesmen then known by the Romans as the Scoti, were swarming in from the west. The heavily tattooed Pictish pygmy-like race, also said to have originated from Scythia (Iranian Steppes), wanted to settle in Ireland, but were forced to live in the northern part of Britain known as the Western Isles. A red-haired people like the Picts, were named Caledonii by the Romans; they occupied Scotland just north of the Roman's northerly frontier. The Irish or Scoti, fought with the Picts against the Romans. In 383 the Romans withdrew their troops from northern England, and twenty-five years later had left Britain for good.

Records of the movement of peoples between Ireland and England were given in the writings of Venerable Bede. At that time Northumbria stretched from the Forth of Firth to the Humber; Britain's Christian inhabitants had been driven into the mountains of Wales, or reduced to slavery in their own land by its new pagan masters, the Anglo-Saxons. As early as 397, Saint Ninian born in Galloway and trained in Rome, converted the Irish who had travelled to the Solway area, and founded a shrine at Whithorn, in Wigtownshire. He was known as the 'Apostle of the Southern Picts'. In 431, Pope Celestine sent St Palladius (of Roman descent) to Ireland, but this first Christian mission was unsuccessful.

The early close connection of Ireland and Scotland was also illustrated by the life of Saint Patrick (Roman Patricius), said to have been born in Alba (Scottish Gaelic for Scotland) of Roman parents. There is much uncertainty over the dates relating to Patrick and the 'elder Patrick', Palladius. The Irish high king, Niall of the Nine Hostages, made a predatory expedition into Britain, and plundered and robbed as he went along the coast. In 432 it is said he made a landing near Dumbarton (fort of the Britons), and carried away Patrick and a number of other slaves. After six years Patrick escaped back to his homeland, but returning later to Ireland. Patrick spent about forty years preaching the gospels, and converting the Irish people to Christianity. Apparently, he visited Patterdale in Cumbria, and in 441 he spent forty days at Lent on the lonely summit of Croagh Patrick (Cruach Phadraig). He became Bishop of Armagh, Primate of All Ireland, and eventually was revered as the Patron Saint of Ireland. The 17 March, the date of his death about 461, is known as St Patrick's Day and is still celebrated by the Irish all over the world. It is said that Patrick first gave utterance to that cry against British oppression.

During this period when Finian the Wise (of Clonard) was popularising the faith, Saint Columba or Colm (Columcille in Irish) had great influence over learning in Ireland. Columba was born in Donegal about 521, and left Ireland at the age of forty-four to convert the north of England. He founded a holy centre on the island of Iona (west of the Isle of Mull) in 563, and gained fame in converting the Picts to Christianity. Iona being within the bounds of Dal Riata, a Gaelic territory combining eastern Ulster and western Scotland (now Argyll and Bute), ensured that Christianity would spread to Pictland and Northumbria via Lindisfarne. Columba also spread Christianity to the European continent. He turned his back on gaining the kingship of Tír-Conaill (north-west Ireland) in order to carry out this mission. Colm died at Iona in 597, leaving the Book of Kells as a legacy of Irish artistic talent of those times.

Eighty years later, Adamnan born in Tyrconnell, became abbot of Iona. As a respected successor to Columba, he was visited by the exiled King of Northumbria, Alfrid. Later, Adamnan journeyed from Iona, crossing the dangerous currents of the Solway Firth, and successfully appealed to Alfrid (now king), to release Irish prisoners who were being kept as slaves in Northumbria. He enacted the Law of the Innocents, sometimes called the 'law not to kill women'. Irish monks and scholars then turned their attention to south of the area controlled by the Southern Picts. The Dalriadan Scots who had left Ireland in the early part of the sixth century, soon obtained a strong foothold in Scotland, and by the middle of the ninth century had defeated the Picts; the Scots and Picts then coalesced under a single chief governing Alba.

From 550 until the Norman's arrival in 1066, there was to be continuing warfare between the Anglo Saxons of Mercia and Wessex, the Norsemen of Northumberland, and the Danes of Yorkshire and East Anglia. Anglo-Saxon King, Ida the Flamethrower, seized the coastal stronghold of Din Guyaroi (Bamburgh) in 547, which became the capital of the kingdom he established known as Bernicia, later part of Northumbria. The island of Lindisfarne, in close proximity to Bamburgh, was to see the early battles between the Britons and the Angles. AEthelfrith, the grandson of Ida, became king of Northumbria in 593. Ten years later he joined forces with Aidan MacGabrain, King of the Dálriadan Scots, and won a notable battle against the Gaels. AEthelfrith was killed in battle in 616 whilst laying waste to Wirral. Edwin, a prince of Deira (Yorkshire), then became King of Deria and Berncia, and the chief power in Britain. He was converted to Christianity in 627, but when he died six years later, Northumbria reverted back to paganism.

In the meantime AEthefrith's sons Oswald and Oswiu fled to Dal Riata where they were converted to Christianity by the monks of Iona. After returning from exile in 634, Oswald killed his elder and pagan brother Eanfrith, becoming king of Northumbria and shaking off the yoke of the Mercians and Britons. He was determined to re-introduce Christianity to the north-east of England, and invited the monks of Iona to his kingdom. Thus Aidan founded a monastery at Lindisfarne in 635, where he became abbot and bishop. Lindisfarne was to become another Iona, with monasteries also founded at Whitby and Melrose. It was said that the Irish monks were the first to convert England to Christianity. At this time when barbarism held sway on many continental countries, Ireland was called by Dr Johnson 'the School of the West'.

In 642, Oswiu following the death of his brother Oswald, became King of Berncia. An Irish monk, Finian, who had trained at Iona, was sent over to Northumberland by the Irish, succeeding Bishop Aidan in 651. In the next ten years he constructed a church at Linisfarne built in the Irish fashion of hewn oak and thatched reeds rather than stone. In addition to the Christian developments, such as the founding of Escombe Church near Bishop Auckland, using stone from an old Roman fort at Binchester in Durham, Northumbrian military and political expansion continued.

In 670 Oswiu died and was succeeded by his son Ecgfrith. One year later he defeated the Picts of Caledonia and the Celts of Cumbria and Dumfries. At this time, Ecgfrith's brother Aldfrith was exiled in Ireland and was educated at Armagh, a world-renowned school of learning. The most important Roman Christian monasteries, St Peter and Paul at Monkwearmouth and Jarrow in Durham were established in 674, while at Melrose and Lindisfarne, St Cuthbert followed the Celtic tradition until his death in 687 as patron saint of the North East.

Three years earlier, Ecgfrith had turned to foreign expansion. He sent a raiding army to Meath in Ireland against the advice of St Cuthbert. Ecgfrith, apparently without provocation, or any design other than plunder, destroyed and robbed monasteries and churches. Venerable Bede condemned this invasion, however noting that tribal warfare was characteristic of the Celtic temperament. The following year Ecgfrith was defeated and slain by the Picts, which Bede considered a judgment of God. Ecgfrith was succeeded by Aldfrith the illegitimate son of the late King Oswiu and an Irish princess named Finn. Great works of Celtic art were encouraged by the new king, with the completion of the Lindisfarne Gospels by Bishop Eadfrith. The Irish national script was imported to Northumbria from Iona.

The English 'Woden' was overthrown in the seventh century by a vigorous encircling movement from the north and south together, with the religion of Columba and Aidan from Scotland, confronting the religion of Gregory and Augustine from Rome. However, in 716, the island of Iona was persuaded to abandon its Celtic Christian ways in favour of the Roman form of Christianity. Bede commented that 'the Scoti [Irish] travelled daily into Britain, and with great devotion preached the word and administered the baptism'. At this time the power in Saxon England lay in the North, and then never again until the nineteenth century when coal and iron became more valuable than cornfields.

In 731, Saint or Venerable Bede, the English monk and priest, based at the Northumbrian monastery of Saint Peter, Monkwearmouth and sister monastery of Jarrow, wrote 'The Ecclesiastical History of the English People'. In this world renowned document, much reference was made to Ireland. When Bede was 17, Adamnan, abbot of Iona Abbey visited the Northumbrian monasteries, and this may have sparked off Bede's interest in Irish historical links with Northumberland. Bede visited Lindisfarne in 734, and died one year later; he was buried in Durham Cathedral with St Cuthbert.

Viking plundering and invasion of Britain and Ireland

Towards the close of the eighth century, Ireland was ravaged by Northern pirates often driven to plunder by famine at home and in search of new territory, a source of metals and slaves for trade. The Vikings or Norsemen from Norway attacked the holy island of Lindisfarne in 793, followed by the Isle of Man and the Hebrides. The Durham monk Simeon described how the Northumbrian abbey was destroyed and monks killed, with some thrown into the sea and others carried away as slaves along with church treasures. In 795 they attacked Iona and the nearby Isle of Rathlin, and in the following years ravaged the west coast of Ireland. The Vikings established a permanent colony at Limerick, and from this stronghold they were able to plunder the surrounding territories, sometimes fighting as mercenaries for Irish kings. In 830 the monks of Lindisfarne were forced to flee the island, carrying with them the coffin of St Cuthbert to avoid it being taken in further Viking raids.

The Annals of Ulster recorded in 832: 'The first plundering of Armagh by the heathens three times in one month'; the Norsemen sailed up the Shannon as far as Lough Ree. At this time the Picts had taken over Dalriada to form a united Scotland with Kenneth MacAlpin as their first king. The Vikings (from Denmark) were already firmly planted

Lindisfarne, Northumberland (northern-horizons.co.uk)

Venerable Bede (Bridgeman Images)

Viking boats (author's collection)

Gallowglass (pinterest.com)

in Mercia, East Anglia and south Northumbria. The Irish distinguished the Vikings as Finn-galls or white strangers, and Dubh-galls or black strangers; the former being the fair-haired inhabitants of Norway, whilst the complexion of the Dubh-galls, or natives of Denmark was slightly darker.

The Norwegian leader Turgesius consolidated his hold on Ireland with the assistance of his Irish (Norse-Erse) allies, and soon stood supreme in Ulster. The monastic settlement on Devenish Island and at Clones near Enniskillen were attacked by Vikings in 837. The Irish round towers were used as a watch-out to give advance warning of raiders. By 841 the Norsemen had established their main coastal stronghold at Dublin, from which twelve years later Olaf the White carried out raids on the western isles of Scotland. Turgesius was recognised as the Irish sovereign, while his chief opponent was native chieftain, Niall, provincial king of Ulster. After the death of Turgesius in 844, the Norsemen abandoned their settlements on Lough Ree, travelled up the River Shannon and fought their way along rivers and lakes to the Sligo coast. Shortly afterwards the Danes from their base at York started incursions in the Carlisle area and into Ireland to settle scores with their Norsemen cousins.

At this time on the continent, the Danish and Germanic Vikings were harrying the Franks, eventually consolidating part of the Gaulic area which became known as Normandy. These conquerors later emerged as the Normans, a dominant force both on the continent and Britain. In England there continued to be battles between Danelaw and Wessex. Alfred the Great defended his kingdom of Wessex against the Danes, and was considered the King of the Anglo-Saxons by his death in 899.

Towards the end of the ninth century, the Norsemen from Ireland began raiding Cheshire. In 902 they were expelled from Dublin and sought a new base in the Wirral, seeking the approval of Queen AEthelflaed, daughter of King Alfred. With the Vikings leaving Dublin were some Irishmen who were known to have thrown their lot with the Scandinavian raiders. The Norsemen also invaded the Solway and the estuaries of the Furness region, settling in the Lake District. In 914, like the Norsemen, the Danes sailed up the Shannon in a great fleet to Lough Ree where they plundered islands and burned Clonmacnoise monastery, and eventually settled near the source the River Shannon.

The Historia of de Sancto Cuthberto recorded how Raegnald, king of the Dubhgalls, gained possession of parts of Northumbria at this time. Five years later he captured York, then becoming king of Northumbria. After many battles against the Irish High King Niall Glúndubh, in 921, Sigtrygg Silkbeard, formerly king of the Dublin Vikings, took over the Kingdom of York. The Vikings were defeated at Brunanburh (either in Northumberland or Wirral) in 937 by Alfred's grandson AEthelstan, first king of England, who went on to invade Alba. When he died four years later, his half-brother Edmund came to power, followed by Olaf. Northumbria then suffered a period of disunity; often peace was agreed on the basis of tributes and ransoms. In 952, Erik Bloodaxe became the last independent king of Northumbria after ejecting Olaf.

In Ireland, at the Battle of Clontarf in 1014, Brian Boru aged 73, the High King leading the Irish, defeated the Scandinavian forces, but he was slain by retreating Vikings. The last gasp of the Viking Age occurred during the reign of Cnut, Viking king of Denmark, Norway and England, with the death of King Harold's brother Tostig in 1066, during the battle at Stamford Bridge in Yorkshire. Thirty years later, the strong relationship remained between Vikings and the Irish demonstrated by Magnus Barelegs, so called because he dressed in the Irish fashion, and was strongly influenced by Irish culture. The Viking's legacy in Ireland was to include the art of ship construction, warfare and the Norse language; however the development of Irish civilisation was much curtailed.

Anglo-Norman and Tudor Invasion and subjugation of Ireland

After the murder of Norman appointed earls in York and Durham, William the Conqueror subdued Northumberland during 1069/70. St Cuthbert's coffin was taken to Linisfarne for safekeeping, and on the keeper's return to Durham, he found the city totally destroyed. Having conquered England and after their crusade to Jerusalem (and their massacre of Moslems), the Normans then turned their attention to Ireland which they were able to subdue in part but never to conquer.

In Ireland, inter-chief rivalry continued for much of the twelfth century. In 1152 Turlogh O'Brien, the chief of Thomond (now Co Clare and surrounding areas) and his clan, were slaughtered by the forces of Turlogh O'Connor of Connaught. Of the 7000 dead, there were many Dalcassian chiefs including nine O'Shanaghans. This victory was shortly after reversed; such was the nature of inter-clan warfare. O'Connor dominated the area for fifty years both at peace and war, to the extent of building some bridges over the Shannon.

However in 1154, Henry II ascended the throne, and became the first English king to visit Ireland; at the same time Adrian IV was the first Englishman to ascend the Papal throne. To Henry's delight the Pope agreed to issue a Papal Bull or Privilege which allowed England to carry out the religious and moral 'reformation' of Ireland. By 1166, local túatha and weaker over-kings, such as the King of Leinster, invited Norman lords from South Wales to assist them against their rival, Rory O'Connor. Brutality was commonplace by Irish and English leaders, with Turlough O'Connor putting out the eyes of his own son, and Henry II commanding the cutting off of the ears and noses of his Welsh female hostages. Up to 1168, friendly relations had existed between Ireland and England, to the extent of the Normans selling slave children to the Irish.

Then the Earl of Pembroke (Strongbow), a new strain of Norseman, landed in Ireland two years later. These Anglo Normans and later English forces were to 'grind down the liberty' of the Irish over the next seven centuries. This unwarranted incursion was the first step leading to the ruthless subjugation of Ireland by means of 'plantation'. For the first time in Ireland a man was called a rebel if he presumed to consider his hose and lands as his own property. Tiernan O'Rourke, chief of Bréifne (Leitrim), was decapitated for such a presumption. In 1189, the year of Henry's death, the English forces entered Fermanagh (Fir Fearmhaigh). During the conquest of Ulster by John de Courcy, captured chiefs were first blinded, then hung. The chief of Ulster, Hugh O'Neill, was the main stumbling block to the English. Even by 1188, Connaught also remained triumphant and un-subdued. By 1211 the O'Neills and O'Donnells were still in control of Ulster, the former destroying an English castle at Clones. However this was reversed the same year with the English re-building castles at Birr and Athlone.

In England, the Magna Carta was signed in 1215, but the new rights were not extended to Ireland. Ten years later the English laid waste to Roscommon and Mayo; so many men died that crops could not be harvested, and the area suffered both famine and fever. Up to 1264, the O'Seánains were a prominent name in the Tirkennedy area of Fermanagh; thereafter the Maguires became the chiefs and princes of Fermanagh known then as Maguire's Country.

In 1247 the clans O'Shanneans, Shannans, and Gilseáns due to late payment, had entertained Bit Giolla 'Losa on behalf of their overlords Garv O'Donnell. Later as under-chiefs to Maguire, MacGulshenan or Gilshenan ruled over a túatha or barony, and were required to give tributes, such as cattle.

During the following centuries the Irish chiefs would call on mercenary soldiers from Scotland called gallowglass (gallóglaigh). Their name was derived from Gallagher, meaning 'foreign helper'. (A Gallagher was to marry into the Shannon family when they reached Newcastle upon Tyne in the 1830s).

In the wars between Scotland and England, the Irish sympathies were always with the Scottish, as when William Wallace defeated the English at Stirling Bridge in 1297, and wasted Northumberland, Cumberland and Durham. Wallace was taunted by the English as being an Irishman; his closest commander was 'Stephen of Ireland'. The Irish were over-joyed on hearing that King Robert the Bruce was about to invade Ireland. However the pride and vanity of the Irish chiefs prevented the Irish and Scots combining to throw out the English. The Anglo Irish lords and English settlers continued to frustrate the Irish plea that the English laws be enforced, knowing that this would allow a subject redress against injustice. Then it was no crime for an Englishman to kill an Irishman.

Brother to Robert, Edward Bruce, at Ireland's request invaded Ireland in 1315, to drive out the Normans. With Edward II recently defeated at Bannockburn, the new Irish king had nothing to fear from the English. However the Bruce campaign in Ireland was to be disastrous, and during the 1317 famine, the starving poor were driven to eating the corpses of those hanged at the cross-roads. One year later Edward Bruce was killed in County Meath and his head was displayed in London.

In Scotland, near Islay, during the thirteenth to sixteenth centuries the ancient family of McSheniog, later known as MacShannon, were the hereditary harpers of Clan Donald. Their name was derived from their church dedicated to St Seánnan, and they held a castle at Dunaverty Point on the south coast of Kintyre in Scotland.

If the O'Neill factions had united they could have defeated the weak English forces. However minor conflicts continued in Leitrim involving the O'Farrells in 1323, the O'Rorkes and O'Reillys in 1324, and the MacRannells in 1342. To prevent the integration of the English in Ireland with the indigenous people described as 'aliens and enemies', the Government launched the Statute of Kilkenny in 1367. It then became high treason to intermarry with the Irish, speak Irish Gaelic or adopt the dress and customs of the Irish. Even though the statute did not have much effect, the Irish chiefs took alarm, and soon the whole of Connaught was back in Irish hands. In 1349, the Black Death visited Ireland as well as most of Europe, which in England led to the Statute of Labourers and the Peasants' Revolt. English labourers carried on their struggle for freedom, and free labourers attempted to ignore the statute and strike for better wages. The English Rising in 1381 ended with the slaying of rebel Wat Tyler. The Revolution of 1399 gave certain people freedoms from the Crown, however Richard II felt secure enough to set out on an expedition of Ireland; however forces were gathering against him at home. The Percies of Northumberland refused to serve under him and fled to Scotland. Richard died soon after.

Philip of the Battle Axe in 1395 had consolidated the Maguire grip over Fermanagh after defeat of the O'Connors; with the castle built at Enniskillen, known in Irish as Ceithlenn's Island, there was a period of stability over the area south of Belturbet to Swanlinbar. At a parliament in Trim during 1447, it was enacted that Irish customs were illegal and penal, and whoever did not shave his upper lip was to be regarded as an enemy. Annandale in Scotland was then suffering from raids between the Douglas and Percy families. With Ireland supporting the House of York, it was to suffer when Richard III lost at Bosworth Field in 1465.

Irish internal conflicts continued; in 1457 the O'Rorkes were defeated by Fermanagh chieftain Thomas Óg Maguire; in 1490 O'Donnell was at war with Maguire, and the latter at war with the MacMahon in 1508. In the early sixteenth century the O'Donnells and O'Neills battled with the Connaught chiefs Clanrikard, O'Connors, and Burke of Mayo; the MacDermots supported O'Neill in 1522. O'Donnell obtained the support of the chieftains of Tirconnell (Donegal) – O'Boyle, O'Doherty, MacSweenys, and O'Gallagher. 1513 saw the English victory over the Scots at Flodden – Ireland once more was under threat.

Poynings' Law of 1495 meant that the Irish Parliament came under direct English control. Henry VIII in his early years was zealous on Church matters, vigorously replying to Luther's attack on the Sacraments. Henry's Chancellor, Thomas More, a Catholic, strongly supported his king; he was said to insult Luther with the following blast: 'throw back into your paternity's shittymouth, truly the shitpool of all shit, all the muck and shit which your damnable rottenness has vomited up'. Henry was rewarded by the Pope in 1521 with the title of Defender of the Faith. Thirteen years later Parliament passed the Act of Supremacy, rubber-stamping Henry's announcement that he was the supreme head of the Church, leading to the desecration of the Irish monasteries. As Rev E A D'alton concluded:

> 'A religion which was avowedly novel, and above all whose high priest was an English king, was certain to be regarded by the Irish with suspicion and ill-favour; but when it further-more involved the destruction of churches, the suppression of monasteries, and the murder of priests and monks and nuns, it was equally certain they would regard it with aversion and hate'.

By 1535, Henry VIII had resolved on the conquest of Ireland. He had already broken with Rome, made himself head of the Church as well as the State, and had plundered the monasteries to the sum of £50,000,000. His commissioners defaced the shrine of St Cuthbert at Durham Cathedral in 1538. This was strongly opposed by the Percies of Northumberland. The confiscation of Church property introduced a new injustice depriving the poor of alms. Three years later Henry arranged for the Irish parliament to declare him King of Ireland. Skeffington, his new Lord Deputy, introduced artillery which was to dramatically change the political scene, in being able to batter into ruins the great Norman houses and the castles which were sheltering the rebellious Irish. Following the appeal by the Pope to defend the faith, O'Neill agreed to join forces with O'Donnell, but failed to prevent Lord Deputy Gray from enlarging the Pale (area directly under control of the English). It should be said that Henry treated Ireland in some ways better than England using conciliation rather than force and colonisation, but nevertheless he considered all Catholics as disloyal.

In 1543, O'Neill of Tyrone was required to swear allegiance to the crown, but to sow discord between the Irish chiefs, O'Donnell, Maguire of Fermanagh and O'Neill of

Clannaboy were exempted from the obligation to 'Tyrone'. There was much strife in Ulster with Tyrone seeking help from the Duke of Northumberland and King Edward. The Scots had long been a menace to the peace in Ulster. Descended from the Scoti, they had extended their sway over all of modern Scotland. The Scots who lived in the Western Islands were as daring and adventurous as the Vikings in former days.

Under their chiefs, the MacDonnells of the Isles made many incursions onto the neighbouring coasts of Ireland. They often hired themselves out to the Ulster chiefs as mercenaries. Towards the end of Henry's reign in 1545, the English were not troubled by the Irish who as usual went back to their own fighting: the O'Donnells against the Maguires and O'Gallaghers, and O'Rorkes against the O'Kellys and Burkes.

By the middle of the sixteenth century the MacDonnells had effected settlements in Ireland, with Rathlin Island in their exclusive possession. Queen Mary disapproved of the Scots or 'Redshanks' residing in Ireland; thus James MacDonnell and his followers were forced to flee in 1558. The heresy law introduced by Catholic Mary and co-monarch of England Philip II of Spain, and the memory of the Anglican bishop martyrs, bred a hatred for the Church of Rome which proved a constant factor in the coming centuries of civil and religious conflicts. In 1559 both England and Scotland became Protestant after rebellion in north, but the Catholic faith drew the Irish closer together in opposition to the outsiders and the threat of extermination.

Shane O'Neill 1560
(hallamor.org)

At this time the leading Irish chief was Shane O' Neill. He refused to help the English against the Scottish settlers on the coast of Antrim, allaying himself with the MacDonnells, the most powerful of the immigrants. In 1562, Shane O'Neill visited Queen Elizabeth in London to safeguard his ancestral rights to Ulster territory. The courtiers marvelled at his appearance and of his gallowglasses (Scottish mercenaries with a reputation for honour), their hair worn long after the manner of their country. One of the courtiers described him as 'O'Neill the Great, cousin of St Patrick, Friend to the Queen of England, enemy to all the world besides'.

On his return to Ulster, like a trapped man, he fought with O'Reily and Maguire and other clans in order to re-gain his supremacy. Shane's mistrust of the English was reinforced after an attempted poisoning; he was to build a castle on the shores of Lough Neagh which he called 'Fuath-na-Gaill', or 'Hatred of the English'. In the end, Shane was tricked and slain by a spy, and his head was spiked and displayed on the north-west gate at Dublin Castle. There were many examples of Irish leaders being invited by Dublin officials, and guaranteed protection, but then murdered as their guests – a premonition of the Massacre of Glencoe.

English and Scottish Plantation of Ireland

In the Plantation of Ulster, a province named 'Scottish Ireland' by French writer Grousset, not only included lands given to others of an alien race and creed, but the small portion of the lands reserved for the Irish was often, by force or fraud, still further curtailed, and many of them were cast forth, without a house to shelter them or lands to till. And while the natives who received land were punished if they violated the prescribed conditions, the planters ignored these conditions when it suited them, and did so with impunity. Plantations in King's County, Leitrim and Westmeath were either 'exempted or affected, and great discontent followed'. At this time England was under threat from Scottish raids with the English army driven back from the Tyne into Yorkshire, and Northumberland and Durham overrun. The Ulster Presbyterians had the same hatred of Catholics as their Scottish kinsmen who were attacking the Catholics in the English northern counties.

In 1565 Henry Sidney (Lord Deputy) and the Protestant bishops published the Book of Articles, which condemned papal supremacy, the Mass, the use of images, candles and beads. No bishop was to be appointed who was unable to speak English, and in order that the natives might learn the language, Protestant Free Schools were established in 1570. With the continuing unrest caused by bands of warring clans including the Scots, the English Government in 1572 decided to carry out a 'plantation' on the east coast of Antrim. They ignored the fact that the land belonged to the whole clan community and not just to the chiefs. The double purpose of the plantation was to keep watch on the Irish chiefs and cut off the Scots from entering Ireland. Sir Thomas Smith, who was given some of O'Neill's lands, sought to console the Irish by saying that these colonies were not intended to destroy the Irish race, but to teach them 'virtuous labour'. Henry Sidney tried to subdue the chiefs, including Clanrickard in Connaught, but O'Rorke of Leitrim described as 'the proudest man on earth', would not submit.

Although Elizabeth I was not a zealous Protestant, the Pope had refused to dissolve the marriage of her father to Catherine of Aragon, and in declaring that marriage was valid, he announced Elizabeth to be illegitimate; therefore she was repelled from a religion that branded her a bastard. Like her father she considered Catholics as traitors. At the massacre of Rathlin Island in 1575, in which Sir Francis Drake took part, four hundred women and children of the MacDonnells were killed. Proclamations were issued inviting younger sons of the landed gentry to go to Ireland. These were given the name of 'Undertakers', and included Sir Walter Raleigh and Edmund Spence. They were not to employ Irish labour, but this was largely ignored. Spence considered the only solution to be the entire extermination of the native Irish. At this time Connaught was under the rule of Richard Bingham, who used cruelty, hangings and confiscation to get his way, and helped Raleigh to butcher the 'shipwreaked' Spanish.

When Bingham first entered Connaught there were few disturbances, but he turned the province into a state of warfare, continuing to wreak havoc up to 1588. Mary Queen of Scots had just been executed. Maguire gave directions to raise an army from the Gallaghers, Bohills and Sweenys. The Spanish Armada was scattered along the Irish coast, and O'Rorke was one of the few chiefs to give the Spanish relief, and in consequent of this the English imprisoned O'Doherty and O'Gallagher chiefs.

Irish chief Red Hugh O'Donnell escaped from Dublin Castle in 1591, and was assisted by Hugh Maguire who picked him up at Enniskillen and rowed him across Lough Erne. The state of Ulster was threatening English rule; Maguire and O'Donnell were already joined by O'Rorke of Breffni (Leitrim), and if Tyrone were to join the Catholic Confederacy, the worst consequences were feared by the English. Maguire had driven the sheriff from Fermanagh and had invaded Connaught, however during the next year Fitzwilliam again invaded Fermanagh and captured Enniskillen and left there an English garrison.

After the departure of Bingham, Hugh O'Donnell exerted his authority as chief of Tyrconnel, laying waste Leitrim, Sligo and Fermanagh in 1594. After his victory at Yellow Ford near Enniskillen four years later, O'Neill became head of the Gaelic Confederacy. However, O'Neill's lieutenant Hugh Maguire (Lord of Fermanagh) was killed in that year, after rising in rebellion against Elizabeth, fearing imposed re-division of lands in Fermanagh.

THE OLD WATER GATE, ENNISKILLEN CASTLE

Enniskillen (lisburn.com)

The upswing of Catholics came to dramatic end on the 14 December 1601 at Kinsale. This became known as one of the black days for Ireland when it was said the faith and country (the Irish battle plan) were bartered to Sir George Carew for a bottle of whiskey. The combined forces of O'Neil and O'Donnell, after a 300 mile winter march to support the depleted Spanish forces sent over by Philip II, were unable to lift the siege. In 1602, Enniskillen was destroyed including the monasteries of Lisgoole and Devenish in Lough Erne. The English were most concerned to crush O'Neill rather than O'Donnell. Thus when Hugh O'Neill, second Earl of Tyrone was defeated in 1603, this signalled the final collapse of the old Gaelic order, leading to the 'Flight of Earls' four years later.

King James VI of Scotland (King James I of England) did not live up to Irish hopes of toleration; he had been trained in the gloomy tenets of Calvin, as preached by Knox in Scotland, with a harshness peculiar to Scotch Presbyterianism. Many of the planters came from south west Scotland and also from the Scottish/English Border area, arriving mainly in Fermanagh. It was said that the planters from Scotland and England were 'generally the scum of both nations, who, for debt or breaking and fleeing from justice, or seeking, came thither'. Some confiscated Maguire lands were given to William Cole (first provost of Enniskillen) by Major Coote. King James saw this strategy solving the problem of England/Scotland border disputes as well as taking control of Ulster.

Enniskillen owed its prominence in 1612, to the Plantation of Ulster. A county town was needed by the English to control the Maguire territory, which had been converted in 1569 by Sir Henry Sydney, the Irish Lord Deputy of Queen Elizabeth, into a county under the name of Fermanagh, which at that time was described as 'lying waste'. It was an unwelcome terrain to strangers, difficult to cross with forests, rivers and lakes. In Elizabethan times, Ireland was an appendage of England apart from the north and north-west which provided shelter for the Irish where it was dangerous for the English to enter. Bitter feuds divided the earls of Norman descent in the South, while in the North the old-Irish chieftains seemed more intent on achieving personal supremacy than in forming a united force against the English crown. Fermanagh was largely planted with moss-troopers from the Scottish border, men used to cattle reiving and fighting, such as the Johnstones and Elliotts of Annandale. Not until 1613 were the Irish considered English subjects; previously they were looked upon as 'outlaws' and 'enemies'. When Chichester became Deputy of Ireland, he wanted the Catholics in Tyrone prosecuted; they were ordered throughout Tyrone and Tyrconnel to attend Protestant churches on pain of forfeiture of goods and imprisonment. This was the time of Gunpowder Plot with Henry Percy Earl of Northumberland one of the conspirators; spies were everywhere. In 1617 Ireland's great leader Hugh O'Neill died.

At the time of Plantation in 1629, Morogh and Hugh O'Shewman (surname derived from Shannon) lived in the parish of Magherculmony near Enniskillen. Thirty years later, census records showed families O'Sheerin and O'Sheanan living nearby at Killeshandra in Cavan, a plantation town. Flax growing and linen manufacture was introduced by Huguenot and Scottish settlers. A Thomas Shannon was an overseer on a farm at Killeshandra, probably involved with flax growing. The climate and soil in Ireland was well suited to flax cultivation, however, flax workers in the mills suffered from a disease caused by flax dust. (In 1781 Robert Burns was a flax-dresser which may have caused his early death).

Lord Burleigh wanted English law and customs to prevail throughout Ireland, but he effected little. Tenants whose plots were held by Irish tenure had no land rights, but were allowed to graze a certain number of cattle on the common lands. They tilled small areas, ploughed with short ploughs tied to the horses' tails (in 1612 a heavy penalty was available for this practice), and their houses consisted of boughs coated with turf. Wealth was in the cattle. In the 1640s, potatoes were beginning to be grown as a garden crop throughout Ireland because they were well suited to the cool climate and wet soils. Raleigh supposedly introduced the potato to an estate in Ireland as well as tobacco to Britain, bringing ill-fortune in different ways for many centuries ahead.

Irish Rebellion 1641 and Cromwell's Settlement

The disgrace of defeat at Kinsale rankled with the Irish, so the 1641 rebellion was the rallying cry as the exiles hastened home – the O'Neills, Maguires and MacMahons of the older stock, and Butler and Preston of the newer; but jealousies and divisions did not allow a combined force to come together. During the rebellion, Presbyterians were killed as Catholics exacted their revenge – 30 killed near Clones and 15 killed at Monaghan. Some Presbyterians backed the rising to achieve religious freedom, and there were cases where protection of Protestants was rendered, for example O'Reilly laid on an escort for 1500 non-Catholics from Belturbet to Dublin. Enniskillen was overrun and Leitrim was in flames. O'Rorke besieged Castlecoote near Roscommon. The siege of Drogheda was raised, and there was only small satisfaction for Catholics when Sir Charles Coote was killed near Trim. The first ironworks at Arigna and Creevela were destroyed but coal mining continued at Tullyniskan in east Tyrone.

There was indignation in England that Irish Papists should have had the effrontery to attack Protestants not long after the Scottish Covenanter's uprising in 1637. Subscriptions were raised to put down the rebellion with the reward of land for the 'Adventurers'. It decreed that the adventurers should be given the forfeited land in Munster and Leinster, on condition that these lands were planted within three years with Protestants 'of any nation but Irish'. In 1642 the Scottish Parliament sent 10,000 soldiers to Ireland to quell the Irish Rebellion.

Covenanter soldiers of Clan Campbell killed local Catholic MacDonalds, including women who were thrown over cliffs onto the rocks below. Lord Maguire was tried in London for his share in the rebellion, and tortured before being hanged. Manus O'Gallogher was hanged at Manor Hamilton in county Leitrim. In 1647, the MacDonalds under siege at Dunaverty Castle were massacred by the Campbells. The MacShennoig harpers may have been forced to flee.

Early in 1649 the English monarchy was abolished, and the Scots who had revolted in the previous year were crushed. Charles I's death warrant was sealed. Owen Roe O'Neill who returned to Ireland in support of the 1641 revolt, was intent on overturning the Plantation. He was poisoned after seven years in Ireland. Cromwell started to effect a 'Settlement' of the Irish population in 1652, involving the confiscation of the whole of Ireland from its legal owners. All Catholics who possessed more than 50 acres were ordered to 'take them-selves and their belongings beyond the Shannon into Connacht', where room would be found for them on 'acres confiscated from the proprietors there domiciled'. The Catholic landlord represented in fact or by custom the chief of his kinsmen, and therefore in most cases his tenants followed him since they feared their existing tenure would be rejected by the new landowner. The Council gave Cromwell a large army and directed him to 'reduce Ireland to obedience'. However his departure for Ireland was delayed by a mutiny of his army. The Parliamentary forces then sailed up the Shannon. These troops laid waste the counties of Kerry, Leitrim, Fermanagh, Cavan, Tyrone, Monaghan, Armagh and Wicklow, with little regard to innocent lives. After Cromwell's final battle in Ireland, he returned to England and to the death of the 'Commonwealth'.

Disbanded following the Act for Settling of Ireland in October 1652, various baronies including Fermanagh and Sligo were allocated to disbanded English soldiers. The county of Clare and the province of Connaught were assigned to the transplanted Irish in October 1653 required by the 'Act of Good Affection'; the provisions of this Act were proclaimed in each 'district by the sound of trumpet and beat of drum'. Fathers and heads of family had to transplant themselves before the first of January following, others of the family by the first of May. Catholic Irishwomen who had married Protestants before December 1650 might stay, but only on condition that they become Protestants; boys under 14 years and girls under 12 might also stay if they were in Protestant service and were brought up as Protestants. The Irish were showing their worth in the first rank as soldiers, scholars and founders of the mining industry. King James II arranged for thirty-five Acts to be enacted which included the 'prohibition of importation of English, Welsh and Scotch coal' into Ireland.

The "crossing of the Shannon" became for the Irish their statement of resistance and honour. To avoid the dispossessed from being able to view their old home from their new residence, none from Cavan, Fermanagh, Tyrone or Donegal were allowed to be planted in Leitrim; those who had lived ten miles east of the Shannon were to be planted ten miles west of the Shannon. Finally, all were to be cut off from the Shannon and the sea, and should not dwell in towns; the islands were to be cleared of Irish and given to disbanded soldiers; Protestants in Connaught were given land elsewhere. The soldiers got the whole of the county of Sligo, and in Mayo the barony of Gallen and part of Tirawley. Perhaps the Irish had the last laugh over Cromwell when in 1728, Primate Boulter lamented that the descendants of Cromwell's soldiers had gone over to Popery.

Oliver Cromwell, 1652 (coffe blossom)

Following Cromwell's campaign, retribution 'to Hell or to Connacht' meant that land-owners implicated in the 1641 Rising had no choice. To get rid of troublesome women and children, the Government contacted Bristol merchants, and a regular and continuous slave trade was carried on. Many women, children, defeated soldiers and priests were shipped off to the West Indies to be sold as slaves. Often the women ended up as wives or mistresses of the West Indian planters, replacing the negresses and maroons (escaped ex-slaves). They were to be the ancestors of the so-called 'Black Slaves' of Monserrat, the Caribbean island where Gaelic was still spoken up to 150 years ago by mixed-race people.

Every facility was given for the Irish soldiers to volunteer for foreign service; most went to Spain where the 'English Government wished the whole nation would go'. Irish soldiers were also to serve in France, Spain and Austria, and everywhere they went they covered their country in glory exhibiting patience, fidelity, courage and reckless disregard of danger and death in battle. The Irish exiles were eager to join England's enemies at Fontenoy, Lexington and Bunker's Hill. Research has shown that between 1691, the arrival of Irish troops in France, and 1745, the Battle of Fontenoy, 450,000 Irishmen died in the service of France.

Attaching blame for social unrest in England, Richard Younge wrote in the Poores Advocate 1654, 'The greatest part of rogues are uncirmcumcised generation, unbaptized, out of Church, and so consequently without God in the world'. Vagabonds became scape-goats for all social problems. They were carriers of rumour, sedition, and disease and they infected others with their "Licentious Liberty". After the Restoration in 1660, there was a morbid dread in England that Protestantism was in danger (the comet in 1664 was an unwelcome sign), with Charles II's wife, mother and brother being Catholic. Although Charles II allowed the Catholics to practice their religion openly, the Test Act of 1673 rendered Catholics incapable of holding office.

Oliver Plunkett, Catholic Archbishop of Armagh, was implicated in the Popish Plot of 1678; he went into hiding but was caught and tried for allegedly conspiring to bring in 20,000 French soldiers and levying a tax on his clergy to support 70,000 men for rebellion. He was executed at Tyburn in 1681, the last Catholic to die for his faith in this manner.

Some of the dispossessed Irish refused to be transplanted and took to the hills, forming themselves into small guerrilla bands who attacked the colonist settlements. These bands, who came to be known as 'Tories', were hunted with rewards posted for their leaders. (Quite separately, the 'Tory' political group appeared in the 18th century at first favouring the Stuarts and later royal authority and the established church.)

King Billy and the Battle of the Boyne

In 1688, James's son-in-law, the Prince of Orange (William III) was invited to England to defend the Protestant faith. This 'defence' was later known as the 'Glorious Revolution'. With rumours that the massacres of 1641 were to be repeated, Enniskillen closed its gates, after admitting the local Protestants and expelling the Catholics. The men of Derry and Enniskillen had already rebelled against James II, even before he had left England. The Irish attempts to besiege Enniskillen were unsuccessful, unlike an attack on Lord Mountcashel at nearby Lisnaskea. William's General Schomberg took Belturbet in December. James's armies were much inferior to those of William, comprising of men little better than Tories or Rapparees, and some who had lately held the plough had been urged to fight for their faith by their priests. William also had the advantage of a wheel-engine, a prototype of a machine gun.

It was said that the Glorious Revolution gave to Great Britain both freedom and efficiency (Protestant work ethic), because it tipped the balance of power permanently on the side of Parliament. The next year, the Toleration Act gave religious peace for a while. With the tacit support of the Pope, William was proclaimed King at Enniskillen and Londonderry in 1689 after fighting near Lisnaskea and Cavan, and then won the decisive battle at the River Boyne in the county of Meath. Two years later following the Treaty of Limerick, about 14,000 Jacobite soldiers (later known as 'The Wild Geese') were required to seek refuge in France, where they formed the Irish Brigade. This drain of Irish men would last 100 years. The Treaty was to provide for native Irish rights and freedoms on condition of the disbanding by Patrick Sarsfield of his forces, but this was not honoured by the Government. Sarsfield died in battle on the fields of Flanders fighting for King Louis XIV; before he expired he was to have said the immortal lines "Oh, if only this were for Ireland".

The first massive movement of Lowland Scots, English, Welsh and Huguenots took place between 1690 and 1715 when 50–80,000 new immigrants arrived in Ireland following the Catholic insurrection of 1641. Also following the famine in the Scottish/English border area between 1696 to 1698, tens of thousands fled to Ireland. Scottish Presbyterians became a majority community in Ulster, but resented their lack of power in the resettlement when the Protestant Ascendancy came into being. Thus 250,000 Ulstermen migrated to America during the years 1717 to 1776; shiploads poured out of Belfast and Londonderry of Presbyterians who considered themselves as treated unfit to receive the rights of citizens in a similar manner as the Papists, and forbidden to teach their children in their own faith.

Glencoe Massacre, Penal Code and Coercion

The year 1692 was to be a dark moment in Catholic history. The MacDonalds of Glencoe known as the raiding group 'Gallows Herd', were the only 'popish' highlands clan in Scotland. A clan chief, John of the Heather, had been buried in Iona in 1338. The treacherous murder of thirty-eight men, women and children of the MacDonald clan by Campbell 'government' soldiers took place on the 13 February 1692. The few surviving MacDonalds fled over snow-clad mountains, some to Ulster changing their name to McDonnell looking for refuge.

A 'crannoge' was an artificial island settlement found mainly in the north of Ireland, for example, at Boa Island in Lough Erne (Fermanagh), used for concealment or retreat. Near St Mogue's Island adjacent Bawnboy in Cavan, a Philip Sheanon was born in 1694. Shannons were now spreading south from their homeland in the barony of Lurg area east of Loch Erne. Records also showed that an Edward and Mary Shannon were born in 1693 at Clones in Tyrone where nearby coal deposits were worked. About fifty years later Mary and James Shannon were born at Donaghmore also in Tyrone.

This was also the time when a number of Acts were passed by the Dublin Parliament, all levelled against the Catholics, which were known collectively as the Penal Code, to prevent 'Further Growth of Popery'. A long series of penal laws were passed in 1695, and nine years later a bill to prevent further growth of Popery involving property restrictions. The entrenchment of 'English Rule' in Ireland was to affect in many ways the life of ordinary people. In 1702, as Queen Anne started her reign, William Molyneux had found 'everybody understanding or answering you in English in the small cabins by the road in County Monaghan'. Nevertheless, the Irish language at that time was still largely spoken as the vernacular in the north and west of Ireland. Burke described the Penal Code as 'a machine of wise and elaborate contrivance, as well as fitted for oppression , impoverishment, and degradation of a people, and the debasement in them of human nature itself, as ever proceeded from the perverted ingenuity of man'.

During the eighteenth century many Presbyterians emigrated to America to escape the restrictions of the Protestant Ascendancy. Lakall and William Shannon arrived in Virginia around 1697, and Charles (a vagabond aged 76) and James Shannon travelled to Boston Massachusetts in 1742, escaping from a severe fever in Ulster.

A few decades later in Fermanagh, the penal laws were still in place. Notice was given that a 'ffrier' [friar] called Shenan who 'had not taken the Oaths' was to be apprehended, in order 'to find by Inquisition' his guilt or otherwise! In 1711, a Clogher priest Philip Maguire was arrested and lodged in Enniskillen gaol; Francis Shenane was noted a Popish priest.

In east Tyrone, small amounts of coal had been dug out of the ground from the middle of the seventeenth century, but the sinking of deep shafts at Blackaville (Tyrone), soon to be known as Coalisland in the 1720s, revealed deposits on a scale not found anywhere else in Ireland. About ten years later, works commenced on the Tyrone & Coalisland Navigation to transport coal to Belfast and Dublin. However this early canal scheme hit many problems and took 55 years to complete. At Coalisland in 1731, a 156 feet deep shaft, called Engine Pit, was sunk under the control of entrepreneur Francis Seymour. This was the time when the massive canal works known as the Newry Navigation, linking the coal to Loch Neagh, involving 15 locks, was completed in eleven years; this pre-dated the Sankey and Bridgewater canals in Lancashire.

In north east England, miners were revolting by burning pit-head machinery, but on Tyneside these riots were constrained by the law of 1736 making it a felony to set fire to a pit. High food prices had sparked off riots by keelmen on the Tyne in 1710 and thirty years later in Northumberland and Durham. In England the use of steam power in mines was just beginning. In Aryshire 'coal-shanking' (sinking) was in progress in 1765. The sinking at Walker Colliery near Newcastle upon Tyne had just started; at the same time at Walker was the earliest recorded strike by miners disputing the yearly bond.

In 1728, Burke's birth-date, the darkest hour of the penal laws, the Catholics were stripped of the franchise, and in the previous year the Test Act was passed requiring proven attendance at Church of Ireland services. A limited number of Catholic priests were still permitted and duly registered; any not so recorded who were found practising were put to death or forced into exile. Penal bigotry went as far back as a proposal in 1623, that if priests refused to leave the kingdom they were to be castrated. The Report on the State of Popery, in the Diocese of Clogher in 1731, said there was then a priest residing in Derryvullan, but it did not give his name. In the nearby parish of Cleenish, the price upon a priest's head would have been a fortune to any of the poor people who might have been tempted to betray him. The greatest danger of detection to which the priests were exposed in Fermanagh, arose from the imprudence of servants in Protestant families, gossiping about the time and place of Mass on Sundays. Many were the stories handed down by tradition, of the adventures of the priests of those days, hiding among the glens and ravines of the Fermanagh mountains, including the skill and tact of the peasantry in outwitting the priest-hunter and his hated yeoman guard.

Following the Act of Union of the Scottish and English parliaments in 1707, and the activities of the Scottish Pretender, the Government became so obsessed with potential plots that even Queen Anne had to protest. Conn O'Neil of County Antrim sought Flora MacDonald to help Prince Charlie escape from Scotland, and for her efforts she was imprisoned in the Tower. The highland clearances started in 1747, one year after

Culloden. Acts were passed for Ireland to promote the planting of trees (rather than men!) and to encourage 'linen manufactures'. In 1757 some bishops called for more toleration, and fifteen years later an Act was passed substituting the Oath of Allegiance for that of Supremacy. Attempts were made to reduce the revenue passed for the support of the royal bastards, discarded mistresses, court favourites and corrupt politicians. Bribes were often used if other ways were not successful, for example when Henry Boyle was made Earl of Shannon.

Author Jonathan Swift protested against the right of the English Parliament to make laws for Ireland – 'government without the consent of the governed' – the very definition of slavery. During his last days in 1745, Swift poured out his wrath against the English treatment of Ireland, of governing exclusively for the advantage of England. Wesley also berated the accusation against the unemployed that 'They are poor because they are idle'. In 1759, at the mere rumour of a projected Union between England and Ireland, there was mass protest in most counties including Fermanagh, Cavan, Monaghan and Tyrone.

For some centuries the north-west of Ireland was looked on as 'beyond the Pale'. It was wild country and formed a good shelter for outlaws carrying out 'outrages'. In 1763 following the appearance of a secret agrarian organisation known as the Whiteboys (wearing white smocks), there was a general rising of the peasants. Rapparees (Irish irregular soldiers or freebooters) and robbers infested North Louth and South Monaghan, and were pursued by the 'Tory Hunters'. The population in Ulster was then composed of Anglican landlords, small Presbyterian farmers and Catholic labourers. The local gentry took little interest in the country and did little to improve it. One of the biggest curses suffered by the tenants was absentee landlordism which bred a horde of middlemen or squireens, and small holders. During his tour of Ireland in 1776, Arthur Young described them as the 'most oppressive species of tyrants that ever lent assistance to the destruction of a country'. They sought to extract the last penny from the tenants already on their knees. A few landlords were different, like Richard Edgeworth, who had just invented estate railroads to carry manure to his fields.

Adam Smith mentioned in the 1760s that the importation of cattle from Ireland had only recently been allowed. The year 1761 saw the first Coercion Act in Ireland, and eight years later, the birth in County Meath of Arthur Wellesley, the future Duke of Wellington. Three months later, Napoleon was born in Corsica. A Monaghan newspaper in April 1765 reported tumultuous risings in Ulster, on the Fermanagh side of Clones; fights often erupted between the peasantry and farmers. In those times to be convicted of minor offences meant being put in the pillory or publically whipped. The pillory was a framework of wood and iron, for example situated at the Cross in the 'Diamonds' of Monaghan and Clones. Many United Irishmen and other political offenders were exhibited on this frame, and its occupants attracted much popular respect; it became an honour to be placed in it. The whipping was very brutal, with men, and sometimes women, tied to a cart and horse; the horse was led from the old County Courthouse up to a hill where a public official tore the flesh on the back of the victim by means of knotted whip-cords attached to a stick. The British Governments were to make use of coercion acts as a quick reaction to fears of an Irish "backlash".

American Independence

It is no coincidence that in the same year of American Independence, a relaxation of the Penal code began. In 1771, severe floods in the north east of England swept the Tyne Bridge away; a ship picked up a cradle washed out to sea and the baby in it was rescued – a good portent in those uncertain times. The Irish must have started to believe that the heavy yoke of English suppression could be removed when they heard of America gaining its independence from Britain. George Washington, the first President of the United States, was descended from a County Durham family. Daniel O'Connell born in 1775 was to play an enormous part in fighting for Irish independence. Also at this time Patrick Brunty was born to a poor Protestant family in County Down, and became the father of the famous Bronte sisters when he settled in West Yorkshire about 40 years later.

In Ulster there was now a growing republican feeling among the Presbyterians encouraged by their relatives in the American colonies, fighting the English for independence.

George Washington 1776 (cn snews)

After Britain's loss of 13 American colonies during the American War of Independence, (1775–1783), Britain built up a new empire – the largest there has ever been. During 1773 to 1793, Irish statutes started to readdress William III's oppressive legislation. Protestant 'Discoverers' could still legally seize Catholic's land, but now this was considered unworthy conduct. In 1777, Catholics in Ireland gained some rights – able to practise religion, establish schools, enter the legal profession, dispose of property, vote at elections, become magistrates, and in general hold most civil and military appointments, but remained debarred from high political and legal positions in Irish government. Grattan's modest aim was to gain Parliamentary independence under the British Crown.

The author's 3-great grandfather Philip Shannon was born in Ireland about 1772; it is likely that he was named after Catholic Philip II of Spain. Probably his grandfather was a Philip Sheanan who died on the 15 December 1771, aged 77 years; his son Terence erected a headstone in his memory at Ballyhaise Killoughter in Co Cavan. The burial took place at a momentous point in history, only four years before the signing of the document declaring the Independence of America. Five Ulstermen signed this document, most with an Irish-Scots Presbyterian background.

A Peter Shannon born at Lisnaskea in 1782, near Maguiresbridge, could have been brother of the author's 3-great grandfather. Also nearby at Kinawley, a Phelix Sheanon in 1824, erected a headstone in memory of Patrick Sheanon born in 1766 at the Mullinaherb parish.

A Daniel Sheannon was forced to sign an Oath of Loyalty recorded in the Catholic Qualification Rolls for Clogher Fermanagh as required by the Catholic Relief Act 1778.

The English had been involved in the African slave trade for about two hundred years, when in 1781, a slave ship called Zong, captained by Luke Collingwood, was sailing in Caribbean waters. Due to the depletion of drinking water, the captain ordered that 132 Africans, men, women and children, be thrown overboard into shark-infested waters. The famous painter, JMW Turner, captured this massacre in his painting of 1840, as part of the Abolitionist campaign. The Society for the Abolition of the Slave Trade was founded in 1787, with particularly strong support from the north of England. In America, the issue of slavery had polarised on each side of the Mason-Dixon Line. Jeremiah Dixon was a surveyor born near Bishop Auckland in Durham who had joined up with surveyor Charles Mason. Even then the North East was exporting its engineering expertise. In 1791, William Chapman from Whitby was re-building all the canals on the River Shannon.

The year 1782 was memorable in Irish history, since for the first time its own Parliament had the power to legislate, a kind of 'Home Rule', after pressure from America. Only two years earlier Burke had lost his Bristol seat for advocating Ireland's rights – Wilkes had said that his oratory 'stank of whiskey and potatoes'. Poyning's Act (obedience to English monarch) had gone; a Habeas Corpus Act secured a speedy trial for prisoners and substantial relaxation of the penal laws, and the repeal of the 1719 Act. Eight years after the 1776 agrarian rebellion, agriculture started to prosper. Commercial restrictions were lifted much to the disgust of English manufacturers who feared that the Irish would flood their markets with Irish goods, however a poor flax season in 1777 indicated a bleak future for the linen industry.

Catholics were allowed to worship in public in 1779, but Government fear of a French invasion caused the formation of a Volunteer Corps in Ulster, which then spread over all Ireland. However eight years later, the Whiteboy outrages were considered sufficient reason for the Government to re-introduce a coercion bill. In Ulster the Peep-of-Day Boys organisation was formed in 1785, which denied Catholics the use of arms; in response this gave rise to the Catholic Defenders. These conflicts extended until the whole of Ulster was torn with strife and discord. At this time even the Dissenters of Belfast were proposing the emancipation of the Catholics.

John Stuart Mill explained in his book 'Political Economy' that 'the whole of the agri-cultural population of Ireland were cottier-tenants [except those under the Ulster tenant-right laws]. There was a numerous class of labourers who (through refusal of proprietors or tenants in possession to permit further sub-division), have been unable to obtain even the smallest patch of land as permanent tenants. But, from the deficiency of capital, the custom of paying wages in land was so universal, that even those who work as casual labourers for the cottiers or for such larger farmers as are found in the country, are usually paid not in money, but by permission to cultivate for a season a piece of ground, which is generally delivered to them by the farmer ready manured, and is known by the name of conacre'.

De Latocnaye described in contrast the opulence of a landowner at Castle Coole, in Fermanagh: 'Lord Belmore has built in this neighbourhood a superb palace, the masonry alone of the building costing him £80,000 sterling. The colonnade of the front eleva-tion is of an architecture too fine, perhaps, for an individual and for a country house. The interior is full of rare marbles, and the walls of several rooms are covered with rare stuccio work produced at great cost, and by workers brought from Italy'. The finance for this luxury came from coal mining established by Charles Coote in the 1600s at Arigna near Lough Allen, the first lake on the River Shannon. The O'Reilly Bros founded an iron foundry in 1788 with coal used in the smelting process. Iron mining started at Arigna but was less successful, and closed in 1838, however small scale coal mining continued until the 1980s.

Thomas Paine 1792
(British Museum)

French Revolution and Wars

In 1789 when 'France had gone mad' (as well as George III), it was reported that Arthur Wellesley was privately reading Locke's essay concerning Human Understanding, and his sister was writing to the Ladies of Llangollen believing she would not see 'poor dear France' again. The Ladies had trembled at the Gordon anti-Catholic riots in London. Wellesley, now MP for Trim in Meath, spoke in parliament for a liberal attitude to Catholics. The Grattanite Whigs had secured some relaxation of the Penal Code, and the economic development which followed destroyed a great deal of the segregation which the Code had been designed to create. The Dissenters, republican by tradition, were enthusiastic admirers of the French Revolution, but Burke feared that 'engine', the guillotine!

In 1791, Theobald Wolfe Tone, descended from Cromwellian planter stock, formed the Society of United Irishmen in Belfast following the 'Volunteer's agitation' of 1783. Their slogan, 'the greatest happiness of the greatest number' was to be made more famous by Jeremy Bentham. Tone made a bitter attack on 'Grattan's Parliament' which left 'three fourths of our countrymen slaves as it found them'. Many of Tone's aspirations for Ireland were contained in Thomas Paine's 'Rights of Man' published in 1791/1792, and were fifty years ahead of the Chartists.

In Edinburgh, the newspapers were brisling with notices of meetings concerning the cruelty of the slave trade. In 1792 Olaudah Equiano, a freed slave, was involved in the anti-slave campaign; he was allowed to go 90 fathoms down the shaft at St Anthony's Colliery at Newcastle upon Tyne. This was the year when Catholics were allowed to marry Protestants, masters to have more than one Catholic apprentice, and Catholics were allowed to build and endow Catholic schools. There was obvious support for France from the Irish, but not from the English lower orders, who still considered France as the traditional enemy, not realising that the war with France was delaying the advance of their freedoms.

Irish MP, Burke, had been one of the first to recognise that the revolutions of America and France were of world historical importance. In many of his tracts, he strongly argued the case against Protestant ascendancy over Catholics. Some Englishmen had welcomed the French revolution in its early stages (1789–91), seeing it as the rejection of Popery. Burke felt he needed to educate the English by publishing his greatest tract, 'Reflections on the Revolution in France'. In his address to Lord Shannon, he called for the State of Ireland to teach parties moderation in their victories.

William Godwin in his momentous Political Justice of 1793, put forward the then utopian expectation that the means and materials of labour should belong to the labourer, and would come about with the new conditions of industry. Even in 1775, the first fragment of socialism was emerging in a paper read before a 'Philosophical Society' at Newcastle by a local headmaster, Thomas Spence. Its basis was that all men have a natural right to equal property in land. Newcastle became too hot for Spence after his lecture was published; for the rest of his life he propagated his doctrine from a bookshop in London including long periods in prison for selling the Rights of Man and other Radical papers. Many remembered Rousseau's famous quote which stated: 'You are lost if you forget that the produce belongs to all, the land to none'.

Surprisingly on Paine's return from America, he brought back with him immediate plans for the construction of a cast- iron arched bridge, which was built at Sunderland in 1796. At this time of war and famine affecting the whole of Europe, and when the militia and pressgangs were threatening the occupation of the artisan, George Stephenson contemplated emigrating to America. The Government, however, were more concerned with Paine's seditious and libellous views than whether the English political system was unconstitutional and tyrannical. Other views were also causing much consternation to both rich and poor.

However, with the declaration of war by the French Republic in February 1793, England felt obliged to grant Catholics the right to vote, and most civil and military posts were thrown open to them. However England also took the opportunity to also wage war on the United Irishmen, and this Society was pronounced illegal in May 1794, and Tone driven into exile.

The Irish state-trials at this time were an endeavour to set up the doctrine of constructive and cumulative treason. Anti-Jacobin hysteria engulfed England; Habeas Corpus was suspended, and Wellesley left Ireland for Ostend and war. The Government's attempts to conscript men for the war met with general resistance in Ireland, resulting in pitched battles fought at Ballinafad in Sligo, Enniskillen in Fermanagh and Athboy in Meath. Following skirmishes over a decade between the Catholic 'Defenders' and Protestant Peep-o'-Day Boys, in September 1795 matters came to a head in the 'Battle of the Diamond' at Loughgall near Portadown, Co Armagh between rival gangs. After the repeal of penal laws restricting Catholic land purchase, Catholic competition for leases had intensified, driving up prices and provoking Protestant resentment. About 10,000 Catholics, mostly weavers, fled to the province of Connaught.

Shortly after their victory, the Protestants founded the Royal Orange Order signalling their strong support for William of Orange. Many Catholics known as Ultachs, took refuge on the bare mountainsides of Leitrim. Others escaped to parts of Mayo, Roscommon, Sligo and even as far as Galway. Those that remained were in a constant state of fear. Their cabins consisted of holes in the bog covered with a layer of turf, and not distinguishable as human habitations from the surrounding moors, until close up to them. A Frenchman in 1792 reported '… a road through the mountains leads to Aghacashel belonging to Mr Johnston where iron, coal, pipe-clay, etc have been discovered'.

Anthony Trollope in his book The MacDermots of Ballycloran described this settlement in Leitrim (the early home of author's wife's families, Keany and Gallagher):

> 'Aughacashel is a mountain on the eastern side of Loch Allen, near the borders of the County Cavan – uncultivated and rocky at the top, but nevertheless inhabited, and studded with many miserably poor cabins, till within about a quarter of a mile of the summit. The owners of these cabins, with great labour, have contrived to obtain wretchedly poor crops of potatoes from the barren soil immediately round their cabins. To their agricultural pursuits many joined the more profitable but hazardous business of making potheen, and they were generally speaking, a lawless, reckless set of people – paying, some little, and others no rent, and living without the common blessings or restraints of civilisation: no road, or no sign of a road, came within some miles of them; Drumshambo, the nearest village, was seven or eight miles distant from them; and although they knew that neither the barreness of their locality, nor the want of means of approach would altogether secure them from the unwelcome visits of the Revenue police or Constabulary …'

United Irishmen and The Act of Union

After the failed insurrection attempts by the Irish during 1796/7, the Government was in a constant state of suspense, and the 'Dragooning of Ulster' followed the Insurrection Act of 1798, with the 'Orange Terror' giving rise to persecution and incidents of ferocious cruelty driving thousands from their homes. The yeomanry corps were little else than Orange Lodges and Peep-of-Day Boy gangs put into uniform. This culminated in the actual Rising and its bloody repression in May 1798. The 'Union of Irishmen, irrespective of creed', drew together Catholics and Presbyterians of similar radical views, but lack of co-ordination was to prove fatal. During this time Castlereagh condoned every illegality, employed the vilest of men as his instruments, and appeared to love cruelty for its own sake.

Wolfe Tone considered that the French Revolution had 'changed in an instant the politics of Ireland', but complained that Irish priests in Munster hated the very name of the French revolution. He met Thomas Paine during 1798 in Paris after the failure of his planned invasion in 1796. After Lord Edward Fitzgerald, a popular leader of the United Irishmen, was shot and died, the United Irishmen led by Tone were defeated at the Battle of Vinegar Hill in June 1798 at the cost of 30,000 lives. Tone committed suicide five months after Fitzgerald's death. Three years later, Robert Emmett, a rebel also from a Protestant family sympathetic to Irish Catholics gaining rights, was executed for high treason. Later Napoleon expressed bitter regret that he had not made more determined efforts in support of Ireland.

The Flax Growers List of 1796 included a number of Shenans and Shannons from north west Ireland, for example Philip Shenan from the Derrybrusk parish of Fermanagh. The author's 2-great grandfather, Peter Shannon, an elder son of Philip Shannon, was born about 1798, the year of the 'Rising' of the United Irishmen. It must have been a time of great anxiety, not the best of times for Philip's wife to be in labour. Shannons were recorded living at Clones in Monaghan, at Stokestown in Roscommon, and at Dromore and Downpatrick in County Down. At this time, linen represented 58% of the total Irish exports.

At Kesh in the Lurg area, east of Lough Erne, the ancestral home of the Shannons, in 1792 a Susan Shannon was born to another Philip Shannon, a blacksmith, and Mary Clarke. Susan went on to marry Charles Murray. About forty years later, there were Murrays who were sponsors to two of Peter Shannon's children in Newcastle upon Tyne. The Murray name had entered Ulster following the Scottish invasion during plantation times.

Coal mining started at Newcastle in south-east Australia in 1801, and three years later a penal colony was established there. It was named after the most famous British coal

Wolfe Tone 1798
(Wikimedia Commons)

mining city, known by the saying 'coals to Newcastle'. During the nineteenth century many of Australia's miners came from north-east England, so Australian place names have included Jesmond, Hexham, Wickham, Wallsend and Gateshead. Then, working in the Australian coal mines was considered one of the worst forms of hardship suitable for the early convicts, and the first consignment was a shipload of 34 Irish convicts who had been involved in the 1798 Rising (all convicts after 1792 were sent to Australia).

During the period 1790 to 1797, a frenzy of canal building gripped England, and at the height of this 'Canal Mania', many companies were competing for labour. Independent MP Denys Rolle wrote: 'From the Immense Numbers of Canals now coming on and the not only absence of a Multitude of the Labouring Class abroad in the War but the vast suppos'd Diminution that there will arise from the destruction in it, a great scarcity of Hands for the Cultivation will be found at the End.....'. He went on to say that some Irish were already worked in harvesting and canal cutting, and he proposed that more should be encouraged to come over. Often canal cutting was started as soon as harvesting was completed. The canal mania hardly touched Ireland because private money was not available there. An exception was the Royal Canal from Dublin to the upper Shannon started in 1789, promoted by a private company but with borrowed State money. By 1800, Telford was advocating iron railways instead of canals, although in 1802 he was still heavily involved in canals designed with William Jessop – the Caledonian Canal, and the

Pontcysyllte Aqueduct in 1805. Twenty-five years later he was still dealing with the Ulster Canal near Leitrim engineered by Jessop. This was the birth of a new class – the mechanic and well-paid engineer.

In 1798, the 'Essay on the Principle of Population' by Thomas Robert Malthus was first published. This essay was to evoke strong working class passions. Its message doomed their lives to 'misery and vice' based on an anticipated population growth that would be unable to keep pace with the means of subsistence. He listed certain restraints on the increase in population which he categorised as 'positive checks' – starvation, sickness, war, infanticide (mainly affecting the poor), and 'preventive checks' – delay in marriage, restraint of sexual passions, contraceptive methods. He also felt that the movement of workers from agriculture to manufacturing would worsen the situation by reducing the supply of food. Ireland's first socialist was considered to be William Thompson, a strong critic of Malthus and capitalism.

Ninety years later, Henry George in his book, Progress and Poverty, also refuted the basis of a Malthusian catastrophe, with Ireland the target of much Malthus's criticism. George stated that it was not the inability of the soil to support so large a population that compelled so many to live in this miserable way, and that 'A merciless banditti of tax gatherers did not march through the land plundering and torturing, but the labour was just as effectively stripped by as merciless a horde of landlords among whom the soil had been divided as their absolute possession, regardless of any rights of those who lived upon it'. He added 'For when her population was at its highest, Ireland was a food-exporting country. Even during the [Great] famine, grain and meat and butter and cheese were carted for exportation along roads lined with the starving and past trenches into which the dead were piled'.

By 1800, Armagh, the centre of the linen trade, was the most densely populated county in Ireland. Also linen-dependent populations had arisen on poor land in Mayo, Sligo, Leitrim and Roscommon. The internal economy of Ireland was rapidly improving; this seemed the last days of dearth and famine. However, the oppressive legislation that was restricting Irish commerce and injuring the seaports compelled the inhabitants of inland counties like Monaghan to use up the produce of their own lands. This led to the dictum of Swift, "Burn everything English except coal", becoming the moto and guide of the Irish.

It was said that Prime Minister Pitt had prepared the Irish for Union with England by repealing the Penal Codes. Despite a petition showing the Irish to be 14 to 1 against Union with England, by the Act of Union, in 1801 Ireland was required to merge with Great Britain to form 'The United Kingdom of Great Britain and Ireland'. The Church of Ireland and the Church of England also became united in law. The Irish parliament ceased to exist; instead 32 Irish peers were to sit in the House of Lords at Westminster, and 100 Irish members in the House of Commons. Daniel O'Connell, in his first speech at a meeting of Catholics in 1800, had said 'he would rather the Protestant fellow countrymen than lay the country to the feet of foreigners', or the re-introduction of the penal laws. The Irish had been forced into the Union unlike the Scots, and ironically the Irish Parliament had never refused to follow England into her wars unlike the Scots. What little industry did exist in the Belfast area was unable to compete with the rapidly developing English economy. Robert Emmett had planned an attack on Dublin Castle in 1802. Daniel O'Connell was a member of the Lawyers' Yeomanry Corps of Dublin who volunteered to hunt for Emmett's insurgents.

In the early nineteenth century, Edward Wakefield noted the Irish peasantry's love of learning: 'Education is more general among the poorer classes in Ireland than it is among the same description of persons in England. In the former the peasantry are more quick of comprehension than the latter. Labourers in England can plough the land or make a fence in a manner which would astonish the Irish, but they are so boorishly stupid that it is difficult to converse with them and they seldom trouble themselves about anything beyond the precincts of their own parish. But the Irish, with less skill in manual operations, possess more intelligence, they are shrewd by nature, and have a most anxious desire to obtain information.'

Apart from 1801, when a potato famine hit Ireland (and bread riots in England), the early years of the nineteenth century (before Waterloo) saw a great surge of agricultural prosperity in Ireland. This was started partly by earlier government corn bounties to farmers in the days of the Irish Parliament, but accelerated by the high farm prices obtainable at the end of the Napoleonic War. Yet in Ireland, where land was virtually the only source of livelihood, and competition for land therefore unlimited, agricultural prosperity meant prosperity only for those who received rents. In the first decades of the century, resentment was focused in sporadic outbreaks of violent resistance to the collection of church tithes (10% of a tenant's produce). Violent confrontations and the sense of underlying alienation continued as a theme of rural life up to the 1840s, mobilised by issues of tithes, land hunger and invasion of common bog or grazing. All the revenue extracted from Ireland by the landlords was drained away for consumption and investment in England.

Arthur O'Connor, a United Irishman, escaped to Paris where he was appointed a general in Napoleon's army. Arthur Wellesley, soon to also know Napoleon, who became Chief Secretary of Ireland in 1807, commented on his birth in Ireland: 'Because a man is born in a stable that does not make him a horse' – perhaps he did not remember Jesus! However in many ways, Wellesley (later Duke of Wellington), had a reputation for tolerance, promising a Catholic nobleman to administer Catholic laws with 'mildness and good temper', and forbidding his yeomanry to celebrate the anniversary of the Vinegar Hill

Anti-slave medal 1795
(The British Museum)

victory over the rebels of '98. He also considered reforms in schooling, drawing Catholic and Protestant children together, and the eradication of tithes and absentee landlords. Unfortunately, his last time in Ireland was 1809 when he left Cork with English troops bound for the Portugal.

During Wellesley's Peninsular campaign, he remarked on the difficulty of the British 'beef addict' troops to survive on the starvation diet of the Spanish peasants. In contrast he noted that the large Irish contingent was happiest in wine country, and the Scotch on pay-day. Among the troops fighting in Portugal and Spain were the Connaught Rangers who were held in high regard by Wellesley. Perhaps reflecting on the beginnings of Orange lodges, he was very suspect of freemasonry, although he had been initiated at Trim lodge as a young man (even Burns succumbed). He also feared the effects of Catholic priests and Methodist preachers. At home the new Tory administration was headed by Spencer Perceval, an evangelical, fanatically opposed to Catholic Emancipation.

England was the first nation to prohibit the slave trade in 1807, and by 1820 similar legislation had been adopted by most European countries. The British campaign for the abolition of the slave trade was gathering momentum, and one of Wellington's duties as ambassador to Austria was to urge King Louis to abolish the slave trade in the French colonies. Having spent most of his recent time abroad, Wellington had not realised the fervour that the campaign had generated in Britain. Lord Castlereagh was also surprised to learn that there were meetings being held in every village to insist upon his exerting his authority to abolish the trade in 'negro' slaves. Wellington was quickly brought up to date by Thomas Clarkson, and had high hopes that the American Congress would be persuaded. When Napoleon briefly returned to power, he immediately abolished the French slave trade.

Grain prices fell sharply after a bumper harvest in late 1813; in the following year there was a catastrophic fall in the price of livestock as high wartime demand disappeared. The Catholic Relief Bill was passed after Lords Grenville, Grey, Wellesley, and Mr Canning refused to take office with Emancipation. It took another sixteen years before the Bill was realised. Among others, Robert Peel as new Chief Secretary, showed his early illiberal views in suppressing the Catholic Board and attacking O'Connell. In March 1815, news of Napoleon's escape from Elba was greeted all over Ireland with great joy. Wellington was involved in discussions with Castlereagh regarding the calling up of the militia in Ireland from fears of insurrection. The British upper classes feared that France would attempt some incitement to rebellion in Ireland, and that priests would instruct their flocks to outrage against the Protestants. This led to the development of innumerable secret societies and confederations of peasants, for example the Ribbonmen, Trashers and Shanavests.

Shelley, a sympathiser of the Irish people, was to leave home in 1818 for Italy, never to return, as the Elgin marbles were brought into England. However thousands of disbanded soldiers and sailors arrived back in Ireland to face high unemployment in urban areas and 'in rural areas the landlords engaged in a war of extermination with the tenantry'. There were 'risings' in Yorkshire and other northern counties in 1817. In County Durham during 1816, a Thomas Mason was sentenced to death for stealing heifers. There was no leniency for the poor.

Famine and Disease 1815 to 1817

Failure of crops in Ireland and over most of Britain in 1815 may have been due to an event that took place in a far-away continent. On the island of Sumbawa in Indonesia, a mountain called Tambora exploded spectacularly, killing a hundred thousand people from its blast and associated tsunamis. Even seven months later the effect of the ash fallout was widespread. Spring never came and summer did not warm the land. 1816 became known as the year without a summer. In Ireland, a famine and associated typhoid epidemic killed sixty-five thousand people. At this time it was said that more lives were lost due to epidemics than by wars.

From earliest times, famine was a regular visitor to Ireland. The causes of famine were often a combination of severely adverse weather leading to potato and crop failure, and the prolonged effects of wars. The subsistence crisis of 1816–1818 was the worst immediately proceeding the Great Famine, and worsened by the economic depression following the end of the Napoleonic Wars. There was a radical change after 1815 due to the price of corn falling, but not rents. Corn was being exported to England despite its need in Ireland. The acre under tillage decreased as cattle became more profitable. Irish cottiers and tenant

farmers faced oppressive rents with little local seasonal work. Barker and Cheyne's Report described Ireland in 1817:

> 'The summer and autumn were humid, cold and ungenial, and agricultural produce, with the exception of potatoes, which were more abundant than in the former year, was almost as scarce as 1816. We collect to have seen, when travelling on the north road leading from Dublin, corn in sheaves rotting on the ground in the month of December, 1817. In some places the poorer classes were compelled to the sad necessity of collecting various exculents, wild vegetables, nettles, wild mustard, navew [turnip], and others of the same kind, to support life; and in places distant from Dublin wretched beings were often seen exploring the fields with the hope of obtaining a supply of this miserable food. In districts contiguous to the sea various marine plants were had recourse to for the purpose of allaying the cravings of hunger. In some districts seed potatoes were taken up from the ground, and hopes of the future year thus destroyed for the relief of the present necessity; and the blood drawn from the cattle on the fields and mixed with oatmeal, when this could be procured, has not infrequently supplied a meal to a starving family. So general was the distress, and insufficient the supply on some parts of the country, that a few unhappy sufferers are said to have died of absolute want of food ....'

In Ireland, the Shannons would have obtained a livelihood by working off the land, as cottiers and part-time weavers or flax growers. It is possible that they also worked part-time in the local iron and coal mines. After the resumption of peace in 1815, emigration resumed and intensified, following the destruction of hand-looms causing

rising unemployment. Two years later an unusually good harvest came too late, and a particularly severe famine and fever epidemic forced the Shannons to flee their native land. From north west Ireland, the Shannon family fatigued by starvation, would have taken about two weeks to walk to the port of Donaghadee, twenty miles east of Belfast.

The 'crossing of the Shannon' had been a statement of resistance and honour, and the Shannons as immigrants were to continue the fight for themselves and their communities.

In Mayo there was a tradition that when a family emigrated, their kinsmen or neighbours took a piece of burning turf from their last fire in the abandoned house and placed it in their own, never quenched fire – a symbolic refusal to believe the probable finality of most departures, however the harsh fact was that most never returned to re-light their fires and restore the broken continuities of Irish life. The following exiles' song recorded their hope that they might return to Ireland:

> 'Farewell Enniskillen, fare thee well for a while,
> To all your bright valleys and every green isle.
> Oh, your fair isles will flourish most powerful and free
> While I from old Ireland an exile must flee.'

CHAPTER 2

1817 Emigration to Scotland

(The Shannons escape from Irish famine and poverty)

'Weave o'er the world your weft, yea weave yourselves,
Imperial races weave the warp thereof.
Swift like your shuttle speed the ships, and scoff
At wind and wave. And, as a miner delves
For hidden treasure bedded deep in stone,
So seek ye and find the treasure patriotism
In lands remote and dipped with alien chrism,
And make those new lands heart-dear and your own.
Weave o'er the world yourselves. Half-human man
Wanes from before your faces like a cloud
Sun-striken, and his soil becomes his shroud.
But of your souls and bodies ye shall make
The sov'reign vesture of its leagueless span,
Clothing with history cliff and wild and lake.'

('Emigration' by William Michael Rossetti 1850)

'There are parts of Connacht where a man plants his potatoes at the proper season and shuts up his cabin and goes to England and labours; and perhaps his wife and children beg on the roads; and when he comes back to dig his potatoes, with wages of his English labour in his pocket, he is able to pay a larger sum in rent than he could have extracted from the soil.'

(George Cornewall Lewis, House of Lords Committee in 1825)

It was said that Columbus visited Ireland in quest of information before his voyage to America. He met a Patrick Maguire who taught him sailing craft and accompanied him on his journey of discovery in 1492, and thus was the first Irishman to step on American soil. Sadly, Columbus was to treat the indigenous Americans as the English treated the Irish, as slaves, in the name of Christianity.

Those leaving Ireland can be categorised into various groups: seasonal workers, armed forces, cattle drovers, navvies, poor law and settlement migrants, convicts and emigrants.

Seasonal Workers

The very lowest of Irish society, who lived on wasteland on the mountains or in the bogs, emerged to get work in the summer months. These seasonal workers were known as spalpeens (Irish for 'penny sythes'), and were willing to tramp long distances in search of summer employment. During the early 1800s in County Kerry, spalpeens were generally hated for lowering wages, and were known to have had their ears cut off. In Drumahaire Co Leitrim they were attacked and beaten. As early as the 1740s, there were large numbers of Irish harvesting in the London area, and in the 1770s likewise. Seasonal migration was thus a vital aspect of pre-industrial agriculture due to irregular farm workloads which required an uneven spread of agricultural labourers relative to demand. Also during the period 1710 to 1790 there was a considerable demand for labour required by enclosure works. Due to Irish harvest failures, Irish labour was attracted in droves to England, and during the Napoleonic wars. Even by 1815, some still believed that emigration could weaken or depopulate Britain, contrary to the frightening population predictions by Malthus. Many in Government considered the emigrant ship as England's strongest safeguard against revolution.

Some non-Catholic workers also sought work abroad. Joseph and Mary Orr Burgess were of Presbyterian faith, and left County Down in 1807 fearing reprisals after the 1798 Rising. They crossed the 'Short Sea' (Donaghadee to Portpatrick) as was common by seasonal workers. They settled in the heart of 'Black Douglas country', the Dumfries

Irish spalpeens en route to Britain (A O'Kelly)

district of Scotland. The family moved several times around the Dumfries farms. Joseph would have attended the annual (Whitsunday 15 May) hiring fair in Dumfries, where employers contracted with labourers for a year's work, and often if married, provided a cottage and small garden. He had four children by 1814, but then committed a felony and his world collapsed. On the 7 Sept 1815 as a convict he arrived in New South Wales. His family had to wait eight long years before they could join him.

During the period 1783–1814, the Irish economy was relatively buoyant with the Ulster linen industry prospering. In the latter years, England was at war with France and depended on Irish exports. The expansion of tillage provided more employment, but the poorer people were the least to benefit. The Presbyterians kept their farms intact by sending their 'superfluous' sons to America, while the Catholics then took advantage of the greater availability of land. In their traditional way, the Catholics subdivided the land into minute portions, and subsidised their income by cattle droving and seasonal migration to Scotland. While the Protestants were attracted to the independence that was offered in the 'promised land', they emigrated only if they could afford to transport whole families, hoping to retain status and life-styles which were under threat in Ireland.

The war with France brought high prices and increased taxation, making a greater demand on rents and tithes. Shortage of labouring work also caused many thousands of poor labourers to enlist reluctantly with the British army and navy. After the 98 Rising, farmers were afraid to grumble and then be labelled as rebels. Catholics were also fleeing to escape Orange Order persecution. A landlord needed only apply to the county court to result in Irish peasants being expelled from the land and their homes destroyed, and then they had to choose between starvation or taking a ship to the British mainland in the hope of casual work. When linen production moved to centralized factories in Ulster, many cottage workers lost their means of living. This contributed to the first big wave of nineteenth century emigration from the poorer parts of the country after 1815.

By 1814, it was reported that in Armagh, Tyrone, Derry and in other Ulster counties, 'the population ....exceeds the means of subsistence, and seems to be the chief cause of the frequency of emigration'. American Independence provided more confidence, particularly for Catholics, who the United States gave financial benefits as well as ideals of Liberty and Independence, but the cost of passage to America was still beyond the means of most poor Irish families. At least after 1815, Irish emigrants did not have to fear British press-gangs or interception by pirates or French warships. During 1815–1819, emigrants were similar in background to those departing Ireland in the late eighteenth century; about two-thirds from Ulster, mainly Presbyterians and Anglicans, of 'superior quality'- 'strong and active farmers', artisans, shopkeepers, tradesmen, and professionals. During August, September and October in the 1820s, there was an annual influx of six to eight thousand agricultural labourers mainly from Connacht and Ulster. Those who arrived by the Portpatrick route, looked for work along the valleys of the Nith and Annan in Dumfriesshire. As they travelled east they took lodgings in the open heaths and fields

From 1834, H D Inglis noted that all who can, emigrated, and were chiefly Catholic. A poor Inquiry's survey concluded that about forty thousand reapers were emigrating annually to Britain, mainly from the impoverished north west counties of Ireland. By 1851 the Irish-born population in Dumfriesshire was about 6%. The Irish death rates were high, since being weak from famine, their resistance to disease was low. From 1800 to 1850 it was estimated that 300,000 Irish had made their way to Scotland. Many decades later, seasonal workers from Ireland were still travelling to Scotland.

Although the Shannons may have travelled to Scotland before 1815 as seasonal harvesters or itinerant labourers (spailpin fanach), there were no records available to confirm this, not unusual for Catholics following the period of penal laws. The fact that they chose to go to Scotland was probably because it was cheaper than heading for Liverpool, and then to America. In the Catholic records the Irish were described as wanderers, strollers, stragglers and travellers. Records of these times show that Wigtownshire and the adjacent counties were the only areas in Scotland where Irish agricultural workers made it their permanent residence. It is perhaps fortunate that the Shannons' stay in Scotland gave them a transition before having to face urban life.

Ireland/Scotland Crossings

From earliest times the peoples of the northern part of Ireland and the south west of Scotland had travelled between their countries, and sometimes settled for short and long periods as conditions allowed. There were Dalriadic immigrations until the invasions by Norsemen three centuries later. Ireland and this part of Scotland were regarded as one race, in language and in literature. The Irish language had had common usage over many parts of lowland Scotland. Over four centuries there had been a backward flow of men from the west of Scotland to the country of their origin. In the seventh century, Ireland was famous for her monasteries as centres of learning which attracted students such as their kindred Scots from Caledonia, Saxons from Britain, and Gauls from France.

Legend says that St Patrick, after being enslaved in Ireland, returned to Scotland via Port Patrick (Port Phadraig in Scottish Gaelic), hence its name. In 1662 it became the chief port in Britain for the shortest sea crossing to Ireland, only twenty-one miles away. During the seventeenth century this port was known as Galloway's Gretna Green with many eloping couples travelling from Ireland. The old connection between the north of Ireland and south west Scotland was strengthened in the eighteenth century by the growth of the cattle trade in Galloway, brought into Scotland from Ulster. The '98' Rising in Ireland had been responsible for a vast inflow of Irish from the west of Scotland. Irish inhabitants of Glasgow were also involved in abortive risings in 1798 and five years later. Afterwards the British authorities tried to break the power of the United Irishmen. The port claimed fame where Thomas Muir, the Radical lawyer, landed in July 1793 before being captured, and sentenced to fourteen years transportation. Muir was the first political prisoner to be sentenced for sedition on the basis of distributing Thomas Paine's Rights of Man. After his trial, Burns wrote in his honour "Scots Wha Hae". Wolfe Tone also travelled this route with a petition for 'Catholic equality with Protestants' drawn up by the Catholic Committee to be presented to King George III.

On the Solway like Ireland, peat had been cut for household fuel over the centuries. Down the coast, Little Whitehaven from the seventeenth century exported coal to Ireland and was one of the largest ports at the end of the next century. There the Lowther family profited immensely from handling Virginian tobacco in addition to Irish cattle and local coals. Many Irish heading for Newcastle, first landed on English soil at Whitehaven; some stayed employed in mining. In the second half of the 19th century, iron-masters were attracted to Whitehaven iron ore mines from Ireland and Durham.

After witnessing the gerrymandering of the Lowther family against Lord Brougham in the election at Ambleside in 1818, the poet Keats moved on to visit Dumfries and in particular to see the places associated with Robert Burns, someone he greatly admired. Other emigrants from the north of Ireland crossed to Glasgow, and then worked their way down the east side of Scotland. In Carlisle, development in textiles encouraged an influx of significant numbers of Irish and 'Scotch' weavers. The main crossing route was to Liverpool, either to find work in England, or wait until they has sufficient funds to take them to the United States or Canada.

In common with the upper Solway, the Irish Sea coast of the Rhinns had many bays where small sailing ships could beach at low tide in favourable weather, yet there were only two natural harbours on this treacherous coast. They shared a common tragic history. Port Logan and Port Patrick were at the centre of a national controversy over the shortest sea-passage to Ireland, which raged for more than a century after the 1760s. The government's main concern was for fast communication with Ireland for mail and troops; the problem was to decide on the quickest and most reliable route across the North Channel. Many different routes had been followed before the eighteenth century, though the established one for mail packets was from Portpatrick to Donaghadee. The hazards to navigation, especially unfavourable winds and currents, caused interminable delays in passage, and soon merchant and landed interests on both sides of the Irish Sea joined the political lobby for a government inquiry.

The first of many commissions, led by a veritable cortege of eminent engineers, reported in 1768 when Engineer John Smeaton found Portpatrick 'almost in a state of nature', except for a small landing place for travellers. He proposed two outer breakwaters to guard the rocky entrance and the reconstruction of the inner harbour. Work was completed ten years later, having cost twice the original estimate. After further misadventures, the Government appointed Telford to carry out another crossing investigation. After a visit to Portpatrick in 1802, Telford reported the site 'was destitute of the advantages requisite for a perfect Harbour for packets to ply from', where winds from every direction except the east caused a heavy swell and 'large reefs of rocks' made entry to the harbour hazardous on any but calm days. It was destroyed by gales during the early 19th century; later Stranraer nearby was considered more sheltered. The survey produced no definite conclusions, but during the 1820s work was carried out on new harbours and roads designed by John Rennie.

Over the period that separated Culloden from Waterloo, agriculture in Scotland went through a revolution. The timely development of steam power at the end of the Napoleonic

Port Patrick 1820
(Tate Galleries)

Wars resulted in steam packets providing cheap passage across the Irish Sea, and opened up the floodgates to the Irish, whose population was to increase phenomenally over the next few decades. As soon as the simple requirements of their conacres were met, the Irishmen crowded the steamers. The Irish reapers on the cross channel steamers were described as 'thick as barnacles'. The fare in the 1820s for the passage was 8 shillings or 2 shillings for paupers. From the mid-eighteenth century, black cattle were driven through Dumfries down to the English markets. Cattle from Ulster joined the stream of those from Wigton.

Although the first steam packet crossing of the Atlantic took place in 1818, the more local crossings by steam started a seven years later, therefore the Shannons would have crossed the Irish Sea by sailing ship to Portpatrick; then they travelled through counties Wigtonshire and Galloway to reach Dumfriesshire. The family consisted of James Shannon's grandfather and grandmother, Philip and Ann, and their children Richard, Thomas, and Rosannah, and Thomas Shenan probably Philip's brother.

In 1818, Philip Shannon and his wife were forty-six and thirty-eight years respectively. Their children Richard, Thomas and Rosannah were not recorded in the local records, but their ages would have been only three, two and one respectively. In the absence of burial records some of their children could have died in Dumfriesshire. Amongst the Irish and Scottish poor, there was an acceptance of sudden death. It was an Annandale reverent custom to talk freely of the dead with the acknowledgement of those "that's gane".

Later, English census records gave their son Richard as born in Scotland, so it followed that younger siblings Thomas and Rosannah were also born there. Their son Peter then nineteen, and other older children, must have remained in Ireland at that time, with the intention of joining the family later on a temporary or permanent basis.

Hiring Fairs

Hand-bills were posted up by recruiting agents in Ireland giving the dates of the next Scottish harvest. Anne O'Dowd noted that 'Seasonal and temporary workers adopted several conventional methods of finding work such as wandering from one farm to the next in the locality visited, acting on information received from others who had worked in a certain area the previous year, and on occasion, writing to farmers who traditionally hired temporary staff each year'. In Ireland at the hiring fairs, the farmers recognised the labourers who were available for work by their general demeanour and dress, by their implements and belongings or by some special emblem or spare clothes in a bundle. The workers often carried the tools of their trade with them such as reaping hooks. The [Old] Statistical Account of Kirkoswald (1792) noted a:

'.... Great number of Irish vagrants and beggars who daily travel the great post road from Ayr to Port Patrick; near to which on both sides stands the greater number of farmers' houses which are oppressed by the importunate and violent cravings of the beggars.'

The hiring fair at Strabane in Co Tyrone covered a large area including Donegal and Derry. Others were at Irvinestown in Co Fermanagh, Clones in Co Monaghan and Omagh in Co Tyrone. There were also hiring agents from Ireland based in towns near the work locations such as Newcastle, Kendal, Darlington, Belfast, Dublin, Liverpool, Bristol and Manchester. In Scotland and northern England, farm servants were hired on a half-yearly or yearly basis, others on a weekly term, such as Carlisle at Whitsun and November. In Scotland in particular, work was not freely available for casual workers except in the Border counties.

In the early years of the nineteenth century, the usual procedure was for workers to assemble at four or five o'clock in the morning at the market square of agricultural towns. Especially in Northumberland and Scotland, the yearly hiring of farm servants for live-stock and dairying persisted to the last quarter of the 19th century. At hiring fairs, the bargain was sealed by the farmer simply buying his man a drink. The hiring agreement in Ulster was unwritten, but always obeyed, although there were also fines applied.

Jim Reilly from Eshnanumera in Fermanagh related that 'A man at the Swanlinbar fair in the Kinawley parish was fined a shilling for every holy day which he took [off]. Connaughtmen were mainly employed raising potatoes in June and July, late potatoes in October and November, and as general farm hands milking and hoeing between the two potato seasons'. Sir William Jardine noted in 1839 that harvesting in October was quite normal in Dumfriesshire and Northumberland where potatoes were an important part of the labourer's diet as in Ireland.

The fact that the Shannons were able to stay more than a few years in Scotland, indicated that they either had built up a good reputation during these years of seasonal work or they had demonstrated that they had good skills and were hard workers. Irish harvesting families would tend to return to the same farms each season.

Navvy migrants

A particular migrant who was to gain notoriety with the British press was the Irish 'Navvy'. English children were traditionally warned that the 'navvyman' carried away naughty children. The word navvy was an abbreviation of navigator, a name somewhat lightly bestowed on the labourers who 'cut the navigation'. Navvies were to dig three thousand miles of canals in Great Britain in the second half of the eighteenth century. Canal construction was overtaken by the railways in the 1820s. From 1818 to 1822, labourers were being canvassed in the north of Ireland for work on the Union Canal in Scotland. A canal scheme from Solway to Newcastle was shelved since it would have needed 117 locks!

In later years there was some temptation for harvesters in Scotland to switch to railway work after their seasonal occupation had finished for that year. Finding navvies for rural areas could be difficult since many agricultural workers found the strict discipline and rough living conditions too demanding, even for higher wages. The work was often dangerous, with men being killed by rock or earth falls or by gunpowder explosions going wrong. Disabled navvies found work by wandering from one site to another keeping the men informed of news and wages. It was said that as the navvies toiled, they were 'the embodiment of physical force in its fullest development of concentrated energy. No man stops to lean for breath on the head of that pickaxe he wields so strenuously; the heave of the shovels was like clockwork. The navvies, bare-throated, their massive torsos covered but by the shirt, their strong, lissom lions lightly girt, and the muscles showing out on their shapely legs through the tight, short breeches, and the ribbed stockings that surmount the ankle-jacks, are the perfection of animal vigour. Finer men I never saw, and never hope to see. Man for man, they would fling our Guardsmen over their shoulders; they have all the height and breadth of the best picked men in a Prussian Grenadier regiment of the Guard Corps, without their clumsiness'.

Poor Law and Settlement Migrants

William Aiton (1811) commented on the reaction of local farmers to Irish vagrants: 'Instead of … their trusty servants, they were obliged to employ' at a high rate, indolent Highlanders or vagrant Irishmen'. Many farmers took advantage of the poor laws in the practice of hiring workers for only fifty-one weeks. The 1817 Report on the poor law, mentions among 'the measures, justifiable undoubtedly in point of law, which are adopted very generally in many parts of the kingdom, to defeat the obtaining a settlement, that of hiring labourers for less than a year; from whence naturally and necessarily follows, that a labourer may spend the season of his health and industry in one parish, and be transferred in the decline of life to a distant part of the kingdom'.

During 1817 to 1818, parish expenditure on poor relief reached nearly £8,000,000, or 84% of the total sum spent by local authorities, sourced by the poor rate. In some areas of England the poor were living in conditions not dissimilar to the Irish. Of course any other newcomers to their area were bound to make matters worse. Migrants were passed from parish to parish until they arrived at the port. In 1824, the Vagrancy Act was passed to sweep the 'wandering poor', including ex-soldiers off the streets. The Vagrancy Act of 1548 had forced the landless and destitute to be made to work in chains, and the Law of Settlement Act 1662 forced the paupers to obtain relief in only one specific parish – ideally that of their birth.

1818 was a peak year for poor relief – subsidising farmers by forcing small independent parish ratepayers to contribute. However in Scotland unlike England, there was no relief until 1845, so country labourers such as the Shannons were dependent on charity when their work came to an end, and while they were searching for employment.

The Mendicity Report of 1815 revealed a system operating in several counties for transporting paupers back to their parish of origin, including old women about to die and heavily pregnant women. However some compassion was shown when the Act of 1795 suspended the orders of removal where the pauper was dangerously ill. A Select Committee on Emigration in 1826 noted the good conduct of the Irish, and occasionally it was reported in admiring tones of the flexibility of the Irish in responding to market forces: 'When hands are wanted the Irish are ready to obey the call for even the distance chance of work here is worth the small labour and expense of a trip across the Channel; and in times of depression they retire and so relieve our suffering population. We thus enjoy in their turn all the advantages of an immigrating and emigrating population'.

There were fears of the rising tide of Irish and Scottish pauperism. Workington in Cumbria was one of the six English and Welsh ports for the removal of Irish paupers including their families even though they were born in England. The farmers who got good value from the migrants had differing views to the parish constables and magistrates. The press saw British public opinion as: 'the land of Ireland ought to support the poor of Ireland – that we have enough to do to pay our own taxes and poor rates, without those of the Irish gentry ...'. Many of the Irish migrants found mining work in Cumbria after working in Durham mines, on route to deportation.

Sarah Miller, aged fifty, a native of Belfast, was sent back home to the Irish workhouse by the Newcastle authorities after thirty years in Scotland and England. A native of Mayo, Mary Hopkins, aged twenty-three and her infant child were also sent to the same workhouse from Newcastle after twelve years in England. At Neston in Cheshire, the old custom house in the second half of the eighteenth century was used as a house of correction for unemployed Irish labourers who were being forcibly returned to their own parishes. The flow of Irish migrants increased, provided that persons born in Ireland or Scotland who became chargeable for relief in a parish in England, could be removed by an order imposed by the local justices of the peace.

Removal, where the Irish were concerned, meant that they were put on a boat and returned to a port in Ireland convenient to their original place of residence. However in practice this law was difficult to enforce since notice had to be given, and as soon as the paupers were aware, they fled from the parish concerned. Later the law was amended to omit persons who had resided more than five years or were relieved due to illness, but authorities were no longer required to give notice to vagrants. Robbins described a boat arriving in Ireland with removals from Liverpool: a young boy with the body of his brother at his side who had died during the passage; their parents had died in the Rochdale fever hospital; and a harvester with his boots and reaping hook at his side who had died in one of the lifeboats.

Convicts for Transportation

Although the partial abolition of pillory had just taken place, the Act of 1816 resulted in poachers running the risk of man-traps and seven years transportation. Hunger drove many Irish to kill rabbits and hares. Free emigration for law-abiding citizens to Van Diemen's Island had been established in 1817. Nicholas Bayly commenting on the female convict ships leaving for the colonies, stated that 'it is customary, when female convicts embark, that every sailor be allowed a woman during passage'.

Peter Cunningham, Surgeon Superintendent, made the following comment on convicts bound for New South Wales from Ireland: 'The Irish convicts are more happy and contented with the situation on board ship than the English, although more loth to leave their country even improved as the situation of the great body of them is thus being removed, numbers telling me that they had never been half so well off in their lives before ...... They laid particular importance to the fact of having a blanket and bed "to my own self entirely," which seemed a novelty to them'.

In October 1833, the convict boat Parmelia, arrived at Cobh in Ireland from Gravesend, ready to receive a cargo of Irish felons for the long journey to Australia. The captain of the vessel was not new to this trade having been master of the female convict transport Edward from Cork in 1829. The transport of convicts was not exclusive to Ireland, with the Parmelia's first excursion dealing with 200 English prisoners, four of whom died of cholera; in 1833 there were three English prisoners, one a Durham-born soldier Thomas Gibson, stationed in Limerick and sentenced for habitual insubordination and drunkenness. Of the Irish, 62 had committed crimes of Ribbonism, including a father and son, the Brennans, coal-miners who had issued a threatening notice, and the McNallys of Mayo. Ten men had been committed for vagrancy. It was recorded that on board the transports, the Irish as compared with the English were 'untainted' by sodomy.

Prejudice and Religion

An Irish traveller compared the unwelcome attitude of the locals to the warmth of his people back in Mayo. People with a fixed abode felt contempt for vagabonds. Flora Thompson, author of 'Lark Rise to Candleford', recalled seeing Irish harvesters during her childhood. A threat to local children who refused to behave took the form of 'I'll give you to them old Irishers' in the same way that children were threatened with 'Boney' [Bonaparte]. Some countries have traditionally shown more toleration to vagrants. De Jonge wrote how the wanderers and 'unfortunates' of Russia were treated with benevolence – peasants would leave outside their well-bolted doors each night a dish of food and a bowl of milk for vagrants and men on the run; the fact that they would not dare admit them into their homes did not mean that they were willing to let them go hungry.

Objection to Irish immigration by Scottish residents was highlighted by Glasgow Chronicle of 9 October 1819 when it published a letter to the editor on the 'Necessity of Emigration':

> '.....I am very well aware that the propagaters of the doctrine that poverty increases as the means of relief increase oppose emigration upon the ground that, if we improve the condition of our labourers, we shall only be annoyed by new inroads of the Irish, more numerous and much more wretched than our countrymen conducted to Canada. This argument ..... proceeds solely upon this – that if wages be raised at any time, they will be immediately lowered by fresh irruptions of the Irish. It would doubtless be a galling spectacle to see the room of our sober, religious, industrious, frugal and intelligent countrymen filled with thse ignorant, hapless, wandering wretches; but effectual measures must be taken to prevent this, and I know of no plan so likely to answer this important purpose as that which you formally proposed in the Chronicle, viz., that all those who are the means of bringing Irish here should be obliged to give sufficient security that they will never in any way become burdensome to the parish. In the present precarious state of the commercial world, no man would undergo the risk unless there was positively a scarcity of hands, and hence we would at once get rid of a dangerous and accumulating evil.'

Two centuries earlier, relations between the Irish and Scots had been dramatically worse. Catholics were badly treated by the Scottish Covenanters in the 17th century since Scottish Roman Catholics were mainly Royalist, and therefore were opposed to the Covenanter's imposition of their Protestant religious views. Many Covenanters from Scotland and Ireland emigrated to America and fought on the side of the Union against slavery. During the Covenanting troubles, Ireland proved a haven of refuge to harassed Covenanters from the south west of Scotland, as Scottish Catholics also escaped to Ireland from persecution in their native land.

The introduction of the Corn Law in 1815 meant high prices for bread, causing deprivation in both Ireland and Britain. In 1814, the Commissioners of Supply for Wigton reported that 'Vagabonds and beggars were apprehended and confined for at least 14 days, and in 1816, the Collector of Customs at Portpatrick was 'anxious to prevent influx of Irish vagrants into county'. Until the mass influx of starving labourers and their families threatened the livelihood of the indigenous people, there had existed a very kindly feeling towards the Irish over all the Western Highland and Western Lowland counties of Scotland.

Coastal Smugglers

Newcomers to Scotland would have been as much aware of smuggling as the natives. For 200 years smuggling, especially in rum and whisky, was rife along the Cumbrian coast due to the lower rates of excise duty on the Isle of Man and Scotland. Following the

Robert Burns 1787
(National Galleries)

Treasonable Practices and Seditious Meetings Acts 1795, Lord Sidmouth had increased the powers of magistrates, and was responsible for the repressive policy embodied in the Six Acts, 1819, which included limiting the rights of public meeting and the circulation of political literature. In January 1820 smugglers were apprehended carrying whisky into Cumberland. They had light tin containers known as 'belly cans' fitted to their body by means of straps, almost undetectable when carried under a greatcoat. Again two years later, men were caught carrying Scotch salt whilst crossing the bridge over the Esk. Salt was smuggled until the tax was removed in 1825. The tax on liquor and salt had been a major factor in encouraging smuggling. The stealing of Cumberland cattle and summary hanging was recorded by Carlyle. Tinkers were seen nestling in out-houses, melting pot-metal, and engaged in rude feuds and warfare, and passing Highland drovers was a common sight. To reduce smuggling, well-armed sloops were deployed at Annan Waterfoot.

In the Scottish Lowlands there had been a tradition of anti-establishment activities, continuing from Jacobean times through to piracy and smuggling, which Robert Burns as an excise-man (Tom Paine was also an excise-man in 1761), was well placed to use as the basis of some of his poems. During the reign of George III, Burns caused much consternation by remaining seated at a Dumfries theatre while the audience rose for the national anthem. This gesture was to be used by his enemies to denounce Burns as a revolutionary sympathiser. He was willing to suffer the scorn in supporting the minority 'newlight clergy', in standing fast to his ideals of liberty against hypocrisy. Burns in 1787, perhaps as he was touring in Northumberland, Newcastle and Jarrow, the year that the Quakers of Britain formed the Association for the Abolition of Slavery, denounced the ambitions of the propertied classes at the expense of the hardships suffered by the Scottish peasants:

> 'See stern Oppression's iron grip,
> Or mad Ambition's gory hand,
> Sending, like blood-hounds from the slip,
> Woe, Want, and Murder o'er the land!
> Ev'n in the peaceful rural vale,
> Truth, weeping, tells the mournful tale:
> How pamper'd Luxury, Flatt'ry by her side,
> The parasite empoisoning her ear,
> With all the servile wretches in the rear,
> Looks o'er proud Property, extened wide;
> And eyes the simple, rustic hind,
> Whose toil upholds the glitt'ring show --
> A creature of another kind,
> Some coarser substance, unrefin'd --
> Plac'd for her Lordly use, thus far, thus vile, below!'

Journey from Portpatrick

The Old Statistical Account of 1790 noted that the great road from Portpatrick to Dumfries passed through the parish of Lockerbie, and was constantly swarming with Irish beggars – no distinction was made between Irish harvesters, hawkers, drivers and immigrants – all relegated to the mendicant class. Bell's 'Description of the Condition and Manners of the Peasantry of Ireland between 1780 to 1890' and the Report of the Whig Club on 'The State of the Labouring Poor', gave vivid illustration of the annual migrations long before the end of the eighteenth century. Lecky writing at that time stated: 'It was still true that, at the beginning of every autumn, the roads were crowded with bare-footed and half-naked mountaineers, who travelling 150 to 200 miles to work for the harvest in England, where they commonly fell into the hands of contractors known as 'spalpeen brokers', who distributed them among the farmers, intercepted a substantial part of their scanty wages and imposed on them an amount of labour which few West Indian planters would have exacted from their negroes.' The Editor of the Dumfries Courier wrote in December 1822 of 'The Irish in the West of Scotland':

> 'An intelligent and benevolent correspondent,' says the Editor of the Glasgow Chronicle, 'who lately travelled in Ireland remarks that he saw no cottages so poor in that country as some that stand on the roadside between Stranraer and Portpatrick.' From this observation, a stranger might be apt to infer that, in point of up-putting – if we may adopt a vulgar Scotticism – many of our Gallovidian labourers exhibit a degree of wretchedness unknown even in a land where, according to a correspondent of our own, the peasantry are so much worse clad than the scarecrows of some other countries that the general adoption of these effigies would go far to create a new species of theft, and add to the other causes of Irish demoralisation. But how, we ask, stands the fact? Many of the hovels alluded to are doubtless abundantly mean and wretched, not only between Stranraer and the Port, but also between Glenluce and the former place, being mostly built with turf, and so little beholden to the labours of the mason and joiner that we might expect to see them upset by the first puff of wind that blows, or ignited by every casual spark that wanders beyond the region of the hearth. But here the important questions occur, by whom are these hovels put up (built, in this case, would be an improper term), and by whom are they inhabited? Now, the answer to these questions is completely fatal to the argument which, we presume, was meant to be established in the paragraph above quoted – namely, that we need not travel so far as Ireland to look for the extremes of human wretchedness; for the sheds, or huts, in question are, almost without a single exception, inhabited by Irish emigres – a class of labourers who, in proportion to its population, abound more in Wigtonshire than any other county in Scotland.'

'Though the many-armed Atlantic divides, by his angry billows, the opposite cliffs of Portpatrick and Donaghadee, still the distance is so short that, for the matter of a few pence, Pat can at any time transport himself from the land of potatoes to the land of oatmeal; and as his slender finances are generally exhausted even by this outlay, we may naturally enough suppose that he will foreswear, as far as possible, the fatigue of inland travel, and attempt to find a job at the first place he touches at. So soon, therefore, as the emigrant acquires a settlement, his first care is to save the expense of lodging by building a turf shed, to rent, if he can hit it, a small piece of potato ground, and assimilate himself in every other respect to the manners and the habits of his countrymen in Connaught and Ulster. And, as the Irish surpass every nation in the use of the spade and mattock, and are, in a word, not only excellent labourers, but are often willing to work at reduced rates, and this liberty is very often granted; so that the shire of Wigton may be described as almost one-third Irish and two-thirds Gallivldian. In these circumstances, no one need marvel at the meanness of most of the huts that skirt the public roads in the Rhinns of Galloway; potatoes will grow on the grounds around 'the Mull' as well as in Tipperary; and as a Hibernian, by migrating a few leagues farther east, neither changes his name nor his nature, the existence of such abodes, so far from proving anything new in regard to the situation of our own countrymen, confirms the general impression of Irish filth and misery. But, if the system of location continue, there is no saying how soon Scotchmen may be obliged to lodge in similar cabins.'

As the Shannons travelled from Portpatrick, they would have camped out on open moorland. It was against a background of local distrust and suspicion that the family of Shannons arrived in the area near Lockerbie and Lochmaben in Dumfriesshire about 1815. It is interesting to note that there was a small village on the route between Stranraer and Lockerbie with the name of Shennanton, near Newton Stewart.

CHAPTER 3

1815 to 1829 Scotland –
Combinations and Emancipation

(Philip Shannon's family settle near Lockerbie)

'Let three millions of the people abandon all that they and their ancestors have been
taught to believe sacred, and to forswear it publically in terms the most degrading,
scurrilous, and indecent for the men of integrity and virtue, and to abuse the whole
of their former lives, and to slander the education they received, – and nothing
more is required of them.'

(Edmund Burke on Penal Laws 1793)

' .... the Irish spirit was unlikely to be quenched by any foreign power, having been
nurtured over thousands of years of faction-fights, pike-skirmishes, private duels by
shillelagh, by dirk and fist'

(Thomas Carlyle 1840)

Irish Newcomers

The Scotland/England Border area has had a history of turbulence, with skirmishes and raiding, a continuing occurrence. In particular Annandale was a lawless
border country. Thomas Carlyle, grandfather of the historian, was at Ecclefechen in 1745,
and saw the Highlanders passing through, and was at Dumfries when they returned back
in flight. In 1797, with the French Revolution fresh in everyone's mind, suspicion of insurrection and uprising was rife; Pitt had brought in the Treason and Sedition Acts (1796).
Under those acts, no language of criticism was safe, and fifty persons could not meet
except in the presence of a magistrate, who had the power to stop the meeting and arrest
the speaker.

The Combination Laws, making it illegal for men to 'combine' against their employer, had
been introduced in 1799 and 1800; this caused a reaction by workers in urban areas with a
petition and protests held in Newcastle upon Tyne. These laws gave the masters unlimited
powers to reduce wages and to make working conditions more severe. The employers were
free to combine against workers but not vice versa. William Wilberforce was to support
the introduction of these laws, while at the same time was campaigning for the freedom
of slaves in far off lands. Daniel O'Connell, an anti-trade unionist, was more concerned
with Irish matters; he took up an aggressive attitude in 1807, with a strong attack on the

[Act of] Union asserting that 'The present administration has emancipated Negroes ....
they should introduce a Clause in the Slave Bill to raise Catholics to the rank of Freemen'.
He then came out against Grattan's 'safeguards' for reduced emancipation, and in 1813
rejected the Catholic Relief Bill. This was to cause a bitter split with Grattan lasting
almost a decade. O'Connell popularised Irish history to his audience (like Walter Scott
for Scotland), and urged the rejection of the 'subdued demeanour and almost crouched
walk'. This sentiment was also expressed by Robert Burns in the lines of his poem, 'A Mans
a Man for a' that'.

From 1817 onwards, organised unions appeared in many parts of Britain, especially in
the western Scottish counties of Ayrshire, Lanarkshire, Renfrew and Dunbartonshire,
fighting wage reductions, limiting output to maintain the price of labour, and in some
places trying to operate a closed shop to keep out strangers. The owners retaliated by
importing [Irish] blackleg labour, which began a tradition of bitter racial and religious
hatred that marred the life in the west of Scotland throughout the nineteenth century, and
up to present times. In 1824 there was a terrifying incident during a strike in Midlothian,
in which a party of blacklegs was ambushed underground and had their ears severed.
Later, probably based on his personal experience of Scottish towns, but equally attributable to northern towns like Newcastle, Thomas Carlyle forebode the worst:

> 'Crowds of miserable Irish darken our towns. In his rage and laughing savagery he
> is there to undertake all work that can be done by mere strength of hand and back,
> for wages that will purchase him potatoes. He needs only salt for condiment; he
> lodges to his mind in any pig-hutch or dog-hutch, roosts in out-houses, and wears a
> suit of tatters, the getting on and off of which is said to be a difficult operation. And
> yet the poor celt-Iberian Irish brothers, what can they help it? It is just and natural
> that they come hither as a curse to us. Alas for them, too, it is not a luxury. It is a
> straight or joyful way of avenging their wrongs this; it is but a most sad, circuitous
> one.'

Adam Smith, Robert Burns and Scottish Mines

From the beginning of the industrial revolution there were a number of Scotsmen that
were to have a profound influence on national events: Adam Smith, Robert Burns, Walter
Scott and Thomas Carlyle. In 1777, Adam Smith, published his treatise on the new
political economy, The Wealth of Nations. This was to attack 'private interests' in conflict
with the 'general interest', and gave technology and industry a new and decisive role, not
only in the economy but in society. Although he advocated 'natural freedom' and 'laissez-
faire' in the market-place, he also maintained that the derived prosperity would benefit
all workers: 'No society can surely be flourishing and happy, of which the greater part of

Wanlockhead miners 1900
(museum of lead mining)

the members are poor and miserable. It is but equity, besides, that they who feed, clothe and lodge the whole body of the people, should have a share of the produce of their own labour as to be themselves tolerably well fed, clothed and lodged'. Unfortunately, in practice the social part of the contract was not honoured.

Adam Smith described the principle of 'division of labour'; for example the means by which the miner made his contribution in digging coal from the bowels of the earth: 'labour is the real measure of the exchangeable value of all commodities'. A collier at Newcastle earned commonly about double of the common labourer 'harvest time' wage; in France, 5 years as journeyman was required to become master. Unlike the French philosophers, Smith's view was that human nature was determined by interests, passions, sentiments and sympathies; the differences in people were less the 'cause' than the 'effect' of the division of labour. On the latter point, Smith anticipated what Marx was later to expose as the fatal flaw of capitalism, the 'alienation of the working class'.

Robert Burns, a resident in Dumfriesshire towards the end of his life, became well known as a poet and champion for the rights of working people. In 1792, Maria Riddell, sister of the deceased mine-owner of the Goldilea estate near Dumfries, made a visit to

Wanlockhead Pit accompanied by Robert Burns, breakfasting earlier at Sanquhar. Maria commented 'The interesting remarks and fascinating conversation of our friend Burns, not only beguiled the tediousness of the road, but likewise made us forget its danger'. Holding tapers, they had to make their way bent almost double; water dripped continually from the roof, and they waded through muddy water that came half-way up their legs. The pit props were slimy; Maria held onto the walls for support and her gloves were soon in ribbons. After about a mile of this they, or at least Burns, had had enough: 'The damp and confined air affected our fellow adventurer Burns so much, that we resolved to turn back, after I had satisfied my curiosity by going down one of the shafts. This you will say was a crazy scheme – assailing the Gnomes in their subterranean abodes! Indeed there has never been but one instance of a female hazarding herself hither'.

It would be about forty years before coal mines would be of interest to the Shannons. Compared to the small-sized mines of Ireland and Dumfriesshire, the collieries of the North East were to grow on a gigantic scale. It was unlikely that Philip Shannon would have found work in the mines near Dumfries due to his mainly agricultural background, and because of his Catholic faith.

The 1606 [Scottish] Act stated: 'no person could fee, hire or conduce any salters, colliers or coal bearers without written authority from the master who they had last served'. Lead had been exploited at Wanlockhead by the Romans. The miners in south west Scotland were predominantly Presbyterian. However in 1835, when Daniel O'Connell was touring the mining towns of Sanquhar and Thornhill, he was given an enthusiastic welcome, showing that the local miners had some Catholic sympathies. A love song called the Collier Laddie, supposedly written by Burns, was popular at this time. It gave the thoughts of a young girl who realised that in choosing a collier as a husband she was condemning herself and family to a life of slavery:

> 'Though you had all the sun shines on,
> And the earth conceals sae lowly,
> I'd turn my back on you and yours,
> And embrace my collier laddie.
> Love for love is the bargain for me,
> Though the wee pit hoose should hae me
> I'll mak my bed in the collier's neuk
> And lie doon wi ma collier laddie.'

Robert Burns was well known for his interest in the other sex as expressed by 'Rab the Rhymer' rather than 'Burns the Gauger'. He spoke of a young woman from Durham called Matthews engaged in the 'oldest profession' in Edinburgh. He also took a particular interest in local politics, for example, the elections in the Lochmaben area, then 'a city containing upwards of fourscore living souls that cannot discern between their right hand and their left – for drunkeness'. On polling day Burns described how he had been required by his landlord to do his bit for the Whig interest:

'I have just got a summons to attend with my men-servants armed as well as we can, on Monday at one o' clock in the morning to escort Captn Miller from Dalswinton in to Dumfries … On Thursday last, at chusing the Delegate for the boro' of Lochmaben, the Duke and Captn Miller's friends led a strong party, among others, upwards of two hundred Colliers from Sanquhar Coalworks & Miners from Wanlock-head; but when they appeared over a hill-top within half a mile of Lochmaben, they found a superior host of Annandale warriors drawn out to dispute the Day, that without striking a stroke, they turned their backs & fled with all the precipitation the horrors of blood & murther could inspire…'

In Scotland, the use of children in mines was well documented, with this practice continuing into the 1820s. Handley described in detail the 'use' of female labour in the Scottish coalfields:

'The miners associated with no outsiders and sought partners in marriage only amongst themselves, for a wife was chosen not for her domestic qualities but for her ability to endure backbreaking toil below ground. Such a custom powerfully increased the tendency to isolation, because no female of any other class of life could be found ready and willing to undergo such slavery. The collier preferred a woman or girl as coal-bearer because she was alleged to be able to carry double the weight of coal that a man or boy could scramble out with. Ascent from the mine was made variously by shaft, the ropes of the ascending and descending baskets being worked by one-horse gin, by traps – the name given to wooden ladders-rising from one height to the next, by spiral staircase or by incline. Where shafts were used no separation was made for ascent or descent. Ventilation was taken care of by leaving abandoned shafts open. Originally the bearers carried their loaded creels, varying between one and two hundredweights, up the ladders to the surface, where each had a coal-fauld in which she stored the coal but had to wait for recompense until the master had made a sale. The hazardous drudges, perhaps thirty times a day, for the bearers up the traps with their heavy loads of coal on their backs and the slender support on the ladder of only one hand because the other held a ten-inch stick with an oil lamp at the end of it, led to such frequent accidents that spiral staircases were substituted. Where the pits were a hundred or more feet deep the masters took into their own hands the raising of the coal to the pithead by means of the shaft, thereby giving some relief to the bearers, who had their coal-faulds transferred to the bottom of the pit shaft, the one-horse gin at the surface having the rest of the work. But they had still to manoeuvre to the shaft their loads from the coal-face'.

Industrial Riots

As new industrial methods overtook the former ways of working, groups of workers were forced by starvation to attack the machines which were destroying their jobs. This led to the 'Luddite Risings' in the textile industries. In Northumberland and Durham the miners came out on strike in 1810, against their bonding. The keelmen were resisting the development of the steam locomotive and the extension of the railways down to the banks of the Tyne and Wear; these railways circumnavigated the rivers and delivered the coal directly into the colliers' holds at loading staithes known as 'drops'. Riots were recorded at the new Sunderland Drops in March 1815 when a body of keelmen demolished the staithes setting them on fire. One man was killed by the falling timber and the crowd was not dispersed until a party of dragoons arrived from Newcastle.

From 1816, Thomas Telford took charge of the building of the road from Glasgow to Carlisle which opened in 1820. It is therefore possible that Philip Shannon worked on the section of this road where it passed close to Lockerbie. Philip and Ann were recorded as residing at either Lochmaben or Lockerbie, villages only a few miles apart.

The area around Lochmaben attracted Irish farm workers. Lochmaben was on a peninsular/crannog surrounded by four lochs, and in one of them was the Castle Loch, said to be the only home in the world of the bait-defying vendace (freshwater whitefish). Lochmaben had a colourful history. An entrenchment at Torwood Muir near Lockerbie marked a Roman marching camp, part of Agricola's invasion of Scotland. Edward Bruce

Thomas Telford 1790
(National Museum Liverpool)

met Wallace at Lochmaben. At the outset of the War of Independence in 1306, Bruce was Lord of Annandale, and Lochmaben was his castle. Hence it has always been considered a royal fortress and therefore the origin of the 'King's Rentallers of Lochmaben' who held their lands on a peculiar tenure owing to their being the descendants of the old domestics of the Bruce. The battle of Dryfe Sands, the last great clan battle of the borders, took place close to Lochmaben in 1593, between the Maxwells and the Johnstones, involving the besieging of Lockerby. Eventually the Maxwells were nearly exterminated by their victors, giving rise to the phrase 'Lockerby Lick'. During the border clashes between Wallace and Edward I, there were garrisons at Dumfries and Lochmaben. When they ran out of supplies, little ships were required to sail up the Nith and the Annan. An area of land between the Esk and Sark was known as the 'Debatable Land'. Its inhabitants were described in a report to Elizabeth's Council as 'a people that wilbe Scottische when they will, and English at their pleasure'.

As an apprentice, Thomas Telford lived in Lochmaben for a short period around 1770, working on proposals for a fast road to Portpatrick. Only a few miles from Lochmaben was the famous village of Gretna Green where young couples crossed the border from England to marry. The 1st Earl of Durham from a long established coal owing family, was married there in 1812, but sadly his wife died three years later. He remarried after three years to the eldest daughter of Lord Grey. On the 16 January 1818, the bells of St Mary's Church at Gateshead rang out to announce the birth of the heir to Lambton family, and were to ring out every year until his death twenty-three years later. In 1819, the marriage took place of Ulsterman Lord Charles Stewart, a widower of 41 years, to 19 year-old Lady Frances Anne Vane Tempest, a coal heiress owning colliery estates at Penshaw and Rainton in Durham, and given away by the Duke of Wellington. When his step-brother, Lord Castlereagh died, Charles Stewart became Lord Londonderry, who was to become the most hated colliery owner in Durham.

In 1818, Grey and Lambton worked closely in their unending fight against the Government's oppression and its continual threat to liberty. Another Radical, Henry Brougham, was always ready to undertake the defence of any man that offended against a growing number of laws which forbade free speech and writing. In 1819, the Government suspended Habeas Corpus, but an indemnity bill was introduced to protect its 'servants'. Shortly afterwards, Brougham was fighting the Government's use of spies and agent provocateurs (servants), especially William J Richards, known as the notorious 'Oliver the Spy'. The Tories were determined to turn the screw, and introduced the 'Gagging Acts'. They were also closing in on Major Cartwright, one of the oldest supporters of Reform.

A Catholic chapel had opened in Dumfries in 1813. The first evidence of the Shannon family in Scotland was a baptismal entry on the 1st of November 1818, in the

Dumfries Roman Catholic records. This gave the baptism of a daughter Catherine to Philip and Anne Shennan, living near Lockerby. In later baptismal entries, the surname was given as both Shennan or Shannon.

These records also gave a family named Gollacher [Gallagher]. Philip's grandson, James, was to marry Isabella Gallagher in Newcastle fourteen years later. In the period 1740s to 1770s, there were Shennans residing at Portpatrick in Wigtownshire; there were also records in 1801 of Rosanna Shannon at Dornock in Dumfriesshire, in 1802 of Agnes Shenan at Borgue in Kirkcudbrightshire, and in 1811 of Janet Shannan at Lochmaben.

The 'massacre of Peterloo' on the 16 August 1819 was to arouse great national outrage and did much to discredit the Tory Government. A crowd of peaceful protesters in Manchester was charged by a company of mounted yeomanry resulting in eleven people being killed and about four hundred wounded. Carlyle in 'Past and Present' supported the 'just actions' of the people. Even the Times newspaper was to draw the conclusion that the massacre was due to the 'masters' who were responsible for the repression of the workmen. There was particular resentment regarding the use of yeomanry rather than the more disciplined regular soldiers, and the congratulations from Prince Regent caused country-wide protest.

Lord Lambton also protested strongly, and organised a public meeting in Sunderland to counteract an earlier vote of thanks by the Durham clergy. Lambton's actions were noticed by another north-east coalowner, Sir Thomas Liddell, who expressed concern regarding Lambton's 'alarming radical tendencies'. A General Election took place in 1818, when Gladstone's father was elected MP for Berwick, and Peel's period as Secretary in Ireland came to an end in August. In November, Queen Charlotte died causing much public grief. In contrast, Queen Victoria was born on the 24 May 1819, with little public attention; her parents the Duke of Kent and Princess of Saxe-Coburg had married in the previous July.

In the north west of Scotland, 'Clearances' were sparking off riots. On the 2 April 1820, a rising by disaffected workers took place in the south west of Scotland. If this had occurred in Glasgow, it could have led to a major insurrection. Like the insurrections in Ireland of 1798 and 1803, it was doomed to failure for similar reasons. Rioting also broke out in the south and west of England. Although no lives were lost, nine were sentenced to death, and 500 for transportation. In the newspapers at this time the 'Ragged Radicals' were causing much commotion. They were demanding a progressive change in the way the country was governed which needed reforming the laws by pulling down the constitution to its foundation and building up a new one. However for the Irish immigrant, his main concern was to earn his bread and butter, and from the end of the Napoleonic War to the beginning of the Chartist risings, he took little active part in political questions that agitated the English working classes. In-fighting broke out between the cautious reformers of the

House of Lords and the Radicals in the House of Commons. Canning's denouncement of parliamentary reform at this time was to have influenced Gladstone for many years to come. As immigration gathered pace in the 1820s, violence increased. The Irish tended to congregate in areas requiring heavy manual labour, but were not directly in competition for skilled work, or initially in mining which was controlled by the native population.

In January 1820, Philip Shannon and his wife Nancy were recorded in the Lochmaben Catholic registers as baptismal sponsors. At the baptism of their daughter Catherine one year earlier, sponsors were named as Thomas Shennan and Rose McCrae. Thomas was probably a brother or cousin to Philip. In 1805 at Lochmaben, a Nancy McRae had married William Shannon. McCrae (meaning shirt of mail) was a local name, indicating that the Shannons were already on friendly relations with the native Scots.

Lochmaben Castle
Painting by Turner,
1834
(Tate Galleries)

On the 22 January 1820 the Duke of Kent died, and George III died six days later. The country was then obsessed with George IV's attempts to divorce Caroline of Brunswick. In June she returned from abroad to demand her rights as Queen. At first there was great public sympathy for Caroline but it was not long before opinion turned. George IV was determined to have a divorce, and on the 8 July a Bill of Pains and Penalties was introduced in the House of Lords by prime minister Lord Liverpool to deprive Caroline of her title and to dissolve the marriage. The London crowd had little feeling for her, but they hated George IV who was soon to show his distrust of both Whigs and Tories. His Queen, a well-known supporter of the Tories, was disliked intensely by the working classes, yet she was escorted by cheering mobs as she drove each day to the Lords for the hearing. The Bill was eventually shelved and Caroline died shortly afterwards.

Robert Owen was at this time developing his 'Plan' for a 'New View of Society'. Instead of pouring out money unproductively on poor relief, he proposed that the Government should raise a fund to establish village settlements, each with around 1,200 inhabitants, in which the unemployed could maintain themselves and add to the wealth of the nation. When the Government refused to consider his plans, Owen was naturally indignant, believing that their decision was due to the influence of Malthus. Naively, he did not realise that his plans were threatening the existing dominance of the ruling classes.

The 1821 Irish census showed a number of Shenans living in the Derryvullan area of Enniskillen, including farm labourers, a wool hatter, weaver, and spinner. (Unknown then, hatters risked early death by chronic mercury poisoning). The flax industry had greatly diminished by 1821, and may have been the main reason for the Shannons falling on hard times, and perhaps having to take other work in Ireland before they moved to Scotland. The Shannons having settled in Scotland would have had to take on work apart from summer shearing in order to survive.

On both sides of the Solway, the cottage flax workers were hit by the introduction of the spinning jenny and factory weaving, and with severe drought, violent aspects of rural depopulation were seen. Even the salt-pans that were a familiar sight along the coast were badly affected by taxation.

On the 17 April 1821, Lambton introduced a motion on the reform bill but this was heavily defeated. At this time, he advised his friend, the Duchess of Kent, that her daughter, and now heir to the throne, should read Miss Martineau's tales, then considered to be radical reading. The Duke of Kent had been rumoured to be a 'necessitarian Socialist' friend of Robert Owen. The Radical newspapers of the day were full of warnings that the Princess Victoria was in danger from the machinations of her 'wicked' uncle, the Duke of Cumberland. Also in 1821, Gladstone's father helped to pass Plunkett's motion on Catholic emancipation. However, a Catholic Relief Bill proposed by Plunkett aided by

Canning, was thrown out by the Lords, and to put down disturbances a coercion bill was passed.

O'Connell attempted to use the visit to Ireland of King George IV to demonstrate Catholic loyalty, and rejoiced to see the discomfiture of the Orange faction when the Lord Lieutenant was attacked during an Orange riot. Castlereagh, who had become one of the most unpopular men in England, died in 1822 by cutting his own throat; a menacing crowd hissed as his body was borne to Westminster Abbey. His reputation was as low as that of Prince Regent. In contrast, the Viceroy, Lord Wellesley, a constant friend of emancipation, had incurred the ire of the Orangemen as they rioted in a Dublin theatre.

In 1822 famine once more hit Ireland. It was not surprising that this resulted in a particularly large surge of emigrants. The Irish autumn of 1821 had been one of unparalleled wetness which had the effect of souring the potato, even then of stunted growth. It was reported that the provinces of Munster and Connaught were suffering a failure of the potato crop due to the excessive humidity, which caused the potatoes to rot after they had been stored in pits, so that the deficiency of food was not discovered until late in the season. The Irish papers recorded that 'Such misery was never witnessed before in the town of Galway, whole clans pouring in from the mountains of Connemara in quest of food.' In the county of Mayo thousands of inhabitants were subsisting on sea-weed, and typhus fever and dysentery were so bad that the living were scarcely able to bury the dead. MacFarlane wrote that 'great subscriptions were raised in England and Scotland ... for the suffering people of Munster and Connaught'.

In 1821, a year of great agricultural distress, the baptismal records gave Philip Shannon and Rose McCrae as sponsors, and again for Philip and Nancy Shannon in 1822. In 1821 a son Daniel was born, but no baptismal record has survived.

An adjoining entry recorded parents James and Agnes Reed. The Reed name was derived from Redesdale in Northumberland, and was common in Ulster .The Reeds were to be closely related to the Shannons later in the north-east of England. Thirteen days after the death of Napoleon at St Helena on the 18 May 1823, the baptism of son Edward (perhaps named after Lord Edward Fitzgerald) to Philip and Nancy Shennan was registered. Sponsors were Philip and Bridget Swords.

These baptismal records were careful to identify (on separate pages) legitimate and illegitimate births, using the terms 'lawful', and 'illegitimate' or 'natural'. All the Shannon children were recorded as lawful, but Philip on two occasions was a sponsor for illegitimate children. In one case, for a boy named Robert, no parents' names were given, and Robert was recorded as 'three years old & ill of the smallpox'.

Before Dr Jenner developed his vaccine for cowpox in 1798 at Edinburgh, smallpox had been the most feared of all diseases, often leaving its victims badly scarred for life. An entry dated 1825, gave 'Maria illegitimate daughter of a "strolling woman" calling herself Bridget Smith and the father Andrew McGhinnes [McGuinness]'. In 1823, a child of Protestant parents was recorded with the comment, 'This child in immediate danger of death'. Another Protestant baptism was included in 1826.

Twenty years after the establishment of the Catholic Society of 1802, Daniel O'Connell, formed the Catholic Association, which was organised until 1829 when emancipation was achieved. It created the first mass-membership in Europe. Through the agency of the priests, a 'Catholic Rent' for the support of the agitation was collected from the pence voluntarily subscribed monthly from all classes of the Catholic population. To some degree, the priests extended their collections to the British mainland. The power and progress of the Catholic Association so alarmed the Government that it was outlawed in in 1825, so O'Connell simply changed its name.

Probably because of the social cleavage between the native born and immigrants it was unlikely that Catholics would have married into a predominantly Protestant population. However, Protestant immigrants from the north of Ireland were accepted by the Scottish as one of themselves. Irish Catholic labourers were inculcated in a bitter hatred of Protestantism and adhered tenaciously to their religion because it was their only legacy. In 1823 a number of Catholic / Orange conflicts took place in Wigton. One year earlier saw the illegalisation of bull-baiting and cock-fighting; in Ireland, the degrading punishment of burial at cross-roads was abolished. Charles Dickens at the age of ten was starting four years in a blacking factory during Christmas 1823

In Leitrim, at the Arigna coalmines near Drumshambo, 200 colliers were employed. These mines were later sold to The English Mining Company. Shortly after, iron works were to start up at Arigna. In Cumberland, Port Carlisle opened in 1823, and three years later Telford's Menai Bridge was opened, a vital connection from Wales to Ireland. No doubt the Government were mindful of the need for speedy transportation of troops to Ireland. In 1822 the system of espionage and repression exercised by the Government was brought to an end by Peel, who replaced Lord Sidmouth.

Following a campaign by Francis Place, and Joseph Hume a Radical MP, the Combination Acts were repealed, but a further law was passed banning violence and intimidation by unions. From 1825 trade unions or friendly societies started activities leading to Doherty's major union of cotton spinners formed in 1829.

Carlyle and Scott

There was another Scotsman who was to achieve equal eminence to Adam Smith. Thomas Carlyle was born on the 4 December 1795, four months before 'Napoleon went forth to conquer' and seven months before Burns ceased to breathe. This son of a stone mason was to become a famous philosopher and historian, and exerted great influence on English, Scottish and Irish affairs throughout the nineteenth century. He was born in the village of Ecclefechan some five miles from Lockerbie. His most famous piece of writing, 'The French Revolution', captures vividly the turmoil affecting Europe towards the end of the eighteenth century which was to reverberate through Britain for many years afterwards.

Carlyle's religious background was based on the ineffaceable teaching of the Burgher Seccession community as dissenters, and he would have been particularly conscious of its minority status. The most witty of Burns poems satirised the ministers of religion of that rigid body. There had been a tradition in the lowlands of Scotland, of the 'covenanters' holding meetings up into the hills out of reach of persecuting moss troopers. Perhaps this may have made him have some sympathy for the Catholic travellers, forced to keep mass

Thomas Carlyle 1860
(National Galleries)

in secret and required to seek work away from their home country. His close-hand view of these travellers influenced his account of the state of desolation in Ireland in the 1830s:

> 'The Irish Sans-potato, had he not senses then, nay a soul? In his frozen darkness it was better for him to die famishing; better to see his children famish. It was better for him to be a beggar, a liar and a knave. Nay, if that dreary Greenland wind of benighted Want, perential from sire to son, had frozen him into a kind of stupor and numb callosity, so that he saw not, felt not, was this, for a creature with soul in it, some assuagement; or the cruellest wretchedness of all.'

Scotland's most famous writer, Sir Walter Scott, was to draw heavily on the heritage and history of south-west Scotland in his novels Guy Mannering (1815), and Old Mortality and The Antiquary (both 1816). In his autobiography he was to comment on his only meeting with Burns, who he described as "looking like a sagacious country farmer of the old Scotch school – none of your modern agriculturists, who keep labourers for their drudgery, but the douce gentleman who held his own plough". During Scott's visit to Ireland in 1825, he was to express surprise at the enthusiastic welcome he received from all classes, as he had previously regarded the Irish as not 'a reading people'. He was also to comment on the 'painful feeling in his mind' at the contrast between the great mansions of the gentry in which he stayed, with the misery of the houses of the general population. Presumably this contrast was not so apparent in Scotland.

Living and working on the land

Both in Ireland and Scotland, the agrarian revolution produced a large class of land-less labourers. The living conditions for the 'temporary' harvesters in south west Scotland would have consisted of 'sleeping rough', and most likely a mud-walled hovel with families and animals occupying the same space. Early Irish huts were called 'raths'. Newspaper reports of the time and Carlyle's writings confirmed this. Labourers' dwellings in the town of Dumfries were situated in closes with little ventilation, dunghills, pig-sties and open privies. They lived chiefly on potatoes, buttermilk and salt herring, occasionally pigshead. The lot of the Scottish agricultural labourer and his family would have been similar to their English counterpart as described by Disraeli in his novel Sybil:

> '...there were few districts in the kingdom where the rates of wages were more depressed, those who were fortunate enough to obtain scant remuneration, had, in addition to their toil, to endure each morn and even a weary journey before they could reach their the scene of their labour, or return to the squalid hovel profaned the name of home. To that home, over which Malaria hovered, and round whose shivering hearth were clustered other guests besides the exhausted family of toil

– Fever, in every form, pale Consumption, exhausting Synochus, and trembling Ague, – returned after cultivating the broad fields of merry England the bold British peasant, returned to encounter the worst of diseases with a frame the least qualified to oppose them; a frame that subdued by toil was never sustained by animal food; drenched by the tempest could not change its dripping rags; and was indebted for its scanty fuel to the windfalls of the woods.'

For families like the Shannons, who were able to settle, their primitive accommoda-tion would have been similar to back home in Ireland, unless their employer provided some out-buildings. In the towns like Dumfries, conditions for vagrants were worse, and would have been like those in the tenements of Newcastle where they were to live 5 years later.

Considering that Ireland was largely an agricultural country, it was surprising how few Irish immigrants took up farming after migrating, mainly flocking to the urban centres. Lowland Scotland had set the pace for efficient and mechanised farming having some decades earlier benefited from imported English expertise. By the beginning of the century, progressive agriculture was almost a Scots speciality. This was a period of Scottish innova-tion in many technical fields.

Back in Ireland, for the poor, breaking the 'law' was the only way to survive. John and Martin Shannon of Kilfaoughna were sent to Roscommon Gaol in 1824 for stabbing two bailiffs sent to seize their cattle for non-payment of rent. Records also showed that convicts Edward Shannon and Martin Shannon were transported to New South Wales in 1825 and 1830 respectively. The Leitrim Assizes sentenced Stephen Gilsenan to six months hard labour for stealing a bank note, and Pat Maguire, sentenced to death for stealing a mare in March 1825, reflected the countrywide disturbances. Compared with Ireland, where economist David Ricardo noted the aristocracy ruled with a rod of iron, the Shannons would have been treated better in Scotland, and therefore not tempted to return home.

A type of bondage was practised in Ireland called the 'hanging gale', which provided six months credit on rent. The debt hung over the tenant knowing that at any time the land-lord could call in the debt, and if not paid, the tenant's cattle would be driven to a pound and sold off after a few days. Horn described the Northumbrian 'bondagers' as 'a splendid race', who were under a different form of bondage. They were normally young women under the age of thirty, and extremely strong, capable of carrying out a whole range of different jobs, including weeding, turnip hoeing, haymaking, harvesting, filling dung carts, spreading dung, turnip cutting, driving carts and harrowing. The farmer liked to 'have his wenches under bondage, because then he could send them afield to hoe and dig in all weathers, and they can't shirk it'. To the anger of local workers, the Irish reapers 'always bargained for money, milk and some beer'.

Alexander Somerville, a Scotsman, who in his youth was a harvester in the Scottish Lowlands, gave in his autobiography a vivid picture of the harshness of life after the Napoleonic Wars. If the harvesters worked for a good master, they were provided with harvest homes known as 'kirnes'. Generally the workpeople lived in hovels without windows. Somerville's parents carried around with them one small pane of glass and had it fixed in each hovel which they occupied as tenants. Somerville described the thatched roof, clay floored, bare-walled comfortless dwelling, in which his parents and eight children huddled together. The 'glory which Europe was mad about' had resulted in very high prices for food and clothes. New shoes were out of the question, thus demanding that old footwear had to be patched up with any old scraps.

At the annual 'winter suppers', which were held on a Saturday night (to avoid loss of his workers through intemperate headaches the next day), entertainment included dancing, droll stories, witty jokes and songs. When the harvest failed, and there was no bread, the children were taught to cry: 'Fairy, fairy, come bake me a scone; and I'll give thee a spurtle (a stick for stirring porridge) to turn it off and on'. In 1817 there was a potato and turnip crop failure, but in 1818 the markets fell, and food became cheaper, and it was possible to get clothes. Corduroy was generally worn by the sons of farm labourers. Northern labourers were better paid than their southern counterparts, and they often had cheap coal which allowed them to keep warm during the colder seasons, and made it possible to prepare hot meals. It was natural to eat porridge and go bare-footed when young in Scotland.

The biography of James Carlyle gave typical working arrangements on Scottish lowland farms: 'Moffat!' said he one day to an incorrigible reaper, 'thou has a feature of a bad shearer: high, and rough, and little on't. Thou maun alter thy figure or slant the bog' – pointing to the man's road homewards. As the men worked in the fields, the rest of the family were kept busy. The women and daughters as well as helping out in the fields and barns, often did washing and baking in the master's house. There was a variety of tasks. A master would require at least one shearer no matter how long the harvest might be; also an out-field worker winter and summer, and a 'stack carrier' whenever the threshing mill was going. This might happen thirty or forty days in the year, and usually in the winter months. For the shearer in harvest, and for the carrying of the stacks into the barn, no wages were paid; but the shearer was allowed breakfast and dinner, and a bushel of grain called 'sugar barley'. Those who ate in the field would have hard bannock of bean and barley meal, washed down with milk. Breakfast was normally oatmeal porridge with 'sour dook', a kind of rank buttermilk; sometimes this was eaten in the fields. Potatoes and salt were eaten at other meals, occasionally a herring but never butcher's meat and seldom bread. The binding of the sheaves was done by the 'bondager' who usually worked ten hours per day. The carrying of the sheaves from stackyard into the barn, which was part of the house rent, was heavy work, and generally done by the women even during pregnancy. Babies were often born in the fields.

There was a custom on the last day of shearing for the master to send bottles of whiskey to the field, to be mixed with water, and given to the shearers, partly in honour of it being the last day, but chiefly to make them drive on at great speed to complete the work. The whiskey had its desired effect. All the workers, male and female, home hands and hired hands (hinds), Scotch and Irish, slashed down the corn, and strove with one another at the work more like mad people than workpeople. The slashing down of the ripe corn was known as 'kemping', but it led to the shearers cutting their own hands and those of their neighbours, and quarrelling often broke out no doubt helped by the whiskey.

Irish and Scottish Education

The statue of 1696 required a schoolmaster to be set up in every Scottish parish. The Irish, neglected by the English government, had taken the education of their children into their own hands. An ambulant teacher was found a cottage; each child paid him 2d a week and a few sods of turf in winter. In 1812 there were 4,600 such hedge schools in Ireland. In 1847 Rev. Thomas Guthrie, social reformer and founder of the Free Church, born in Annan Dumfriesshire, was founder of the Ragged Schools. These schools were designed to give free education to the poor. Later Lord Shaftesbury and Dickens supported the ragged schools.

Did the Shannon older children receive any education in Dumfriesshire? It is possible that Philip and Agnes Shannon knew some English but not how to write. In those times, educational opportunities were limited, and even more so for travelling people. The chances of the Shannon children receiving any formal teaching was small, however, one of the benefits of a Catholic upbringing was the activity of priests in these 'uncivilised parts'. As in Ireland, hedge schools provided some basic education for children during the 1820s.

In 1822 Robert Stephenson returned to Newcastle after studying in Edinburgh – his father saw the merits of Scottish education. Some schools were established by subscription with each child paying one penny a week. Adam Smith was to record that the Scottish parish schools had taught 'almost the whole of the common people' to read and a great proportion of them to write and 'reckon'. Adam's use of 'almost' suggests that Irish children were excluded. There were no parochial schools in England and Ireland as there were in Scotland. Somerville described a parish school in the south-east of Scotland that was housed in an old dilapidated thatched hovel similar to those occupied by the farm hinds or labourers. The standard of teaching was remembered as being good, 'excepting the inordinate and cruel use of the taws (leather strap) for punishment. Rarely was there a parish library; books then available tended to be religious novels or on subjects of history, divinity and biography. The question of whether the education of the poor was on the whole beneficial was the subject of Gladstone's maiden speech at Eaton in October 1825; he urged that the upper classes should do their duty for the poor.

Thomas Carlyle attended Annan Academy as pupil in 1804 (as author did about 150 years later), and as mathematical teacher in 1814. He initiated the London Library in 1840. It was not until 1838 that a Roman Catholic school was erected in Dumfries. For Lockerbie, under 'Poor and Parochial Funds', the Statistical Account recorded that during winter, coals were provided for the poor, and it mentioned that the people were very liberal and benevolent to their own poor, but that they were continually being annoyed by an immense influx of vagrants and beggars from 'distant places'. During 1824–25, the eldest two Bronte sisters were to die of consumption (tuberculosis) after suffering the strict regime of Cowan Bridge boarding school in Yorkshire.

Combination Laws

During the period 1818 to 1828, working class unrest continued, particularly evident in the north east of England where miners came out on strike against bonding and working conditions, but farm workers were less active. Hammond felt that 'All circumstances make the spirit of combination falter in the country. In towns men are face to face with the brutal realities of their lives, un-softened by any of the assuaging influences of brook and glade and valley. Men and women that work in the fields breathe something of the resignation and peace of Nature; they bear trouble and wrong with a dangerous patience. Discontent moves, but moves slowly, and whereas storms blow up in the towns, they beat up in the country. That is one reason why the history of anguish of the English agricultural labourer so rarely breaks into violence'.

Castlereagh's Select Committee in 1817 rejoiced in the discovery that 'notwithstanding the alarming progress which has been made in extending disaffection, its success has been confined to the principal manufacturing districts, and that scarcely any of the agricultural population have lent themselves to these violent projects'. Nevertheless, by the end of the 1820s there were still English villages where the overseer would harness men, women and idiots to the parish cart. Little had changed since Goldsmith's 'Deserted Village'.

The repeal of the Combination laws started a wave of strikes in south west Scotland. This mainly involved weavers, but also included some colliers. This led to a Bill in 1825 that severely limited 'intimidation' by striking workers. A Vagrancy Act became law banning begging. In Ayrshire there was a sizeable army of vagrants and licensed beggars known as 'gaberlunzies' who were permitted within the bounds of a certain parish; maimed or deformed beggars were referred to as 'objects'. The fear of spies was widespread; agent provocateurs were reported to have been operating in the border area near Carlisle.

For some of the years when the Shannons were living in Dumfriesshire, Thomas Carlyle was living close-by. The local Carlyle families were farmers, and with Philip Shannon working as an agricultural labourer, it highly likely on market days such as held at Annan, that they could have rubbed shoulders, or even had a conversation about Irish horses or cattle!

In March 1825, Carlyle accepted the offer received by his family to take up residence at Hoddam Hill in Dumfriesshire, a farm two miles from Mainhill, which his brother Alexander then managed. Thomas spent his time translating German. Hoddam, close to Ecclefechen, had just revealed its thin seams of coal. Carlyle described this period as idyllic as he went off on long rides on his Irish horse "Larry". His thoughts were on a certain Jane Baillie Welsh, a descendent of John Knox and William Wallace. They married on the 17 October 1826 but children were not to follow. A William Carlyle was recorded in the Catholic register as a sponsor in 1828 at Lockerby. He may have been a relation of the famous Thomas. It was likely that William was a Presbyterian, since non-Catholics were also recorded in the Catholic registers.

Philip Shannon's family continued to grow. He was recorded as sponsor on the 16 May 1825, and on the 18 November 1827; finally on the 16 March 1828, the baptism of a daughter Mary was registered to Philip Shannon and Agnes Kellach(er) at Lockerby. It can be assumed that Philip's wife had not changed since names like Ann and Agnes were often interchangeable. It should be noted that in 1828 Philip was aged 56 and Ann 52. For Ann, this was very old for child bearing and it was unlikely that she would have any more children. There was every likelihood that Mary died young.

Mary McInally and Catharine Swords were sponsors in 1827 (Isabella MacInally was a sponsor to Shannons at Newcastle in 1849). A Helen Kellacher married Owen Hanlon [Monaghan name] at the Dumfries Catholic chapel in 1829, and in the previous year, baptism sponsors had been John Hanlon and Catherine Kellecher. The first entry of Kellacher was given in 1826, when Peter Kellacher was recorded as a sponsor.

The name Kellegher or O'Kellecher originated from the pre-tenth century Irish name, O'Ceileachair. The first recorded Ceileachair was nephew to Brian Boru, High King of Ireland. The Kelleghers were former inhabitants of County Clare and they may have travelled up the River Shannon to settle in north-west Ireland at the same time as the Shannon families. (In 1866, Thomas Sheenan was baptised as son of Patrick Sheenan and Catherine Kelaher at Derrylin in Fermanagh, which showed that Shannon/Kellegher family connections still continued in Ireland after Philip left).

The vicious winter led to the deaths of the Duke of Kent. In 1825 Lambton was helping his brother-in-law, Lord Howick, fight an election in County Durham against H.T. Liddle, son of Lord Ravensworth, a coalowner. The Tories were opposing Catholic relief on a 'No Popery' ticket. A Pope decree had come out against secret societies, with implications for trade unions. In 1826 there were poor law riots, even though Francis Place and Joseph Hume had pushed through the Repeal of Combination Act in 1824. Place's main objective to avoid the need for strikes was not realised. However, the Act was to have a tremendous impact on workers' liberty to meet and discuss their common grievances, although the Repealing Act of 1825 was to bring back the common law of conspiracy.

The plight of distressed weavers in manufacturing districts caught the attention of Gladstone as a student when he supported his friend's proposal to send relief. Early signs of trade unionism were evident with uprisings starting up all over Britain. Robert Owen became disillusioned with his efforts in Britain to create a 'socialist' system, and emigrated to the United States. This first emergence of trade unions was to be short-lived, and they were to collapse by 1835. Although Wilberforce was a passionate enemy of slavery and the slave trade, he supported the Combination Act which was passed in 1799, outlawing workers combining to strike. This was to be the situation until 1824. Violent aspects of the rural population could be seen on both sides of the Solway. Even as late as 1827 Lord Londonderry was arguing against the game law reforms.

In 1826 a severe drought had strained the situation to breaking point, and the price of oatmeal rose to an exorbitant figure. The meal-dealers felt the wrath of the mob when their houses suffered great damage. Three years later the citizens of Dumfries saw a riot when William Hare was being escorted out of the country after turning King's Evidence in the notorious trial of Burke and Hare. William Burke from Tyrone came to Scotland to work on the Union Canal as a navigator in 1817. He met up with Ulsterman William Hare who had also worked on canals as a labourer. In 1828 they were convicted of 16 murders in Edinburgh based on interning buried bodies to sell off for medical research.

In 1826 a bad harvest hit both Ireland and Scotland, and the worst typhus outbreak since 1817–1818. The building speculations had ended in panic and commercial bankruptcy. There was a dearth of jobs, with labourers in Edinburgh returning to the country where they had to accept any wages that were offered. Cobbett in his travels described the hovels of the agricultural workers in the south of England as similar to Ireland. A society called 'The General Association established for the Purpose of bettering the Conditions of the Agricultural and Manufacturing Labourers' which was trying to revive the policy of minimum wage first put forward by Whitbread in 1795, gave evidence before the Select Committee on Emigration in 1827. As an illustration of the injustice being suffered by labourers, in 1825 the wages of agricultural labourers were generally 9s a week, and the price of wheat 9s a bushel, whereas in 1732 the wages of agricultural labour were fixed by magistrates at 6s a week, and the price of wheat was 2s.9d a bushel.

The 1826 General Election found most educated opinion in England in favour of civil liberty for Catholics, but the old 'No Popery' prejudice still held sway with most of the population. This was not helped when Catholic advocate Prime Minister Canning died in August 1827, and Cobbett standing at Preston and was soundly defeated. It was also an election year in Ireland, and the appeal to the Irish peasants that Catholicism and priests would 'beat property' and the Protestant landlords, resulted in their candidates' election in Co. Dublin and Roscommon. However, on the 8 March 1827 the Catholic Relief Bill was defeated in the House of Commons. Nearly two weeks later a disappointed Beethoven died of dropsy in a bitterly cold Vienna. 'The ideals of the French Revolution were his own all his life'. He had been brought up as a Roman Catholic and became deaf in 1798, the year of the Irish Rising.

Catholic Emancipation

In Ireland, O'Connell was pleased to see that Wellington had left emancipation a free question. Francis Burdett's motion in favour of the Catholics in 1828 was carried in the House of Commons, although it was defeated in the Lords. In O'Connell's election campaign, Father Tom Maguire of Leitrim came to help, and priests of every parish were working day and night to urge all to ignore the landlord's threats. Wellington after much effort was able to force the King to give his assent, warning of civil war fears. The year 1828 heralded the formation of a new government under Wellington. The Institution of Civil Engineers gained its royal charter, reflecting the great innovative strides being taken in all areas of engineering as the Industrial Revolution gathered pace. Scottish ironmoulders had joined together in a union-based friendly society in 1829.

Since 1791, the Act allowing Catholics official religious toleration did not relieve them from the various restrictions on their political activity. When Canning succeeded Lord Liverpool as Prime Minister in 1827, Peel and Wellington resigned from the cabinet, not being willing to serve under a 'Catholic' Prime Minister. After the Dissenter's Bill in 1828, the Catholics had their turn the following year. O'Connell's success in the Clare election convinced Peel and Wellington that emancipation had to be conceded. They steered the Catholic Emancipation Bill through Parliament, and for this the anti-Catholic lobby had castigated the Victor of Waterloo as letting 'the Papists into Parliament'. Peel was considered a turncoat by many Tories of a Protestant persuasion.

O'Connell was elected un-apposed in July 1829 after a new writ was issued for Co. Clare, but he refused to swear the oath of supremacy. He was meditating on a new campaign for the repeal of the Union. The first effect of emancipation on the Irish peasants was disfranchisement of the 40s freeholders. The troops prevented a civil war between the Catholic and Protestant partisans. Many Tories 'swallowed' the Emancipation Bill hoping this would buy freedom from further disturbances in Ireland, but the imposed limitation of franchise to householders, who paid £10 or more in rent de-franchised, four-fifths of the Catholic voters resulting in renewed bitterness. However the Emancipation victory had infused the Irish with new hope of freemen. The English radicals had learned a vital lesson as Thomas Attwood declared in 1829:

> 'The Duke of Wellington has taught us how to command reform. By union, by organisation, by general contribution, by patriotic exertion, and by discretion, keeping always within the law and the constitution. These are the elements of Reform. By peaceful combination of means like these the Irish people have lately obtained a glorious and bloodless victory ....'

Peel brought about the formation of the national police force in 1829, and his policemen were soon known as 'bobbies' or 'Peelers'. He had set up a similar Peace Preservation Force in Ireland when he was Chief Secretary from 1812 to 1818. One of the main initial tasks of the Metropolitan police was to control political demonstrations and riots which became common over the next few years during the battle over the first Reform Act 1832. The view of Government was that only draconian measures would keep the lower classes in line. On English farms the landlords preferred to use Scottish bailiffs (Scots were planted in Ireland since they had a reputation for being very tough). Arthur Young noted that the farms of England, like those in Jamaica, were supplied with drivers from Scotland. Cobbett's prejudice against Scotsmen, the race of 'feelosofers', was expressed in his comment that all the hard agricultural work was done by Englishmen and Irishmen.

Steam Power in Mining and Railroads

In 1744 it was reported in Whitfield, Northumberland, that the roads consisted of trackways for ponies, and in 1780 it took one week to travel by stagecoach from London to Newcastle. Pack-horses had been the normal means of moving goods, and ponies were used in pits from 1760. One of the original waggon-ways, also known as 'Newcastle Roads', was Tanfield Tramway built in 1671, and not far away, the oldest still existing railway bridge, the Causey Arch, with a span of 100 feet, was constructed in 1726.

The exploitation of deeper mines had started in 1825. The problems of flooding in deep mines had been encountered in the Cornish tin mines, and as far back as 1698, Cornishman Thomas Savery had demonstrated his atmospheric engine in front of King George III. He described his device as 'an engine to raise water by fire', and was known as his 'Miner's Friend', but was of limited power for deep flooding. Thomas Newcomen began the development of the steam-operated engine, which was first used in a colliery at Dudley Castle. Newcomen then adapted it to be used with a massive waterwheel with increased efficiency. The third generation of steam engines was developed by Scotsman James Watt.

North East England then took a lead in the use of steam power. One of the factors that caused the North East to pioneer the development of the railways was that the canal system had never caught on locally as in other industrial areas. Where water transport was available, it was considered uneconomic to carry coal by road for more than 15 miles. With no alternative system of transporting coal overland across the steep country next to the Tyne other than along the traditional 'waggon-ways' by horse and cart, the North-East coalowners had much to gain from a more efficient and cheaper means of transport.

The influence of steam was penetrating everyone's vocabulary – Carlyle described Coleridge as "A steam-engine of a hundred horses' owner, with boiler burst". Trevithick's high-pressure steam engine of 1800, a big improvement on Watt's stationary engine and Newcomen's atmospheric engine, was developed further to produce a flanged wheel traction engine at Gateshead-on-Tyne in 1805. By 1814, Blackett and Hedley's Puffing Billy engine was working on a smooth rail at Wylam Waggonway, and it was George Stephenson, a self-educated engine man at Killingworth Colliery, who was to convert this crude colliery engine into a revolutionary means of public transport. In 1822, Stephenson built the Hetton Locomotive for use at the local colliery. He was able to interest a group of coalowners and merchants led by the Quaker Edward Pease, who were planning a horse-drawn railway from Darlington to the Auckland coalfield and then to deep water at Stockton on Tees. Pease was given liberal support from two other principal Quaker families, the Blackhouses and Richardsons.

It was with the help from Edward Pease of the Society of Friends, and Engineer George Stephenson, that was to culminate in the first steam-hauled public railway for freight only, which opened on the 27 September 1825, from Shildon to Stockton-on-Tees. About thirty years later James Shannon arrived in the Auckland area, where colliery sinking was due to start based on rail access to the coast for coal export.

The 1830s saw the start of the railways and steamships – the first conquest of physical distance by mechanical power, and a dramatic increase in man's control of nature. George Stephenson charged the modest sum of £115 for the survey of the Stockton-Darlington line which was extended to Shildon. Where previously only one solitary farmhouse had stood among green fields, staiths were erected and other conveniences for the loading of coal. This was to be the start of the development of Middlesborough.

Stephenson was often required to present the case for a new line to parliamentary committees, and stated his arguments and facts with a Northumbrian dialect and 'burr' scarcely intelligible to southerners. Since most distinguished engineers of the day had taken the position that his schemes were impracticable and absurd, it was no easy task for him to bring home his convictions and convey his meaning in the face of sneers and interruptions and whispered doubts about his sanity. Many landowners feared the development of the

George Stephenson 1830
(Durham Record Office)

Edward Pease 1830
(Durham Record Office)

railways, as a revolutionary force beyond their control, which would rapidly change their way of life. In January 1830, work started on England's first coast-to-coast railway, the Newcastle & Carlisle. A House of Commons Committee on the Coal Trade in 1800 had considered a project for a canal between the Solway Firth and the Tyne, due to the attacks on colliers by French privateers.

The importance of the railways was summed up in Our Iron Roads by Frederick S Williams referring to the quote by George Stephenson: "Now; lads, you will see the day when mail-coaches will go by railway, and when it will be cheaper for a working man to travel on a railway than to walk on foot". John Bright also commented that "Railways have rendered more services, and have received less gratitude, than any other institution in the land". Robert Stephenson in 1828, returning home from South America, met Mr Trevithick, from whom he gathered much information based on the mines of Cornwall, and this by its application to the construction of locomotives, assisted to his ultimate success in that field. No doubt the long experience of Cornish mine sinking was of particular interest to the companies about to exploit the deep coal resources in the Newcastle area.

Why did the Shannons decide as a family to move from Lockerbie to Newcastle as 1830 approached? In a country area, people rarely travelled outside of their parish, and this immobility created an inclusive community, with a natural distrust of outsiders like the Shannons. Poverty and unemployment must have been major factors.

During the Shannon's time in Scotland they would have heard news of the worsening situation in Ireland with agrarian violence and evictions. If their son Peter was already in Newcastle, Philip's decision to move there was the easiest and obvious option. It was likely that the Shannons had not been able to make any savings in Scotland, so the possibility of travelling to Liverpool for a passage to America was not even considered.

Until 1756, Newcastle and Carlisle were only connected by a bridle way. In 1770, the traveller Arthur Young made his views known regarding the road that ran south of Newcastle: 'A more dreadful road cannot be imagined. I was obliged to hire two men at one place to support my chaise from overturning'. However due to the introduction of turnpike trusts between 1795 and 1830, roads had improved enormously. There were large tracts of the north of England served by causeways only just wide enough for one animal. Until the use of railroads, the pack horse, which could carry up to three hundred-weight of coal, was the only means of overland transportation. At that time the daily cost of keeping a horse was twice the wage earned by a labourer.

How did the Shannons travel from Lockerbie to Newcastle, a distance of about 100 miles? After twelve years in Dumfriesshire, they had few possessions requiring the means to transport them. The Shannons probably hired a waggon or horse-drawn cart, or a pack-horse for their luggage. There is no doubt that the Shannon's journey from Portpatrick to Lockerbie was on foot, and it is likely that the family used the same means to get to Newcastle.

A day's journey on foot was generally taken to be about twenty miles (a standard Roman's daily march) – so the Shannons would have taken a week to travel the whole distance. On their journey they would have used the drovers routes, which mainly avoided paying the tolls. They may have stopped at Brampton and Hexham on their way, and there is evidence of families with the name of Shannon or Shenan having settled in these Border towns. As the Shannons travelled to Newcastle they would have seen signs of the start of construction near Carlisle and Blaydon of the Newcastle to Carlisle Railway.

CHAPTER 4

1830–1833 North East England – Cholera and Reform

(Peter Shannon marries Isabella Gallagher)

'Men are grown mechanical in head and in heart, as well as in hand.'

(Sign of the Times Carlyle 1829)

'Hunger drives him [the Irishman] to England. In the mechanical, egoistic, ice-cold hurly-burly of the English factory towns, his passions are aroused. .. in the narrow courts and alleys .. live the poorest of poor … the majority Irish, or of Irish extraction …'

(Letters Engels 1843 & 1844)

With Stephenson's Rocket in the news, Carlyle asserted that men had lost their faith in the spiritual, preferring the practical and material world. William Cobbett had always believed that country 'improvements' were designed to depopulate the countryside in order to create an industrial proletariat. The Riot Act was read by Major Cartwright when bonfires in Northamptonshire were lit in the road to prevent waggons with fencing materials passing, which were due to be used for 'enclosure' work. Protests against enclosures took place as far north as Carlisle and in Dumfriesshire. Southey considered that the urban poor were more easily roused to riot and revolution (as the French had revolted in 1830) than their rural counterpart since the town workman had no loyalties; in times of economic difficulty there was no chance of the townsman raising his own food and he was likely to respond with desperation and violence.

In the 1830s, Irish migrants were the subject of a lengthy sociological study by George Cornewall Lewis, focusing on the morality of the Irish. He concluded that the quality of the Irish workers was based on their 'willingness, alacrity, and perseverance in the severest, the most irksome, and the most disagreeable kinds of coarse labour …'. Even when the Irish were found in skilled industries such as tanning, the preparation of hides was considered particularly dirty and unhealthy work. The Irish were attracted to the heavy iron industries south of the Tyne, but more scattered in the colliery areas. From the correspondence between mine agents, John Buddle of Wallsend and John Peile of Workington, it was clear that they were of the opinion that the Irish were not ideal for mine work since they were not bred to the work: 'Irish and other Trampers only turn to mining when they cannot get any other kind of employment, and were ignorant and careless of danger'.

There were slum conditions before the Irish arrived in English towns, however they brought along their rural habits such as keeping pigs. The Irish were given the worst accommodation. Cobbett considered the examples of idleness and drunkenness of the poor was due to a sense of hopelessness and the break-up of the old communities, with no stake in life. To counter this argument, Arthur Young in 1799 had advocated the settlement of poor families on waste land – the beginning of garden allotments which much later became very much part of the County Durham landscape, with pigeon crees (sheds) and greyhound racing. By 1830 about 40% of parishes provided an allotment scheme. Allotments or field gardens were advocated in the 1830s for agricultural labourers, to supplement their wages and keep them away from poor relief and the beerhouse. By 1881 there were 691,410 allotments, with the railwaymen and miners particularly keen on gardening.

The economic boom of the 1820s came to an abrupt halt in 1829. More significantly, there was chronic under-employment and unemployment in agricultural areas, and the bad harvest of 1828 was followed by a still worse one in 1829. A bad harvest meant not only high bread prices but less to spend on manufactured goods, and so less for the industrialists and their workers; in other words a slump in trade. It was known in some agricultural areas for the proprietors of the neighbourhood to destroy the cottages on their estates, in order to be exempted from the maintenance of the population. Mechanical threshing had cut the traditional winter occupations.

Arthur Young in 1776 maintained that the occasion of the first riots was due to the importation of Irish labourers, a practice then some years old, that might well have inflamed resentment at a time when the governing class was continually contending that the sole cause of distress was excessive population, and that the best solution was the removal of labourers to the colonies. It would be surprising if the news of the riots down the south of England had not stirred the temperature of Newcastle workers. The year 1830 produced a wave of agrarian disturbances mainly in the south known as the 'Last Labourer's Revolt'. The threshing machines of John Bennett, Wiltshire MP, had been recently destroyed. In 1817 he had threatened to pull down his cottages to avoid settlement proposals. Although threshing machines were the main targets for destruction, other forms of industry were at peril. For instance, also in Wiltshire a cloth factory was damaged by seventeen-year old John Ford. Hayricks were being burnt as far north as Carlisle. By Christmas 1830 the Government's reprisals were well under way, and clergymen were going back on their agreements with workers to reduce the tithe payments. 'Opinions' were considered dangerous!

In 1810 Cobbett had been unable to defend himself successfully, on trial for some articles on Ireland in his 1803 Register. However at his trial in July 1831, he was able to turn the tables on the Government when the charge concerning his support for the Swing riots was thrown out. Luddite attacks in Lancashire, Yorkshire and Nottinghamshire were a backlash to the loss of traditional controls by the labour force. In country areas the riot leaders tended to be industrial workers such as coal miners and metal-workers. These protests mingled with reform agitation and trade union activity. Although the Catholic Church was strongly opposed to oath-bound secret societies and trade unions, by the 1830s there were Orange and Ribbon elements in most sizeable Irish communities of northern England. The first Irish in Newcastle, who settled in the All Saints area and later at Sandgate in the St Thomas parish, were served by local priests.

E.P. Thompson considered that the main reason for urbanisation was more the pressure of increasing population rather than industrialisation, but also to escape rural poverty. Sir James Graham, a Carlisle MP originally from Annandale, and supporter of Lord Grey's reforms, saw evidence of local suffering: 'Where [he asked] is the furniture that used to adorn the poor man's cottage? All is gone. Pinching hunger and despair now hold their place in the labourer's habitation. The weaver in Cumberland earns but 4s.2d. a week, out of which he has to supply his family. Oatmeal, water, and peas are his sole food, and for these he has to work fourteen or fifteen hours a day. The country has come to the point where something must be done'.

The winter of 1829 was particularly harsh, and poor labourers were driven to desperation by their condition. A friend of Brunel recorded a bitter winter crossing from France to Britain in a small packet boat. In February even the King spoke of 'distress in some parts'. Also in some counties of Ireland, such as Roscommon, Leitrim and Sligo, there were reports of great hardship. The 'Golden Age' impression of the country before the industrial revolution gave a misleading picture of agrarian life. The long hours of back-breaking work had resulted in a stupefying existence. The Irish were now more easily persuaded to take up work in the mills, mines and factories to 'better themselves'.

There was still a fear of Popery, which anti-Catholic politicians and sections of the press helped to foster. The Home Secretary under Wellington was known as 'Orange Peel', for his strong objection to Catholic Emancipation. In 1829 a rare incident was reported; an Orangeman by the name of John Routledge was charged with shooting a Captain Maguire; he was sentenced to death, and hanged at Enniskillen gaol.

Compared to the well documented movement of people between Ireland and Scotland, it was more difficult to determine any particular historical pattern of people's travel between south-west Scotland and north-east of England. There had been many border clashes over the centuries, such as between the Percy and the Douglas families in 1448, and the position of the border had changed a number of times, but this only affected the east side of the country. Walter Scott was very much captivated by the old fighting Borderers and the harrying of cattle in Tynedale. The cattle trade between Ireland and the mainland probably extended to Northumberland and Durham. Scott had ridden on his stout galloway in the Border Cheviots and Northumberland, through bog and brake, over the 'dim moory Debatable Land' as told in 'Liddlesdale Raids' and the 'Minstrelsy of the Scottish Border'.

The similarities in language of the two areas, for example in the use of the word 'bairn' for child, confirms generations of regular communication between the peoples. Scotsman James Murray in his linguistic studies concluded that there was not much difference between his own Border speech and that of Northumberland. The advent of railways was to diminish the burrs and brogues of the regions. When a Commission of Enquiry took evidence from a Tyneside miner, an 'interpreter' had to be present. George Stephenson had similar problems with his accent when presenting his proposals before parliamentary committees. As a young journalist, Dickens had to deal with the Scottish tongue as he covered a reception for Earl Grey in Edinburgh during 1834. Mrs Gaskell recalled that Patrick Bronte spoke with a strong Scotch accent. This went back to plantation times.

It was well known for Irish immigrants to make for town communities already established by relatives or friends, and often they would end up living in the same street or building, while the same relatives or friends would provide invaluable contacts for employment. The life they could expect in a tenement single room was hardly less squalid than a highland bothy or Irish cabin, apart from the fresh air. In the book Wealth of Nations, in which self-interest was the main theme, Smith noted 'the creation of great cities and manufactories' wherein the industrial worker was 'little attended to', where he lost his 'character', and underwent 'mental mutilation'. Disraeli's 'Sybil', described the transition of the agricultural workers to the mines, and noted the fears of the miners with regard to the new arrivals: "Ah! them's the himmigrants," said Caroline, "they're sold out of slavery, and sent down by Pickford's van into the labour market to bring down our wages.' (Pickfords were operating even in those days!). This urban energy was noted in Bronte's book Shirley:' .... manufacturing lads i' th' north is a deal more intelligent, and knaws a deal more nor th' farming folk i' th' south.' William Morris had divided feelings about cities – urban squalor but wealth of culture. He considered the city capable of alienation (as had Marx), turning people into automations and deadening human passions.

Newcastle was a historical bridgehead and owed its initial foundation to its position on the River Tyne. Its name was derived from the Norman Castle built over 800 years before. From Roman times its location was recognised as critically important. Hardyng in his Chronicle, referred to William Rufus, third son of William the Conqueror:

Newcastle bridge 1829 (magnoliabox.com)

'He buylded the Newcastell upon Tyne
Scottes to gaynstande, and to defende
And dwell therein, the people to enclyne,
The towne to builde and walle as did append
He gave them ground and golde fulgrete to spend
To buylde it well and walle it all aboute,
And fraunchised therein to pay a free rente out.'

Many famous travellers had visited Newcastle, describing the town in glowing terms, such as John Wesley, but Daniel Defoe noted with concern the activities of press-gangs. The River Tyne dominated Newcastle, and the main bridge crossing at that time had been built in 1781. The previous bridge was destroyed in the great flood of 1771 after having survived over five centuries. The famous civil engineer, John Smeaton, was engaged by the Newcastle authorities to advise on the best location and type of bridge to replace the damaged one. Vested interests from Newcastle and Gateshead exerted heavy pressure; the main problems with the destroyed bridge were its narrow width and the steep approach roads.

The River Tyne (Tin or Twin) and its quaysides was a scene of great activity, with sailing and collier boats serving this busy industrial town. The town would have been very smoky and noisy mainly due to the rapid introduction of steam engines in mining

View of Newcastle 1831
(Bridgeman Images)

and manufacturing. Somerville described the 'debris of civilised mankind' employed on Tyneside harbour works 'as gathered from every quarter of the Scottish and north of England compass, with stonemasons, some literally without a shirt and without tools, who wasted their entire wages on whiskey'. From 1830 to 1880, there was a rise in mass entertainment and pub culture. Abolition of beer duty took place in 1830, resulting in religious pressure for teetotalism. Up to the 1842 Mines Act, mineworkers were paid in a public house.

Newcomers to Newcastle like the Shannons, would have been struck by a mixture of sounds, smells and sights. The industrial grime and filthy housing were located alongside beautifully designed streets, for example Grey Street, considered one of the most elegant thoroughfares in Europe. During the 1830s Richard Grainger re-developed many of Newcastle's streets. For country people not used to large towns, the Shannons would have been intrigued by the street lighting lit by gas, produced from coal since 1818.

Life was primitive and rough, and men spent what little available free time mostly in drinking. For the working classes, the most popular form of relaxation was musical entertainment in public houses. Other pastimes included fighting, with Irish Catholics and Protestants ready to show their mettle. Bull-baiting in Northumberland was still legal up to 1833. Miners enjoyed their precious spare time. Some pastimes originated in Ireland, including greyhound racing and hare-coursing, and the playing of bag-pipes. Another form of entertainment, brass bands, started at this time, and was adopted by the Salvation Army sixty years later. The brass band movement, boosted by the railways and the invention by Adolph Sax of piston-valve instruments, was to become the delight and pride of the northern industrial workers.

In 1827, a Prussian immigrant called Henry Bolckow arrived in Newcastle, and was to join up with partner John Vaughan to form the massive iron foundry in the new north Yorkshire town of Middlesborough. In the same year, Newcastle had been described as 'the improving spirit of the age', as Richard Grainger, John Dobson and John Clayton were starting to put together a development plan for the city centre. Newcastle had seen considerable growth and industrial expansion, but had retained the structure of small workshops that blurred the divisions between masters and men and supported sufficient harmony and cohesion to nourish an interclass radical alliance. There was a massive working-class involvement in reform which centred on the traditional pre-industrial groups rather than in those spawned by factory and machine.

By the middle of the eighteenth century the British were already famous for their machines which as a foreign tourist Abbe Le Blanc noted: 'really multiply men by lessening their work .... Thus in the coal pits of Newcastle, a single person can, by means of an engine surprisingly and simple, raise five hundred tons of water to the height of a hundred and eighty feet'. The steam engine in its primitive form had been already in use – it was a product of the mines. By 1769 a hundred 'atmospheric engines' had been erected round Newcastle, and fifty-seven were at work. However, the more modern James Watt type engines, which were to be the real foundation of industrial technology, were to make a slow introduction into the mines. In London, important sections of industry were brought to a standstill if adverse winds in the Thames estuary delayed the arrival of the Newcastle coal convoy. Adam Smith noted that the coal-trade from Newcastle to London employed more shipping than all the carrying trade of England. London contained fifteen per cent of the English population and had an insatiable appetite for food and fuel. Coal grew almost directly with the number of urban fireplaces.

Coal mining had been practised around Newcastle for centuries, probably starting with charcoal burning. It had been considered little more than a branch of farming; indeed the mine could not be operated without the farm since stabling and forage was needed for the horses used at the pit. Young in 1770 gave an idyllic picture of the lives of the 'peasantry' in England: 'Now there is not a collier without his farm; each from three or four to 20 acres of land. Most of them keep a cow or two, and a galloway: raise the corn etc. they eat; are well fed, well clothed, industrious and happy. Their time is spent at home instead of the alehouse'. Writer George Borrow met a Durham 'mining captain' [a Cornish term] who

Old Collier 1830 (en wikipedia.org)

described Durham county in the 1820s as follows: 'One part of it was full of big hills and mountains, where there were mines of coal and lead with mighty works with tall chimneys spouting out black smoke, and engines roaring with big wheels going round, some turned by steam, and others by what they called forces, that is brooks of water dashing down steep channels. Another part of Durham was a more level country with beautiful woods, happy-looking farm-houses, well-filled fields and rich gorgeous meadows, in which stood stately with brown sides and short horns the Durham ox'.

Mining in the 1830s was still a comparatively small occupation, probably numbering less than 20,000 British workers, with coalminers scarcely more numerous than miners of copper, lead, tin and iron. A third of the output from coalmines was for domestic use. During the nineteenth century coalmining progressed towards deeper workings, larger colliery undertakings, and the mechanisation of ventilation and vertical haulage. Advance in underground haulage was based on the introduction of pit ponies but there was the retention of hewing as skilled manual labour. Miners having a specialist trade were to be at the forefront of the trade union movement, and generally, trade unionism was the preserve of the skilled craftsmen until the 1870s.

The Shannons as labourers did not present a risk to the miners' jobs. Once the Shannons had children born in Newcastle, they were tied to the parish where they lived, unless demand for their labour over-rode questions of settlement. 'Bastard' as well as legitimate children provided rights of settlement. Since Newcastle had a size-able Catholic presence, religious prejudice might have been less than in country areas.

During the sixteenth and seventeenth centuries, Durham and Northumberland had been one of the few areas where Catholic 'Recusants' had suffered less persecution. This was due to the Catholic landlords who had given protection to Catholic tenants and their dependents. There was evidence that other Shannons had been in Newcastle for some time; records showed that a John Shannon was buried at Killingworth Colliery in 1823 at the age of 75 years, and a Thomas Shannon was imprisoned in 1828 for stealing.

Two North East families had a great influence on the people of Northumberland and Durham; Earl Grey of Howick, and Lord Lambton. Grey had been pressing for parliamentary reform since 1790, and had taken over the leadership of the Whigs. Grey's marriage to Mary Eliz Ponsonby, daughter of a leading Irish Liberal family, strengthened his sympathies for Catholic emancipation. Grey resigned as Foreign Secretary in 1807 as a result of the refusal of George III to grant Catholic emancipation, and was out of office until November 1830 when he became Prime Minister. The Lambtons, a long established aristocratic family in Durham, had shown radical tendencies as early as 1792, when William Lambton with Earl Grey, founded the Society of Friends of the People. The aim of this society was 'firstly to restore freedom of election and a more equal representation of the People in Parliament, secondly, to secure to the People a more frequent exercise of their right of electing their own representatives.'

The Lambton's main source of wealth was coal, and in 1792 a new pit was sunk at Lambton, near Chester le Street, and in the same year his heir, John Lambton was born, later to be known as Radical Jack. Having just taken the seat previously occupied by Sir Henry Vane Tempest, in 1815 he opposed the retention of the Corn Laws, even though he stood to gain from the inflated prices. His opposition was on the grounds that the miner and the labourer could not afford to buy bread. This was the year of Waterloo, when beacons around the hills of Durham were alight in celebration of the famous victory, except for the Lambton house where John Lambton's wife was dying of consumption. A parliamentary friend, Henry Brougham, advised Lambton that the best way to come to terms with his loss was through continued public service. Lambton had visited Paris in the winter of 1815, and was never to forget the 'naked tyranny of the Bourbon restoration', then seated on both the thrones of France and Spain. This experience was to be critical in developing his radical views.

In June George IV died to national rejoicing and was replaced by William IV. Also to die in the same month was William Huskisson, leader of the 'progressive' wing of the Tory Party, who having caught a chill at the King's funeral, was to tragically step in front of a train at the opening of the Manchester to Liverpool Railway. Huskisson had been a foremost promoter of the 'railroad', with George Stephenson as the chief engineer. The 1830s saw the start of 'general' unions, whereas at that time the 'pompous trades and proud mechanics' described by Sidney Webb held aloof in their narrow 'trade' affairs and friendly societies. There had been some earlier development of trade societies in the handicraft trades as the protective regulations of guild and state began to break down. This was the case for the journeymen printers who adapted their apprenticeship regulations, entry fees and other 'aristocratic' features such as collective bargaining. The first combination in the Durham district was called the Collier's United Association which only lasted a few years, and was succeeded by the 'Pitmen's Union of Tyne and Wear'. A strike which started in 1830 lasted intermittently through much of the following year.

The Shannons had moved from an agricultural area where political activity was rare, to a bustling industrial town where political agitation was at the melting point, particularly on the question of reform. Lord Grey and Lord Durham, were at the forefront of the campaign leading to the 1832 Reform Act. At this time the Irish immigrants were reluctant to get involved in politics other than catching the latest news of Daniel O'Connell and Ireland; their main concern was to earn a living. There was no tradition

of weaving in the North East, and other skilled local occupations were foreign to the Irish.

The Northern Typographical Union for letterpress printers, formed in 1830, was the strongest union among printers in the north of England, followed soon by the union of boilermakers. The printers' union probably formed due to the demand for petitions, and this may have been the time when Edward Shannon was recruited as an apprentice printer. It is unlikely that the Shannon men had much difficulty in finding work in Newcastle, at the centre of expansion in the north east coalfields.

The Political Union societies were well organised bodies of northern workmen who wished to secure the vote and to educate their members to be worthy of it. The first local trade union for miners in the North East was formed in February 1826 (previously in secret), with the knowledge that they would have to do battle with a formidable opponent – that collection of powerful coalowners who dominated the Tyneside coalfields. These owners were known as the 'Grand Allies'. The British landowners were unique in owning the mineral rights (apart from silver and gold which belonged to the crown), and enormous fortunes could be made. Unlike on the continent, the British proprietor owned the mines under his land rather than the king drawing royalties. Lord Londonderry, the leading coalowner, described 'The United Colliers' as 'entirely established' and if not resisted by the coalowners, the latter would have to 'surrender at discretion to any laws the Union propose'.

In May 1830 at Hebburn Colliery, machinery was thrown down the shaft, with 'blacklegs' in terror below. There was to be a long and bitter battle between the miners and the mine owners over the continuing deaths and injuries down the coal mines. The Felling disaster which took place on the 25 May 1812 was one of the worst with ninety-two killed, out of a death toll of almost a 1,000 recorded deaths in the first thirty-six years of the nineteenth century. Further mine explosions were to take place in July 1813 at Fatfield Colliery with eight killed, and again in October at Harrington Mill Pit with twenty boys and four men killed. There was great consternation when in December, there was another explosion at Felling killing twenty-three and injuring twenty-one. A 'Society for Preventing Accidents in Coal Mines' was formed at Sunderland in October 1813, with the Duke of Northumberland as its president, and John Lambton was amongst the vice-presidents which included the Marquis of Londonderry, Robert Surtees of Mainsforth, the historian, and mine owner Sir Matthew Ridley. The coalowners had other concerns – trade with Europe in revolution.

An Evangelical and Tory Radical, Richard Oastler, published a letter on 'Child Slavery' in the Leeds Mercury (1830) which started his campaign for legal regulation of the working day. Under pressure from the 'Swing Riots', the Whigs were beginning to emerge as an effective force, pledged to some form of parliamentary reform. The July Revolution in France, with the overthrow of Charles X, encouraged the English Radicals to hope that 'The battle of English liberty has really been fought and won in Paris'. In the autumn after three months of disturbances, Wellington doomed the Tories by pledging his complete opposition to reform, and this was followed by a frenzy of insurrection around Britain. Henry Brougham and Lord Durham were two Whigs advocating considerable widening of the franchise whereas Lord John Russell and Lord Grey wanted to move more slowly.

Distrust of their political masters led to eighteen months of agitation. One of the essential planks of the Reform was the re-distribution of parliamentary seats to provide the new enlarged industrial towns with some political representation. As an example of the parliamentary inequity, Rye with 14 voters had the same representation as Durham with 6,000 voters. On the Duke of Newcastle's vast estates it was an accepted rule that anyone who did not vote for his nominees could expect to be turned out of his house. Gladstone's father holding similar views, sent a pamphlet to Peel explaining that negroes were happier when forced to work. In 1833 when they received their freedom, Sir John Gladstone was paid £75,000 for 1609 slaves. He also had forthright views on the political make-up in parliament:

> 'As for the whigs, they can all talk and make speeches, but they are not men of business. The ultra tories are too contemptible and wanting of talent to be thought of. The radicals cannot be trusted, for they would soon pull down the venerable fabric of our constitution. The liberals or independents must at least generally side with the duke; they are likely to meet each other half way.'

The political unions organised demonstrations with a strongly anti-clerical tone in view of the fact that 21 out of 26 bishops voted in the House of Lords against reform. On the 2 November 1830, Earl Grey rose in the House of Lords to express his regret that the King's Speech had made no reference to Parliamentary Reform. The Duke of Wellington replied that he had complete faith in the present system. The battle lines had been drawn. The people's reaction was as hostile in the north as in the south. Yet on other issues Wellington's views were more enlightened. On the 14 November, the Wellington Government was censored by the young Gladstone in an Oxford debate for its cowardice in accepting Catholic emancipation. With reference to the forthcoming elections, Grey was heard to say: 'The Black Spot on our horizon is Ireland'. Gladstone was to express the same view many decades later. On the 16 November, the Wellington/Peel administration resigned and Earl Grey took over as prime minister for the Whigs. Shortly afterwards Grey gave Lord Durham the task of putting together the Reform Bill.

The first documentary evidence of the Shannon's arrival in Newcastle was an entry in the Catholic church baptismal registers on the 4 December 1830, when

Peter (abbreviated to 'Pet:') Shannon was recorded as Godfather at the baptism of Catherine O'Bryan (probably corrupted from O'Brien). Interestingly, the adjacent entries included baptisms for John, Peter and Rozanne Gallagher (Isabella Gallagher was shortly to be Peter Shannon's wife). The register recorded many other Gallaghers which was one of the most common surnames in Ireland, especially in Donegal; its population was predominantly Irish speaking.

The next appearance of Peter Shannon was in his marriage record about one year and six months later. It would seem that he had travelled directly from Ireland to Newcastle, perhaps on hearing that his father Philip, mother Ann, and younger members of the family had moved on from Scotland. Peter may have been married previously in Ireland since he was aged about thirty-two in 1830. When the Shannons arrived in the Lockerby area, Peter would have been 18 years old, and perhaps had decided then to stay behind in Ireland and to live independently from his parents.

In December 1830, O'Connell was arrested and was charged with conspiracy when the Government became alarmed by a French invasion fleet at Bantry Bay in Ireland. As Carlyle commented, there were many urban areas which attracted the 'wild Milesians' to England and Scotland, with Irish communities known as 'Little Irelands' in such cities as Manchester, Liverpool, Glasgow, London and Edinburgh. This was also true for Newcastle upon Tyne with the Irish residing close to the Quayside. Newcastle's streets were described as a 'mass of filth' with refuse tipped from the courts. A parliamentary

Tyneside Collier Wedding 1830 (theguardian.com)

investigator commented on a typical 'rookery' at St Giles in London, a notorious Irish slum:

> 'Rows of crumbling houses flanked by courts and alleys, culs de
> Sac etc. in the very densest part of which the wretchedness of
> London takes shelter. Squalid children, haggard men with long
> Uncombed hair, in rags with short pipe in mouths, many
> Speaking Irish, women without shoes or stockings, wolfish-
> Looking dogs; decayed vegetables strewing the pavement, low
> Public houses, linen hanging across the street to dry.'

Before workers were taken on, most mineowners in the north east of England insisted on the men signing a 'bond' which committed them usually to a yearly hire period, during which they were not allowed to seek other work and were required to accept the wages and conditions decided by the owners. When men tried to escape the bond and find work at other pits it was impossible for them to evade the close network of surveillance operated jointly by the mineowners. Durham was the last area in Britain to hold on to the yearly bond. Miners were commonly paid 2s 6d to start, some or all of which would be forfeit if they broke the arbitrary regulations imposed by the coalowners. With hewers only earning about 2s. 3d per shift, a penalty of a few pence for lightweight tubs paid to the 'keeker' or weighman had a crippling effect on the colliers' wages.

In the North East, housing was provided as part of the miner's bond of hiring, so when they lost their jobs they also lost their homes. At the end of 1840, out of 141 pitmen jailed in Newcastle, 64 had been imprisoned for breaking the terms of the annual bond to the masters, 32 for vagrancy and 4 for poaching. Before 1824 when combinations were illegal, the miners formed a loose association called 'brothering', which involved a secret oath of mutual support. In the early days of the century, it was known for miners to have their throats cut or bellies ripped open if they broke the oath.

In addition to the bond, often the mineowners compelled the workers to spend all or part of their hard earned wages in the owners' shops and stores. This system which further 'enslaved' the miner was known as the 'Truck System' (in Scotland known as 'Sutlery'), and the associated shops, 'Truck or Tommy Shops'. Generally the prices of goods were extortionate so the miners rapidly fell into debt. Also the quality of the goods was often poor, thus the saying 'tommy-rot'. Right from the inception of the union, miners in the North-East coalfields complained vociferously about the iniquities of the bond. The owners used the binding as a subtle weapon for imposing onerous conditions, but also for weeding out agitators. Martin Jude, a prominent agitator during the 1840s, was effectively barred from working in any of the North-East pits. He took up as Landlord of the Three Tuns pub near the Newcastle Quayside.

News about the industrial scene in the North East was quickly spreading. Thomas Carlyle in his novel, Sartor Resartus, published in 1831, mentioned the 'opening of new mine shafts'. The safety fuse for igniting gunpowder had just been invented by William Bickford in Cornwall. This was to save many miners' lives. Seaham Colliery, one of the new coastal pits, opened that year. Due to the congested state of the River Wear, Lord Londonderry had abandoned Sunderland as an exporting port and had built a new port at nearby Seaham in 1828. There had been a succession of coal mines opening during the previous decade; Houghton (1820), Hetton (1820) – Robert Stephenson as Resident Engineer, Ouston E or Birtley – known for blacklegs (1824), Monkwearmouth (1826) – a very deep mine beyond mining knowledge at that time, Eldon (1829), Tanfield Lea (1829), Crookhall (1830), South Hetton (1831).

Lord Eldon was Lord Chancellor of England until 1827, and his brother Lord Stowell, a prize-court judge, were sons of a coal-factor at Newcastle upon Tyne. In January 1831 Lord Grey gained King William's approval of a Bill of reform that had been drawn up by Sir James Graham, Lord Durham, Lord Duncannon, and Lord John Russell. Lambton had the foresight to argue that the Reform Bill should have provision for secret balloting, but during his illness this requirement was dropped from the bill, allowing intimidation of voters to continue. The Whig 1831 reforms included the abolition of sixty 'rotten' boroughs.

In February 1831, 10,000 pitmen met at Chester le Street, and a month later a much larger number from forty-seven collieries met at Newcastle and resolved to present a demand for redress of long-felt grievances. Chief among these were the truck shops, the insecurity of their tenure of tied cottages, the punitive system of fines for improperly filled corves (coal baskets) and the agreements concerning standby pay to bonded men who were unable to work because of engine failure or similar causes. Apart from meeting a specific grievance that boys' working day of fourteen hours be reduced to twelve hour, the owners offered no accommodation on the other demands. Shortly after, 20,000 miners assembled at Black Fell near Washington, chiefly to agitate for the removal of the bond system. The miners were led by Thomas Hepburn who was elected a full-time union official. They were astonished to see the third Marquis of Londonderry arrive with an escort of soldiers, accompanied by magistrates. After being threatened with the Riot Act, the men's representatives agreed to meet the owner for talks in Newcastle.

The union struck the pits for several weeks, and secured in the end sufficient concessions for the strike to have been considered a success for the miners. According to the Tyne Mercury it was quite clear that 'the servants have triumphed over the masters in the struggle'. The hero of the contest was Hepburn, who was a firm upholder of moderation and non-violence. Apart from minor and isolated incidences, the strike with 17,000 men 'idle', was conducted in remarkably good order. Troops had been stationed at Morpeth, and dragoons at Houghton.

On the 1st March, Lord John Russell gave a great speech on Reform. When the Whigs won by one vote on the 22 March 1831, with vital help from O'Connell after a seven day Commons battle, Macaulay described the scene in the House of Commons: 'Lord Londonderry brandishing a horse whip was restrained by fellow Tories clinging to his coat-tails'. To many workers around the country doing without a meal to share the price of a newspaper, this news was received with wild excitement. King William IV was the beneficiary of much of this popular enthusiasm. The forthcoming General Election of May 1831 caused great political excitement with many civil disturbances. At Hartlepool there was a riot between local and Irish navvies. In Ireland, during 1831 brothers John and Thomas Cough aged 12 and 10 years were sentenced to 7 years transportation for stealing some Irish linen despite their mother pleading for mercy.

Lord Lambton was one of the few coalowners who was regarded by the colliers with some respect, if not affection from some of his men. Compared to Lord Londonderry, he did make a sincere effort to take care of his workers, and during strikes his colliers were the only men who continued to work, despite threats from men at other collieries. Lambton formed a Lambton Colliers Association which must have been one of the first collieries to provide their workers with accident insurance and a basic pension, largely out of his own pocket. There were exceptions to this goodwill, like the scrawled note sent to the Lambton Pit whose men were still working, including mention of the father of the 'pitman's poet' (Skipsey):

> 'John Radison you give these lins to the workman Or els you will suffer byb the by
> we suppose you Are bound against your grements you think you have don right but
> when our turns is out if you dont come among the men the forst generall meeting
> you and your brother willly in one Church-yeard and that will be such a church as
> a number of men like you has not lane in this long time .... if you don't think fit to
> come after these Directions we must forse you to the grand-stand and you must
> take the punishment put upon you .... We suppose that b culbert Skipsey was the
> first that got bound and if he does not come a monge the men he shall be the first
> to die.'

The very success of the United Colliers Union seemed to have increased the coalowners' determination to destroy it before its hold on the industry became too complete. Hepburn was banned from further union activity and later became a Chartist speaker. Early in 1831, 9000 coal miners from Staffordshire, Yorkshire and Cheshire and parts of North Wales joined the National Association for the Protection of Labour, with John Doherty as its leader. Other areas of Britain experienced rioting, in particular Bristol, where Brunel was to see at first hand the indecision of the riot troops, reluctant to fire on their own people. In June there was a riot by miners and puddlers at Merthyr Tydfil. Following the

Merthyr Riots of 1831, its leader Dic Penderyn was hanged, and the Red Flag was raised for the first time in Britain.

When Lord Grey resigned on the 8 May, the public feared for reform; overnight the King changed from being a popular hero to a bogyman. Only a week before, girls were being christened Adelaide after the Queen. In London, public meetings were held every day declaring by unanimous resolutions that no taxes should be paid until the bill passed into law. There was a run on gold, and the Government was receiving reports that the troops could not be relied on. There were mass meetings in Durham in favour of further 'extensions' and even a vote for every man. Grey was reluctant to press the King too far on the need to create more peers if necessary, to ensure the passage of the Reform Bill through the House of Lords. This aversion to bold action by Grey was to cause the gradual worsening of relations with his son-in-law, Lord Lambton. Grey had left the House of Commons in 1807 on succeeding to the title, and in Wellington's words 'he was lost by being in the Lords'. Much of the actual fight for reform then fell to Lambton. During June to September every clause of the second Reform Bill was hotly contested by the Tories, and when it was defeated in October there was a wave of national indignation, and six months of revolutionary agitation. On the 10 October, rioters burned Nottingham Castle. There was a huge meeting in Regent's Park and all over the country meetings of protest and houses of Anti-Reformers were attacked and bishops' palaces singled out.

An Irish politician, Feargus O'Connor, was starting to agitate for a broadening of the Whig Reform to include universal suffrage, annual parliaments and vote by ballot, as well as total repeal of the Union. The Political Union of Birmingham was formed in 1831 to fight for parliamentary reform, and similar unions multiplied throughout the country. On the 31st October the middle class Radicals of the political union of London met in Lincoln's Inn Fields, with Sir Francis Burdett in the chair. They tried to unite all the political unions supporting the Reform Bill into the 'National Political Union', but were opposed by the 'National Union of the Working Classes', who wanted more radical measures including manhood suffrage and the ballot. These activities and demands were feared as revolutionary, and their planned meeting in London for November was prohibited by the Government.

The Great Cholera Epidemic started with cholera reaching Sunderland from Hamburg late in 1831, and then started to spread throughout Scotland and England. The Welsh strike breakers were particularly hit by cholera. Apparently, Dumfries suffered an especially severe 'visitation' indicating travel between this town and Durham. News of cholera spreading across Europe was reported in the Roscommon & Leitrim Gazette of August 1831. By September deaths were reported in Sligo. Medical opinion was confused as to the treatment as well as the cause of the cholera, resulting in various remedies: pills, clysters, mustard poultices, hot-air baths and preventative belts. The use of camphor and musk and 'anti-spasmdics' was publicly urged and advertised, and despite the partiality which the disease showed for the intemperate, there was a wide belief in the efficacy of copious doses of brandy. Already rendered suspicious of the 'resurrectionist' practices of the period, the people became apprehensive of quarantine and enforced removal to hospital. They resented the rapid and undignified burial of the dead for they were accustomed to regard elaborate and often expensive obsequies as a mark of respect. There were rumours that cholera victims were destined for dissection tables and that Catholics were being buried in Protestant cemeteries. The infamous deeds of Burke and Hare in 1828 had instilled a fear in the public mind.

There was anger by the local authorities at the indifference to the epidemic shown by government until the disease reached London in early 1832. John Stuart Mill was to describe in the 'Chronicle' in 1849, the infamous slum known as Jacob's Island, in east end of London, which was called the 'Capital of Cholera', where the epidemic of 1832 struck, and where Dickens located the grisly scene of Bill Sikes' death in Oliver Twist. It was observed that cholera was more destructive in towns and that it appeared to discriminate, concentrating upon the poor. Many Catholic priests in 1832 died tending the sick. The poor grumbled that since the new poor laws the church pews were not free to all.

Dr Snow, an eminent physician and resident of Newcastle at this time, made the comment: 'The duration of cholera in a place is usually in direct proportion to the number in the population. The disease remains but two or three weeks in a village, two to three months in a good sized town, whilst in a great metropolis it often remains a whole year or longer'. Cholera spread to Ireland. The victims of the cholera pandemic extended to America in the autumn of 1832. Irish immigrants from Donegal, Tyrone and Derry working at mines and on railway construction in Philadelphia (USA) had been subject to strong anti-Irish prejudice. When they fell victim to cholera they were attacked by local vigilantes, and many were battered to death. Fifty-seven Irish workers working on Duffy's Cut were buried in a shallow trench at the side of the line without ceremony or funeral.

In March 1832 the Northumberland miners went on strike. In response, one clergyman and mine owner evicted all his tenants even though there was raging cholera at the time. So perhaps good reason for newcomers like the Shannons with Irish Catholic credentials to keep a low profile.

In early January 1832, King William had at last agreed to the Whigs' request for the creation of more government peers to enable the reform legislation to be passed by the House of Lords by a comfortable majority of 116. In late February there was vigorous opposition to the Irish Reform Bill by the Protestants, with a petition signed by 230,000 persons. After some back-tracking by the King, the amended Reform Bill was eventually passed in the Commons on the 26 March. The second reading was carried on the 14 April 1832 by a majority of 9. O'Connell, who had entered parliament in February 1830, had played a major part in the 1832 Reform Act and the Abolition of Slavery Act by supporting the Whigs. The North East was to share in the good news, with the opening of Durham University.

Before 1832, the working classes as a body in the North had been profoundly indifferent to ideas and causes, but this all changed when the Reform Bill passed into law. The new borough of Sunderland was to have two representatives in Parliament, and Gateshead, South Shields and Tynemouth were each to gain one representative. Bentham, the architect of the workhouses, died one day before the Reform Act became law for England and Wales, and a few months after the appointment of the Poor Law Commission. There were separate reform acts for Scotland and Ireland, the former being least affected. However, the working classes soon came to believe that the 1832 Reform Act had been a betrayal, and that trade unions were the only means left to achieve their objectives by industrial action.

The early trades union activity in the North East had led to the Great Strike of March 1832. Five of the seven strike leaders transported to Botany Bay from Jarrow were Primitive Methodists. William Cobbett during his Northern Tour described the hidden world of the coal districts: 'Here is the most surprising thing in the world; thousands of men and thousands of horses continually living underground; children born there, and who sometimes, it is said, seldom see the surface at all, though they live to a considerable age'. The longevity of miners was possibly true when applied to the eighteenth century, but workers conditions had dramatically changed for the worse. By May 1832 labour disputes were rife in the North East.

In June 1832 magistrate Nicholas Fairless of South Shields was pulled off his horse and suffered fatal injuries. Pitmen Ralph Armstrong and William Jobling were accused, but only Jobling was caught, and later hanged. His body was left to putrefy for three weeks in a metal cage on Jarrow Slake until removed by relatives under darkness. This was a morbid warning to striking miners. At this time a new Anatomy Act became law in response to an illegal trade in corpses. Previously only the bodies of executed murderers could be used by doctors for scientific research. Cobbett raised the fear of paupers that they would then become the targets of a 'legitimate' trade whereas the rich were not affected.

At Birmingham, two hundred thousand persons, under the leadership of Thomas Attwood, the eminent banker, and the father and hero of political unions, petitioned against Government policies. It was rumoured that the Birmingham union was to march to London. Alexander Somerville, then serving with the Scots Greys, were given orders to rough-sharpen their swords – the intention to inflict a ragged wound. Somerville was to write to the War Office warning the Government that the Scots Greys would not prevent the people from carrying out their constitutional right. This may have helped to turn the tide for the reformers; on the 17 May the private secretary to the King confirmed that sufficient numbers of Whig peers would be created to enable the Reform legislation to go through. Somerville for his trouble was later court marshalled and had to suffer one hundred lashes.

Like many Irish couples, Peter Shannon probably met his future wife in Newcastle as part of the Irish 'diaspora'. On the 13 May 1832, Peter Shannon, married Isabella Gallagher in St John's Parish Church. (Strangely, at the same church another Isabella Shannon had married Peter Smith two years earlier). For the Irish, their marriage would have been considered late, since Peter was over thirty. The birth date of their first child, Mary Ann, might provide another reason for the marriage at this time. It is possible that Peter had known Isabella in Fermanagh where there were substantial numbers of Gallaghers.

Vagrants compared with the 'labouring poor', were treated as being degraded, vicious, and dangerous. Their recurrent image was of a 'pestilence', not only as a metaphor but as a literal fact. Vagrants swarmed over the country carrying with them 'tramp-fever', a disease resembling typhoid and cholera, and with that a 'moral pestilence ... as terrible and devastating as the physical pest which accompanies it'. Mayhew described how paupers were put to work breaking up paving stones as a 'labour test', a variant of the 'less-eligibility' test, which came easy to an agricultural labourer but was a great hardship for a starving tailor. Among the Irish Catholic tillers of the soil, most marriages were arranged, and the marriage-tie was binding.

In July 1832, Joseph Skipsey the future 'Pitman Poet', was born at Percy Main near North Shields in the midst of a turbulent strike. The pitmen wanted 2s 7d a day and a twelve hour day (with waiting time at the shaft that would make at least thirteen hours most days). However the coal owners obtained the help of special constables to force such extremists back to work. Joseph's father, Cuthbert Skipsey, an overman at the pit, stepped between one of the constables and a man he was bullying, and was shot dead by the constable for his intervention. The constable was jailed for six months, but Mrs Skipsey was left without pension or relief, needing to feed her eight children on nettle broth until they were old enough to go down the pit.

A pit sinker named Anthony Wandlas, was injured during the riot. In October, he and brother Alex, and father Alex, as part of a group from Tynemouth who received Cobbett's Weekly Political Register, sent a congratulatory address to Cobbett for the lecture he had delivered to them in September. Thompson stated that in the 1840s, the miners of Northumberland and Durham were thought to be better educated than most workers, although labelled non-religious meaning non-Anglican. Compared to other working-class

Daniel O'Connell 1834
(bbc.co.uk)

groups who did not restrict their families, miners rarely neglected their children's educa-tion. Miners felt there was no compelling reason to reduce the size of their families, and there was always a demand for miners' sons to go down the pit as the industry expanded. More sons meant more income and there was always the risk of pit deaths. In the small mining villages unlike the towns there were few distractions and alternative pleasures.

During 1831 to 1834, the chief aims of Irish leader Daniel O'Connell were the Repeal of the Union and relief from the 'tithe' burden. In August 1832, Feargus O'Connor, spoke at a 'Great Public Dinner' held at Enniskillen explaining why as a Protestant he was opposed to tithes. He declared 'My object is to purify the religion I profess by lopping off its rotten and redundant temporalities'. In June and August, Acts were passed converting the tithe into a fixed annual payment. During September when Government agents started their valuations, there was fierce resistance and several killings. The 1832 General Election was held during the turmoil, and 82 members from Ireland were elected, pledged to abolish tithes. One of the acts passed by the new government was the very unpopular measure to pay the owners of negro slaves twenty millions sterling. This issue caused some anxiety for young Gladstone at Newark, nevertheless he was successful in winning his first seat. His first marathon speech at the House of Commons in March 1838 was in defence of negro apprenticeship on West Indian plantations.

Of this period, novelist Padraic Colum had described the burdens suffered by the women of Connaught: 'The hard conditions of Connacht have helped the Connacht women to development and personality. The size of the holding of land does not permit the man to develop his constructive and organising faculty. The women becomes the personality among the Connacht peasantry. The civilisation is of her creating. It is the civilisation of the hearth…… The tragedies of the Connacht life come closest to the women: as a child she sees her elder sister who has reared her leave for America; as a wife she lives alone while her husband works abroad, and often her child is born while its father is labouring in the fields of England and Scotland;….'.

Marriage was commented on by his Majesty's Commissioners, inquiring into the Conditions of the Poorer Classes in Ireland (1835). Early marriages were considered useful since 'a man looks forward to being supported in age by his family … before he is beyond labour'. The great marrying season in Ireland was Shrove-tide, and agreement between parents was often finalised by "dirtying the baste". Another favourite proverb of the peasantry in regard to matrimony was "Either marry very young, or become a monk very young". Early marriages were the rule in Catholic Ireland, and the poorest marry at the earliest possible time. It was said that farmers married later than agricultural labourers. Four generations may be seen in many of the poorest cabins in the west – strong filial affection. It was considered essential in the humblest circles that for the honour of the family, the guests at the wedding, which included sometimes the whole of the country-side, should have lots of eating and drinking: "I'd sell every stitch to me back and go naked, in order to get married dacently".

In all classes, death could strike at any time. On the 12 June 1832, Lord Lambton's second daughter by his first marriage died of consumption. In the next eight months he was to lose a son, mother and daughter. The Shannons would not have to wait long to experience the anguish of losing loved ones, but first the joys of birth. Mary Ann, the first of Peter and Isabella Shannon's children was born on the 27 December 1832 (February 1833 based on burial records). She was baptised at the church of St John on the 4 February 1833. Isabella's maiden name was recorded as Goliher, probably as it was spoken in Gaelic – O'Gallchobhair. Mary Ann was soon to be a victim of cholera which had travelled from Sunderland. At Killingworth Colliery, near Longbenton, triplets Elizabeth, Annie and Mary Mason died only 6 days old, also victims of cholera.

Following the Irish Coercion Bill which aroused immigrant protest at the beginning of 1833, the Whigs started to address themselves to Irish issues – law and order, and the liberalising of the Irish Church. The tithe system meant that the Catholic peasant already pinned at or below subsistence level was forced to give part of what little he had to support the Anglican clergymen in luxurious idleness. Sydney Smith had commented on the ludicrous situation he had observed in Ireland when 'the bell of a neat parish church often summons to worship only the parson, and an occasionally conforming clerk, while two hundred yards off, a thousand Catholics are huddled together in a miserable hovel, and pelted by the storms of heaven'. On the 28 January 1833 Lambton informed Grey of his objections to Stanley's Irish policy on Church Establishment, and this was to eventually lead to Lambton's resignation.

Gladstone dined with old Wilberforce only a few days before the latter's death in July. The campaign which had started in 1823 to free the slaves in the British Empire was achieved in 1833, with the Bill introduced by Lord Stanley, a Whig MP, later Earl of Derby. The slave-traders were given compensation at £37 per slave. Also the high-tide of Methodism and the Oxford Movement promoted a Bill to reduce the working hours for children aged between 13–18 years to 48 hours. John Keble denounced the Irish Church Bill which provided for the suppression of 22 sees of the Irish Protestant Church. Keble and Newman published a series of the Tracts for the Times – the church was in turmoil.

There was a major change in Thomas Carlyle's life as he and his wife moved in late 1833 from Dumfriesshire to start a new life in London. In his book Sartor Resartus, Carlyle set out his philosophy on reform; he welcomed the Reform Bill but felt that it was only 'burning the edges of the dunghill'. In 1833 the Conservative Party was formed after the passing of the First Reform Act, and Robert Owen formed the Grand National Consolidated Union, the first London-based attempt at a general union.

CHAPTER 5

1834–1836 Pauperism, Poor Laws and Workhouses

(Birth of James Shannon)

'The time has come when the Irish population must either be improved or exterminated. With this strong, silent people have the vehement, noisy Irish now at length got common cause made. Ireland now for the first time in such strange, circuitous ways does find itself embarked in the same boat with England, to sail together or sink together; the wretchedness of Ireland, slowly but inevitably, has crept over to us and become our own wretchedness. The Irish population must get itself redressed and saved, for the sake of the English if for nothing else.'

(Carlyle 1835)

As Darwin disembarked from the Beagle at St Julian in Chile and later the Falkland Isles, James, the second child of Peter and Isabella Shannon, was born on the 31 January 1834 at St Peter's Quay, Walker, a heavily industrialised district of Newcastle upon Tyne, adjacent the river. (A Thomas Shannon had been a naval rating aboard the Beagle in 1830). The register at St John's Church, the parish church in Westgate, recorded James Shannon's baptism 17 days later. Catholics would still have to wait a few decades before they were able to be baptised and married in their own church, even though St Andrews Catholic Church had been established in Newcastle after the Reformation in 1798.

St John the Baptist (Established) Church in Newcastle upon Tyne was built in 1287, and was re-built between 1813 and 1823, serving the townships of Benwell, Elswick, St John and Westgate. It was described by Gray, Newcastle's first historian, as a pretty little church, 'commended by an arch-prelate of this kingdom because it resembled much a cross [in plan]. With its well-worn stone, small size and simplicity, it reminds one of a country church, and with its churchyard and fine trees, the only oasis of green in central Newcastle, this resemblance was increased'.

These were volatile times in which to be born, with the Great Reform Act still in its infancy. The Act made no mention of vagrants. Robert Owen was offering hope to the masses by putting forward a new social order based on labour being the source

of wealth and the measure of value. Peter Shannon had been living in Newcastle just over three years, and not yet earning the 'good' pit wages, so would not have agreed with the sentiments of this old Tyneside song:

> 'When Aa came to Walker work
> Aa had ne coat or ne pit sark
> Noo Aa's getten two or three;
> Walker Pit's deun well for me.'

Bringing up children off the narrow crowded wynds and closes (known in those days as 'rookeries') of Britain's urban centres, was a desperate struggle for the poor people who inhabited these areas. Similar dock areas were depicted in Dickens's Oliver Twist published in January 1837. Queen Victoria in 1838 tried to persuade Lord Melbourne, Prime Minister, to read this novel but he declared that he did not wish to read about 'low life'. This book described Oliver's birth in the workhouse as a new burden on the parish, a powerful indictment of the New Poor Law dreaded by Irish immigrants.

When James Shannon was born, his mother's first child, Mary Ann, was only thirteen months old. The celebration in the Shannon household would have been modest compared with the thirty-six thousand bottles of wine consumed at St James's Palace that year. A few weeks later, a future famous poet, artist, and socialist, William Morris, was born into a comfortable middle class family near London. Also born in London at this time in similar circumstances as Morris was Charles George Gordon, later better known to the public as General Gordon.

Slavery throughout the British Empire was officially abolished in August 1834, symbolising the Nation's 'washing of hands' for its past crimes. Strangely, this did not include the territories of the East Indian Company which had just lost its trading monopoly with China. Edward Gibbon Wakefield had just formed the South Australian Association to encourage emigration. However there were many hazards on a ship bound for Australia. Convict Thomas McCaffrey, who was transported for seven years, was suffering from pernicious diarrhoea and died on the 12 January 1834. Also 700 lives were lost in the North Atlantic when eighteen emigrant ships went down. Quite different concerns were occupying the thoughts of Lord Brudenell (later Lord Cardigan of Crimea fame), when on the 1st February 1834, he faced a court-martial for gross misconduct. Even though this led to the removal of his command, he was still able to buy his way back into history.

Irish matters were never far away from Parliament's thoughts which had just denounced Irish Repeal; on the 13 February Daniel O'Connell requested a select committee inquiry in support of the Irish in their resistance to paying tithes to the Irish Church. Two weeks later Lord John Russell and Lord Brougham raised the question of the appropriation of the revenues of the Irish Church for secular purposes. Even Disraeli in 'Crisis Examined', denounced the bloated proportions of the Irish church, but not many months later he was to make one of his many changes of mind to suit the political climate. This religious crisis in the country was instigated by the writings of Keble and Pusey, and was to be a running sore for the Established Church. In May, Edward Littleton, son-in-law of Wellesley and campaigner against the truck system, introduced a bill to commute tithes into a land tax amounting to eighty per cent of the tithe. One year later a Tithe Bill was passed.

Isambard Kingdom Brunel was better known for many construction works in the south of England such as the Great Western Railway, as contractor Thomas Brassey won his first contract to build a railway in the Midlands. However, an Act in 1834, authorised the construction of a new dock at Monkwearmouth, which was to be designed by Brunel for Lord Londonderry. Later, this coalowner employed master sinker, Joseph Coxon, from a well-known 'sinker' family, to carry out sinking for coal at Seaham Harbour. Steam power had been long in use in Durham mining whereas its use had just started at Coalisland in Tyrone.

A national catastrophe occurred on the 16 October 1834 when the Houses of Parliament were burnt down. Five days later, at the age of 1year 8months, James Shannon's sister Mary Ann died at Ballast Hills near St Peters Quay. It is likely that she died of cholera which was still endemic in the North East. James's father Peter Shannon and most of Peter's children were to be buried at Ballast Hills.

Ballast Hills, near Walker, had come by this name due to ballast being dumped off the colliers (boats) after their return journey from London or Whitby. The material was thrown out of the ships' holds into wagons waiting alongside, which were run up to the summit of Ballast Hills, and emptied out there. At the foot of this great mound of shot rubbish, Samuel Smiles noted that George Stephenson worked as a brakesman in 1803. There was once a pretty lovers' lane near Ballast Hills, much frequented by apprentices and their lasses, and during the week the area provided an excellent drying ground for household washing. It later became the main burial ground for that part of Newcastle.

In the Derryvullan district of Enniskillen, the Tithe Applotment Records of 1835 recorded tenants Barney, Bryan and Hugh Shannon, and at Drummackin in 1838, Thomas Shannon. Not far away at Drunmurrish in Monaghan, a Phil Shannon was recorded in 1829. The enforcement of tithe payments was unpopular in England, but in Ireland the payment to an alien church provoked many acts of violence. 'Thus the Whiteboy Association assumed the role of a vast trades union for the protection of the Irish peasantry'.

In 1834, the young John Bright, a Quaker and Radical, made the first of many visits to Ireland; he compared the situation there with the hard times of England: 'What I remember of our journey was the crowd of beggars that gathered round the coach at every place where we stopped to change horses. Nothing like it could be seen in England'. The Irish peasants lived always so near the border-line of starvation, and the tithe burden inflicted cruel hardships on them. This rate was levied for the support of the Established Protestant Church, which the Irishman hated, not only as heretical, but as a symbol of the foreign (that is to say English) domination. In France like Ireland, there had been an affinity between the peasants and their priests. This starkly contrasted with the Anglican clergymen and their flock, when in times of hardship the parson would mainly uphold the interests of the landlord. The method of treating the parson's profession as a comfortable career was closely associated with the system of aristocracy, and therefore sacrosanct for most politicians. Many had numerous livings which they rarely attended, similar to the absentee landlords of Ireland.

Lord Durham was experiencing labour troubles following resentment from the Durham Miners' Union that his men had worked through the unrest of the previous two years. In January 1834, referring to the Union delegates for the local district, Lord Durham commented; 'I know them by their acts to be the most unprincipled rascals'. He was upset by stories that his men had been ill-treated and that they were dissatisfied. He felt he was being attacked by both the Whigs and the Tories. A month later a disturbance took place at Snipper's Gate Colliery, near Hetton in Durham, following the owners of the colliery ejecting a number of the workmen from their houses for refusing to work according to agreement. In the course of the day a number of colliers assembled at the premises, and in their attempt to frustrate the authorities, a general battle ensued, in which a number of constables received severe bruises and wounds from the pitmen, many of whom were armed.

The country was soon to hear of the arrest of the five Dorset agricultural labourers on the charge of administering a secret oath during swearing-in of members of their Friendly

Society. The Tolpuddle labourers were sentenced and awaited transfer to the prison haulks, despite appeals by Daniel O'Connell in Parliament. This was a Government back-lash to the recent 'Swing' insurrection as the authorities watched for further southern unrest. They were determined that trade unionism should not establish itself in the south as it had in the north. Disillusionment with the Reform Bill was turning people from political to trade union action. Factory unions were urging their workers not to work more than an eight-hour-day from the 1st of April, and in the same month three peasants were killed in Newcastle West (Ireland) during tithe disturbances. O'Connell referring to Ireland, pointed out the moral force that trade unionism could exert, particularly in respect of cheap labour being imported from Ireland, which was putting extra money into the masters' pockets. Mineowner Lord Londonderry supported the Duke of Newcastle in the House of Lords against the increase in organisations calling themselves 'trade unions'.

In May, reports received by the Irish Government described the distress caused by the failure of the potato crop in some parts of Ireland, particularly in counties Mayo, Galway and Kerry. However England's attention was more on the news from the Kaffir War which had just started. During the debate on the Repeal of the Union in 1834, the first question was raised by Daniel O'Connell in the Commons. Sir Robert Peel responded by ridiculing the Irish, and created much amusement on the Government benches by reading the record of the ceremonies said to have been adopted at the crowning of the ancient Irish Kings at the time of the first Norman invasion of Ireland in 1117. O'Connell could have pointed out that for many centuries when Ireland was a civilisation, England was still in the dark ages.

Gladstone obtained his first office in the Wellington-Peel minority government as Peel set forth his 'Tamworth Manifesto', explaining that the Tory party was far from reactionary and had no desire to tamper with the Whig Reform Act. The continuing pressure caused by O'Connell's campaign for Repeal of the Act of Union caused Lord Grey to resign in June. Lord Melbourne's new Whig government came into power benefiting from the disarray in the Tory party over the Reform and the Irish question. Melbourne, although sympathetic to the need for equal treatment of Catholic and Protestants, was quite clear that in the final resort, the support for the Union, and therefore for the Protestants, was paramount. He was also aware in general terms of the effect of urban strife, and consid-ered that a growing population, many whom were subject to economic dislocations of the new industrial world, was putting an intolerable strain on the provision of relief. In particular, he referred to Irish men 'who neither mind Lord or Laws'. John Russell was working towards reconciliation with Ireland under the Litchfield-House Compact, by which means the Whigs had surrendered to O'Connell the Irish patronage, who in return secured them the Irish votes.

Melbourne still yearned for the 'days of responsibility and duty' in employment, but this had been replaced by contract work. The country was in a deeply disturbed state with the Government trying to downplay the implications of the 'Captain Swing' riots. Justices of the Peace were faithfully executing the Poor Law and enforcing the Riot Act with militias and constables on the basis that 'poverty should be relieved but it should know its place'. William IV and Lord Grey were pressurising Melbourne to act against the trade unions, but he did not consider the unions a threat unless they advocated violence or showed that they intended to set up a national conspiracy. When the Tolpuddle Martyrs were convicted of conspiracy in March 1834, a few weeks later a large trade union protest march took place at the Copenhagen Fields in London. The dread of transportation and the measures to prevent convicts returning home were dramatised in Dickens' Great Expectations. This show of strength by the trade unions was to be short lived when Robert Owen's Grand National Consolidated Trade Union collapsed later that year.

The Poor Law had a long history. By the Act of 1722, parishes, or unions of parishes, were authorised to construct workhouses, and to withhold relief outside them. Under the Acts of 1782 and 1795, it became the practice to reserve the workhouses for the aged or impotent, and to relieve the able-bodied in their homes. The result was that 'relief' was applied and granted as a supplement to wages, and great numbers of the working classes were pauperised. With the growth of the factory towns, the evil of poverty became intolerable. The poor law commissioners found that the labourers felt that unlike other sections of society, they alone had nothing to lose or gain. In order to obtain employment they had to dress in rags.

The Poor Law Amendment Act of 1834 (for England but not for Scotland) was designed to end outdoor relief with the start of segregated workhouses, based on a 'bounty on unthrift, idleness, bastardy and beer-drinking'. This was the first major legislation since the Act of 1579 when overseers for the poor were appointed for each parish and a rate was levied on every person of substance in that parish to provide a fund for the poor. A Board of Guardians were set up under the 1834 Act to supervise the relief of poverty in the 590 groups or unions of parishes into which the country was divided. Some Boards, particularly in the north, refused to put men who were temporarily unemployed into workhouses. The poor had to choose between starvation and loss of liberty. It was recorded that Newcastle women objected strongly to the poor law separating those 'that god had joined together'. Children were not educated in workhouses, and bells were not tolled when the burial of paupers took place. During the eighteen century there had been forty-seven bank holidays, whereas by 1834 this had been reduced to four.

Jeremy Bentham's moral code was based on the theory of the 'greatest happiness of the greatest number'. Robert Owen and Edwin Chadwick were two of his disciples. Chadwick's inquiry into the old poor law set out sound principles, but often these were used as a means of abolishing outdoor relief indiscriminately. Owen worked on the principle of 'collective happiness'. In contrast, William Cobbett, a hero of the working classes, who was coming to the end of his life, called the recent Act the 'Poor Man's Robbery Bill', and the poor nicknamed the workhouses the 'Bastilles' after the French prisons. Hammond noted that the workhouses were dreaded by the poor for the dirt and disease and devastating fevers that swept through them, described by Crabbe's poem, The Parish Workhouse:

> 'Theirs is yon House that holds the Parish-Poor,
> Whose walls of mud scarce bear the broken door;
> There, where putrid vapours, flagging, play,
> And the dull wheel hums doleful through the day;-
> There Children dwell who know no Parents' care;
> Parents, who know no Children's love, dwell there!
> Heart-broken Matrons on their joyless bed,
> Forsaken Wives and Mothers never wed;
> Dejected Widows with unheeded tears,
> And crippled Age with more than childhood fears;
> The Lame, the Blind, and, far the happiest they!
> The moping idiot and the Madman gay.
> Here too the Sick their final doom receive,
> Here brought, amid the scenes of grief, to grieve'

In Yorkshire, even a conservative like Patrick Bronte, (father of Charlotte, Emily and Anne), opposed the Workhouse Act, fearing it would cause widespread starvation, and the people deprived of relief would break out into open rebellion. The Bronte children at the same time were expressing their 'anti-Catholic emancipation' feelings, probably following their father's views. Notwithstanding, the fact that Catholic Emancipation had been enacted in 1829, this issue was still stirring emotions on the street as well as in Parliament, with the Ultra- Right Tories eager to revoke the Act. This may have led to the 1834 Poor Law Inquiry including a special study of Irish immigration.

Another burden on the 'poor' were the Corn Laws enacted in 1815. These were designed to protect farmers from foreign imports. However, they had a devastating effect on the working class in Great Britain. The main issue was the deteriorating condition of the poor, and in particular those able-bodied poor people receiving relief from the Government based on the 1795 Act, which offered relief 'to any industrious poor person or persons ....', and elevated the pauper to labourer. The 1834 Royal Commission Report stated that the Speenhamland system had encouraged the poor to marry early and have more children. However, Malthus was proved wrong when the increase of population between 1811 and 1821 began to level off.

Before workhouses were imposed on Ireland, 'sweathouses' were locally provided, giving the poor a little relief from rheumatism and stiffness of the joints. They were used during the 18th and 19th centuries, particularly in Ulster, with 42 located in Fermanagh. The 1835 Statistical Report for the townland of Sheetrim in Monaghan, described a kind of steam-bath erected by an old man, Stephen Shannon. It consisted of freestone rocks, partly cut out of the solid rock with the front part built up with mud, lime and rough stones. A flat stone covered the top, finished in sods to keep in the hot air. The entrance was small and only sufficient to allow a man to creep in on all fours. It had the appearance of a beehive, an ancient Irish structural form. These workhouses had been introduced into Germany in Druid times by Irish missionaries and were known there as 'Irish Baths'.

A new Tory member of Parliament, Benjamin Disraeli spoke out against the new Poor Law: 'in England being poor is a crime'. However, Disraeli's Young Englandism 'advocated the kind of democracy not of right but of sufferance – not of independence but of charity – a well-fed slavery in which the people like tame animals, should lick the hand that caressed them, and obey the bidding of their masters'. The Act for the Abolition of Slavery had been passed but it was not fully effective till 1838. In South Africa the Boers being slave traders, bitterly resented the emancipation of slaves, and thousands of them during the period 1834 to 1837 trekked from Cape Colony northwards, settling in the territory which extended from the Orange River to Limpopo. About forty years later, America was to be torn by similar racial issues.

In November, Lord Grey was accusing his son-in-law, Lord Durham, of having joined the Radical 'class'; but Durham had immense popularity in the country. Conveniently for the Government, at this time the Lambtons had been sent on a mission to Russia. In November the Poles under Russian rule were uprising – some had to escape to Prussia. On the 10 November Lord Spenser died and his son (Althorp) entered the Lords. Peel's administration which followed only lasted to April 1835, since the Whigs had co-operated with the Radicals and O'Connell to defeat the Tories. The Conservative members to their great annoyance found themselves sitting alongside the Radicals and the 'queer lot' who had just arrived from Ireland. O' Connell was observed by the Tories 'swaggering about the floor of the House attended by his tail of obsequious followers, talking and gesticu-lating to other members of his party on the benches in a conscious pose of authority'. During a debate in Parliament in August, Joseph Hume compared the criminal acts of the Orange Lodges, regarding oath-taking, with the Tolpuddle Martyrs who were undergoing sentence in Australia for lesser transgressions.

For an un-skilled labourer looking for employment, what was available in Newcastle during the early 1830s? Peter Shannon in his early thirties was unlikely to obtain 'below surface' mining work requiring previous experience. No doubt he and his brothers, and father started labouring near the coal pits such as at Walker, Wallsend and Longbenton, or at the major ironworks of Losh, Wilson and Bell at Walker established in 1807.

Up to this date the typical collier was considered to be the lowest type of Briton – morally and intellectually. It was no small coincidence that with the introduction of the Irish into the collieries, the mining population became among the foremost in political awareness and began to compare more favourably with other classes of labour. Irishmen were generally barred from entering areas of skilled labour, their main assets being their strength, willingness to work in intolerable conditions and at low wages. Handley had written of the Scottish miners in the early nineteenth century, and the conditions he described equally applied to the miners of Newcastle at that time:

> 'There are twice as many Scots miners as Irish due to the considerable degree of practice that is required and that beginning early in life. It seldom happens that a man can bring his body in the positions required if he begins after twenty-two or twenty-four; much of the work is done with the body bent down or resting on the side; but the simple tasks of drawer who dragged the coal from the pickman to the bottom of the shaft [shank], and redsman [roadsman] who kept the tunnels clear of impedimenta the Irish far outnumbered the natives – they are fully more obedient and tractable than the natives and not so much given to combine, do not find difficulties in learning something new and no hesitation going down the mouth of a coal pit. ....In addition, the iron industry and its allied craft of coal mining were the only branches of labour where the Irish immigrant may be said to have competed with the Scottish worker for employment – but the demand usually exceeded the supply; the meagre recompense was not the fault of the interloping stranger but the powers of the master and the maladjustment of labour and its lack of organisation inevitable in the infancy of the industry. When time remedied these weaknesses the Irish worker proved to be not a superfluous snatcher of bread of the deserving native but a stalwart fighter against infringement of industrial standards.'

English industrialists including mine owners were very happy to use the cheap and willing Irish labourer, and these newcomers were soon to share the dangers with the miners already established in the pits. Coal mining in Durham was gaining momentum. After a disastrous early attempt at sinking in 1831, Haswell Colliery shaft was completed four years later. In 1835 the shafts to Urpeth and Thornley collieries were being sunk. The latter colliery became known as a 'Chartist colliery', and the earliest to try arbitration with mineowners. The East Hetton (Kelloe) shaft was sunk one year later.

An inquest was held at Hetton in 1836 into the explosion at Eppleton Colliery which claimed 20 lives. Although the Davy safety lamp was available at this time, the company

Wallsend Colliery 1844 (t.h.hair)

explained to an inquest that the men preferred candles to lamps as they provided a better light, and that this was perfectly safe as long as the ventilation was intact. The conclusion of the inquest was that a young trapper was guilty of neglecting his duty!

In 1835, an explosion at Wallsend Colliery cost the lives of members of a Mason family:

Luke, 19, putter	William, 15, trapper	Thomas, 12, trapper
Peter, 17, putter	Robert, 13, trapper	

For some diseases there had been improvements in treatment compared to the first half of the eighteenth century when 75% of children born alive had died before their sixth birthday. By the beginning of the nineteenth century this mortality rate had dropped to about 40%. This was due to improved medical science with the introduction of inoculation against smallpox, but also due to better farming methods involving enclosure, and new roads meant that fresh meat and milk were becoming available in towns during the winter. The inhabitants no longer lived in fear of scurvy. Yet there was little serious attempt to apply the lessons of 1832 to the control of other epidemic diseases, and when in 1837 the economic depression returned and 'fever' became more virulent, the measures of prevention and alleviation had to be built up again amid the same confusion of defective powers and ineffective legal prohibitions. Even in the 'upper classes', there was an attitude of acceptance of fate; in October 1835, Princess Victoria had a severe attack of typhoid.

Protestants were especially resentful and felt betrayed during the period 1835 to 1841, when an alliance took place between Irish MPs and the Whigs. The Liberal Irish under Secretary Thomas Drummond reversed the policies which had governed Ireland for over a century. The worst features of the Anglican establishment were dismantled. The Protestants began to fear the impending struggle between 'poverty and property'. The living conditions of the Irish in British towns since the large influx in the last decades of the eighteenth century had not changed much by the 1830s. In 1835, the Municipal Reform Act was passed. This landmark legislation required town councils to be elected by their ratepayers – the first step towards local government. Previously control had been exerted by the Lord of the Manor and local magistrates, who now were not able to cope with the enormously increased population. Insanitary 'rookeries' with no provision for drainage or water supply, would slowly come under local authority control.

A second daughter, Helen (a popular name in south west Scotland; the Ballad of Fair Helen was sung for generations around Annandale), was born to Peter and Isabella Shannon on the 7 August 1835, and a second son, Daniel, on the 6 December 1836. He may have been named after his uncle and Daniel O'Connell. At Daniel's baptism, his uncle Richard Shannon was recorded as Godfather. His Godmother was Rose Hanlon. (Back in 1829, an Owen Hanlon had married Helen Kellacher in Dumfriesshire. Also in 1837 at the birth of Peter Shannon's son Peter, the Godmother was Ann Hanlon). It would appear that after five years in Newcastle, the Shannons were still living in the same area near Westgate.

Due to the efforts of certain members of Parliament, attention was increasingly being focused on coal mining activities. A Select Committee was appointed to consider 'Accidents in the Mines', but there were still mine owners like Lord Granville to contend with, who in 1835 gave orders to discharge all men belonging to a union. But, though the industrial system 'pounded men and women into a single body' for certain purposes, they remained men and women, pursuing not one interest but many. They did not lock themselves in trade unions; but they were to be found in chapels, in friendly societies, or on the race course, and in the public house. Many of the speakers at miners meetings were Methodists. They were able to gain converts to their cause by getting involved in the issues of the day, and this included stopping fights between intoxicated workers. Lord Durham, still serving in Russia and due to return in two years, was missing out on recent changes affecting the North East, following the 1832 reform.

Dissension between the church sects was dividing their parishioners' loyalties. For example, in the Howarth (Bronte) area, there were vigorous protests against paying the church rate in September. When Daniel O'Connell made a tour of Scotland in 1835, he was greeted by the ringing of bells as he passed through Sanquhar, Thornhill, Dumfries and Annan. After 1835, the Whigs' survival was dependent on the Radicals and O'Connell's Roman Catholics. The Duke of Wellington in 1836 was bemoaning the fact that power was tilting away from 'decent' Tory Anglicans to Whig manufacturers, shopkeepers and atheists.

The founding meeting of the London Working Men's Association took place on the 28 February 1836. This was to be the fore-runner to the Chartist Movement, which started as a political gospel and turned into a 'vast revolt of the hungry and the intolerably oppressed'. The chairman was Robert Hartwell, a journeyman printer, and the speakers included two other printers, a cabinetmaker (Lovett), a shoemaker, a carpenter, a pamphlet seller, a tailor, and two unspecified 'working men'. G.D.H. Cole described the Chartist founders as skilled, well-paid craftsmen with 'bellies full enough and minds well stored enough' to await patiently the fulfilment of their political gospel, in contrast to the handloom weavers, factory workers, miners, and unemployed labourers who could not afford that luxury and who had more urgent material needs. The Londoners wanted the Charter but the main body of the Chartists wanted bread, or as JR Stephens was to say, it was 'a knife and fork question'.

In 1836, the Orange Society of Great Britain was dissolved, and although the Irish one continued as a system of unaffiliated lodges, few were willing to defend its activities, even Peel with all his love for ascendency. Drummond saw the need to provide further relief in Ireland, and in 1837, Lord Morpeth introduced a bill for the expenditure of £2,500,000 in the building of Irish railways, but the Tories defeated the measure. With 73 votes, O'Connell was criticised that he did not use this more effectively in Ireland's interests, however he always argued that as long as Drummond kept the Orangemen down he was content.

Dickens' book Pickwick Papers was published in November 1836, and no doubt he was glad to hear of the reduction in stamp duty. During the period up to 1837, Carlyle had struggled with the writing of the French Revolution. He was faced with one of the worst moments of his life when he learned that the housekeeper of his friend JS Mill, had accidently burnt the manuscript of the French Revolution which Carlyle had lent him. The Carlyles were close friends to writer Harriet Martineau, a Whig sympathiser who lived in Tynemouth, and John Forster born in Newcastle and son of a Unitarian.

At Newcastle in 1836, Rosanna Shannon, daughter of Philip Shannon, married William Fenwick, a joiner. Ann Fenwick was to marry Richard Shannon one year later. Fenwick was a Border name with long established Catholic connections. Fenwick was also a Northumbrian and Scottish habitational name from the Old English word fenn meaning 'marsh'.

Unusually in Durham, 1836 saw the opening of the railway and colliery at Brooms near Cornsay. However, from 1836 to 1837 there was a period of depression. The growing number of workhouses was a sign of the vicious law that punished unfortunates for being poor. This new Poor Law was denounced as a Malthusian bill designed to force the poor to emigrate, to work for lower wages and to live on a coarse sort of food. Lord Durham, who had long been an opponent of the new Poor Law, was bestowed the Order of the Bath, as King William's last order. The forgotten masses of the Industrial Revolution soon had another advocate in the person of Feargus O'Connor, who, although he would never forget the Irish peasants and their problems, was to turn his main attention to the English scene.

CHAPTER 6

1837–1840 Chartism and Corn Laws

(Death of Peter Shannon)

'England lay in sick discontent, writhing powerless on its sickbed, dark, nigh-desperate, in wastefulness, want, improvidence and eating care, till, like Hyperion down the eastern slopes, the Poor Law Commissioners arose and said, 'Let there be workhouses, and the bread and water of affliction there!' It is a simple invention, as all truly great inventions are. If the paupers are made miserable, paupers will decline in number. It is a secret known to all rat-catchers .... A briefer method is that of arsenic, where otherwise permissible.'

(Carlyle Chartism 1845)

The great depression of 1837 arrived just as the workhouses in most parts of the country were ready to receive their unhappy occupants. Also bad harvests coincided with a curtailment of the finance available for railway enterprises. In November, Marx was criticised by his father for his sensitivity to gloom, grief and heartbreak as Marx developed his theories on alienation and communism as a 'one-sided realisation of socialism'. Marx presented religion as 'the sigh of the oppressed creature, the heart of the heartless world – the opium of the people.…. To be radical is to grasp the root of the matter. But for man the root is man himself'.

Consett steelworks in Durham started in 1837, and soon the Government had to 'steel' itself for the start of a mass protest movement. This was the nationwide start of Chartism, due mainly to the failure of Owen's trade unions and disappointments in the Reform Bill. Disraeli as a Tory MP, formed a radical 'Young England' group in support of Chartism. The General Election triggered by King William's death had left the Whigs with a small majority, assailed on all sides. A Committee on Combinations was formed in 1837, and the Tolpuddle Martyr George Loveless, now back in England, stated 'England had for many years been lifting her voice against the abominable practice of Negro slavery. Numbers of great men have talked, have laboured and have struggled until at length emancipation has been granted to the black slaves in the West Indies. When will they dream of advocating the cause of England's white slaves?' The drafting of the People's Charter was one encouraging response.

In England, between the late 1830s and early 1840s was a period of crisis both economically and socially. Chartism was said to have been a reaction to the declaration from Liberal Party leaders that they did not intend to push Reform any further. In November Feargus O'Connor started the newspaper Northern Star, with its first campaign against the New Poor Law. The 'Voice of the People' also began to be produced. The invention of the electric telegraph in 1837 helped to speed up the reporting of foreign news. There were changes in the poor law bastardy clauses to allow recovery from the punitive father the cost of maintenance of the illegitimate child. Tyneside suffered little from the economic trough of 1837–39, yet it generated a Working Man's Association, led by the pitmen's leader Thomas Hepburn, and the 'Northern Liberator', an impressive and influential Chartist journal. Irish politician Brontere O'Brien, who had argued against the 'sacred month' in 1839 as likely to provoke the authorities, became an advocate of a more socialist approach to counter 'wage slavery'.

Peter Shannon died at the age of 38 at 10pm on the 24 November 1837, near the quayside at Newcastle upon Tyne. (Burns and Byron had died at a similar age which Lord Beaconsfield called the 'fatal age'). After only five years marriage, his wife Isabella was left a widow, with the threat and disgrace of the workhouse. At this time in All Saints, only a few Irish were receiving parochial outdoor relief. Just as well that Isabella did not live in Scotland where women still worked underground in the mines. In Ireland, women and girls were never used down mines. At the loss of his father, James Shannon would in a few years have been in a position similar to that of the twelve year old boy, who told of his work down the East Lothian colliery:

> 'Mother took me down four years ago, as my father died of typhus. I work with three brothers and one sister, usually 10 to 12 hours, many times longer, as we wait our turns for the gig to draw up the cart; I am not very strong, as my thigh bone was broken two years since by the cart. All the family had typhus within the last three years, and I had it twice. Putting is very sore work; the coal weighs four cwt., and the cart is nearly as heavy. Mother has ceased to work for two years; she is fashed with pains in the stomach, owing to hard labour'.

Only four days before Peter's death, his younger brother Richard married Ann Fenwick at the parish church of St John in Newcastle; this could not have been a happy occasion with his brother seriously ill. Richard's occupation was given as 'Servant' and his father's occupation, 'Gardener'. Ann Fenwick's father, James, was a Tanner, a very dirty and unhealthy occupation. Surprisingly Richard Shannon was able to sign his name, especially since he was to work as a labourer all his life. All of Philip Shannon's sons could write; his daughter Catherine in 1839 signed her marriage certificate with a cross. Richard might have worked on the nearby Ouseburn Railway Viaduct in Newcastle which was constructed during 1835/6.

Peter Shannon probably died of cholera or typhus fever, almost certainly due to the unsanitary conditions prevalent in Newcastle at that time. The cause of death was given as 'Inflammation of the Bowels'; doctors were reluctant to use the word cholera on death certificates since local government authorities wished to avoid causing public alarm. On Tyneside, Bishop Riddell, who had baptised James Shannon, lost his life administering to the Catholic poor the most vulnerable to fevers. Peter's death certificate gave his place of death as Queen Street, in St Nicholas parish. (This street probably named after Victoria's accession to the throne, was to be a casualty of the later clearance for the construction of the High Level Bridge in the late 1840s).

The informant of death was a Mary Cowley (Peter's widow was expecting a child in hospital), who lived at Head of Side, the top of steep short lane leading down to the quayside. Eleven years earlier, in the Cock Inn at Head of Side, the Colliers of the United Association had convened a meeting to put their 'Appeal' to John Buddle Esq and other colliery owners in the Newcastle district regarding the harsh 'bond' or contract conditions under which miners worked, but without success.

'The Side' was one of the most ancient thoroughfares in Newcastle. 'No sooner had Hadrian built the Tyne Bridge, then a stream of passengers began to flow from the "Head of the Side" to his viaduct'. In 1733 it was described as 'stretching downwards from St Nicholas' Church to Allhallows' or All Saints' (Butchers' Bank), ... with a very great descent from the Head of it, until you come to the middle of it, from which place it opens in a spacious breadth, and so continues to Sandhill, once the centre of the medieval city. The Side was from one end to the other filled with shops of merchants, goldsmiths, milliners, upholsters, &c'. This historic thoroughfare also contained the Meters' Arms, the birth-place of Admiral Collingwood, Nelson's comrade in arms. It was an area where the rich lived in close proximity to the poor. Engels wrote six years later that 'the majority of the [poor] families live in cellars are almost everywhere of Irish origin'. Abandoned Irish women and prostitution was not unusual in North East ports, especially for widows with small children.

A direct connection between impoverishment of the poor and epidemic fever was put forward by Thomas Southwood Smith in his Treatise on Fever published in 1830. Smith, a devout Utilitarian, was a follower of Jeremy Bentham and friend of Edwin Chadwick. James Kay reported in the 1840s that it was incontrovertible that typhus was a major killer in areas which 'are ill ventilated, unpaved, or which contain heaps of refuse or stagnant pools'. William Farr, the first Register-General, was appointed in 1837. One of his earliest decisions was to require doctors to cite the causes of death following an official classification. Chadwick was known to be responsible for abolishing outdoor relief, and there were public demonstrations against him during the 1837 General Election.

Edwin Chadwick 1870
(Spartacus-educational.com)

Chadwick first thought that work shyness to be the primary cause of poverty, but by 1838 it was clear to him that the major factor was frequent illness, particularly from fevers, and premature death, all too often involving dependents for whom the Poor Law Union would have to accept responsibility. He became convinced that intervention in sanitary provision could make a significant contribution to improved health. Typhus unlike cholera, did not generally affect the middle classes. In the Sunderland workhouse, it killed off half the inmates in a single year. The Edinburgh Observer in 1839 gave detailed advice on the alleviation of typhus fever which was affecting most cities and large towns.

On the twentieth of June 1837, at two o'clock in the morning, King William IV died and was succeeded by his eighteen year old niece, Victoria. Referring to the young queen, Carlyle recorded that he was 'heartily sorry for the poor bairn'. If the Orange Order had got its way, Princess Victoria would never have succeeded to the throne. It had been rumoured that they were conspiring to exclude the heir-apparent, fearing that a young girl, notoriously under Whig influence, would be unable to cope with the rising tide of Radicalism.

William IV died of asthma, never recovering from a violent asthmatic attack in April. (At that time his condition was described as 'lungs turgid with blood, heart valves ossified, the liver enlarged, and the spleen double its normal size'). Typhus, a classic winter disease, was carried by louse bite; typhoid and typhus were influenced to a minimal degree by nutrition whereas diarrhoeal diseases and cholera are strongly conditioned by the nutritional condition of the affected person. On the 12 December, Thomas Carlyle wrote to his brother Dr Carlyle on the completion of his biography of Sir Walter Scott, and noted how he had suffered from 'catarrhs, November fogs like Erebus'.

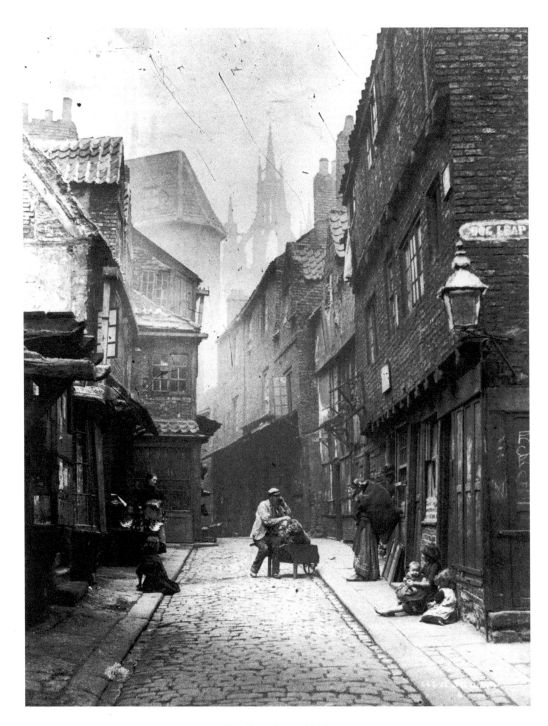

Dog Leap Stairs 1900
(Getty Images)

It was said of Irish workhouses, that a diet of buttermilk rather than fresh milk led to vitamin deficiency causing blindness. Overcrowding and poor hygiene was given as the source of 'hospital fever' – usually typhus – which then spread to the surrounding community. Scraps of food left by infected patients were often distributed to the poor. The inhabitants had nowhere to dispose of refuse water, excrement etc other than throw it on the street. A Gateshead resident Peter Putwright, expressed his anger over dirty conditions, comparing Gateshead and Newcastle:

> 'There is a good deal of dirt in Gateshead; more, I consider than would be tolerated in Newcastle. All the butchers in Gateshead hang their meat out so far that any passenger runs the risk of spoiling his coat and hat, nay, even his pantaloon or breeches; from the contact into which he must frequently come with grease and blood continually troubling all who go by. It is quite impossible to detail the histories of dunghills or pigsties, of want of drainage, of dirt and filth of every description, of open drains becoming the very nuisances they were mean to prevent, of places which have recently been found uninhabitable on account of damp, of the shocking state of entries and yards, of confined air and imperfect ventilation, of the immense number of instances of unwholesome numbers living in single rooms – of uncleared middenheads and noisome manufactures – of foul water, ashes, animal and vegetable refuse and dead cats, of filthy and abominable sloughs and unapproachable privies – of lanes made into privies altogether, and of such a want of accommodation that one portion of Gateshead have to go along the Tyne Bridge to the Newcastle side for necessary relief!'

Unfortunately Newcastle was not much better; out of a population of 4,600 in the district of Sandgate, only 100 had access to a private privy. The whole drainage of Gateshead and Newcastle went into the river. In the tenements, the water supply usually amounted to one tap in a common yard. There was 'considerable apathy on part of the landlords and a deal of stealing among the tenants'. The Superintendent of Police reported that there were 26 lodging houses mostly in the low and crowded neighbourhoods, with seventeen Irish lodge keepers, seven English and one German. In one room 18ft square was occupied by 18 human beings, adults and children, with 11 of these in a state of continued fever. The report noted that 'it was worse than the packing of negroes in a slave ship. Men and children were completely naked and women wore a shift which .. had [more] the appearance of an oilcloth than an undergarment'. The users of such boarding houses were 'sturdy vagrants (posing as) shipwrecked mariners, widows with a large family or begging little impostors'. It was rare to find an unfortunate artisan driven to work far from home, except the Irish labourer, in such places. Inhabitants invariably stopped up all openings by which fresh air could penetrate.

At this time, Brunel was facing a disaster during the tunnelling for the Box Tunnel between Chippenham and Bath, where thirteen shafts were being sunk. For a considerable distance the tunnel passed through freestone rock. In November 1837 the water flowed so freely from the rock fissures that the steam engine used to pump it out proved insufficient. One division of the tunnel became filled, and the water rose fifty-six feet high in the shaft making it necessary to suspend operations until the following summer when another steam engine was brought in to assist. The dangers of shaft working were to cause many deaths on canal, railway and mining works.

A Select Committee on Transportation was at last looking into the horrendous treatment suffered by convicts transported overseas. The 1837 Report on the Poor in Ireland estimated that 2,385,000 persons in Ireland were in a state of semi-starvation every summer as they waited for the new potato crop at the end of the season. In contrast a manservant working in a middle-class house made the following moralizing entry in his diary, four days after Christmas 1837, having fed well on 'surloin of beef, roasted broccoli and potatoes and preserved Damson pie:

> 'The company comes generally about ten or eleven o'clock and stays until one or two in the morning. Sweethearting matches are very often made up at the parties. It's quite disgusting to a modist eye to see the way the young ladies dress to attract the notice of the gentlemen. They are nearly naked to the waiste, only just a little bit of dress hanging to the shoulders, the breasts are quite exposed excpt a little bit comeing up to hide the nipples. Plenty of false hair and teeth and paint'.

It is worth noting that civic registration of births and deaths had just commenced in July 1837. The deaths of Catholics in England were generally registered in the Catholic Chapels, notwithstanding that their burials were entered in the Anglican Register of the parish where they were buried. Dissenters were now not required to be married by Anglican parsons. During the winter of 1837 Gladstone found comfort in Psalm 128 (Blessed are those that fear the Lord). This was the period when Darwin was wrestling with his religious upbringing when formulating his evolutionary principles which he kept under wraps until 1859.

At his fifth attempt, Disraeli entered parliament in 1837, five years after Gladstone; they were to remain bitter enemies. A passage from Disraeli's book, Sybil, described a similar scene to the one which had confronted the Shannons in that year:

> 'These wretched tenements seldom consisted of more than two rooms, in one of which the whole family, however numerous, were obliged to sleep, without distinction of age, or sex, or suffering with the water streaming down the walls, the light distinguished through the roof, with no hearth even in winter, the virtuous mother in the sacred pangs of child-birth gives forth another victim to our thoughtless

civilization; surrounded by three generations whose inevitable presence is more painful than her sufferings in that hour of travail; while the father of her coming child, in another corner of the sordid chamber, lies stricken by that typhus which his contaminating dwelling has breathed into his veins, and for whose next prey is perhaps destined, his new-born child. These swarming walls had neither windows nor doors sufficient to keep out the weather, or admit the sun or supply means of ventilation; the humid and putrid roof of thatch exhaling malaria like all other decaying vegetable matter. The dwelling rooms were neither boarded or paved; and whether it were that some were situate in low and damp places, occasionally flooded by the river, and usually much below the level of the road; and that the springs, as was often the case, would burst through the mud floor; the ground was at no time better than so much clay, while sometimes you might see little channels cut from the centre under the doorways to carry away the water, the door itself removed from its hinges: a resting place for infancy in its deluged home. These hovels were in many instances not provided with the commonest conveniences of the rudest police; contiguous to every door might be observed the dung-heap on which every filth was accumulated, for the purpose of being disposed of for manure, so that when the poor man opened his narrow habitation in the hope of refreshing it with the breeze of summer, he was met with a mixture of gases from reeking dung-hills.'

If Peter Shannon had been working as a colliery labourer, then his widow had no security of tenure. In cases like this the treatment was short and brutal – eviction. However, should the widow have had sons older than four and a half years, then the master's charity would usually have been forthcoming. He would have offered her children work, and allowed her to retain the colliery accommodation. In Isabella's case, she could have offered James at nearly four years old as a trapper (operating underground ventilation doors), with the promise of more sons in the years ahead.

At Skinner Burn, Isabella's second son Daniel had died nine months earlier than his father at the age of only 2 months on the 5 February 1837. At this time, the dead body of a man found in the river, was identified as a mariner at the 'Dead House' [mortuary].

Only two weeks after the death of her husband Peter Shannon, his wife Isabella gave birth to their third son, Peter. The birth certificate recorded that the birth took place in a 'lying-in hospital' – probably because of her recent bereavement and the danger of infection from the fever at home. This particular hospital had been in existence since 1760, first located in Rosemary Lane, near St Johns Church. Peter probably died soon after birth. By a strange coincidence, as Peter Shannon was to lose his son Peter, a Clement Mason in Lanchester Durham was to lose his son Clement in 1837.

A Lying-in-hospital was described in Dickens' Hard Times. At this time only paupers died in hospital. Infection was rife in hospitals with 'hospital fever' – usually typhus, spreading to the local community. The first lying-in or maternity hospital in the British Isles was built in 1790 in Dublin. In London, until 1828, St Bartholomew's charged all patients entering its hospital a deposit of 19s 6d burial fees. At the beginning of the nineteenth century there were two kinds of hospital: voluntary hospitals and poor law infirmaries. Some of the voluntary hospitals which were supported by public charity had been founded in the Middle Ages; the poor law infirmaries had been set up by Boards of Guardians to care for the 'destitute sick'. Standards of hygiene, medicine and nursing were very low in all hospitals, with filthy wards, untrained nurses and surgeons in bloodstained coats. There was little attempt to segregate the infectious from the non-infectious inside hospitals. Sir James Young Simpson, who introduced chloroform as an anaesthetic, wrote in the 1840s,: 'The man who lies on the operation table in one of our hospitals runs a greater risk of dying than did the British soldier on the battle-field of Waterloo'.

A court case was reported in late 1840 where the principal witness was Rosanna Rox, wife of Daniel Rox, an Irish labourer. 'She stated that she lived in the dogger's entry at the Head of Side, with her husband, and Sophia Quin her mother. About a fortnight previous her mother took very ill, and on making her case known to Mr Heslop, the relieving officer of the parish of St John, he sent Mr Turner, surgeon, to attend to her, but on seeing her, said [her mother] was dying. On Thursday, the 17th, her mother having died, she again applied to the relieving officer for a coffin, upon which she was told a coffin would be sent to her on the Saturday, and the ground and every other thing requisite would be prepared for her mother's interment, and while waiting for them on Saturday afternoon, five men with a coffin and pall came in, about four o'clock and stated that they were authorised by the parish officer to come and to take the body away and bury it imme-diately, for everything was ready, and the priest and the clerk were waiting to perform the service. [A] Witness, however, objected to her mother being buried that day, as it was then dark, and desired that the men should leave the coffin, and that she would get buried on the Sunday following, but the men refused to comply, placed the body in the coffin, and forcibly carried it away. Witness and a friend then followed them, thinking they were going to take it to the Ballast-hills burial ground, but instead of that they carried it to the Surgeon's hall, Manor chare, where, on their arrival, the gate was opened, the body taken in, and witness and her friend were pushed outside, one of the men saying at the same time, that 'they had nothing more to do with the body'. Witness was then told by a person standing by that they were going to dissect her, upon which she informed the police, who, after a fruitless endeavour to obtain admittance into the hall, informed the mayor, when his worship went personally and demanded an entrance. The door having been opened, [the] witness went in, and the first thing she saw was the shavings which had been in the coffin, lying on the floor, and the lid of the coffin standing against one side of the room. She also saw dead clothes lying under the table, all torn, and upon her brother, who was with her, taking up the lid off a place, she saw the body of her mother lying in warm water, but she was so much overcome by the sight that she fainted and fell. When she recovered herself, the body was replaced in the coffin, and taken home, and on the next day she was decently buried. At the ensuing sessions the defendants were found guilty of illegally obtaining possession of a dead body'.

Fevers then became epidemic again in the years of economic depression; in 1826, 1836–37, 1842, and in 1847–48. The term 'fever' covered a variety of symptoms which the science of the period was trying to sort out into typhus and typhoid, relapsing and spotted fever, each with its characteristic mortality rate. Popular opinion and some doctors blamed the miasmatic exhalation from decaying matter in the adjacent dung-heaps or filthy courts. Some medical men argued that poverty, underfeeding and mental depression made the disease epidemic, and called for a more generous public assistance as the best preventative. Others identified it with the jail, hospital, camp and ship fevers of the eighteenth century, and regarded as simply due to living in crowded and filthy quarters. The low class lodging houses known as 'flea-barracks' by the Irish were obvious centres of the disease. Surviving on a very poor diet, the working classes were frequently visited by the disease (visitations), especially in autumn and beginning of winter, with 'low and nervous fevers, in short, putrid and gaol distempers, that often cut off men, leaving families behind'.

A report for the Magheraculmony parish of Fermanagh stated that worsening conditions were now forcing the emigration of the yeomanry or better class. Four years later in 1837, a Catholic family, Charles Murray, his wife Susan (daughter of a blacksmith Philip Shannon) and their six children embarked on the ship Barque Susan at Londonderry for Port Jackson in New South Wales. Charles gave his age as 38, six years younger than his true age, to ensure a funded passage. They were never to return to the fertile drumlins, heathery moors, meandering rivers and lakes of Fermanagh. Also heading for Australia were prostitutes from around Enniskillen sentenced to seven years transportation.

During 1838 an event off the coast of Northumberland, was to capture the attention of the nation, which illustrated the similar perils which faced fishermen and lifeguards at sea and pit sinkers down shafts. On a wild and stormy night, a small steamer was wrecked off the Farne Islands, a group of small islands eight miles south of Holy Island (Lindisfarne). On the 5 September, the lighthouse keeper, William Darling, and his daughter Grace, from their lonely watchtower, saw the wreck which was about a mile away. After persuading her reluctant father to attempt a rescue, they both rowed to the beleaguered men. Grace Darling's bravery was soon known country-wide, and when she died four years later of consumption, a monument was raised to her memory:

'And out of her lonely grave
She bids us this lesson prove -
That the weakest may wipe some tears that flow,
And the strongest power for good below
Is the might of unselfish love.'

The origins of Chartism could be said to have developed by Mr Duncombe, MP of Finsbury, who raised a question on the adoption of a ballot and the shortening of the duration of Parliaments. In 1838, six members were conferred by the London Working Men's Association to produce a charter. O'Connell eventually handed the 'People's Charter' to their leader William Lovett, a cabinet maker, and told 'Agitate for it and never be content with anything less'. The Charter drawn up in the form of a Bill to be put through Parliament, contained six demands: annual parliaments, manhood suffrage, vote by ballot, no property qualifications for MPs, payment of members of parliament, and equal electoral districts. Fergus O'Connor became involved at an early stage with the Chartism movement and soon there were a number of periodicals being issued around the country including the Northern Liberator in Newcastle, urging 'better to die by the sword than perish with hunger'.

Carlyle became inspired by the Chartist movement, and in 1838 thought of writing an essay on the 'claims, conditions, rights and mights' of the working classes. After some discussions with John Stuart Mill, he began to write the book, 'Chartism', eventually published in 1839 after the first Chartist petition had been rejected by Parliament. It was 'wildly declamatory, truth without soberness', containing some of Carlyle's finest writing. His main thrust was the denunciation of democracy as 'a self-cancelling business', leading infallibly to despotism in the absence of the blessed alternative of government by Aristocracy, defined as 'a corporation of the best and bravest'. Carlyle in his pamphlet Chartism, warned the British Government on their continuing immoral treatment of the Irish, but matters closer to home were about to explode. Carlyle's book which apparently had been in his head for 10–20 years, noted that the working classes did not need universal male suffrage and democracy but the guiding hands of wise leaders, but added that he did not wish to bring back the villages and castles of a former age.

In parallel with the Chartist Movement, the Anti-Corn Law Association was formed in September 1838 by Richard Cobden MP. Industrialists argued that the Corn Laws dangerously inflated food prices and labour costs which in turn threatened manufacturing competiveness. Lord Melbourne was becoming anxious over the demonstrations of the Chartists and the Anti-Corn Leaguers, and wrote 'I suppose the present Irish prices will make the Corn Laws a serious question, which it never has been since the year 1815'. Militants were using materialism to underwrite their anti-clerical propaganda. For most working classes, the High Church had become too remote, and other sects had filled the void. Erasmus Darwin used the expression 'a featherbed to catch a fallen Christian' religion to describe Joseph Wedgewood's Unitarianism. John Bright, another nonconformist, was persuaded by Cobden in late 1841 to become an anti-corn law national agitator. On the 27 November 1839, John Bright married another 'Friend', Elizabeth Priestman at the Friends Meeting House in Pilgrim Street, Newcastle upon Tyne. Chartist meetings often took place in Methodist chapels. Lovett noted that 'The National Union of the Working Classes' of 1831, was organised on the plan of the 'Methodist Connection'. Chartist meetings were starting to worry the authorities, especially when a Rev. J R Stephens, Methodist minister of Ashton-under-Lyne, openly incited a crowd to discharge their firearms.

Queen Victoria was crowned on 28 June 1838, with the coronation oath confirming the maintenance of the Protestant religion. During her early reign it was said that Lord Melbourne had misled her and blunted her social conscience by inferring that all the discontent in the country was due to a handful of agitators. The Jamaica Bill was causing the Government much anxiety in early 1839. Despite the previous year's decision by Parliament to purchase from the West Indian planters the freedom of the slaves at an enormous cost, the abominable traffic was still being carried on in Africa. The legislation to counter the resistance by Jamaica to accept the abolition of slaves was opposed by both Peel and the Conservative Opposition, as well as David Hume and several members of the Radical party; the latter based their opposition on the question of infringement of liberty!

The Government lost the Bill and resigned, but got back in by the support of the Queen. Portugal continued to resist British efforts to stop the slave trade, but Lord Brougham managed to persuade the Duke of Wellington to support a Bill. Gladstone in July 1838, delivered in the Commons a brief and aggressive statement of his objection to the renewal of the Maynooth [educational] grant, because it contravened the main principle on which the Established Church of England and Ireland was founded. Earlier he had caused great offence to O'Connell and the Catholic party by his objections to the provision of Catholic chaplains in prisons.

In 1838 the Irish Poor Law was introduced, modelled on the English version brought in four years earlier. Dr Kinealy explained that the two Poor Laws differed in three important respects: firstly, Irish relief could only be administered within the confines of the workhouse, with no provisions made for outdoor relief; secondly, no general right to relief existed in Ireland, so that if the workhouse became full, the Poor Law was not obliged to provide alternative relief; and thirdly, no Law of Settlement was included in the 1838 Act. Tithe payments were now charged on rent. The Irish Poor Law passed into law on the 31 July with Home Secretary Lord John Russell greeting the establishment of Irish workhouses 'as a measure of peace, enabling the country to prohibit vagrancy'.

Molesworth noted that 'Irish tithes, Irish corporation reform, Irish poor-laws, and other Irish questions were occupying their usual disproportionately large share of the attention of the legislature'. He recorded in his History of England that 'The winter of 1837–8 had been one of great and unusual severity, producing a reduplication of complaints of the hardships of the new poor-law, and of proposals for its modification'. One proposal was to check the emigration of labourers from the country to the manufacturing districts. Most of the agitation was coming from the farmers who wanted cheap labour. The Brontes recorded heavy winter snows in the January of 1838, with the country paralysed by a general strike organised by the Chartists, and anti-Poor Law riots in the following August. Darwin noted that the Poor Law and pauper riots on everybody's lips, and workhouses being attacked; there were fights between Church and Dissenters over education.

The Borderer's Table Book recorded in January 1839, a fire in Blyth's Nook, Newcastle; the bed and bed clothes of an Irish family, occupying a room in a tenemented house there, had taken fire; the flames however were subdued with little other damage than the destruction of the bed, and few other articles of furniture. Following the 1840 Select Committee on the Health of Towns, in 1842, Chadwick published the 'Report on the Sanitary Condition of the Labouring Population of Great Britain' to protestations of disbelief. Many of the wealthier classes were living in the immediate vicinity of the tenements on which his revelations had been based. In fact one of the remedies was to design new streets to cut through the 'rookeries' which contained the worst areas of unsanitary conditions. His main concern was the 'miasma' emanating from the decaying matter, the 'fetid effluvia', 'poisonous exhalations' and 'reeking atmosphere' which he contended was the source of the physical, moral, and mental deterioration of the poor. The newly appointed Health Boards began enforcing certain preventative measures but with limited success. The 'lower Irish' were accustomed to keeping pigs in or near their dwelling houses and to sell manure as well as meat. This practice was 'untouchable' by police action or by common law. An indefinite accumulation of dung had been allowed in stable lanes, but as places of public access these had now to be cleaned up every week and if they led to human dwellings, removal was required every second day on pain of confiscation.

Disraeli expressed his opposition to an education grant in favour of laissez-faire in education. In March 1839 he sympathised with the Chartists but voted against universal suffrage. The year 1839 had seen the formation of the Female Political Union of Newcastle, perhaps due to the fact that Lovett had reluctantly been persuaded to drop female suffrage from the Charter. In Spring, the Chartism National Convention was held at Westminster Palace Yard, where a monster petition was handed in to Thomas Attwood MP by John Fielden Radical MP. The unexpected termination of events of May 1839, had seen the re-establishment in power of a party confessedly too weak to carry on the parliamentary government of the country. When in July the first national petition was rejected there were fears of civil war. Thornley Lodge was renowned for militant action, and was the only pit village to have participated in a bold attempt at a general strike in 1839.

The railway from Carlisle to Newcastle had just opened. The Government soon began to realise that trains had become an essential part of their strategy in deploying troops wherever the trouble arose. In this climate of fear and apprehension it was not unexpected, when in late 1839, a rebellion took place. In Newport John Frost led the rebellion, supported mainly by South Wales miners, men of great strength and determination strongly attracted to the 'physical-force' party. The Government quickly and harshly dealt with the ringleaders and prevented similar uprisings planned to take place in Newcastle and other northern towns in November. After a trial on the 6 June 1840 which was watched with great interest throughout the country, Frost was sentenced to hang; this was later commuted to transportation. Chartist meetings became infrequent and the periodicals disappeared.

On the 10 February 1840 Queen Victoria married Prince Albert causing some scepticism amongst the upper classes. Catherine Shannon had also married Ralph Reed at St John's Church in Newcastle on the 1st December 1839, about two years after the marriage of her brother Richard. As with Peter Shannon and Isabella Gallagher, they married in the Established Church; even though the Reeds were also of Catholic origin. Ralph was recorded as a ship's carpenter and his father John, a joiner. Carpenters, and especially shipwrights, had skills much sought after, and were therefore paid higher than many other skilled workers. Many joiners came from Scotland.

Palmers, the shipbuilding company, was starting up in South Shields and due to become the largest in the world. In 1838, the brother of Ralph Reed, Andrew Reed, had married Sarah Storey at the Established Church in Gateshead. Andrew was a Vitriol Maker (Turpentine Distiller), the same occupation as that of Sarah's stepfather, James Storey. Andrew was probably working for his father-in-law. Ralph Reed, as a ship's carpenter, would have suffered the pollution from the paper and chemical industries located on each side of the Tyne.

For centuries, boats called colliers had plied in all weathers to and fro from Newcastle to London, so giving plenty of work for shipwrights. There had been ferocious rivalry between the coal merchants on either bank of the Tyne to defend their rights of trade. The coal reached the boats by means of substantial timber structures called staithes, which led from the waggonways to the side of the boat; the 'keelmen' had the arduous task of loading the coal into the boat, and the coal whippers unloaded the colliers.

Complaints at the release of large quantities of hydrochloric acid into the atmosphere forced many manufacturers to build high chimneys. Ironically, a young ship's carpenter very ill with consumption was reported to have benefitted from the breathing of the hydrochloric acid gas! Many of the workers were Irish immigrants whose arrival caused housing problems. So many factory owners put up rows of small cottages, often described as 'model cottages for working men and their families'. The Felling Chemical Works in 1845 even went as far as building some baths, where for a moderate charge 'the worker might go and have a hot bath and a cold plunge after it'. (The colliers waited another century before they got their pithead baths). A local dialect song called 'The Changes on the Tyne' was a reminder of earlier times:

> 'Baith sides of the Tyne, aw remember'
> Were covered wi' bonny green fields,
> But now there is nought but big furnaces,
> Down frae Newcastle to Shields
> And what wi' their sulphur and brimstone,
> Their vapour, their smoke and their steam,
> The grass is all gaen, and the farmers
> Can nowther get butter or cream."
> There's Losh's big chimley at Walker
> Its very awn height makes it shake.
> And if Cookson's again tumble over,
> It will make a new quay for the Slake'

The ironworks of Walker was also a major employer. Since 1615 the glass industry had flourished with the use of 'Newcastle Cole', resulting in a growing demand for alkali and other chemicals. Thus Liddells of Ravensworth, the owners of Walker Pit, were not only able to sell coal, but also to pump out and sell a concentrated brine from a spring in one of its shafts. Unlike most mine owners, the alkali masters had a sense of public duty and many were active in the Reform Movement, and provided schools and recreational facilities for the men and their families. Equally, the men seem to have had a 'tribal' sense of loyalty to their masters. In 1843, for example, when the South Shields firm of Cookson's was being heavily prosecuted for damage to crops and pasture, their workmen held a grand procession to the Town Hall to enlist sympathy for their employers. In 1916, Frank Ward of Saltwell, Gateshead, wrote the following verses showing his attachment to Friar's Goose Works:

> 'O give me back my boyhood's days
> Those far off days of yore,
> When I romped about the Goose Pit Yard
> And played on Tyne Main Shore.
> How oft I'd slip the factory gate
> When I heard old Bravey snore!
> And rush **Tom Shannon's** ugly stick

To gain the Ball House floor.
Old Jimmy Boyle I yet can see
At number six pan door.
And see the black salt boiling up
As he sings of Erin's Flower.
How many hours I've stood and watched
Todd's engine great and grand -
Just like a woman possing clothes
With piston rods for hands.
I'll ever see and ever hear
The blowing of them all
The 'Sulphur' and the 'Weldon's'
And the pumps behind the wall.
Alas! alas! that I can see
What can be seen there now
The good old Goose dismantled
And the old hands lost to view.'

From the mention of a Tom Shannon working at Friar's Goose Colliery, (possibly a relation of James Shannon), and Jimmy Boyle, both surnames from the Enniskillen area, it was clear that a large contingent of the chemical industry workforce were Irish. The 'ugly stick' used by Tom Shannon obviously left a deep impression on young Frank!

The harsh disciplining of young workers or apprentices was not uncommon, as illustrated in 'Sybil', when the lock apprentice described how his master had broken many ash sticks during beatings. The shillelagh was a traditional stick or cudgel made of blackthorn or oak. MacDonagh in his book 'Irish Life and Character', tells a tale by the Father Tom Maguire:

> 'He was asked by a rather simple-minded farmer what a miracle was; and he gave a very full explanation, which, however, was not quite satisfying, for the man said, "Do you think yer riverence could be after givin' me an example of a miracle?" "Well," said the priest, "walk on before me and I'll see what I can do." As the farmer did so, Father Tom gave him a knock on the head with his stick. "Did you feel that, Mick?" said he. "Wisha, why wouldn't I feel it, yer riverence," replied Mick, surprised that the priest should ask him such a foolish question. "Faix, I felt it hard enough." "Well Mick," said Father Tom, "it would be a miracle if you didn't.'

The Government was determined to crush the working class agitation for Chartism, and they saw the rising in South Wales as a test case. On the 16 January 1840, a special assize was held at the Monmouth Court House. The prisoners John Frost, Zephaniah Williams and William Jones were standing trial for High Treason against the Sovereign.

The sentence of guilty was declared as follows: 'It has been proved in your case, that you combined together to lead to the hills, at the dead of night, into the town of Newport many thousands of men, armed, in many instances, with weapons of a dangerous description, in order that they might take possession of the town, and supersede the lawful authority of the Queen, as a preliminary step to a more general insurrection throughout the Kingdom'. So these men found themselves in the condemned cell only days before the royal wedding.

Throughout the country there were campaigns to raise Chartist support, but it appeared that Daniel O'Connell had refused to participate due to lack of allies and witnesses. Frost was aware of the long animosity between the labouring Welsh and Irish and had striven to bridge this unhappy divide between fellow Celts. As early as 1798, when the Irish Rebellion was led by Father John Murphy, the Welsh regiments under English officers had suppressed Irish peasantry and joined with German Hessians in committing outrages against defenceless Irish populations. Since then Irishmen had undercut the wages of the artisan Welsh, and this had resulted in continuing bitterness. Nevertheless there had been wagon loads of petitions sent to London and torchlight meetings up and down the country. Government feared an armed Chartist outbreak and even an attack on the Monmouth Gaol.

Waiting to be transported, Frost and his fellow prisoners were double-ironed and chained together at the waist as they loaded pit props for the Welsh mines. In 1615 the history of 'transportation' had started, and many Catholic martyrs found themselves 'married to the Three Sisters' – that is, bound naked to the blood-soaked triangles of Van Dieman's Land. Between the years 1660 to 1820, some 190 capital offences were added to the 52 already existing; death was the sole punishment for these; it was available to hanging judges for crimes varying from embezzlement to murder (attempted killing was only a misdemeanour up to 1802, unless maiming resulted), and piracy to damaging a fence, or concealing the birth of a bastard child. By the eighteenth century systematic transportation began to take the place of capital punishment. Hanging at Tyburn had been reduced significantly; William Cobbett could no longer complain of the foul stench of a woman burning!

Human abuse in foreign lands was shortly to be revealed to the British public. In 1840 David Livingstone was sent out to Bechuanaland by the London Missionary Society, and discovered the Victoria Falls during his travels up the River Zambezi. His ultimate objective was 'to bring justice and peace into the darkness of Africa', and particularly to seek out and destroy the roots of the slave trade pursued by the Arabs.

CHAPTER 7

1841–1844 Child Labour and The Great Strike

James Shannon starts work down pit

'.. after his mother had introduced him into the world, she returned to the factory and put her infant out to a nurse, that is to say, paid threepence a-week to an old woman who takes charge of these new-born babes for the day, and gives them back at night to their mothers as they hurriedly return from the scene of their labour to the dungeon or the den, which is still by courtesy called the "home". The expense is not great: laudanum and treacle, administered in the shape of a popular elixir, affords these innocents a brief taste of the sweets of existence, and keeping them quiet, prepares them for the silence of their impending grave. Infanticide is practised as extensively and as legally in England, as it is on the banks of the Ganges;'

(Sybil Disraeli 1845)

'I have known a boy fall asleep with his arms clasped round the [shaft] rope, and gone to the bottom of a 100 fathom pit, and the banksman took him off again when he came back. He was not aware of it 'till then awakened by a slap. They don't show any repugnance to go down. It is fine fun for them.'

(colliery manager and mining engineer John Buddle parliamentary committee 1841)

Radical Jack, who had long concerned himself with abuse of the poor, succumbed to the family weakness, consumption, and was buried in Sunderland on 10 August 1840 to the acclaim of both the rich and poor of Durham. In contrast, two years earlier Daniel O'Connell had voted against a proposal to shorten the hours of child labour in factories.

At the beginning of 1841, James Shannon was approaching seven, and even at that tender age it was not unusual for children to start work down the coal mine as a trapper. Colliers' families without a father would starve if mothers and their children did not get work. The 1841 census revealed Isabella Shannon at the age of thirty-two working as a labourer in the Westgate district of Newcastle, and living with her remaining children, James and [H]Ellen.

Trapper 1842
(National Coal Mining Museum)

The 1842 Commissioner's Report mentioned the account of a child worker at Walker Colliery, a 'gassey' pit, 'where the foul air blinded him sometimes'. James was lucky not to have been a victim of an explosion at nearby Bigges Willington Colliery in 1841. In this disaster four trappers were killed, with an average age of 10 years.

A pit sinker named Thomas Mason was working nearby at Kibblesworth Colliery just south of the River Tyne. James Shannon was not to know that in twenty years he would be a pit sinker working under the name of James Mason!

In desperate situations, families resorted to poaching, risking the severe penalties. This was illustrated in the novel, 'Twopence a Tub' by Susan Price, when young Thomas Shannon, a collier at Old 'Oss Pit near Dudley in Staffordshire, set traps for rabbits to supplement the family meals. At this time the only education available was that afforded by the Methodist Sunday School or provided by the state or private benevolence, so the likelihood of schooling was very remote for working class children. By coincidence, in 1840, a report on the shortfall in education of miners' children in Wales was produced by a Government official, Seymour Tremenheere, but this was ignored by Government. The following verse from 'Pitman's Happy Times' looks back at these times when work dominated most of the hours available:

> 'We didn't heed much lairnin' then,
> We had ne time for skuel;
> Pit laddies wark'd for spendin's syek
> And nyen was thowt a fule.'

Evidence has shown that iron harnesses were worn by children dragging coal laden tubs along narrow underground roadways at Monkwearmouth Colliery and other collieries. The abuse of child labour was a consideration in the 'fighting charter' adopted by Northumberland and Durham miners when they formed the 'Pitmen's Union of Tyne and Wear' in 1831. They were able to force the mine owners to agree to a twelve hour working day for boys instead of one without limitation. This victory, however, was short-lived when a year later a second strike was 'broken' and the working hours reverted to the usual sixteen. More than a decade was to lapse before this was to be re-examined. In July 1833 Althrop's Factory Act (a modified Ten Hours Bill for children) was passed, but this did not apply to the mines; it would also take some years before its recommendations were enforced. One of its main concerns was the lack of provision of education and religion in new colliery towns.

A large number of the mine explosions was found to have resulted from young 'trappers' who had fallen asleep. In a submission to the Commission, George Stephenson wrote: 'It is a difficult task to improve the mode of ventilation. There is always a great number of (ventilation) doors required in a large mine, and any one of these doors being left open by a boy falling asleep may cause some part of the mine to be charged with hydrogen gas, and an explosion from that district may follow ....'. He did not anticipate that the Committee's response would be that his comment was 'proof of the necessity of not employing boys for that purpose, of six, seven, eight, nine and ten years, as too commonly done'.

In the 1841 census, Richard Shannon and Rosanna Fenwick (formerly Shannon) were living next door to each other on Percy Street in Newcastle upon Tyne. Richard was aged 25, born in Scotland and working as a labourer, with wife Jane, aged 30. Rosanna was aged 25 living with husband William Fenwick aged 30, who was working as a joiner. Ten years later the census recorded William Fenwick as a widower; Rosanna had died sometime between 1841 and 1851 (no death certificate available).

At Alnwick in Northumberland, Thomas Shannon aged 30 was recorded as a Shoe Maker (journeyman), and his wife Elizabeth. Also at nearby Bamburgh, once capital of Northumberland, lived an agricultural labourer called Daniel Shannon aged 20. Thomas and Daniel may have been sons of Philip Shannon.

In January 1841, John Roby Leifchild, an inspector by Royal Commission into child employment arrived in Newcastle, then in the throes of transformation under the direction of entrepreneur builder Mr Richard Grainger. Leifchild's reception in the colliery villages was distinctly chilly, similar to the bleak weather, with the rivers Tyne and Wear frozen over. In addition he had great difficulty understanding their 'foreign' dialect with words such as hitches, hoggers, crook yer hough, kibbles, neuks, mushy styen, baits; he had to face the local distrust and doubts about the purpose of his mission. Leifchild noted the miners' distinct physical characteristics – 'small of stature with body curvature, the result of working in low places. They were inclined to bandiness (bow-legged) and pigeon chested, and the eyes hawk-like. The children were small, bony-faced, pale, showing the effects of heredity. He saw them as a tribe of 'blackamoors' returning home with the dust of the pit on them'. Malnutrition was the reason for many of their features.

Leifchild moved into the outlying areas and saw the pit villages in the making, firstly used by the pit sinkers, followed by the jerry builders who erected the long rows of one-up and one-down cottages, to house the incoming miners. Then the colliers and their families would move in on wagons piled high with furniture. Some would be established colliers moving to a new village for the sake of change or, perhaps, slightly better wages. Leifchild saw the balance as 'the very scum and offscourings of a peculiar, mysterious and unlettered race'. These were likely to consist of poor Irish and Scots falling to the lure of 'high' wages to leave forever the rural areas of their birth. Also attracted for similar reasons were the tin miners of Cornwall and Welshmen from the mining valleys. As in the towns, the new villages suffered from lack of sanitation, and cooking facilities consisted of one communal oven per row. Despite these primitive surroundings, generally 'their furniture was reasonable and bedding clean'. He described the pattern of daily life in the villages with the constant surge and retreat of men at the behest of the pit.

The 1841 census revealed Philip and Ann Shannon then living at Rosemary Lane in the parish of St John, with their son Edward aged 18 years, and their married daughter Catherine Reed aged 22 years. Both parents were noted as born in Ireland, with Philip aged 68 years a labourer, and Ann aged 60 years. Since working on farms in Scotland, he like his daughter-in-law Isabella, had been forced to take up general labouring. Both dependents were given as born in Scotland, and Edward's occupation was recorded as 'Printer'.

It can only be assumed that Edward Shannon living so close to the city centre, was taken on as an apprentice at a young age. (In 1718, Benjamin Franklin became an apprentice printer working at the age of 12!). Two years later, the miners' own paper the Miners' Advocate started publication. This was probably printed by the miners' union own printer, T.Dodds, located at 77 The Side. The term 'chapel' used by printing unions revealed the union's past association with Methodism. Edward's faith or Irish origins had not prevented him becoming a printer.

Catherine, who had married Ralph Reed in 1839, seems to have continued to live with her parents after her marriage, and at the time of the census her husband was working at Jarrow as a shipbuilder's journeyman. Even when iron ships started to be built in the 1840s, there would be still plenty of carpentry to be carried out.

Access to printing facilities would have been a very useful asset for a Chartist sympathiser, and many printers were Chartists. John Mason, a shoemaker from Newcastle, was the chairman of the Northern Political Union. Due to his Chartist activities, he was forced to leave for New York in 1842. John Bates (another sinker family name) from Yorkshire, was a coal miner and Chartist; he also fled to New York in 1848 where he founded the first miners' union in America based on Chartist principles. In south Staffordshire, Mason from Tyneside had warned Chartists against Anti-Corn Law League cries of 'Cheap Bread', and to stick to the Charter. He was charged with sedition and riot in July 1840 at Newcastle upon Tyne but was found 'not guilty'; Mason was later imprisoned for six months for making the following speech:

> '...the laws of this country were made by the aristocracy; that the people had no voice in the election of their representatives; that the laws which were to be obeyed by all should be made by all; that the individuals who worked the hardest received the least, and that those who worked the least received the most'.

With the demand of a growing population for cheap reading matter, the paper industry was booming. As early as 1825, a pamphlet was produced by Northumberland miners called 'Voice from the Coal Mines'. There was a wide use of illustrations in publications, and it is said that the illustrations to the report on the employment of children were sketches supposedly done on the spot by the assistant commissioners. Very effective and widely reproduced, the most famous was of a naked child on all fours hitched by leather straps to a wagonful of coal. These stark images helped to bring about the passage of the Mines Act. George Cruikshank's illustrations in Dickens novels were similarly effective and an incentive and aid to those learning to read. At this time Dickens wrote Barnaby Rudge, which featured the anti-Popish Gordon riots of 1770, and perhaps revealed then his fears of Chartist mob action, especially the Physical Force section.

O'Connell urged his Repeal Association of Ireland to help support Lord Morpeth's bill on voters' registration, since it would greatly increase the number of Roman Catholic voters as opposed to the alternative Bill of Lord Stanley who he described to be 'as false as the black heart of its inventor'. After amendments by Lord Howick, the Bill failed to be carried and so was put off for future battles. However legislation was passed to substitute transportation in place of hanging for forgery, embezzlement and rape. Also in 1841, duties on foreign timber and slave grown sugar were reduced. On the 4 June Melbourne lost on a motion of no confidence by a single vote. The Whig ministry resigned in September, and Peel became Prime Minister, much to the distress of Queen Victoria on losing her first prime minister. This was soon forgotten with the birth of her first child, Princess Royal in November.

After Burnhope in 1837, colliery shafts were sunk in Durham at Willington, Edmondsley and Westerton colliery associated with the pits and drifts in the Binchester area; Littleburn, Whitburn, and Wingate, were sunk in 1840. The plans for a new shaft at Monkwearmouth Colliery were approved one year later. Also at this time, the underground haulage system in collieries was changed from corves (wicker baskets) to rolleys (small iron wagons). 1842 was a bad year for colliery accidents in the North East:

5 January Elvet Colliery – 2 men trapped by inrush of water
14 January St Hilda Colliery – caught fire, 22 men and boys died
15 March Cowpen Colliery – 4 men died in shaft accident
19 April Willington Colliery – major disaster, 32 died due to gas explosion
Colliery deaths were not required to be formally recorded until 1843.

There had been a succession of 'accidents' at Willington: in 1829 an explosion killed 4 men with the release of floodwater from old workings; in 1831 an explosion killed 3 men with 14 severely burnt; and in 1840 an explosion killed 1 man with 3 men and 5 boys severely injured. The colliery viewer remained convinced after the last explosion that such accidents were inevitable and that it had to be accepted for the 'national good'. The fact that thirty-two men's lives had been entrusted to an infant did not strike the officials as being irresponsible. The 'Trapper's Petition' was to be in vain:

> 'Why must I sit behind the door
> So many hours away from you,
> And hear the putters shout and roar
> And naught but shut and open do?'

Leifchild interviewed a trapper aged six years, who had already worked underground for six months. His father was a hewer and his two brothers worked as a putter and driver. He arose at 3 am and walked to the pit to start his duties at 4am. Working a sixteen hour shift would mean he got home by 10 pm. The following verse sums up the drudgery of their young lives:

> 'I'm up in the morning afore it is light
> And down in the pit in the dark ;
> And tho' I get home afore it is night,
> I'm asleep from my terrible wark.'

Injuries were common, with a boy describing how he lost a finger at Felling Colliery, broke a leg at Walker, and cut his face at Percy Main. Roof and tramway accidents resulted in broken ribs, maimed legs and damaged hands. This was the age of village stocks to enforce law and order. 1841 to 1843 was a period of depression with Carlyle in 1840 publically raising the issue of 'the Condition of England'. Dickens' Christmas Carol was published shortly afterwards.

The Molly Maguires although originating in north-west Ireland, developed a sister organisation in America founded by Irish and Irish-American coal miners. During the 1840s, the 'Mollies' of Donegal were active in Fermanagh, Leitrim and Roscommon, following the tradition of Catholic secret societies such as the Ribbonmen and Defenders. One of their activities was digging up land so it could only be used for conacre, or the rundale system when the land was divided up by the tenants themselves. In 1841, at a meeting in Newcastle upon Tyne, Fergus O'Connor had repeated the assertion that if the government insisted on using force, the people would be entitled to reply with force. The trial against O'Connor for seditious libels published in the Northern Star began at York on the 17 March 1840, based on a report that he had urged the people at a meeting in Manchester in July 1839 to seize their rights by force. He was arrested, but after eighteen months in prison, O'Connor was undaunted.

On the 30 December 1840, James Storey Reed was born to Andrew Reed and Sarah Storey at Bill Quay at Heworth just south of the Tyne; two years later Thomas was born to Ralph and Catherine Reed in Newcastle with Edward Shannon as sponsor. (During 1665 it was recorded residing in Enniskillen, a James and Andrew Reed).

On the 20 February 1841 another Edward Shannon aged only 14 days died as an inmate of the Tynemouth workhouse. His mother, a widow, was left to bring up her remaining three young children. She may have been admitted to the workhouse when she went into labour. A few weeks later the census revealed that she was working as a washerwoman, and lodging with her children in the same house as the informant of her dead child.

Chartism received the most consistent support from persistently distressed workers like handloom operatives. 1841 had been a crucial time for the Chartist movement with a split developing between its two main spokesmen, into the Physical and Moral Force sections. Feargus O'Connor denounced O'Connell as 'a self-interested dictator of Ireland who kept agitation going for his own profit, and had been bribed by Manchester manufacturers to give up the Ten Hours Bill'. O'Connor's followers came to blows in Manchester, and the police had to be called to protect a Chartist meeting from the Irish (O'Connell supporters).

O'Connor and fellow agitator James Bronterre O'Brien wished to end landlordism altogether, whereas O'Connell himself a landlord, envisaged a utopia where landlords did their duty indulgently. O'Connell had boasted in Parliament in July 1840 that when England had faced a Chartist rising in November 1839, Ireland had remained 'perfectly tranquil'. Nevertheless there was bad feeling between England and Ireland, for in those days to be ultra-protestant was to be anti-Irish; it greatly aggravated the storm about the Maynooth grant in 1845, and then the far wilder storm about the papal aggression six years later.

The Carlyles were staying near Annan in late 1841, and also for a week with Harriet Martineau at Tynemouth. Unused to coal mining areas, Jane Carlyle described their journey home to London: 'the yelling flight through some detestable smoky chaos, and midnight witch-dance of base-looking nameless dirty towns'. Jane considered Harriet 'a humbug with her virtue-doing and penny-ladyisms'. Newcastle upon Tyne School of Design was to be established in 1842, with John Ruskin having shown an interest in Newcastle's architecture. In the same year Dickens visited America on his first lecturing tour, sailing by the first Cunard steamship, the Britannia, whose maiden voyage had been in 1840. He was horrified by the slavery he saw, and considered that the Southerners were clearly hostile to the English, especially as the English navy had just released at Nassau slaves from a Southern ship, The Creole, on its way to New Orleans.

1842 was probably the worst single year of the whole nineteenth century for working class 'distress', when one person out of every ten in the country was a pauper. Referring to his own constituency in Stockport, Richard Cobden reported on 40,000 utterly unemployed; he also drew attention to Hinckley in Yorkshire where only 21 out of 1,500 stocking frames were fully employed. The 'protectionist' duke recommended to the operative classes that 'they should take an occasional pinch of curry powder in a little water to allay their inconvenient cramming for food'. The 'plug' riots were taking place, and similar riots were spreading to the northern coalfields. The removing of the plugs from the steam-engine boilers proved to be very effective since the work could not be easily resumed. The miners had gained a reputation for being very stubborn once they joined a strike, so that other workers often looked to them for support. At first, colliers considered the Charter's five points as something abstract which did not relate to their immediate concerns about tommy-shops, long hours and intimidation by mine owners and their agents. There were attempts to extend Chartism to Ireland after protesters were killed at Preston.

In January 1842, the Thornley Colliery Union had issued an order 'to adopt measures for resistance to the tyranny of the coalowners and their veiwers'. Later in the year at this colliery, a Chartist rally had denounced the dangerous state of the workings where miners were issued with candles instead of safety lamps. The 1842 Report recorded that Blaydon Main Colliery was also notorious for Chartism.

The detestation of the Corn Laws was shown in Longtown near Carlisle, where an effigy of Sir Robert Peel was burned. In 1842 the first Income Tax was imposed, and free trade was given a boost by the removal of all trade protections other than the Corn Laws. John Bright and Richard Cobden were to renew their energies to get rid of this remaining obstacle to what they saw as the means to prosperity for all. They were able to make use of the penny post, available since 1840, to disseminate the anti- Corn Law propaganda. At this time the middle classes and artisans were attracted to Cobden and Bright's aims whereas the working classes mainly found their cause in the trade union action.

The landowners were utterly convinced that free corn would destroy rent, close their mansions and their parks, break up their lives, and beggar the country; they had natural forebodings that protectionism would soon share the fate of Protestantism, and that capitulation to Cobden would follow capitulation to O'Connell. Gladstone was more in tune with the people when he commented to his wife Catherine:'...... when we may reflect on the thorough rottenness socially speaking of the system which gathers huge masses of population having no other tie to the classes above them than that of employment, of high money payment constituting a great moral temptation in times of prosperity, and the reductions in adversity which seem like robberies, and which the poor people have no discipline of training to endure'.

Parliament opened on the 3 February 1842 with much anticipation by the Anti-corn Law League, but they were disappointed when Peel stated that a repeal of the corn laws would have the effect of adding agricultural distress to manufacturing distress. He then announced that a sliding scale system for ascertaining the excise would be modified. After four days of debate Peel got his way, but there emerged a new force in politics in the person of Richard Cobden whose stature was to grow during the following years as he led the campaign for repealing the Corn Laws. Cobden as owner of a printworks, reported that many masters were still evading the laws to suppress the 'truck system':

> 'On Saturday the people go into a room to receive their wages. They are paid at the time in money; but instead of returning by the door at which they entered, they have to pass into another room, in which sits a person who keeps the books of the truck-shops, and to whom the workman has to pay every farthing that has been expended during the previous week in buying goods and clothes; and if it is proved that any of the men has purchased one single farthing's worth of goods from any other shop than that which belongs to the master, he is, without word of explanation, discharged'.

In Ireland during 1842, the first issue of The Nation was published. Great efforts were made to effect a combination of English Chartists and Irish Repealers. On the 2 May 1842, a petition for both the Charter and the repeal of the Union between England and Ireland was presented to the Commons by T S Duncombe, Radical member for Finchley. This petition received over three million signatures, two-and-a-half times the number of the 1839 petition. It had to be carried into the Houses of Parliament by forty men

Putter 1842
(bbc.co.uk)

and contained over three million signatures, ninety-two thousand of which came from Newcastle and district. This second petition was to be also rejected.

The 1842 Commissioners recorded a day-school attached to the Walker Iron-Works conducted by a Primitive Methodist preacher. This school accepted children between the ages of 5 and 12 years old, teaching reading, writing and arithmetic. James Shannon may have attended this school. If James had started down the pit as a 'trapper', he would have opened and closed a trap-door needed for ventilating the mine. Older children were employed as fillers, to load the tubs and skips after the men had hewn the coal, and as putters (or hurriers) to push the tubs from the coal-face to the foot of the shaft.

The [May] 1842 Report on child labour in mines denounced the employment of women in the pits where it still existed. (North East pits had ceased to use women from the end of the eighteenth century). Parliament was shocked by the graphic illustrations of young boys and girls working below ground. The sexuality of these images made it certain that immediate action would be demanded. Mainly in Scotland, it cited cases of women and men, completely naked, working side by side; examples of immorality in mines; and women who actually gave birth while underground. The most telling indictment of the report, applicable to men, women and children was the appalling conditions in which they were forced to work. When Lord Ashley delivered his great speech on the report, it was reported that 'strong men wept'. As the century progressed, these conditions worsened as shafts went deeper to obtain the coal. In the 1840s the government started to look into health problems particularly affecting large towns. Also in 1842, a 'Report on Sanitary

Condition of Dumfries' was published. This noted that a considerable proportion of the poor were Irish, almost all labourers.

On the 7 June 1842 Lord Ashley (later Lord Shaftesbury) gave his speech in the House of Lords for the introduction of a Bill for regulations controlling the admittance of persons in mines and collieries below the age of thirteen. The impetus for a national inquiry into the condition of children working down mines was the explosion at the St Hilda Colliery, South Shields, on the 18 June 1839. A townsman named James Mather instigated the 'South Shields Committee to Investigate the Cause of Accidents in Coal Mines'. After three years of the most thorough scientific investigation, their report attracted the attention of the mining industry's leading figures. The report covered the ventilation of mines, the efficiency of safety lamps, the need for the Government inspection of mines and the provision of medical treatment after explosions, and the use of infant labour in the mines. It was noted that of the fifty-two victims of the St Hilda explosion, there were six boys under twelve years of age. Although Lord Ashley's Bill passed through the House of Commons without dissent, in the House of Lords only Lord Londonderry raised any objections but failed to get a seconder. To avoid delaying the passing of the bill, an amendment to lower the age to ten years for employment of children was accepted.

In October, the 1842 Election, the 'Battle of the Constitution' took place. After so much Chartism activity, the establishment at Wakefield of the Miners Association of Great Britain on the 7 November 1842 was an important landmark in the history of trade unions. This Association was the first union to use the courts of law systematically to

Lord Ashley

defend its members' interests. This was achieved largely through the efforts of an energetic and able solicitor called W. P. Roberts, who was strongly sympathetic to the labour movement. Marxist historian Raymond Challinor pointed out that with the formation of the Miners Trade Union Association, Chartist activity intensified. Disturbances started among North Staffordshire miners and spread rapidly to the industrial north and to Scotland. The Northern Star showed that a large proportion of the mining population had signed the Chartist petitions in 1842. The Chartists' nominations from Byker, Northumberland were put forward by five miners including Martin Jude and John Hall who became treasurer and general secretary respectively. The North East was to become one of the best organised regions of the Chartist movement, dominated by advocates of 'physical force' Chartism. A massive wave of repression followed the 1842 general strike, sweeping many Chartists into prison. By mid-summer most of the advocates of force in the North were under arrest.

There was turmoil at the Palace and in the Church forcing the politicians to act. Queen Victoria had no sympathy with the Chartists. She wrote to her prime minister stating that 'she is surprised at the little (or no) opposition to the dreadful riots in the potteries.....at the passiveness of the troops.....they ought to act, and these meetings ought to be prevented'. The Queen's orders were carried out with savage vengeance. For burning down a coalowner's house, six men were transported for twenty-one years each. Also at this time, it was recorded that Peel reluctantly agreed to a trip to Scotland by Victoria and Albert due to the 'rioting in the North'. Peel also advised Victoria to placate the people by living without ostentation since Radical papers were comparing pauperism in the cities with luxury at the Palace. In 1844 she decided against visiting Ireland after being warned by Daniel O'Connell that she would see 'Repeal' written up wherever she went. When the 'Repeal of the Union' movement collapsed without bloodshed, the Queen eagerly supported Peel's plans for Irish amelioration. She could not understand why Ireland could not be ruled like Scotland, and found it dreadful that 'Government by troops' was necessary and that Irish landlords were evicting peasantry.

The period, 1839 to 1843, was to be known as the 'Hungry Forties' for obvious reasons. In 1843 although there were difficult harvests, the Corn Laws prevented the import of corn. Sidney Webb wrote that 'in almost every respect the wage-earner was suffering from the surviving evils of the old order, while losing all its advantages; he was already exposed to the many disadvantages of the new era, while enjoying few of its benefits'. In the first few weeks of 1843, Carlyle wrote the book 'Past and Present' having been spurred into action by the appalling sight of able but unemployed paupers outside of a poorhouse during a tour of the countryside the previous summer, and fearing that England was on the verge of revolution after reading newspaper reports of insurrection in Manchester. The book written with 'red-hot' passion, was an unequivocal indictment of an economic system that drove men to the workhouse. Denouncing the morals of 'demand and supply', he proposed instead the principle of 'a fair day's-wages for a fair day's-work'. Carlyle encompassed all men within the single category of 'workers', but also put forward the notion of 'hero-worship' as a fundamental fact of human nature, the manifestation of spirit in man, the 'perpetual presence of Heaven in our poor Earth'. He endowed work with a religious quality, making it the condition of man's spiritual as well as material and social existence. As Engels and Marx elaborated later, Carlyle denounced the malignant influence of 'laissez faire', self-interest, and 'cash nexus'.

In 1843 John Bright was elected in Durham, and in his maiden speech he highlighted the grievances of 'twenty thousand pitmen in the North....' and denounced the Protestant Church in Ireland. Shortly afterwards he was to show Thomas Carlyle his mills, and Bright noted their differences of view and how Carlyle occasionally slipped into the Annandale accent. In view of the large amount of travelling he would have to do in future campaigns, Bright no doubt was pleased at the passing of Gladstone's Railway Act which required trains to have 'provision of seats and protected from weather'. George Stephenson was in favour of this measure whereas surprisingly Brunel was against. Despite these hiccups, former transport hardships were disappearing with the last stagecoach leaving London in 1846. The railways were making an important contribution to the politics of mass democracy. No longer did the Government feel it necessary to station troops close to the likely trouble spots, and thereby creating tensions, knowing that it had the means of rapid mobilisation.

On the 13 May 1843, a mass recruitment Chartist rally was held at Shadons Hill, in Northumberland. 20,000 miners were there to hear their leaders' speeches against the harsh conditions of the bond. By signing the bond, the miners were not allowed to 'keep either Galloway, ass, or dog'. By November, Thornley Colliery had come out on strike. The danger of violence erupting caused the Miners' Advocate to urge the men to remain peaceable. It reported a parliamentary debate where Lord Howick, son of Lord Grey, had asked the government to take action against the colliers' union. Sir Robert Peel, the Prime Minister, had replied that 'the colliers, as yet, have kept within the law'. O'Connor ('champion of the horny hands and the fustian jackets') appreciated the crucial importance of the need for the Chartist movement to co-operate with the trade unions and on no account interpose the Charter as an obstacle to their proceedings.

In December The Miners Advocate (originally Miners Journal) was forced to close, unable to pay the penalty for being untaxed. A Repeal petition took place in 1843; Peel allayed his party's fears by confirming that he would resist the demand of the repealers even at the cost of civil war. The re-enactment of the Arms Act was resisted strongly by the Radicals, and also by Lord Clements, heir to the earldom of Leitrim. The 'Battle of Magheracloon' in

Monaghan, resulted from the police firing on tenants demonstrating against rent increases. Throughout 1843 O'Connell stirred Ireland to its roots and aroused the interest of the whole world as he directed the campaign for the Repeal of the Union. One of the devices before the Monster Meetings was organised processions. Thackeray during his visit to Ireland in 1843 was subjected to a practical joke by a peasant who explained the 'GPO' signs as standing for 'God preserve O'Connell'. In a Cork procession there was featured two boys, one painted black and the other white. The black figure bore the label Free, since Westminster had abolished slavery in the West Indies. He displayed to the crowd his broken chains. The white figure, representing the Irish, wore intact chains, and a label round his neck which proclaimed: A Slave Still!

Education was an issue raised by Lord Ashley in Parliament; he reported after surveys of the children attending daily schools at the cost of the state or by religious bodies, there was remaining over one million children capable of education that were receiving no instruction whatsoever in a daily school. Included in the voluminous submission, he commented on the 'dangerous classes of Manchester', and the fact that many other European schools had already established state schools and were far in advance of Britain. These proposals were intended for all denominations in the manufacturing areas, and was to be the important first step towards the goal eventually realised in 1870. The Catholic faith had placed no importance on educating the masses, and thus 'Methodism was to make them the weapons of the owners'. However, at Newcastle the Catholic Cathedral of St Marys had just been completed, built 'by the pennies of the poor'.

Carlyle also saw the Union with England to be root of most of Ireland's suffering: 'To hear the loud and even louder voice of poor Ireland for many years back, it must be clear that there is one thing wanting to make that Ireland happy: total disseverance from this Island; perfect and complete Repeal of the Union, as it is called. If, some night, the Union could be shorn asunder, repealed and annihilated for ever, the next morning Ireland, with no England to molest her, would wake and find herself happy.....Ireland would be a mighty pretty nation, likely to take a high figure among the nations of the world'. Carlyle also had a word for the absentee landlords: '.... the Irish aristocracy, if it will preserve its land much longer, shall rapidly come home from foreign capitals, cease drinking punch and playing roulette at Bath or Leamington, dismount from its idle hunting-saddles, descend from its idle drawing-rooms into the neighbouring hunger-cabins; and see how on these terms it will manage Irish poverty, for on these terms only can or shall it be managed henceforth'.

At this time future Fenian Thomas Meagher had read Carlyle's The French Revolution and was fired up with the desire to assert the Irish sovereignty. Carlyle was to visit agitator John Mitchel in Dublin in 1845. As the agitation and defection from the magistracy grew, an alarmed Government began to move troops into Ireland and re-enacted the Arms Act of 1793. A monster meeting due to be held at Clontarf on the 5 October was cancelled after Wellington and Peel issued a proclamation forbidding the meeting. Afterwards repeal agitation subsided. Years later it was said that 'Ireland was won at Clontarf; and at Clontarf it was lost again.' O'Connell was indicted on January 1844 but released from prison three months later.

During the Great Strike of 1844, the coalowners tried to split the miners' ranks by refusing to negotiate with the union and asserting that there were 'Chartist agitators who proceed from colliery to colliery, sowing disaffection among the pitmen for their own selfish ends'. The full weight of the state apparatus came down firmly on the side of the coalowners. The miners realised that they were to be stigmatised as Chartists whatever they did, so after this strike the union leaders became more open in their political beliefs. Engels believed that earlier trade unions had sought acceptance and respectability from the established order, but miners had always been considered social outcasts and therefore had nothing to lose in being linked with a revolutionary movement.

After 1844, O'Connor had a waning influence on the working class. After the failure of Chartism, the workers started to consider smaller combinations such as the Co-operative Movement just beginning at Rochdale. Ireland continued to be Peel's greatest headache; he announced that a commission was to look into the occupation of land in Ireland as a signal that pacification measures were in the offering. Gladstone's Railway Act (1844) laid down the principles of reserving to the state the full right of intervention in the concerns of the railway companies, and gave the state the option to purchase a line at the end of a certain term. In June 1844 the Newcastle and Darlington Railway opened.

At the sinking of a second shaft at Monkwearmouth, new methods of transport machinery were in use. Unusually, sinkers and engineers worked alongside hewers and putters. It is open to debate whether these workers found common cause during the strike. In August 1844, Irish Lough Allen mines and Arigna were producing 7840 tons coal per acre, at 4s per ton. Also East Tanfield and Eden were sunk in the year of the 'Great Strike'. For Braddyll and his partners, owners of Murton Colliery, the strike which lasted five months was the last straw, and in 1846 they were declared bankrupt.

Disraeli's novel 'Coningsby' published in 1844, covered the period of great political upheaval in England from the 1832 Reform Act to the 1841 General Election. Engel's 'The Condition of the Working Class in England [1844]', was not published in England until 1892, and therefore did not play a part in shaping the British public consciousness. Although he listed the workers' humane qualities of friendliness, generosity and open-minded, he also noted their drunkenness, brutality, licentiousness and criminality. Engels explained his book as a 'bill of indictment' against the English bourgeoisie. He described the 'The Great Towns' as containing hordes of people crowded together, streaming past

Engels 1877
(Britannica.com)

Marx 1875
(theguardian.com)

each other, yet brutally indifferent to each other and entirely separated from each other. Engels concluded that these same cities, the breeding places of misery and vice, were also the 'birthplaces of the labour movements'. He also commented on the immigration from Ireland as having the immediate effect of degrading and barbarizing the English workers, but this 'deepened the chasm between workers and bourgoisie, and hastened the approaching crisis' and revolution. In his writing 'Chartism', Carlyle tried to give hope to a severely oppressed people:

> 'Poor Ireland! And yet let no true Irishman, who believes and sees all this, despair by reason of it. Cannot he too do something to withstand the unproductive false-hood, there as it lies accursed around him, and change it into truth which is fruitful and blessed? Every man can and shall himself be a true man: it is a great thing and the parent of great things: as from a single acorn the whole earth might in the end be peopled with oaks! Every mortal can do something: this let him faithfully do, and leave with assured heart the issue to a Higher Power.'

But England had brought this on herself, so Carlyle fumed: 'More stringent than O'Connell eloquence, or O'Brien pike-manufacture, the Law of Nature itself makes us now, in every fibre, participant of Ireland's wretchedness. Steam passage from Ireland is occasionally as low as fourpence per head. Not a wandering Irishlackall that comes over to us, to parade his rags and hunger, and sin and misery, but comes in all senses as an irrepressible missionary of the like to our own people; an inarticulate prophet of God's justice to Nations; heralding to us also a doom like his own. Of our miseries and fearful entanglement, here in Britain, he, the Irish lackall, is by far the heaviest; and we cannot shake him off. No, we have deserved him: by our incompetence and unveracity – by our cowardly, false, and criminal neglect of Ireland – by our government of make-believe and not of truth and reality, so long continued there, we have deserved him; and suddenly, by the aid of steam and modern progress of the sciences we have got him.......The mad cry of Repeal you can put down, – change it into another as mad, or less, or still more mad; but him you cannot put down.'

In the House of Commons on the 16 February 1844, Disraeli also had Ireland on his mind as he stated: 'I want to see a public man come forward and to say what the Irish question is. One says it is a physical question, another a spiritual. Now it is the absence of the aristocracy. Now it is the absence of railways. It is the Pope one day and potatoes the next. A dense population inhabit an island where there is an established church which is not their church, and is a territorial aristocracy, the richest of whom live in a distant capital. Thus they have a starving population, an alien church, and in addition the weakest executive in the world. Well, what then would gentlemen say if they were reading of a country in that position? They would say at once, 'The remedy is a revolution', but the Irish could not have a revolution and why? Because Ireland is connected with another and more powerful country. Then what is the consequence? The connection with England became the cause of the present state of Ireland. If the connection with England prevented a revolution and a revolution was the only remedy, England logically is in the odious position of being the cause of al the misery of Ireland. What then is the duty of an English minister? To effect by his policy all those changes which a revolution would effect by force. That is the Irish question in its integrity'. Peel was anxious to 'tranquilise' Ireland; he was disappointed that after all his sacrifices to get the Emancipation bill through, Ireland continued to agitate.

When O'Connell raised the standard of 'Repeal', the Irish in Britain threw themselves into the struggle with characteristic ardour. Following imprisonment after the Great Conspiracy Trials during 1842, P M Brophy of the Irish Universal Suffrage Union was sent to organise the Cumbrian miners during the 1844 Strike. He had a difficult struggle with mineowner Earl Lonsdale over blacklegging. A strike-breaker or 'blackleg' was considered the Judas of the community, perhaps less for the imported Irish blacklegs. The Catholic Church refused to baptise the children of Irish Chartists, withholding the sacraments from those who failed to renounce the membership of the Irish Universal Suffrage Union. Issues like this were probably the reason for the loss to the Church of many Irish workers who had strong political views.

Lord Durham [John George Lambton]
1835
(National Portrait Gallery)

In the same year there was an explosion at Haswell colliery killing outright 95 out of 99 men, including three generations of the Briggs family dying, grandfather Thomas 61, John 25 and James 10 from Sinker's Row. Four workers near the shaft were protected from the blast by the nearby pit ponies and large metal tubs. The eminent scientist, Michael Faraday was appointed to investigate the disaster at Haswell. At Eppleton Colliery, a sinker named Nicholas Cowey died whilst sinking Jane Pit due to a shaft collapse.

During the 1844 Strike, the solidarity of miners was shown, including contributions from Lancashire miners despite Haswell Colliery becoming known as a 'blackleg' colliery. The Thornley Strike Funds included many subscriptions even from pit sinkers who generally did not get involved in strikes since they more often were on the move, and also from a trapper:

Chilton Sinkers   8s 0d;
Ludworth Sinkers   16s 3d;
The late Trapper boy 2s 6d

The colliery owners brought up to surface their pit ponies, an indication that they would not give in easily. As a punishment, the colliery owners introduced a monthly bond to weed out strikers, and this was enforced until 1866 when the annual bond was re-introduced.

The monthly bond had caused an unstable workforce due to the undue freedom of movement.

Marx's daughter, Laura Lafargue in 1880 translated a poem composed by George Werth about the 1844 Strike. Willam Hornsby of Shotton Moor also wrote the following poem:

> 'A dialogue I'll tell you as true as my life
> Between a coal owner and a poor pitman's wife
> As she was walking all on the highway
> She met a coal owner and this she did say
> Good morning, Lord Firedamp, this woman she said
> I'll do you no harm, Sir, don't be afraid
> If you'd been where I've been the most of my life
> You wouldn't turn pale at a poor pitman's wife
> Then where do you come from, the owner he cried
> I come from Hell, the woman replies
> If you come from hell, then tell me right plain
> How you contrived to get out again
> Aye the way I got out, the truth I will tell
> They're turning the poor folk all out of hell
> This is to make room for the rich wicked race
> For there is a great number of them in that place
> And the owners is the next on command
> To arrive in hell, as I understand
> For I heard the old devil say as I came out
> The coal owners all had received their rout
> Then how does the old devil behave in that place
> Oh sir, he is cruel to the rich wicked race
> He is far more cruel than you cold suppose
> He's like a mad bull with a ring through his nose
> If you be a coal owner, sir, take my advice
> And agree with your men, and give them a fair price
> For if and you do not, I know very well
> You'll be in great danger of going to hell
> For all your coal owners great fortunes has made
> By those jovial men that works in the coal trade
> Now how you can you think to proper and thrive
> By wanting to starve your poor workmen above
> So come ye poor pitmen and join heart and hand
> For when you're of work and trade's at a stand
> In the town of Newcastle all cry out amain
> Oh gin the pits were at work once again.'

In 1844, Penshaw Monument was erected, dedicated by citizens of Newcastle to the first Earl of Durham, the great Whig politician, who had helped to start the process of reform in 1832. He had died eight years after the first Reform was passed.

The 1844 Great Strike starting in April and lasting six months, was defeated by the importation of many blacklegs, also called 'candymen', from all over the country. The miners in the new east pits were more radical, and held out longest. After the sufferings of the strike, in November 1844 a second child was born to Catherine Shannon and Ralph Reed. Catherine was still residing at 3 Rosemary Lane in the St Johns area of Newcastle. The baby girl was named Ann, probably after Catherine's mother. The sponsors were Richard and Rosannah Shannon. Ralph was still working as a shipwright after being recorded in the 1841 census working as an apprentice shipwright at Jarrow. The strike would have seriously affected work on the river.

CHAPTER 8

1845–1848 Railway Mania and the Irish Famine

(Isabella Shannon marries John Lawrence)

' …. Ireland, Ireland! that cloud in the west, that coming storm the minister of God's retribution upon cruel and inveterate and but half-atoned injustice! Ireland forces upon us those great social and great religious questions – God grant that we may have the courage to look them in the face, and to work through them.'

> (letter to wife by Gladstone 1845)

' … the negroes of Antigua had subscribed £144 to the relief of the starving poor in Ireland…'

> (Roscommon Newspaper 1846)

'I have not in my travels seen anything uglier than that disorganic mass of labourers, sunk three-fold deeper in brutality by three-fold wages they are getting. The Yorkshire and Lancashire men, I hear are reckoned the worst, and not without glad surprise, I find the Irish are the best in the point of behaviour. The postmaster tells me several of the Irish do regularly apply to him for money drafts, and send their earnings home. The English, who eat twice as much beef, consume the residue in whisky, and do not trouble the postmaster.'

> (Navvies on the Caledonian Canal Carlyle 1846)

'I understand that rotten potatoes and seaweed – or even grass – properly mixed, afford a very wholesome and nutritious food. We all know that Irishmen can live upon anything, and there is plenty of grass in the fields even if the potatoes should fail.'

> (unsympathetic Royal Duke 1847)

From 1845 to 1847, Britain was caught at the peak excitement of Railway Mania, 'down the ringing grooves of change' – no other invention revealed so visibly the power and speed of the new age. George Hudson born in Yorkshire, was elected as Conservative member for Sunderland against an Anti-Corn Law League candidate. His railway empire was to make him a fortune after the hectic speculation in the early forties; by 1849 it was starting to collapse, yet his electors stayed faithful. He retained his seat until 1859.

Hudson was eventually discredited, and committed suicide. The London mail coach had been withdrawn in 1846 due to the 1830s mail contracts having gone to the railways. It should not be forgotten that 'horse' power still played a vital part of the nineteenth century economy, providing a feeder service for passengers and freight to and from the stations, and in the coalfields.

No doubt James Shannon's mother was excited at the thought of her forthcoming marriage. James would have been 11 years old. Nearly eight years after the death of his father, his mother Isabella re-married on the first of June 1845. (David Livingstone had married 6 months earlier). Her second husband, John Lawrence [registered as Lawrance], a bachelor of 39 years, was a labourer living at Crook Hall in County Durham. The marriage took place at the Catholic Chapel of St Cuthberts Broom, in the parish of Lanchester. Isabella, as a widow, gave her mark. Unsurprisingly, John Lawrence was able to sign the certificate since his father, also John Lawrence, was given as a 'Clark' (probably a colliery clerk). Catherine Reed and a John Maguire had been marriage sponsors at Auckland one month earlier.

Isabella's father was recorded as Anthony Golighar, (a corruption of Gallagher), which indicated the way Isabella pronounced her name. Anthony's occupation was given as a plasterer, a skilled trade. The marriage was also registered in the Catholic Church's own registers, confirming that John Lawrence [spelt Laurence] was also Catholic. The majority of the Irish in the Broom parish were from Ulster, and the highest numbers were natives from counties Monaghan, Leitrim and Mayo. The abode of John Lawrence's father was given as Glasgow; he had probably emigrated from Ireland.

Witness to another Broom marriage which took place on the 25 February 1845 was Mary Shannon. Also on the 6 November 1847, a Margaret Shenan was married whose parents were Thomas and Bridget, and on the 24 November 1851 a Patrick Shannon was married whose parents were given as Owen and Bridget. This sudden increase in Irish marriages in Durham was due to the Great Famine, and there is little doubt that this tragedy in Ireland would have been the subject of much discussion at these weddings.

The 'Condition of Ireland' was a discussion thrust to the top of the political agenda, and for many years ahead was to be considered by Gladstone and others to damage England's international reputation. It was used by a number of Europe's politicians to point the finger at England whilst defending their own acts of suppression. Whilst travelling in France, Gladstone had met French statesman Guizot, who had rebuked him for the treatment of the Irish by the British. However Gladstone took very little action on Ireland for the next twenty-one years. Crimes of violence in Ireland had increased from 1495 in 1844 to 3642 in 1845, especially in counties Tipperary, Clare, Roscommon, Limerick and Leitrim. Peel had long believed Irish discontent to be a haemorrhage draining away the life blood of national prosperity, and he needed to counter-balance the campaign by O'Connell for repeal of the Union. In 1845 Thomas Davis, leader of Young Irelanders was beginning to assert a new more independent direction, when he died of scarlet fever aged thirty-one.

Disturbances in Ireland resulting in fatalities were reported by Irish local newspapers: in October 1841 Michael Shannon was drowned in the Sligo Estuary, and in September 1843 Michael Gallagher was shot dead at Drumshambo in County Leitrim. Unrest continued to grow in Ireland; in May 1845, three Molly Maguires were killed and two wounded during an attack on the police also at Drumshambo. Two months later the local assizes recorded 106 cases including one homicide, 17 attacking houses, 17 robbery, 7 burnings, 27 threatening letters, and 6 killing cattle. The Roscommon & Leitrim Gazette reported on the 14 February that an 'itinerant beggar' called Margaret Shannon had been found dead beside the River Boyle, and a few weeks after, William Maughan of Knockadoo was beaten for conveying baggage for the army; the ears were cut off his horse.

To the upper classes, Protectionism in 1845 was like Protestantism in 1828, a point of principle to be fought for with all possible means. Nevertheless Lord Enniskillen was criticised for his obsession against Popery and Papists; there was much opposition from the Government's own supporters, as well as dissenters outside Parliament, to the intention to give concessions to Roman Catholics in Ireland. During Gladstone's audience with Queen Victoria, he gave his resignation due to his opposition to the Maynooth Bill, which intended to increase funding to a Catholic seminary. Prince Albert was an ardent 'free-trader', and at this time the royal pair were very popular, particularly with the middle-classes whose watch-words were duty, industry, morality and domesticity.

Dickens had already taken the lead in exposing the corrupting influence of industry and big business, and other writers followed. Disraeli's 'Coningsby' and 'Sybil' were published in 1845, confirming his sympathies for the Chartist cause. He was also to popularise the 'two nations' metaphor, by drawing attention to the 'poor' who were considered a foreign nation by the 'rich' – 'inhabitants of different planets'. Already, Carlyle in Sartor Resarus had divided England into 'dandies' and 'drudges'. In similar vein, Elizabeth Gaskell's Mary Barton came out in 1848, and later her novel 'North and South'. Gladstone noted that the main feeder for Chartism was want of employment. The Irish took part in Chartist disturbances in Lancashire where cotton amounted to 40 to 50% of the value of British exports.

In 1845, Branwell Bronte wrote a poem called "The Emigrant". Perhaps this was his premonition of the famine years ahead. It was said that in Wuthering Heights, Heathcliffe may have been based on an Irish vagrant or famine victim whom Mr Earnshaw had rescued from the Liverpool streets. Ominously in Ireland, the first signs of failures of the potato crop were beginning to be reported. Irish crop failures in the west of Ireland had occurred in 1806, 1822, 1831, 1835, 1836, 1837, and 1839. By 1845 the population of Ireland had increased to about nine millions, and after the Famine this was to go down to four and half millions. Warnings of the dire state of Ireland and the need for urgent action by the Government had been given over the years by Swift, Arthur Young, John Stuart Mill and Thomas Carlyle, but went unheeded. In October, Peel became aware of the reports of the Irish potato blight and considered that the 'removal of impediments to import' was necessary. When Wellington heard that Peel had been converted to Free Trade he exclaimed 'Rotten potatoes have done it all'. 200 years before, the Irish had introduced the potato to Scotland using the 'Irish ridge method' or 'lazy-bed', and now Scotland as well as England was feeling the effects of the potato blight.

By autumn, Gladstone made a proposal to visit Ireland since 'it is likely to find this country and parliament so much employment for years to come, I feel rather oppressively an obligation to try and see it with my own eyes instead of using those of other people'. Newman and Gladstone's sister had changed to the Catholic faith. Philip Pusey who was about to join the Catholic Church, stated his belief that 'in these agrarian outrages, the Irish peasants have been engaged in a justifiable civil war, because the peasant ejected from his land could no longer by any efforts of his own preserve his family from the risk of starvation'. With dreadful foresight, Cobden used the words: 'three weeks of rain when the wheat was ripening would rain away the corn law'.

The combination of the Irish famine, a poor harvest in England and Russell's public announcement on the 22 November of his conversion to Repeal, forced Peel to take the issue of the Corn Laws with greater urgency. Eventually, not having the full support of his cabinet, and considering that it would be best to leave it to Russell to carry the Repeal, Peel resigned on the 16 December 1845. Russell tried to form a ministry and failed, and reluctantly Peel re-assumed control, but was soon in trouble when on the 28 February two thirds of the Conservatives voted against their leader. At this time of high parliamentary tension, there was anger when Gladstone tried to extend the policy of transporting criminals to Australia. One month earlier, Disraeli aided by Lord George Bentinck (known together as the Jew and the Jockey), delivered a devastating attack on Peel, rallying the protectionist forces of the Conservative Party. The Irish Arms Bill was the final measure which led to Peel's downfall. The election that followed had more Chartist candidates than ever before.

Before the final collapse of his government, Peel had ordered the purchase of £100,000 worth of corn to be sent to Ireland and warehoused in British army stores throughout the poorer regions of Ireland. However, this Indian corn was so hard to crack that it had to be chopped in steel mills, but there were no such mills in Ireland! It was very difficult to cook, and if improperly done, caused severe and even fatal bowel disorders. In Munster, starving dogs were being killed like vermin as they began to attack the bark of trees.

So the 'hungry transit' from spring to autumn still continued thirty years after the Shannons had left Ireland. Deaths in mining also continued. Pit sinker Joseph Mason, died at Seaton Union Pit in 1846 during blasting stone with gunpowder. Despite all this gloom, on the eighth of March, Isabella's first child to John Lawrence was born. Ann Jane's birth place was given as Westgate, Newcastle, and she was registered by her mother on the third of April. John was still working as labourer.

Belatedly, there were some relief schemes being organised in Ireland such as the Shannon Navigation Improvement Works between Boyle and Jamestown to give immediate employment to 500 to 1500 labourers. Also work started on the Ballinamore-Ballyconnell Canal employing 7000 during the famine years. However Ireland could never compete with England, the centre of the industrial revolution. William Armstrong in Newcastle had just developed the hydraulic crane. Carlyle was impressed with the Irish navvies working on the Caledonian Railway. Many of the hazards that confronted the navvies and pioneering engineers were of the same nature as those being overcome in sinking mine shafts. On the 19 July 1843, Brunel's revolutionary ship, the SS Great Britain, floated out of Patterson's dock at Wapping. Brunel had plans for railway development in Ireland following strong Irish support for railways when lines were being constructed in Wales. The famine put paid to those dreams of a profitable Anglo-Irish traffic. This abrupt stop may have contributed to the victory of the narrow gauge and the 1846 Gauge Act. Ireland was also to be the reason for grief, when on the 22 September, Brunel's second great ship, the Great Britain, foundered on the sandbanks of Mourne in Co Down. Fortunately, with the help of the local people, the ship was eventually re-launched on her way to providing a regular Atlantic crossing service.

Quebec was the centre of the trans-Atlantic trade. Later, Philadelphia was one of the United States ports to receive emigrants – both place names later adopted by County Durham. Irish male immigration to Liverpool from November 1846 to May 1847 was 196,338, and by the end of 1847 the total number of immigrants (excluding those who went to America) was 296,231 – all apparently 'paupers' as described by the official report. According to the 1847 Report of the Health Committee, the condition of these people "suddenly dropped into a town" (referring to Liverpool), already overcrowded and notoriously unsanitary, was vulnerable to typhus, smallpox and measles. Ten Catholic priests succumbed during the year to the disease contracted in the course of their ministrations to the sick people. The French traveller, Paschal Grousset, commented on the unique place held by the Catholic Church in the history of Ireland and the role played by its clergy in 'resistance to the oppressor'.

After thirty-one long years, 25 June 1846 saw at last the repeal of the Corn Laws. Peel's (Irish) Coercion Bill, however, was defeated, and resulted in Peel's resignation. Palmerston became Foreign Secretary for the third time. Lord Melbourne, no longer prime minister, voted by proxy to support the repeal, having opposed it for so long, agonising on his decision up to the last moment. However, these measures were taken too late to have a significant effect on the Irish famine. Corn was being exported to England from Ireland although it was desperately needed for its own people. Making grain cheap meant that it took more Irish-grown grain to make up the landlord's rent. The man who had contrived till then to save a little grain for his family, had now to part with it all or starve, or alternatively, be evicted. Thus the English remedy brought thousands more beneath the famine line; and made evictions easier than ever. Irish grain was shipped by relief committees to Ireland and re-sold there at half its cost. The starving peasants had no money, so it was bought up by speculators who re-shipped it to England, where the relief committee bought it a second time, and so while speculators made money, the people starved.

Contrary to the Irish Poor Law regulations, in September 1846, half of the country's unions had started to administer outdoor relief. The new 1847 Extension Act placed the responsibility for providing relief exclusively on the Poor Law guardians, but many unions were running out of funds. Kilrush Union achieved notoriety for evicting as many as 300 people each day, who then became dependent on external poor law relief. In Carrick-on Shannon it was reported that 'the children exhibit the effects of famine in a remarkable degree, their faces looking wan and haggard with hunger, and seeming like old men and women'. The poor hung onto their small strips of land till the last moment, since they knew that once they entered the workhouse or fever hospital their cottage would be 'tumbled-in', in their absence. Even some Catholic 'strong farmers' evicted their tenants, and small number of Protestant landlords provided soup kitchens but on condition that the Catholic recipients gave up their faith.

In 1847, a year when trade was depressed, the House of Lords established a select committee to study 'Colonisation from Ireland'. They were told by a Presbyterian clergyman that: 'If you bring people over who have been accustomed to work for 6d a Day, and place them in competition with those persons here who are obtaining 2s 6d or 3s or 5s a Day, the necessary Consequence will be that those Irish Labourers will consider themselves well paid with 1s or 1s 6d a Day, and your Labourers must come down to that

Great Famine 1849
(Bridget O'Donnell and family)
(en wikipedia.org)

standard. Either you will raise the Irish to the Condition of the English, or you will pull the English down to the Condition of the Irish'.

A virulent scurvy was also common. It was known as 'black leg' by the Irish since it caused the blood vessels under the skin to burst. Famine dropsy, also took its share. Another dietary disease made hair fall from children's heads but grow in patches from the faces, so that one of the Society of Friends working in Skibbereen near Cork said that the starving children looked like monkeys. In late July the Government brought in the 'Soup Kitchen' Act which established a Relief Committee in each district. To cheapen food, the Corn and Navigation Laws were suspended until November. Many English members blamed the Irish landlords, but were unwilling to relieve Irish distress with Imperial funds. Peel, whose influence was still considerable, told the Prime Minister that he better turn to other work rather than draining the Irish bogs. Nevertheless, Peel helped to defeat a measure introduced by Lord George Bentinck, whereby £16,000,000 was to be advanced by the

State for the construction of Irish railways. A much lesser railway measure was passed, and also measures to facilitate emigration and temporary suspension of the corn laws. Despite the urgent need for relief, Peel remained a conservative, as back in 1817, he had dined and feasted with Orangemen when a Bill passed through Parliament cheapening and making it easier for the process of eviction.

At this time, Robbins described the distressingly high temperature of typhus patients, and how the doctors sought to cool them quickly. A Father Brady, parish priest of Bornacoola, Leitrim, recommended that 'the sick person be seated on a stool in the kitchen, that buckets of water be thrown over him and that he be dried and put back to bed'. Not surprising that a local paper reported that a few of Father Brady's patients died! In 1847, fever was prevalent in Leitrim to a 'fearful extent'. A Fermanagh newspaper reported a similar situation in Lisnaskea. The death rate was so high that in some counties Catholics and Protestants were being buried together in mass graves. At the public kitchen associated with the Enniskillen workhouse, in June the 'stirabout' was being made with water from a cesspool.

The winter of 1846–47 was the coldest that anyone could remember. Mortality rates were highest in south Ulster, west Munster and especially Connaught, areas inhabited by petty subsistence farmers, cottiers and labourers who often lived far away from relief centres, and who had little money to buy food even when available. There were ragged bands of starving families marching on the poor houses demanding to be admitted. In January 1847 Lord John Russell explained the government's plans for relieving the distress in Ireland, involving giving employment and wages to the suffering Irish and bringing forward a poor law. However, evictions increased alarmingly: from 1845 to 1847 there were 3,000; from 1847 to 1849, 25,700; and from 1849 to 1852, 58,423. These figures hid the desperation of the famine victims to hold on to their land and homes, as recorded by the Poor Law Commission Report of 1847:

> 'The class of poor and destitute occupiers, who are debarred by law (from poor law relief) unless they give up their land, struggle, notwithstanding their great privations, to retain it; and endeavour by every effort to pass through the seasons of difficulty by which they see a prospect of their former mode of subsistence returning, provided they continue in the possession of their land. The use for a long time of inferior food has in such cases sometimes induced disease fatal to the occupier himself, or one or more of his family.'

The disaster that was unfolding in Ireland was even beginning to permeate the royal conscience with Queen Victoria recording that the sufferings of the peasants were 'really too terrible to think of'. She noted the hopelessness of the situation: '... in the midst of all this, the Landlords appropriate the people's corn! after all we have done to supply the needy with food! God alone can bring help, for no human means seem able!' Burials were taking place to save the expense without clergy or coffins. The return of cholera and typhus and other similar diseases were no longer deemed a 'visitation of God'.

The Queen soon found that the starving Irish were turning to 'human means' for salvation of which she could not approve. What she called the 'insubordination of the poor' began to loom larger in her mind than the 'mismanagement among the higher classes', though in deference to Irish feelings she rationed the Palace bread to one pound per head. Some landlords provided soup kitchens but some only available for Protestants. At last due to the Irish Famine and the 'Andover scandal', the poor laws began to be humanised. However sympathies turned with the murder of Irish landlords and demonstrations by 'Young Ireland' towards the end of 1847.

In the 1847 Election, Feargus O'Connor was elected, and was still a force to be reckoned with. The Peelite numbers were reduced by half. The Dissenters failed to get their MPs elected, but the Ten Hours Act was passed which helped to persuade the working classes that their views were beginning to be taken seriously. The notorious 'Gregory Clause' in the Poor Law Extension Act denied relief to anyone farming more than a quarter of an acre, which meant that such people had to abandon their homes if they accepted aid. There were horrible stories of starving dogs and cats eating babies. The £4 Clause made the landlord responsible for the landholding tax on any holding valued less than £4. This led to landlords evicting tenants/cottiers, but in the long term the landlords were weakened by lack of rents and 'strong farmers' were the beneficiaries. In September Russell's government sent 16,000 extra troops to Ireland to maintain martial law in many troubled areas, signally the failure of the government's relief measures.

During 1847 John Stuart Mill published his 'Principles of Political Economy' which was due to become a set book on economics. It was characteristic of the author that he arranged for a cheap edition without royalties in order to bring the book as much as possible within reach of the purses of working men. That such a dry writer should have been so widely read is a testimonial to the seriousness of his age. Mill was well in advance of his times in advocating female suffrage in his book 'The Subjection of Women'. During his brief parliamentary career, he introduced an amendment to the second reform bill in favour of Women Suffrage. However in Ireland such reading was far from their immediate concerns. John Bright continued to plead the cause of Ireland in the House of Commons with arguments now familiar but then rare in the extreme:

> 'If Ireland has been rightly governed, if it has been wise and just to maintain the
> Protestant Church established there, you ought, in order to carry out your system,
> to establish Prelacy in Scotland and Catholicism in England; though if you were
> to attempt to do either the one or the other it would not be a sham but a real

insurrection you would provoke. Driven by poverty, Irishmen emigrate in great numbers, and in whatever quarter of the world an Irishman sets his foot, there stands a bitter, an implacable enemy of England. That is one of the results of the wide spread disaffection that exists in Ireland...But take all the lives that have been lost in the last twelve months in Europe amidst the convulsions that have occurred, take all the cessation of trade, the destruction of industry, all the crushing of hopes and hearts, and they will not compare for an instant with the agonies which have been endured by the population of Ireland under your glorious constitution. We must retrace our steps – we must shun the blunders, and I would even say, the crimes of our past legislation. We must free the land; and then we shall discover, and not till then, that industry hopeful and remunerated, industry free and inviolate, is the sure foundation on which can be reared the enduring edifice of union and peace.'

On the 5 April 1847, Clement Mason aged 51 (the future husband of Isabella Lawrence) and his son Thomas aged 23, were convicted of larceny at Durham assizes, and both were imprisoned for 3 months. The penalty was relatively small when compared to the sentence of 7 years imprisonment for larceny given to a John Howe in 1816. Larceny, then under English Common Law, was the act of wrongful removal of personal property from another person, that is theft. The fact that the charge was not given as 'simple larceny' might have meant that the act of theft included some violence. It was also relevant to note that the act was not described as a 'felony', a more serious crime, however the lesser term 'misdemeanour' was not used. Even a short time would have been unpleasant in overcrowded prisons of those times. Minor offenders were often put with hardened criminals awaiting transportation. Prisons were rife with debauchery, riotous quarrelling and gambling. Unlimited quantities of alcohol and women were made available.

At this time there were tensions at collieries between the arriving Irish and the indigenous workers, with large scale disturbances reported in the British local papers. Nevertheless there was little history of general animosity towards the Irish Catholics. However in Durham, the Berry Edge Riot of 1847 near Consett necessitated the stationing of troops over a four day period. Many men were arrested and charged with riot; of the 195 men sent for trial, none were jailed, but ten were bound over to keep the peace for £20 each. Clement Mason may have taken part in this riot.

A story has passed down the author's family that James Shannon fell out with the Irish and the Catholic Church at an early age. This may have happened following the 1844 strike, when Lord Londonderry brought in many workers from his estates in Ireland as strike-breakers, which would have bred bitter resentment towards the Irish.

In June 1847 the first Communist League conference took place in London, and Marx and Engels began drafting their Communist Manifesto. The basis of their projected revolution was the theory of progressive pauperisation of the working class under capitalism. Shortly Marx and his family would be ordered out of Belgium. Marx's wife, Jenny, was arrested for vagrancy and locked up with prostitutes. Inspired by Engel's Irish mistress, Eleanor the daughter of Marx was later to show great enthusiasm for the Irish freedom fighters.

The Irish old order was about to disappear. Daniel O'Connell's last address to Parliament was on the question of the Destitute Persons (Ireland) Bill; he pleaded that if this bill was not passed, then Parliament would be responsible for the loss of twenty-five percent of the population of Ireland. He then left for Rome, the metropolis of the church of which he had been so loyal and devoted a champion. However he was never to see Rome as his illness suddenly became worse. His heart travelled on to Rome and his body was carried back to Ireland for burial where the bells of all the RC chapels rang out. His memory remained despised by the Protestants who had ridiculed him as the 'big beggarman', and in England his services to the emancipation of the Roman Catholics were respected by few compared to the appreciation abroad.

A Peter Gallagher was recorded in 1851 working as a labourer in the iron works at Berry Edge, and a Patrick Shannon as a blacksmith. Also, a Mary Shannon aged 20, was living at Berry Edge employed as a house servant. The census gave her born in Ireland. This could have been the same person who had acted as a witness at the Brooms marriage in 1845. Could she also have been Philip Shannon's daughter, Mary, born at Lochmaben in 1828? There was no record of her at Newcastle in the 1841 census. The Brooms chapel had opened in 1802; the Catholics were previously served by a private chapel owned by the Swinburnes, a long established Catholic family.

At this time Great Britain was considered the "workshop of the world", with the country mining over half the world's output of coal. At the height of 'railway mania' in 1847, there were over a quarter of a million engaged in railway construction. One year later Britain was producing half the pig-iron in the world due to the demands of shipbuilding. George Stephenson the pioneering railway engineer, died in 1848. At the bottom of Westgate Road near Newcastle Railway Station, a monument was erected to Stephenson in 1862, and around the base were the figures of a miner, engineer, navvy and smith. The first piles to the High Level (Railway) Bridge, which his son Robert Stephenson designed, were sunk in 1846 using Nasmyth's Titanic steam hammer; this bridge, first proposed by Hudson, was completed in 1849 as one of the wonders of the Railway Age. Almost 5,000 tons of cast and wrought iron were supplied by Hawks, Crawshaw and Company of Gateshead and Losh, Wilson and Bell of Walker. 1848 saw the end of the railway gauge debate; some said that Stephenson's dour and conservative approach won out against Brunel's flare.

In 1847, Monkwearmouth Colliery, formerly owned by Richard Pemberton, was taken over by Messrs. Bell, Stobard and Fenwick. This colliery was to develop into one of the largest in the country. Not far away at the colliery village of Usworth, the Lawrence's second child, John, was born on the 28 August, seventeen months after their first child. His father was still a labourer. Isabella was the first of the Shannon family, and not the last, to venture south across the Tyne in search of better prospects.

On the 24 February 1848, the French king, Louis Phillipe, abdicated as France once more was in revolution, with two thousand killed and thousands more killed subsequently. His successor, Napoleon III was nephew of the great Napoleon, and had been a special constable in England during the Chartist rising of 1842 (as was Brunel). This event gave rise to expectations especially in Ireland that the overthrow of the English government was possible. Amongst the Chartists who were still numerous in the working classes, was the hope that this would provide the opportunity they yearned for. The turmoil which ensued on mainland Europe was to give Britain a competitive edge in world markets.

Britain's legislation did not have the French 'Right to Work', and England's unemployment remained high during the late 1840s. It is worthy of note that in revolutionary France, the Code Napoleon enforced employers' liability for accidents, whereas in Britain there was no compensation for fatalities and only a common law claim for injuries only when the victim could prove negligence on the part of the employer, who was likely to have been a small contractor with little means of paying. Although Edwin Chadwick championed the navvies' cause, workmen's compensation was not introduced until the last years of the century. In 1848, Murton Colliery suffered its first major disaster when a lighted candle ignited a fire-damp blower with the loss of 14 men and boys.

A huge Chartist demonstration took place on the 10 April 1848 based on the Charter and including an article for the re-establishment of the Irish parliament. There was a considerable Irish element among the Chartists, and during the whole of June, new confederate clubs, composed entirely of Irishmen, were being formed, and members being enrolled. Thus Bernard McNulty, writing from the Felon Repeal Club Room, at the Corn Market in Newcastle upon Tyne, announced that one hundred and twenty-four members had enrolled in about twenty minutes. McNulty was described as 'sturdy, large-hearted son of the northern province of Ireland, and one of the best types of Irish in Britain who by working his way by sheer force of ability and integrity had entered the front rank of life in the town of his adoption'. He had been born in 1820 in County Tyrone; when Chartist hopes subsided he emigrated to the United States.

The revolutionary fever hit Ireland in 1848, with Fenians being tried and convicted of treason and sentenced to death, later commuted to exile in Van Diemen's Land, as with 'Young Ireland' leaders O'Brien, Meagher and Mitchel. O' Brien's aid-de-camp, twenty-four-year-old James Stephens, a civil engineer, was wounded but managed to escape to France. A Papal decision to re-establish Roman Catholic dioceses in England produced sharp and hostile reactions from Protestants. It was at this time that the Irish Tricolour of Green, White and Orange emerged. It was modelled on the French flag, but to Meagher's design, and put together by the daughters of '98 exiles and women descendants of the 'Wild Geese'. In the Irish rising of 1848, the starving population was in no fit state to take up arms, thus it failed as their heros had failed in 1798. Before sentencing, Fenian Thomas Francis Meagher made the following statement mainly for Irish consumption:

> 'My Lord, this our first offense, but
> Not our last. If you will be easy with us
> This once, we promise, on our word as
> gentlemen, to try better next time … sure
> we won't be fools to get caught'

A few Irish landlords such as the Seymours and the Marquess of Sligo were sensitive to their tenants' distress and borrowed to pay the poor rate, but when Lord Clarendon applied for a Treasury loan to meet the new emergency of the 1848 blight, Lord John Russell replied negatively giving 'the reason being rage against Ireland on account of its faction, its mendicancy, its ingratitude'. The Phoenix, a symbol of Fenianism, rose from the pyre of the 1848 French insurrection. O'Brien became determined to establish a republic of Ireland.

The emergence of socialism was often associated with this time, even though the word 'socialism' was coined as far back as 1827. By 1848, socialism was closely identified with Owenism, so much so, that when Marx and Engels were drawing up their Manifesto, they were obliged to call it 'Communist' rather than 'Socialist'. In the 1820s, Owenism was a largely middle-class movement, but by the end of that decade it was more involved in working class unions and helped the opening up hundreds of co-op stores. After 1835, the Owenists and 'Guardian' Radicals led by O'Brien, split on the issue of national ownership of land. During May 1848 Gladstone was careful to clear himself from any associations with 'socialism', which may have arisen from his rescue of the coal whippers employment arrangements in 1843.

Christian Socialism based on the teachings of Jesus, love and co-operation, was born in this year of revolution. These socialists considered the cause of inequality to be associated with capitalist greed. Marx's Communist Manifesto just published was to create revolutionary ripples across Europe. William Morris was to be deeply affected by both Carlyle and Marx. Those who considered themselves 'native Irish' as opposed to their 'alien oppressors', identified the three major characteristics as language, religion and 'rightful' title to the soil. James Fintan Lalor recognised that his people's helplessness was due to both political and economic causes, and advocated a social revolution to destroy 'landlordism' and redistribute Irish land. Lalor demanded 'Ireland her own, from the sod to the sky'.

Of the eight baronies in Fermanagh, that of Magheraboy (which ran from Enniskillen towards the west and took in villages Derrygonnelly, Grisson and Belcoo) was worst affected by the Famine losing 31% of its population. The barony of Lurg (which included villages Kesh, Ederney and Lack) declined by 27%. Tirkennedy (which included the Enniskillen and Tempo) only declined by 13%.

The Catholic Church blamed the famine on the people themselves for their own sinfulness. In the same vein, the Times newspaper openly embraced the effects of the Irish Famine which they said would prove to be a 'great blessing', advocating replacement of impecunious tenants with 'thrifty Scotch and scientific English farmers'. Also following enactment of the Gregory clause, the Times enthused 'In a few years more, a Celtis Irishman will be as rare in Connemara as is a Rd Indian on the shoes of Manhattan'. However, many said: 'God sent the blight, but the English made the Famine'.

The long-lasting effect of the Great Famine were the memories left by the emigrant population who travelled by 'coffin ships' to America. A descendant in Canada erected a monument with the following inscription:

> 'Thousands of the children of the Gael were lost on this island while fleeing from foreign tyrannical laws and an artificial famine in the years 1847–8. God bless them. God save Ireland.'

CHAPTER 9

1849–1853 The Great Exhibition after the Great Hunger

(Death of John Lawrence and Philip Shannon, Isabella Lawrence marries Clement Mason)

'These are the Sappers and Miners who ran
To test the girders on Paxton's plan;
And helped the Workmen, that busy array -
Two thousand and more as I have heard say,
Who readily, steadily, toiled away,
And finished before the first of May
The Crystal Palace that Fox Built'

(This is the House that Jack built – parody by David Bogue 1851)

The seeds of the Great Exhibition or 'Peace Festival of Industry' were beginning to germinate when Prince Albert started to show publicly his great interest and admiration for the engineering achievements in his adopted country. In 1849 he opened the Albert Dock in Liverpool, which not many years before had been the harrowing scene of famine ravished people arriving from Ireland. There were a number of ports which dealt with emigration, and North America was the main destination.

The passenger lists for departures from Liverpool and Belfast included a few Shannons, Shenans and Gallaghers (with their occupations):

[Vessel] Yorkshire	1 April 1847 from Liverpool
Jas Shannon	27 M Labourer
Thomas Shenan	27 M Unknown
[Vessel] Rosa-Linda	20 May 1848 from Belfast
Philip Shannon	46 M Farmer
Elizabeth	10 F Unknown
Isabella	13 F Unknown
[Vessel] W.M.Vail	29 June 1848 from Liverpool
Thomas Shannon	35 M Farmer
Margaret	32 F (wife)
Bridget	08 F child

Peter   06 M child
Michael Gallagher   30 M Labourer
[Vessel] Montezuma 12 April 1849 from Liverpool
Peter Shannon   37 M Labourer

Although about 85% of emigrants to the US were labourers and servants, the continuing potato blight made many small farmers give up hope of Ireland ever recovering and accepted that emigration was their only resort. They were escaping from the threat of pauperism rather than starvation. For those of hardly any means, the Gaelic poor and elderly, headed for the cattle boats and coal barges to the British mainland. For some there was no escape; many Irish people were dying from starvation in Ireland or dying from fevers in England.

The previous year had seen the start of another cholera epidemic, but it came back with a vengeance in 1849. In the Belfast Union, cholera had already caused seven deaths, with 71 inmates affected and 9886 persons on out-door relief. Cholera was also reported in Athlone, Monaghan and Longford. A cure for the disease was given in the local paper: teaspoon of the tincture of rhubarb and 16/18 drops of laudanum mixed with a tablespoon of water. At the Woodhead Tunnel in Derbyshire where navvies were suffering from vomiting, cramp, collapse, shrivelling of the fingers, sinking of the eyes and rice-water evacuations, the doctor was prescribing hot coffee and brandy. In 1849, Elizabeth Blackwell became the first woman to qualify as a doctor; perhaps the desperate situation

Emigrating passengers 1850
(charter.net)

forced the medical authorities to liberalise their entry requirements as later with Florence Nightingale.

One year after the latest French Revolution, the Shannon family was again hit by tragedy. On the tenth of June 1849, step-father John Lawrence died at Trimdon Grange Colliery. The death certificate gave the informant as his widow Isabella Lawrence present at the death, and recorded the cause of death as "typhus fever 17 days". It is possible that the cause of death was cholera, as with Peter Shannon twelve years previously. Conditions in colliery villages were little better than the Newcastle tenements.

The Shannon family were again deprived of their head and main breadwinner. The household now included Isabella and the two recent 'Lawrence' children; James Shannon, the only survivor of her first marriage, at fifteen years was probably working at a coal pit, and lodging nearby. Sinking at Shincliffe or Old Durham Colliery had just started, so James could have already moved southwards with the Lawrences. If she had survived, Helen would have been fourteen and still living at home looking after the 'Lawrence' children.

Trimdon Colliery had a history of pit shaft deaths. In 1846, two colliers William Wilson and Henry Wind, both 24, died when the shaft rope broke sending them to the bottom of the shaft. Another sinker, F. Barker, died in a shaft accident leaving a wife and four children. About four years later, sinker Matthew Oliver, was killed when the shaft rope broke. Until hessian ropes were replaced by wire ropes (resisted by the miners), this type of tragedy often took place.

In 1854 James Shannon was to marry Lydia Calvert. About 3 weeks after the death of John Lawrence, Lydia's father Alexander Calvert died at West Howle near Ferryhill, seven miles from Trimdon. The death certificate recorded Alexander's occupation as a Pitman, and at 51 years, he would have been still working up to his heart attack. The informant was Hannah Calvert who came from Muker in Yorkshire, the original home of the Calverts.

Victorians cared passionately about religion, and the moment of passing from this world to the next was not to be hushed up. However Prince Albert, known for his 'gloomy morality', was to advise his wife Victoria in 1846 that they should show their religion by leading moral lives rather than 'slavishly attending services in Church'. The working classes always tried to ensure that there was some money for a 'decent' burial, by paying into burial clubs. However in populous areas, it was common to keep the body in the crowded tenements a long time before burial, which was carried out close-by. Irish custom required whatever the cause of death, that the body was not buried until sufficient sums had been collected to pay for the wake. In 1817, a woman held no less than three wakes for her daughter, and before the funeral 'a fever got into the house and there were six buried and eighteen or twenty ill'. The first benefits of trade unions and friendly societies were funeral expenses.

Engels describing the starving and desperate city workers, recorded that 'they were irreligious for the same reason that they were illiterate, because they were denied education other than the futile attempts of the Church to inculcate the incomprehensible dogmas of conventional religion'. For many workers like factory workers and miners, any free time on a Sunday was spent sleeping after their exhausting labours during the week. Misery and misfortune was loosening the faith of illiterate workers. Even Gladstone brought up in the established church, and under the early influence of Newman who had rejected Locke's theory of toleration, admitted in 1839 that 'the land was overspread with a thick curtain of prejudice'. However at this time he considered any extension of representative principles to be irreligious.

In 1849, a pamphlet was published with the title 'On the Mode of Communication of Cholera'. Its author, Dr John Snow, suggested that the infection from the sick could be transmitted to food and that it might also be carried by water. He was born in a poor area of York, where his father worked in a local coal yard. Snow became an apprentice surgeon at Newcastle in 1831, and later was appointed assistant surgeon at Burnhopfield Colliery in Durham. Snow went on to making improvements in the administration of chloroform as an anaesthetic. Thomas Rammell, Government Health Inspector for South Durham, was to report in late 1852 the alarming death rate – 'mortality at the enormous rate of 28.6 in 1000' and deaths of children under five at 43% of the total number. The main cause was identified as 'The public drains ...very limited in extent and rudely constructed'. Lodging houses came in for special criticism, the Irish houses being the worst. There were many cases of typhus fever and cholera, especially in the colliery village of Crook.

Marx arrived in London penniless during August 1849 as Queen Victoria and Prince Albert made their first royal visit to Ireland, despite there being cholera in Dublin. Three months earlier the Queen was shot by a 'mad Irishman', the fourth attempt on her life. Other deaths in 1849 included Queen Adelaide widow of William IV, and Sir Robert Peel who was thrown from his horse.

The Shannon family in Newcastle were also in mourning. Philip Shannon had died at the good age of 77 years, on the 13 August 1849 at Rosemary Lane, in St John's parish. Philip's death certificate gave the cause of death as 'Asthma several years Dropsy 3 months Certified' (similar to cause of King William IV's death), and the informant present at the time of death was Isabella Macanally (a surname from Donegal). It would appear that Philip and his wife Ann had remained in Newcastle since arriving

from Scotland nearly twenty years before. Ralph Reed's daughter Ann had been born at Rosemary Lane in 1844. The Shannons and Reeds were probably neighbours.

In those days of hardship and poverty, to reach the age of 'three score year and ten', was quite an achievement. It was only in Philip's latter years that he had to suffer the filthy urban conditions without the relief of country fresh air and water. The fact that he and his wife survived the 1832 cholera epidemic and subsequent fevers was probably due more to good fortune. Politician John Bright was later to comment on 'the people of the north being a more sturdier race' [as compared to those from the south of Ireland].

The Griffiths Valuation carried out in Ireland 1848–64, recorded a Philip Shannon living in the parish of Derryvullan near Enniskillen. Not far away at Doon in the parish of Kinawley, a Patrick Kellegher was recorded.

Charles Kingsley, a Christian Socialist, in his novel 'Two Years Ago' described the cholera epidemic in 1849. Thomas Carlyle in his writings Past and Present, had castigated the short-sightedness of the authorities in dealing with a case of typhus in Scotland: 'A poor Irish widow – her husband having died in one of the lanes of Edinburgh – went forth with her three children, bare of all resource, to solicit help from the charitable establishments of that city. At this establishment .. she was refused, referred from one to the other, helped by none, till she had exhausted them all, till her strength and heart failed her. She sank down in typhus fever, died and infected her lane with fever, so that 'seventeen other persons' died of fever therein in consequence.'

The 'Great Famine' was at last showing signs of subsiding, with the year's potato crop showing little evidence of blight. Thomas Carlyle on his tour of Ireland accompanied by Charles Gavan Duffy, founder of the newspaper 'Nation', was to describe a country devastated by the worst human disaster in the century. Patrick Bronte in 1849, reflecting on the death of his children, bemoaned the fact that "consumption has taken the whole five", with Charlotte Bronte the only surviving child at that time. For the Lambton family, the 'Consumption Worm' could not be defeated. It was responsible for the early deaths of Radical Jack's first wife, his son and three daughters. 1849 also marked the second outbreak of English cholera. First impressions were that the poor people had been affected worst with 3,489 deaths of working men compared with 558 tradesmen deaths, and 135 gentlemen deaths; but Fraser's Magazine drew attention to the proportional death statistics – 1 in 120 working men, 1 in 150 tradesmen, and 1 in 200 gentlemen. The Economist warned that there was no justification for further centralisation of power in the form of an expanded Board of Health, a measure that could only play into the hands of 'Chartists, red republicans, and socialists'!

Bright also visited Ireland in 1849, and afterwards drew up the Tenant's Rights Bill. Russell's government, learning from the famine, hoped to stimulate capital investment in Irish land. In July 1849 the Encumbered Estates Act was passed which allowed owners and creditors to dispose of their property much more easily. However, the Act swept away the personal knowledge possessed by the old landlords of the improvements made by the more diligent and enterprising tenants. This resulted in the re-emergence of Whiteboyism, or under its new name, Ribbonism, an organisation committed to fight the Capitalist landlordism, and also by parliamentary agitation to obtain for rented land the 'Three F's': fixity of tenure, at a fair rent, with freedom of sale for his own improvements.

Massive construction projects had been in progress in Newcastle. During the previous two decades Newcastle had seen great changes as its streets and buildings started to reflect its commercial prosperity. Overlooking St John's Church, Central Station was opened in August 1850 by Queen Victoria. There had been great celebrations on the 6 October 1849 at the opening of the High Level Bridge over the Tyne also by Queen Victoria. The station was designed by Newcastle architect John Dobson, and was a magnificent demonstration of the might of the railway revolution, with its two miles of platforms and outstanding ironwork. The bridge was the brainchild of the famous civil engineer, Robert Stephenson, and was integral with the re-development of the railway station.

During the construction, a large number of buildings on each side of the Tyne had to be cleared, including some very old structures in the vicinity of the old castle. Stephenson at the opening dinner, recalled his beginnings as an assistant engineer on the Stockton and Darlington Railway. He held up the rapid development of the railways as bearing testimony to the indomitable enterprise of the nation. His father would have spoken of the contribution to this achievement by the navvies using only the pick, shovel and horse power; it was only after 1887 when steam excavators began to be used in Britain.

In 1849, Carlyle's 'The Nigger Question', was published to controversy, and in 1850, 'the Latter Day Pamphlets' – both repudiations of liberalism and utilitarianism. His hysterical outcries at the nomadic wanderings of the Irish emigrants demanded a complete change of approach by the Government. (It is unlikely his personal experience of his Irish servant's drunken ways made him bracket all Irish in the same way). America was beginning its self-analysis of the 'negro issue', with the compromise Fugitive Slave Act coming into law, and four years later the Kansas-Nevaska Act. Britain was bullying Greece over the Don Pacifico affair, which caused a diplomatic incident with Russia and France. During the period 1846 to 1854, Bright had been advocating working class enfranchisement, a cause which Carlyle considered a diversion from man's central need, the focus on spiritual principles.

In 1850, Gavan Duffy through his Irish newspaper, 'The Nation', was able to galvanise both Protestants and Catholics in support of a Tenants' Right League. Even the Fermanagh Mail, a Protestant newspaper in a strong Orange area, acclaimed the movement without reservations. This happy co-operation was to end in betrayal, when a former leader of the Catholic Defence Association and 'The Pope's Brass Band', William Keogh, accepted the position of Solicitor-General for Ireland, and the Tenants' Rights Bills were to die in committee in 1852.

After Peel's death in 1850, the Earl of Aberdeen became leader of the Peelites; most Conservatives supported free trade; these included Gladstone, Palmerston, Russell and Edward Cardwell. This time was to see a change in the character of Chartism, when the left-wing of the movement, headed first by Julian Harney and later by Ernest Jones, captured the National Charter Association. They remodelled Chartism as an avowedly socialist party, intensely class conscious and linked by ties of friendship with Continental revolutionaries exiled in England. They adopted an explicit 'declaration of social rights', calling for among other things, the nationalisation of land, mines and fisheries, the extension of state credit to all, and humane provision for the destitute. The country at large was moving towards trades unionism and co-operative movements, and collaboration with the middle classes in politics. The North-East was one of the areas where Chartism showed its greatest staying power.

In November 1850, the Roscommon & Leitrim Gazette reported that the Shannon-Erne Canal was progressing and due to open the following September. There were 800 labourers and 70/80 tradesmen employed daily. Two years later the first steam boat made an appearance on the Shannon Navigation to Lough Allen with the possibility of use by the local mines. In Newcastle upon Tyne, a riot took place at Sandgate between the 'Connoughtmen' Irish and the Northumbrians over a 'No-Popery' sermon. However, one year later there was little support for an Orange procession even though an offer of relief for Irish paupers was based on changing religious faith and education. The Nonconformists were unwilling to follow the Church's anti-Catholic stance.

At this time, the boom in English Catholicism contrasted with the chapels and churches of the established religion only attracting one out of ten of the population. A Catholic school had just opened at South Shields. Newman, a former Anglican theologian, had a few years earlier joined the Catholic Church, and in 1851 Manning and Hope followed suit. Manning eventually rose to be a cardinal. Gladstone was greatly distressed by these defections, but it had a tolerating influence on his future position, knowing that his own episcopal church in Scotland was dissenting. The Government was shown to be equally divided when the No Popery Bill encouraged negotiations to form a coalition government to be broken off. There was fierce anti-Catholic backlash against the so-called Papal

Aggression of 1850, when the Pope Pius IX restored the hierarchy of the Catholic Church in England and Wales.

Ten months after the death of her second husband John Lawrence, Isabella married widower Clement Mason at the parish church of Trimdon, on the 30 March 1850. The marriage certificate now gave the occupation of Isabella's father as quarryman, presumably still alive in Ireland (previously a plasterer). Clement's father, John Mason, a collier, was given as 'deceased', and Clement signed the certificate with his mark.

Clement was working as a collier at Trimdon Grange Colliery (sunk in 1845) at the time of his marriage. Isabella was still living in Trimdon following her recent widowhood. This may have been the start of a break from the Catholic Church for the Shannons. After Clement had been released from prison only nine months earlier, he would have read in the local newspapers of gold diggings just started in Australia; they would have contained adverts for passages, but meeting Isabella changed his options. Isabella's prospects with two young children would seem to have improved, provided Clement's criminal record was a thing of the past!

Clement Mason's first marriage had taken place at Lamesley near Chester-le-Street back in 1821 to Margaret Armstrong Reed. The marriage of master sinker Matthew Coulson in late 1820 was recorded in the Lamesley marriage register just before that of Clement Mason. This may have been the first connection of Clement with the Coulson sinkers. Clement went on to marry Isabella Young in 1840 at Low Downs Hetton. (Clement's son, Clement, married Anne Young in 1848 at Castle Eden). Clement Mason was to be Isabella Shannon's third husband, but Isabella was not his last wife! Clement's earlier marriages were recorded in Quaker registers.

On the occasion of Guy Fawkes Night, an especially sensitive date during these times, Russell referred to the 'Pope's aggression' as insolent and insidious. This was to cause an uproar in the country similar to the Gordon Riots. Bright supported by Gladstone sternly rebuked Russell on his inflammatory pronouncement. Gladstone said that this would offend and indict eight millions of his own countrymen, recklessly create fresh discords between the Irish and English nations, and perpetuate animosities that the last five and twenty years had done so much to assuage. Even the Times 'blew up the coals', describing Russell's position as humbug and a pack of nonsense.

Later Gladstone called for religious liberty, and advocated that the country's Roman Catholics should be treated as brethren to gain their affections. Despite the efforts of Gladstone of the Established Church, and Bright a nonconformist, an anti-Catholic bill was passed, but it was to remain a dead letter until it was abolished by Gladstone's government in 1871. The old Catholics liked a quiet and gentlemanly religion, and were somewhat disturbed by the attention which the new elements in their Church were devoting to popular authoritarianism for Irish labourers, and to the drama and opulence of new churches for middle class converts.

A teacher of science in 1850 recorded that 'The toiling mining population of Durham and Northumberland proceed over the hills in rain, sleet, and frost, that they may learn the great truths which civilisation has made manifest'. The early 1850s was a relatively prosperous time with bread in plenty – the effect of the removal of the Corn Laws, but conditions underground had not improved despite the high expectations after the 1842 Report. However due to the series of colliery explosions since the report, public opinion was now firmly against the mine owners and for genuinely active legislation. This resulted in a further bill gaining Royal Assent on the 14 August 1850, requiring registration of plans, the notification of facilities, and appointing of inspectors of mines with power to enforce the Act by legal proceedings. Nevertheless, in Inspector Tremehere's Report of 1851, he admitted that the Act had been deliberately flouted, with small boys still being taken down pits in Northumberland and Durham and working shifts of twelve to fourteen hours. In 1852 he was reporting the deaths of under-age boys in explosions, and added that the truth about their ages had emerged only because inspectors had attended inquests.

Newcastle in 1850 was the world's largest shipbuilding and repair yard. Ralph Reed, a Ship's Carpenter, at Westgate, St Johns, died on the 21 August. Ralph had died of consumption, 8 months certified. Jane Mason was the informant, present at death, who lived at Pudding Chare, St Johns (In 1861, a Jane Mason was the wife of a Husbandman, Thomas Mason, living in Westgate). There was a record in 1852 of a Catherine Reed who was imprisoned for 9 months on a charge of larceny or theft. After her husband's death nearly two years earlier, she may have fallen on hard times; she was recorded as a Shopkeeper in the 1851 census.

Following the formation of the National Association of Trades in 1845, remarkable progress was made in 1850 with the amalgamation of trade unions under the name of 'The Amalgamated Society of Engineers, Machinists, Millwrights, Smiths, and Pattern-makers' leading to the Trades Union Act. The expansion of coal mines in Britain was gaining pace. Ayrshire had then nearly eighty collieries, and in Lanarkshire, Irishmen occasionally had their introduction to the mines as substitutes for strikers.

Children were also at risk above ground. Gladstone's daughter Jessy died of meningitis and convulsions on the 2 April 1850. The assassination attempt on Queen Victoria's life on the 22 May was laid at the door of Marx, but this assertion was not convincing when during the previous seven years there had been seven assassination attempts. In the

Trollope family, from April 1850 up to 1851, there were many deaths from tuberculosis. It seemed that the well-off as well as the poor were suffering.

Isabella Mason was recorded head of the household and 'Housekeeper' in the 1851 census at Longbenton in Newcastle, with her children John and Ann Lawrence (spelt as Lorence); living with them a spinster Elenor Burn aged 34 years. Isabella's birthplace was given as Ireland. Another interesting point was that the family was now living at 70 Gosport Row, Longbenton (a district of Walker) in Newcastle, perhaps showing that in times of family distress, Isabella had decided to live closer to her mother-in-law, Ann Shannon.

Strangely, Clement Mason was recorded in the same census as lodging (away from his wife) at 120 Gosport Row, with the family headed by his son Clement. Both Clements were given the occupation of 'Coal Miner Hewer'. Clement's sons John (eldest) and Thomas, were also working as a hewers at Longbenton. It seemed at this time that Longbenton was attracting many miners from Durham. Families of Masons were already long established in the Newcastle area; one had lived close to George Stephenson in 1803.

Isabella's daughter Hellen has not been found in the 1851 census; also son James was not found, whether as Shannon, Lawrence or Mason. At the age of seventeen, James was probably working as a hewer in south Durham, as described in the following verse:

> 'The bonnie pit laddie
> The canny pit laddie
> The bonnie pit laddie for me O
> He sits on his cracket
> And hews in his jacket
> And brings the bright silver to me O'

In the absence of documentary evidence, it could be assumed that Ann Shannon was still living in the same area of Newcastle ten years after the 1841 census. It is likely that James's grandmother were living on her own and close to her son Richard. A clue to her likely circumstances was given in Disraeli's book Sybil when the Irish washerwoman Mrs Carey, commented on the way young people treated their parents in the competitive environment of industrial towns, and were often abandoned:

> ''Tis the children gets the wages, ... and there it is.'

Richard Shannon was recorded in the 1851 census living in the St John's parish of Newcastle with his wife Jane, who at the age of 40 years was four years older. Her birthplace was given as Morpeth in Northumberland and his as Dumfries, Scotland. In the absence of other documentary evidence, Richard's birth date can be estimated as 1815. This suggested that the Shannons had settled in Scotland as soon as the Napoleonic Wars ended. His occupation was given as Railway Labourer; he could have worked as a navvy.

It should be noted that at the time of Richard Shannon's marriage in 1837, his occupation was given as a servant. However in those days, 'servant' described many occupations, and even a coachman would fall into that category of workman. Domestic service was still the largest area of occupation for women, and agriculture for men. Richard may have heard of new developments at strategic railheads like Lockerbie in 1847 without realising its previous connection with his family.

At this time in Pudding Chare, near Westgate, a labourer Peter Shannon aged 30 years, was a lodger. He may have been a relation to his namesake who had died in Newcastle fourteen years previously. Ten years later another Peter Shannon was found working as an Ironworks Labourer at Middlesborough.

A boost for the North East occurred in 1851, when vast deposits of iron ore were found on the seaward slopes of the Cleveland Hills. This was the start of the Middlesborough iron and steel industry , which attracted workers from all over the country, as the start of the deep coal mines further north had done a quarter of a century before. 1850 saw the completion of the Britannia Bridge designed and engineered by Robert Stephenson. This bridge was crucial to the railway route to Holyhead and Ireland. The locomotive 'Lord of the Isles' was constructed for the Great Western Railway and nicknamed 'Emperor of Russia' due to its enormous capacity for consumption of oil and tallow as shown at the Great Exhibition.

Railway companies took great pride in their trains, and when coals were first carried by railway on the London and Birmingham line, they were covered by sheets for fear they should be seen. When George Stephenson heard that a director of that line had said that 'They will want us to carry dung next', his anger was aroused and he replied – "You tell B---- from me, that when he travels by rail they will carry dung now". On the North Eastern and Great Northern lines, coal was carried in wagons most of which belonged to the companies; hence the uniformity of build and appearance. In other areas, coal owners or merchants were allowed to provide their own wagons leading to an endless variety of shape and size.

The Chadwick Report 1842 had confirmed that it was 'more unhealthy' to live in a town. The short-time working disguised the real wages of coal miners, iron puddlers and general labourers. Compared to other occupations, railway workers were paid very poorly. Their poor wages and long hours (12 hour day was standard), was considered to be compensated by having a 'job for life'. With royal approval, engineering was at the forefront of

Great Exhibition 1851
(London Museum)

industrial expansion, with the railways the prime mover. The first 'new model' trade union, the Amalgamated Society of Engineers (ASE), was formed in 1851. It was a quarter of a century since the first passenger line in 1825, and in 1851 there were 6,800 miles in operation and a railway labour force of 2,500. By 1852 a direct line had been opened up from London. The ASE was modelled on that of the Journeymen Steam Engine and Machine Maker's Society, the 'Old Mechanics'. There had been three periods of railway boom; 1824–25, 1836–37, and 1845–47. In 1836 thirty-five Railway Acts passed into law. The 'Railway King', George Hudson, in 1849 was at the peak of his £816M business, but inevitably the growth was unsustainable, and he fled abroad in 1855. Even in 1857, a Leopold Redpath of the Great Northern Railway was convicted of fraud and transported for life to Australia.

As far back as 1836, Whitehaven and Carlisle had been dominated by Irish incomers, and by 1851 the Whitehaven district alone contained 4,175 Irish settlers with 525 of those in the burgeoning iron-ore centre of Cleator and Cleator Moor. At this time Michael Davitt and family arrived in Lancashire. His mother had learned in Ireland that all her sons over 3 years old were to be separated from her in the poor house, and to avoid this she decided to travel to England. Michael worked in a cotton mill for six years, but his arm got caught in machinery and he had to have his arm amputated, receiving no compensation. He was lucky enough to be befriended by a local Chartist and obtained a good education which served him well as a prominent Fenian and IRB organiser in later life.

The Great Exhibition took place in Hyde Park in 1851 as the showpiece for the British Industrial Revolution. The North-East played its part in the exhibition with the provision of newly invented roll-plate glass from James Hartley's Wear Glassworks of South Shields. A former garden boy, Joseph Paxton was the designer of the famous cast-iron and glass structure. After a chance meeting with Robert Stephenson on a train in June 1850, Stephenson was persuaded to back Paxton's unusual design. In the autumn of 1850, Charles Fox, former assistant to Robert Stephenson, received the order for the erection of the Great Exhibition. Engineering was of special interest to Prince Albert, following the famous sixteenth century German mining engineer, Agricola. Some months earlier he had given a speech to the 'Society for the Improvement of the Conditions of the Labouring classes'. The Prince Consort was the driving force behind the exhibition, but met much resistance from Conservatives who expressed fears 'about bringing large numbers of the populace together'. The British Ambassador in Russia reported to Palmerston that the Tsar had refused passports to his nobility who were intending to visit the exhibition due to fear of 'contamination' from political agitators. The exhibition was intended to be a festival of work and peace. Samuel Smiles was a publicist of the mid-Victorian creed of 'self-help', and the Prince its impresario, planned to marry art with commerce. He praised the simple grandeur of engineering above the richness of architecture. However, a famous Punch cartoon at this time showed the contrast of the poverty in the country with the success of the exhibition.

William Morris refused to enter the exhibition revealing his early independent views on art and industry. Dickens was also uncomfortable about the exhibition as he contemplated his next novel, Bleak House, with its total abhorrence of England's social order. Ruskin fiercely attacked the whole structure of the nineteenth century England, an indictment of the brutalizing cycles of contemporary commerce. This was initially serialized in the Cornhill, Thackeray's popular monthly magazine, until then considered too inflammatory by the publishers. Shortly after the hugely successful exhibition, Queen Victoria and Prince Albert made a triumphal progress through the North of England. When the first 'Crystal Palace' had closed in October after only four months open to the public, a place was sought to relocate the exhibition and eventually a site was chosen in Kent. Following the running of many excursion trains to the Exhibition, these trains became increasingly common, and were used by working-class families to have a cheap day at the seaside.

The niece of the Rector of Beckenham, Frederick Chalmers, recounted how "early in the year 1853, a large number of Railway 'excavators', amounting at length to nearly three thousand, were gathered from different parts of the kingdom, to work at the grounds of the Crystal Palace at Sydenham", the second location for the exhibition. These major works also attracted labourers from the mining industry. The construction industry was still medieval in many of its practices, and little thought was given to the safety of its workforce. It was reported that a 'fearful accident befell a large number of the Crystal Palace workmen. Scaffolding gave way, and in its fall crushed out the strong young life from some of these manly forms in a moment.' A large number of navvies at Sydenham were later recruited by Paxton for the Army Works Corps to serve in the Crimea.

On the 2nd December 1851, Louis Napoleon's coup d'etat took place in Paris, and he was proclaimed Napoleon III, Emperor of France. The following day, Palmerston, without consulting anyone, intimated to the French Ambassador that he approved of Napoleon's action. This latest incident brought matters to a head when Prime Minister John Russell, urged on by the royal couple, dismissed Palmerston, despite the latter's powerful and popular reputation. Prince Albert was accused by all sections of the press as the person responsible for this supposedly traitorous act. (This press onslaught against Albert was to continue up to early 1854, when public attention turned to the Crimean War). The early weeks of the new year saw the disintegration of Russell's government. The Peelite rump preferred to stay with the Liberals rather than move over to the Conservatives.

Emigrant steamships started their service to North America, and within a decade would replace sail on the Atlantic crossing. However in Australia, an anti-transportation vote showed that Irishmen there were not under the same 'spell' as their countrymen back home. Fenian Meagher escaped to America in January 1852 (the year of the book Uncle Tom's Cabin), and Fenian Mitchel shortly after. The last ship from Britain sailed for Van Diemen's Land in May 1853. Evans noted that anti-Catholicism was on the increase reflecting the surge in Irish immigration, with priests apparently retaining a more effective hold over Catholic working men than Protestant clerics did over theirs. Russell's

Ecclesiastical Titles Act was an attempt to stem the flow of anti-Catholicism which had made traditional Bonfire Night celebrations literally inflammatory in 1850. Primitive Methodists traditionally strong in mining areas were endorsing the temperance ideal.

In English workplaces, quarrels and fights between English and Irish, Catholics and Protestants was still a frequent event. Engels although finding 'total indifference to religion', 'No Popery' was still a powerful issue, and in late 1852 two Catholic chapels in Stockport were ransacked and desecrated by a mob of working men. This hostility between English and Irish diverted their energies from ways of improving their common hardships, and this was often taken advantage of by unscrupulous employers. When Gladstone was protesting at the condition of Neapolitan prisons, King of Naples, Schwarzenberg, replied in kind by pointing to the English treatment of the Irish. An inquiry was set up in April 1852 to look into the 'organised torpor' of Oxford University, where protestant colleges had been subsisting on Roman Catholic endowments. This led to the Oxford University Reform bill of 1854. J S Mill explained the purpose of higher education:

> 'To rear up minds with aspirations and faculties above the herd, capable of leading on their countrymen to greater achievements in virtue, intelligence, and social well-being; to do this, and likewise so to educate the leisured classes of the community generally, that they may participate as far as possible in the qualities of these superior spirits, and be prepared to appreciate them, and to follow in their steps – these are purposes requiring institutions of education placed above dependence on the immediate pleasure of that multitude whom they are designed to educate. These are the ends for which endowed universities are desirable; they are those which all endowed universities profess to aim at; and great is their disgrace, if, having undertaken this task, and claiming credit for fulfilling it, they leave it unfulfilled.'

Parliament dissolved in July 1852 to decide on the great issue of the repeal of the Corn Laws. In the country at large it was accepted that these bad laws raised the price of bread to the toilers in order to raise the rent for territorial idlers. On the 14 September 1852 the Duke of Wellington died; at the same time the General Election took place. Forty Irish members were elected and pledged to Tenants' Right and Independent Opposition. These members included Gavan Duffy for New Ross and John Francis Maguire for Dungarvan. With Whigs and Tories of equal numbers, the Irish held the balance of power. In January 1853, John Bright was pressing Lord John Russell on a new reform bill. Stamp duty was abolished following the abolition of advertisement duty in 1853. Dickens obsessed by his childhood experiences, attacked Cruikshank for adapting old nursery tales for temperance propaganda purposes. He was turned off religion by boring church services.

The South Durham coalfield had started to open up in the early 1840s due to the new railway connection from Stockton in 1843, providing a wider market for the coal via the sea. A spate of chapel building and renovation for Methodists and Quakers followed. St Wilfrids Catholic church at Bishop Auckland was built in 1846; previously Roman Catholic services were held at Croxdale. Nearby, Ushaw College had been founded in 1808 by French scholars from Douai, who had fled the French Revolution. This area had a growing number of Irish arrivals, due to the mass influx of Irish since the famine of 1847. The centre of Bishop Auckland was described at this time to be dirty, overcrowded, disease-ridden and overpoweringly smelly, with both the poor and wealthy living in close proximity. The poorly resourced and poorly experienced police force of those times had a difficult task in coping with the disturbances, which were bound to erupt with a workforce of varying cultures, and inflamed by alcohol. The Irish families rarely occupied more than one room, with a staple diet of bread and boiled potatoes. The stones used in building the houses both for the rich and poor, came from the coal shafts.

Towards the end of 1853, James Shannon, probably known as James Lawrence, had arrived in the Bishop Auckland area. He may have already have been employed in sinking, and Clement Mason could have provided the contact with William Coulson, a master sinker who was working in the area. The Coulsons and Masons were long established sinker families. The 1852 Report on the Inspection of Coal Mines in South Durham and Northumberland included an account of a George Green that could well have described James Lawrence in 1850 (a Joseph Green was later a sinker friend of James who worked in Brazil):

'I am 16 years of age. I work in the Blackboy pit, near Bishop Auckland; I have worked in it five years. My father was dead when I first went to work. I went down first to drive the galloway; it did not tire me much; we sit on front of the waggon; it moves upon a railway. When we come up to the front of the shaft we take the horse out and yoke him at the other end, and go back to the flats, being the place to which the putters bring the coals; the putters push the carriages upon the rollers. I had 1s 3d a-day. The proprietors find the candles for the drivers; we light one, and stick it in a little box thing, and put the box on the rolley, it has a hook and it is stuck into the rolley. We use every day eight candles, of 30 to the pound. The trap boys open the doors for us; sometimes they fall asleep, and we baist them a little to make them mind their work, only to fear them a little. They know they are to blame, and they take it quietly. I get up at two in the morning, and take something to eat and drink before I go out; I take a coffee and a pie or anything, and eat it before going out. I generally make my own coffee. Pretty near three I set out, and walk two miles and a quarter to the pit, and I get to the pit in half an hour. Eight of us are lowered in the cage at once to the foot of the shaft; we get the horses ready, and start to our work at four. The horse keeper has them fed for us, and we yoke them ourselves, and go on to the flats. The stable is near the shaft, nearly a mile from the flats, and we are at the flats by four. The putters then put a tub of coals on the rolley, then we lead the horse's head a little further, and the putters then put on another tub of coals; the tubs are wood, and that is the load of one rolley; we then lead forward the horse a little more, and other two tubs are put on the second rolley, then we lead forward another time, and other two tubs are put on the third rolley; the horse draws three rolleys, with two tubs on each; we then take off the horse, and take him round to the other end, and yoke him to it. I set myself on the timber to which the horse is yoked, and take my whip and drive along at the trot to the foot of the shaft; there are men there who take two tubs, and put them into the cage. We stand and wait until the other cage comes down, and then two more tubs are put into that cage, which is pulled to the top of the shaft, and by that time the first cage is down again, and our remaining two tubs are put into it. Empty tubs which come down are put upon our rolleys, and I take the horse and yoke him to the other end, and go forward again to the flats. If I see another horse coming with a load I make the horse stand up at the sidings till the other horse is passed, and I drive on to the flats. I generally go backwards and forwards 15 times in the day. We carry with us a tin bottle of coffee when we go down, and a pie, and a bit of bread, but no salt, and we sometimes carry these with us, and sometimes hide them in a hole in the coal, and begin to eat.'

CHOLERA.

Every House in the Village must be immediately White Washed, Outside and Inside.

Hot Lime will be provided, free of charge.

Every Nuisance to be at once removed.

The Houses to be freely Ventilated, and Good Fires maintained.

Chloride of Lime to be had, free of charge, at the Colliery Store House.

Medicine to be obtained on the First Symptom of Bowel Complaint, and on no account to be deferred.

Thornley Colliery,
Sept. 19th, 1853.

From the Office of J. PROCTER, High Street, Hartlepool, and Victoria Terrace, West Hartlepool.

Cholera poster (Durham Record Office)

It was a distressful time for the Queen with scurrilous broadsheets about the unhappy royal pair, causing their adviser Stockmar to accuse the Tories of being 'degenerate bastards', and the Whigs 'sheer Republicans'. The monarchy was a vital factor in the formation of a coalition in 1853. On the 7 April 1853, during the birth of Prince Leopold, chloroform was used under the direction of Dr Simpson of Edinburgh, pioneer of this advance in medicine. Later haemophilia, the inherited blood disorder which affected the Royal Family, was to haunt the Queen until her death.

It was still commonplace for young workers to be badly injured or die from infection. Following the introduction of vaccination by Edward Jenner in 1796, compulsory vaccination of babies against smallpox was carried out in 1853 at Leasingthorne, and at Thornley precautionary measures were issued by the colliery against the threat of Cholera!

CHAPTER 10

1854–1859 Crimean War and Darwinism

(Death of Ann Shannon, James Lawrence marries Lydia Calvert)

'..the cabins of the [Irish] peasantry were pulled down in such numbers as to give
the appearance, throughout whole regions of the south, and still more to the west,
of a country devastated and desolated by the passage of a hostile army'.

(New York Quarterly Review 1854)

In 1854 Britain became embroiled in a war with Russia as Palmerston argued the need for 'balance of power'. Gladstone, however, warned against the 'glory and excitement about war ... [which] tend to blind men to those evils'. William Morris had recently arrived at Oxford University with twenty-five years to go before revolutionary Socialism was to ignite his passions. Lord John Russell put forward his new Reform Bill – the enfranchisement of more of the middle class and some of the working class, but nevertheless the Coalition Government dropped this moderate reform. Drinking restrictions on Sunday were applied to public houses in 1854. An outbreak of cholera forced the Government to send to Newcastle a Commission of Enquiry into the filthy conditions.

In England there was general unrest in January as Dickens went himself to see the twenty-three week battle of strike and lock-out that had been fought in Preston between owners and workers in the cotton mills. In the Old Curiosity Shop, Little Nell had glimpsed the maddened, rioting workers in the Chamber of Horrors, scene of infernal forges in Birmingham. From the days of Oliver Twist, Dickens had long detested education which destroyed imagination as a blind worship of fact. Hard Times just published in Household Words revealed his new-found rejection of the virtues of self-help – the symbol of money as the false measure of human worth in a corrupt society. Despite Brunel's Paddington Station opening to public acclaim, it gave lie to the enlightened picture of Britain presented at the Great Exhibition, and showed the effects of the remorseless capitalist machine on working people lives. In May, at Newcastle there was an enthusiastic welcome for the visit of Garibaldi, in dispute with the Holy See of Rome, but not by the local Irish who saw it as their duty to defend the Pope.

In America, Abraham Lincoln started the crusade against the Kansas-Nebraska Act which allowed states to extend the institution of slavery. Fenian John Mitchel had

Victoria & Albert 1861
(life.royalalberthall.com)

recently escaped from Australia to the United States, where he began publishing the Irish Citizen. This publication was to become involved in the slavery issue and the controversy surrounding the book, Uncle Tom's Cabin. Mitchel, son of a Presbyterian minister from Londonderry, was a supporter of the South and considered the slaves there better off than the Irish cottiers. Most of the Irish migrants who had escaped from Ireland to New York lived in the slum areas.

A future Irish bishop, Dr Nulty, saw 700 evictions in a single day in Westmeath. In one house, patients were delirious with typhus fever, but even that house was pulled down; and as the shades of night fell, the evicted, young and old, cowered under the hedges, drenched with the heavy autumnal rains. In the county of Mayo, a whole countryside was emptied of its inhabitants by Lord Lucan, who was to gain further infamy during the Crimean War to match the infamous acts of his forebear, Bingham. In Parliament, under Lord Palmerston with landlord sympathies, there was little hope that the few Irish members such as John Maguire could alter the eviction policy. John Doherty who had fought for workers' rights as former leader of the spinners union in Manchester, died at the early age of 56. Michael Davitt and Charles Stewart Parnell, who were to take over the battle for workers' rights, were both born eight years earlier.

Queen Victoria and Prince Albert re-enacted their wedding vows in 1854. This year was of special importance for the Shannons when James Lawrence (Shannon) married, but seven months earlier he had suffered the loss of his grandmother Ann Shannon on the 7th of February at Low Friar Street, St John, in Newcastle. Records showed that Newcastle was the centre of the cholera horror in 1854. Ann Shannon died at the age of 83 years from 'Anasarca' (massive swelling under the skin similar to dropsy, often in the feet caused by organ failure). The informant was Ann Bell, who was present at the time of death, and her residence was given as "Cross Keys entry", St John. The death certificate recorded the occupation of her deceased husband, Philip Shannon, as a labourer.

Only 3 weeks before, another Shannon by the name of Alexander aged 28 died in St John's Infirmary, Newcastle, recorded as 'accidental death' by the coroner. He was unlikely to be a direct relation of Philip, since his first name suggested Scottish ancestry. A Thomas Shannon aged 59 died at St Andrews Auckland.

With the fall of the Whig ministry in February, Isaac Butt's request for the pardon of Smith O'Brien, convicted of sedition in the 1848 rebellion, was granted by Palmerston. Pardons were also granted to Fenians Martin, O'Doherty and three Welsh Chartists, Frost, Williams and Jones. In May, Catherine, the wife of Fenian Thomas Meagher, died of typhus in Ireland at the age of twenty-two years (her husband had escaped from Australia in 1852). With the imminent declaration of war in Crimea by the British, the Irish Americans were frustrated by the lack of action by the Irish groups back home. Frost, who was refused permission to return home, had travelled to America. Mitchel had been given an enthusiastic send-off in Melbourne by Irish miners. His republican politics were reinforced by his experience on the Californian and Nevada goldfields. In September, the only insurrection in Australian history took place, led by an Irish miner Peter Lahor in the goldfields of Eureka Stockade, Ballarat. Peter was the brother of Irish republican James Fintan Lalor.

Leasingthorne, a small village beside Bishop Auckland was to be a place of special significance for James Shannon, because it became his residence at the time of his marriage. James started working at Leasingthorne Colliery shortly after 1851. (The sinker's cottages at Leasingthorne were known as Stone Row since they were built from the first stone raised from the pit shaft as it was being sunk in 1835 and seven years later). Another marriage was to take place in 1854 on the 29 June, that of Charlotte Bronte. Unfortunately this marriage was only to last nine months when Charlotte with child died of tuberculosis, a similar fate to that of her sisters, who had all died of consumption.

Leasingthorne colliery had opened as the North East coalfield was producing 15.4 million tonnes of coal out of a UK total of 47 million tonnes. In 1850, the Times newspaper described County Durham as 'little more than one huge colliery', although Hobsbawn noted that miners largely remained villagers. From Slater's Directory of 1848, the collieries within five miles radius of Bishop Auckland included Woodhouse Close, St Helen's, West Auckland, Greenwood and Gordon, Adelaide Deanery, South Durham (Eldon), Black Boy, Leasingthorne, Westerton, Whitworth, Hunwick, Willington and Bowden Close. The 1852 Inspector's Report noted that the south Durham mines were less dangerous than the gassey pits of Newcastle. Further shafts were sunk at Burnhope Colliery, and Wardley in 1856. Across the Irish Sea in October 1854, Thomas Geogheran of 18 years was killed at Arigna Colliery in Leitrim. Most Irish mines were not 'gassey' therefore at little risk from explosions.

Chalmers writing about the workers at Crystal Palace recorded that 'The warmest interest was taken by the navvies in everything touching the welfare of our army'. Soon there were reports of former mates dying of cholera in Crimea as well as men dying of an 'attack of inflammation' on site at home. A site worker native from Sunderland was described as dressed in the 'dusty fustian of a working man', having left his wife after a quarrel, had turned to drink and moved south. A report in November revealed that 2000 patients had died in Crimean hospitals where only six shirts had been washed. On the 14 September, French and British troops landed in Crimea in high temperatures, shortly to face a severe winter. About a week later the Battle of Alma took place. Shortly afterwards, Prince Albert accepted Napoleon's invitation to visit his camp at St Omer, and in October, the Royals at Balmoral were enjoying a premature victory fire.

James's future wife, Lydia Calvert, came from Shildon, a colliery village in South Durham, near the rail-line from Stockton to Bishop Auckland. Their marriage took place on the 25 September 1854 at the Norman parish church of Merrington. In line with the national mood, it was a time of celebration for the new couple. James signed his name as James Lawrence, a labourer (probably at the colliery). It can only be assumed that James still held affection for his recently deceased step-father; after all he had continued to use the name of Lawrence since the age of eleven. It is therefore not surprising that James's father was recorded as John Lawrence.

Both bride and bridegroom were aged twenty-one, and like most working class women of those times, Lydia was not able to write, signing the marriage certificate with her mark. It was passed down the family that James Lawrence was 6 feet 4 inches tall, whereas Lydia Calvert was small in height and size; apparently when James stretched out his arms, Lydia was able to walk underneath with some clearance. It was said that her daughter Isabella resembled her. It is likely that Clement and Isabella Mason were guests at the wedding, but unlikely that the remaining Shannons had travelled from Newcastle and Sunderland. Naturally, the main topic of conversation of the wedding guests would have been the Crimean War, with news of disembarkation of British troops at Balaklava on the 14 September. Reports of cholera in Turkey raised fears for local men serving in the forces.

MacDonagh recorded of the Irish that 'with that singular contrariness of character which makes them so incomprehensible as a race, love by no means decides all marriages that are made in Ireland. The match is often arranged in a ludicrously cool, business-like and mercenary fashion, between the parents, the young people themselves rarely being allowed, and indeed rarely expecting, any voice in the matter.' The 'old Irish rule to marry for riches and work for love' was one which was followed by Irish 'strong farmers'. Proverbially reckless western peasants 'takes unto himself a mate with as clear a head, as placid a heart and as steady a nerve as if he was buying a cow at Ballinasloe Fair'.

'Marrying-in' (arranged by family) was usual for Catholics, but most marked for the Dissenting sects. Therefore for James from a Catholic tradition, to marry Lydia from a Wesleyan Methodist family suggested that their attraction was strong. They both had agreed to marry at a Protestant church which indicated a compromise on their respective faiths. It would be intriguing to know whether James Shannon's children at first were brought up as Methodists, since later the family were Anglican. Perhaps the influence of Methodism helped James to eventually gain the position of master sinker, which required a responsible attitude and engineering skills as well as physical attributes.

From the 1850s, cokeworks were opening up, with many Irish labourers working at Winlanton and other Durham collieries. Although a cokeworks was a 'surface' occupation and therefore safer than working below ground, it nevertheless was very unhealthy because of the smoky environment. John and Thomas Shannon from Monaghan were working as cinder drawers at a cokeworks near Brandon and Esh from 1861 to 1871. Another unhealthy industry, the alkaki works at Westoe in Durham, also attracted many Irish labourers, such as Henry Shannon from Derry and James Cassidy from Leitrim. In 1854 Mary Moran was married at Brooms, Co Durham; Mary's parents were from Drumshambo, Co Leitrim.

At this point it may be opportune to provide some details of the Calvert family. The Calverts originated from the North Yorkshire dales, and like the Shannons were attracted by the prospects of work in the North East coalfields following exhaustion of the Yorkshire lead mines; they had arrived in the south Durham area some years before James Shannon. The livelihood of the people in the Yorkshire Dales often was a combination of lead mining and sheep farming, and therefore they already had some experience of mining before moving to Durham. The famous locomotive engineer, Timothy Hackworth, a Wesleyan, had set up the Shildon engineering works in 1825.

Lydia's sister Dorothy was baptised at the Wesleyan chapel at Barnard Castle in 1828, at the time of the new railway link. The first civic records of the Calverts in Durham were given in the 1841 Census. Ten years later, Lydia Calvert was living in a household headed by a Thomas Brown, a coal miner born in Chester-le-Street. In 1841, Lydia was recorded as sixteen years old, born at Shildon in Durham, and working as a house servant. Lydia's father, Alexander Calvert, working as a collier near Shildon, was a Wesleyan Methodist.

One of the marriage witnesses at Lydia's wedding who made his mark was John Brown, Lydia's brother-in-law. In a neighbouring area John Brown and his wife Dorothy (Lydia's sister) were residing, and lodging next door was Lydia's brother, Alexander Calvert, also born in Shildon. Thomas and John Brown may have been brothers or cousins. Her name-sake, Lydia Lawrence mother of D H Lawrence, also came from a Nonconformist background. Many miners were attracted by the highly emotional, hell-and-damnation meetings of the Primitive Methodists, known as the 'Prim Ranters'. The Ranters attracted many converts among north-country miners and small hill farmers. However, there was much antagonism against the lead miners taking the jobs from Durham miners.

As the grimness of the industrial life started to bear down on the workers in the 1820s, the influence of the Methodists became especially appealing. They started with a great spiritual revival, building chapels and congregations and leading to a social awakening in trade unionism and politics. The Methodists were feared by the Established Church who hardly counted in the spiritual life of the districts where mines and factories began to collect vast populations. From Methodism sprang the Sunday Schools which taught the rudiments of reading and writing, not just to the children but to whole generations of men who were to take a lead in their communities. Thus it was the 'Methodies' that formed the leadership of the unions. The miner-Methodists were described as Dissenters, but it was not so. The mining communities, because of Church neglect over the years, had nothing to dissent from! The attitude of the masters was one of ambivalence towards the 'Methodie' miner. In times of dispute, it was the Methodists who led the men, but they were good, conscientious workmen, not given to abuse of drink or loss of work. However their impact was only partial in the 1830s when cock-fighting, dog-fighting and drunkenness was still rife. Methodists helped to organise more than 2000 petitions for parliamentary reform in 1817 and 1818.

On the 3 October, the sudden ringing of bells in Llangollen gave the news that Sebastopol had been taken, but the good news was short-lived as the seemingly interminable siege

Crimea/navvies 1855
(Windows Line Photo Gallery)

began with disasters and disgraces on the part of the British to follow. Recruits for Crimea were being sought from the lowest ranks of society and the half-starved poor from the towns and villages of Ireland. The Irishman noted that 'There is hot work going on at present up in the Black Sea, and brave men, especially Irishmen, are in great request. Yes, brave Irishmen are always in great request with England when she has a battle to fight. At other times they are left to lie in the mud with chain round their necks'.

The Crimean War was to gravely highlight how corrupt and unfit the upper classes were to carry out their responsibilities in an area where they had always contended 'birth' was the essential credential. The incompetence of the aristocrats during the war produced a popular revival for democracy under Bright's leadership once hostilities had come to an end. A significant number of Irish workers must have volunteered to go to the Crimea since the Illustrated London News made the point of how many Irish soldiers there were in the Crimea and how few Irish navigators were available back home. Similar shortage problems must have arisen in 1793, when a Commons motion was tabled which would have banned canal digging at harvest time when navvies were needed to help get in the corn.

The Civil Engineer Corps, Peto, Betts and Brassey was established in early December employing navvies (including sinkers), masons, carpenters and blacksmiths to construct a railway from Balaclava to Sebastopol. Suddenly the press were describing the navvies as heros! The Illustrated London News remarked that 'It must be consolatory to Mr Carlyle and the mourners over the degeneracy of these Latter-Days, that there is at least one institution, and that pre-eminently English one, which, despite climatic drawbacks and all sorts of deteriorating influences, exhibits all its original stamina and pristine healthiness – to wit, the British navvy'. An Irishman and journalist for the Times, William Howard Russell, reported on the early horrors of the Crimean campaign.

A Crimean engineer described a 'navvie henchman, a stalwart Northumbrian, with a fine homely breadth of North-country accent, and a profound pride in his navvies. Frank had the portion of the line between Sebastopol and Denthead, the heaviest work in the whole section. Hither come the best men, where the work is all piecemeal, and the best paid because it is the most severe. There had been a slip in the cutting, and twenty-five men were clearing out the slipped ground, working by the yard'. As with miners, the navvies were provisioned through a 'truck shop' for beer and 'tally'.

At this time other Irishmen were working on the continent. William Thomas Mulvaney had become manager of the Hibernia and Shamrock Mine in the Ruhr; he spread the Irish culture and later opened Erin Colliery in Westphalia Prussia. Back in 1835, he had married in Fermanagh, after starting work on The Shannon Navigation.

On the 6 October a great explosion took place at a worsted factory in Gateshead where various chemicals were stored. The ensuing damage was widespread including the destruction of the medieval buildings on the opposite quayside in Newcastle. Even the miners at Sunderland came to the surface in alarm. This led to a call for the demolition of the Newcastle quayside area which had not substantially changed since medieval times. Shortly afterwards a strike took place around Wearside which lasted ten weeks. Also nearby in South Shields on the 21 October, Professor Airy at 1260 feet below ground at Harton Pit was setting up delicate instruments to test the density of the earth – just as well it wasn't Gateshead.

Perhaps due to a dip in workload or the great fire at Newcastle quayside in 1854, Edward Harland was appointed manager of the Belfast shipbuilding yard having learned his trade at the Robert Stephenson Works in Newcastle. From a 100 workers, the shipyard was to employ 10,000 workers in 1897. Robert Smillie born to working class parents in Belfast in 1857, became a future leader of the Scottish Miners' Union.

James and Lydia's first son John was born on the 13 December 1854 at Leasingthorne. John had been conceived well before their marriage, perhaps the reason for James's

departure from the Catholic Church. The birth was registered by his mother on New Year's Day; her name was given as Lydia Lawnes, and his father James Lawnes, a pitman. Their recorded names were almost certainly due to the registrar not hearing correctly the informant, Lydia. The baby's name came from James's step-father John Lawrence.

Binchester Colliery near Bishop Auckland was probably the first colliery where James Shannon worked as a sinker's labourer in 1855. William Coulson was actively controlling these works with George Stott, the engineer in charge of a well-known boring company based at Ferryhill. Three years later Coulson was boring at Woodhouse Close Colliery nearby. James may have attended the Etherley Mechanics Institute in 1854 arranged by colliery owner Mr Stobart; it was said that the working men preferred their own speakers, and not just provided by their masters.

In England, as forecast by Charles Dickens, the new Sabbatarian Bill was causing serious riots in Hyde Park. Dickens had always championed more leisure on Sundays and cheap theatres for working people, and encouraged the use of the mechanics' institutes. However he refused to support the idea of popular entertainment for moral elevation or instruction.

Despite the public outrage regarding the care of soldiers serving in Crimea, the Government's decision to end the 1848 Health of Town Act was applauded by the Times. 'We prefer' said its leader-writer, 'to take our chance of cholera and the rest, rather than to be bullied into health ...'. The Act's instigator, Chadwick, was soon forced into retirement. Nevertheless, in the Bishop Auckland area, the Local Board of Health met for the first time in September 1854, and one of their main aims was the establishment of a clean water supply. It was to take nearly three years for this to be achieved, somewhat slower progress than by Florence Nightingale on foreign shores. Mary Seacole (an unforgettable name for miners), from Scottish and creole ancestry, volunteered to serve as a nurse for the British servicemen in Crimea, but was turned down because of her ethnicity. Undeterred, she travelled independently to Crimea where she set up a British Hotel for the wounded, and practised a version of Jamaican herbal medicine. After the war she returned to the Caribbean destitute, but was saved from poverty after fund-raising by the British public in 1857.

In November 1855, the abolition of stamp duty on newspapers had an immediate effect on the increase in circulation and then the power of the popular press, perhaps the reason for Edward Shannon eventually moving to Sunderland. Proprietor Joseph Cowen started the Newcastle Daily Chronicle in 1858, and its readership spread to north Durham.

People of all classes had an insatiable appetite for news from Crimea. It is not surprising that the Association for Advancement of Education in the mining and manufacturing districts of Northumberland and Durham was formed at this time. The name of Florence Nightingale soon became public knowledge because of her heroic deeds in Crimea. She had arrived in Constantinople on the 4th of November, ten days after the Battle of Balaclava. Her reports on the grave inadequacy of the nursing care for the injured soldiers caused consternation for Queen Victoria and the country at large. Lord John Russell, the Duke of Newcastle and Lord Raglan were the main targets for criticism. On the 24 January 1855, John Russell resigned over the conduct of the war, and the Queen Victoria reluctantly accepted Palmerston as replacement at the War Office.

As well as soldiers on the battle-field, cholera was affecting the navvies working in Crimea. The navvies back home were also dying from cholera which was sweeping through Europe. On the 2 March 1855, Tsar Nicholas died, it was said of a broken heart at the carnage of Inkerman and Balaclava. Dissatisfaction with the progress of the war rumbled on, with Lord Raglan dying of fever in June. Florence Nightingale was also down with fever in Balaclava but recovered. Even at war there were rumours of religious dissension with the Crimean nurses being Roman Catholic, while the nurses at Scutari were suspected of a 'regrettable propensity towards the tenets of Dr Pusey'. Roebuck's Commission, with its threat to democratize the Army, was shelved to avoid embarrassment. Gladstone argued against continuation of the war. The 'Manchester School' were also strongly arguing for peace. By August 1855, the Crimean War was coming to an end, and the stories of both crass incompetence and great bravery were beginning to leak out. A letter from a soldier stationed at Frenchman's Hill, Balaklava, revealed the suffering:

> 'I now write to inform you of my bodily health, and spiritly welfare, tho I am very poorly to day, but thank God that I am spared to write to you, hoping this will find you all in good health as it leaves most of our company; tho we have lost some men very sudden, one drowned on the 15 August by coming on board drunk, when we lay in the water, and Robson was ill at six oclock in the morning and died at one, and we have six more very ill at the present, and i hope that God will remove the heavy hand of death from us, if it be his will, and if not, I hope that the Lord Jesus will receive our souls to glory and I have not been landed a week until the 24th and we have 3 more men dead in the same way, it is the cholera ....The disease is raging, and death devouring us daily, and the grave is swallowing us up.......'

After Christmas, the French army riddled with sickness would not fight on. Sebastopol fell after a siege of 350 days, and shortly afterwards an unsatisfactory peace was declared in Paris on the 30 March 1856. Four months later Florence Nightingale returned to England, but 300,000 had perished. Although the British Army did not triumph in the battlefield, its soldiers for the first time won the respect of the British people. As British soldiers were welcomed home, Gavan Duffy saw no future in Irish republicanism and left with his family from Liverpool to start a new political life in Australia, the country which he had struggled so long to avoid as the destination of transportation. Outrages had declined from 20,000 in 1847 to 3,500 in 1858. In 1856, bonfires marked Fenian Michael O'Brien's route through Limerick having received a free pardon.

Limited Liability Company Acts of 1855 and 1862 greatly assisted the businessman find capital to invest in the expanding industries. In 1856 the coal and iron industries were still expanding in contrast to Ireland where Engels on a visit there noted the total absence of industry. Victoria and Albert found time to visit the Paris Exhibition during August 1855. Prince Albert would have been pleased to have learned that year of Bessemer's invention of mass produced steel, a forerunner to mass produced goods. He would also have approved of the Philosophical Lecture given at Thornley School Room in December 1852, dealing with electricity, galvanism, electro-magnetism and pneumatics. Entry charges to the lecture room ranged from 1s for adult front seats to 3d for children back seats. Twelve years previously, Thornley had been the hot-bed of trade unionism, one of the new colliery villages springing up in East Durham. It had rapidly expanded with a population of 50 in 1831 to 2,730 by 1851. A Methodist chapel had just opened. Ten years earlier an explosion at the colliery had killed nine men and boys. A trapper boy of 9 years who fell asleep was blamed for the tragedy.

In Thornley, on the eighteenth of August, a second son James was born to James and Lydia. Also born in 1856 was the first leader of the Labour Party, James Keir Hardie. Unlike for their first child, the birth certificate gave their surname as Shannon; the informant was Lydia Shannon. The obvious explanation was that the parents had decided to provide the registrar with James's true surname since this was a legal requirement. However, it is difficult to understand why after being married under the name of Lawrence they should wish to change their surname, having used this name for their first son, and presumably were using Lawrence in daily life. However, having moved to a new area, this would have allowed them to adopt a new name more easily. Also if James had wanted to escape his employer's 'bond', then a name change might have proved convenient, with the chance of earning more money at a new pit.

Another explanation for recording his son as Shannon was the tightening of Government legal employment requirements for emigrants. One very significant change in James Shannon's occupation in 1856, as recorded in his son's birth certificate, was his new job of "Sinker". The 1861 census revealed a large population of Irish in Durham; some of these could have been brought in as blacklegs during the Great Strike of 1844. Thornley had a reputation for its strong views from the days of early Chartist activity, similar to Seghill, and had engaged the lawyer W P Roberts. This had been his first case against the colliery owners, and he was to become a worthy champion for the miners' legal rights.

In 1854, William Armstrong at his Newcastle factory, had produced his first gun, just in time for Crimea. The Inspector of Factories for Scotland reported great difficulty in the operation of the Factory Acts because of the large number of young Irish emigrants presenting themselves for employment with fictitious 'birth certificates'. By the hiring of young Irish labourers, factory owners were getting around the legal ban on employing young persons under 18 years to look after machinery required to be kept in motion during the night. Later the Registrar General was to comment on the great variation of Irish names, not only in spelling and form but also entirely different names were being used synonymously by the same person or by members of the same family!

Sinkers were considered the 'elite' of the workers in a colliery. Their work was primarily involved in sinking the new mine shaft for providing access to and between the coal seams. In some cases ventilation shafts were required. The sinker was very distinctive in his working dress, wearing a leather hat with back and side flaps and leather shoulder protection (called "backskin") to prevent him from getting soaked. During sinking of the shaft, the sinkers would have to work in terrible and dangerous conditions, often with water streaming into their workings as they endeavoured to secure the timber ring beams. The means of access used by the sinkers were open iron tubs called 'kibbles', 'kettles' or 'hoppits', which were lowered or raised by means of the pit head winding gear.

In travelling up or down the shaft, up to four or five sinkers would occupy the tub, sometimes with one leg inside the tub and the other leg outside. Access to the early shallow mines known as 'bell pits', was achieved by simply being attached to the end of a rope lowered down the shaft by means of a crude windlass or 'jack roll'. These bell pits were worked extensively in Durham, often by monks on the estates of Dean and Chapter. The advent of steam power at the end of the eighteenth century had made it technically possible to control the large water heads resulting from the operation of deep mines.

Trevelyan noted that 'Shafts thirty feet deep were sunk by the earliest island miners, who laboured down at the bottom with stag-horn picks and shoulder-blades for shovels, hewing galleries through the chalk and extracting the precious flints which then made man the master of the world'. In more recent times, the skills of sinking had been first required on the canal tunnel shafts. Miners who were often used for this work, set their charges of gunpowder by the light of candles, and then feared for the inrush of water. Ventilation was provided by lighting a fire under the shaft to provide an up-draught, which in turn would cause a down-draught at other shafts. Durham and Northumberland were one of the few coal-mining areas where canals were not the principal means for transporting the coal.

At the beginning of the nineteenth century, waggon-ways were used to convey the coal to the Tyne or Wear, where keels 40 feet by 19 feet broad were ready to transfer the coal to the colliers (boats). A canal from Darlington to Stockton was under consideration, but this was overtaken by the development of the railways. For the next fifty years in the remainder of Britain, the railway was to supersede the waterway as the main form of transport. In 1857, the Bishop Auckland to Durham line turning east to Shildon was constructed. The Darlington to Stockton Line had a reputation for total immunity from accidents, some said to be attributable to the teetotal principles of the Quaker proprietor, Joseph Pease.

Railway construction works also required the skills of the shaft sinker, as given by early records: 'During the tunnelling required for many of the railways, it was necessary to descend into the 'bowels of the mountain'. At the mouth of the shaft will be seen the ponderous engine and pumping gear. A visitor takes a candle stuck in a lump of clay, and prepares for his subterranean journey. Having deposited himself in a tub, and overcome the giddiness which the descent may induce, he observes the lining of the shaft, and the straining of the pumps attempting to lift the volume of water continuously pouring down from the crevasses and fissures of the earth and rock. This creates a sort of Scotch mist, sufficient to wet a "Southern man" to the skin; but, what is remarkable, it does not extinguish the fragile candles, which burn with singular brilliancy'.

Advances in mining practices had taken place during the eighteenth century with Elector Frederick Augustus of Poland founding an Academy of Mines on 1789. In Adam Smith's Wealth of Nations, he listed the activities associated with the sinking of mine shafts: erecting engines for drawing out water, and making roads and waggon-ways. In Britain a publication in 1708 called 'The Compleat Collier: Or, The whole ART of Sinking, Getting, and Working, Coal Mines, &c. AS Is now used in the Northern Parts, Especially about SUNDERLAND AND NEW-CASTLE BY J. C.' gave in fascinating detail the early practices of coal mining. This was the first British sinking manual after the treatise by sixteenth century German mineralogist Georgius Agricola. A summary of 'sinking' was given as follows:

> 'When coal has been proved underground by boring, the next operation in coal mining is the sinking of the shaft. A four-sided pit was first cut in the surface soil, but as sinking proceeded towards the stone it was shaped to an octagon, and the shaft through the stone itself was circular in plan. The sides above the stone were timbered with fir balks and lined with deal boards to prevent falls of earth. When the sand was met with it was usual to hold it back by ramming clay between it and this wooden tubbing. (Tubbing was the mining term for the practice of lining a shaft with a waterproof lining to prevent the ingress of water.) When the sinkers came to wet strata, they sometimes packed undressed sheepskins between the

boards and the stone, and sometimes the sides were lined with bricks, behind which spiral channels, known as garlands, were constructed to carry to the pit bottom water which would otherwise have forced its way into the shaft. The square shaft at ground level was 'nine quarters' across, or 6ft 9in., and if we deduct from this the timbering, it only leaves a diameter of about 6ft for the finished pit.'

To minimise 'down-time', repairs to the pumping equipment down shafts was carried out without its removal. When James Shannon was a sinker at Thornley, working under master sinker James Coxon, he had dived underwater to repair or replace the leather buckets known as clacks. This required tremendous strength, courage, and good lungs! Also good for shouting instructions down a shaft! (James Coxon had been convicted of manslaughter in 1836 at the age of 28 and given 6 months imprisonment).

In 1856 James Shannon had also worked at Wingate colliery close-by, since during the mine disaster at Wingate in 1906, his sinker son, James Mason, led a rescue party and was able to remember the escape routes which he had learned from his father.

In Ireland at this time, popular unrest was being channelled into a secret society known as the Pheoenix – so called because, like the fabled bird, it intended to rise from the ashes of the burnt-out 'Young Ireland' movement. James Stephens, who had acted as an aide to Smith O'Brien in 1848, indirectly created the Fenian movement. In 1857, Stephens an exile based in the USA and Paris, prompted the Phoenix men to start drilling and preparing to collect arms. However in 1858 the police swooped and arrested all the Phoenix leaders. The Fenian Brotherhood started their campaign for the overthrow of British rule in Ireland. These events undoubtedly stirred the emotions of the Irish living and working on the British mainland, and led to suspicion from other workers. (Cathal O'Shannon, a member of the Irish Republican Brotherhood, on Easter Sunday 1916 mobilised with a hundred Volunteers at Coalisland in Tyrone).

The Irish were not alone as the target for unpopular feeling towards foreigners; Albert did not receive the title of Prince Consort until 1857. The Government's attention was suddenly diverted from 'troubles' at home to the Indian sub-continent. Just as the troops had returned to England from Crimea, the Indian Mutiny broke out, and during the next year the abolition of the East India Company took place, and the overhaul of Indian army by Viceroy, John Lawrence. The 1857 General Election was fought on the issue of Palmerston's premiership. Gladstone, Cobden and Bright were unseated, perhaps due to their position on India and Ireland. Joseph Paxton, then a Liberal MP, was luckier for having backed Cobden to bring down Palmerston's government; he managed to retain his seat. During Gladstone's period out of Parliament, he busied himself with his prostitute 'rescue work' and giving lectures. A plot to slay the French Emperor made Palmerston introduce a Conspiracy to Murder bill in 1858. This was so unpopular that Palmerston was forced to resign.

The need for legislation on sanitation was soon realised, when in June 1858 the stench from the River Thames was such to cause a rapid evacuation of the Houses of Parliament. A fortnight later Disraeli introduced a bill for the financing of new sewage drains – eleven years after the establishment of the Metropolitan Commission of Sewers for that purpose. Civil engineer Joseph Bazalgette after experience of drainage in Ireland, took charge in London. Britain was attracting other Irish imports to England. In 1857, a mining engineer Richard Sutcliffe who had worked in the Tipperary coalfields, moved to Barnsley in Yorkshire. He later invented a coal-cutting machine and underground conveyor belt, which made the labouring work of miners much easier, but unfortunately increased the dust health hazard.

This was a year of financial slump and recession. After Brunel's exertions to launch the Great Eastern at the end of 1857, he escaped his tribulations for a while on a trip to Egypt, where he met Robert Stephenson, who was also in very poor health. Palmerston resigned on the 20 February 1858. However Gladstone was to take heart from 'public opinion' to pull himself out of his 'well of depression'. Ribbonism clashes broke out on the streets of Sunderland.

On the thirteenth April 1858, Ellen (possibly named after Helen, her deceased aunt), was born at Batts Row, Bishop Auckland to James and Lydia. As in the case of their second son, the birth certificate gave their surname as Shannon, and James's occupation as colliery sinker. James had proved his credentials as a sinker, and had moved on with his family to the next new mine to be sunk, probably at New Brancepeth. Thomas Kellet was master sinker at Page Bank, Brancepeth, and John Longstaff at Etherley Dene.

Batts Row was located in an area where many Irish lived, mostly agricultural labourers. Running south from Batts to Back Bondgate was an old pathway called Dog Loop. It used to be an old Bishop Auckland joke to bet some unsuspecting person you could beat them in a race from Bondgate to Batts. Once you got ahead of them into Dog Loop the race was won, because it was so narrow that no-one could pass you.

The 'Fancy Franchise' Bill, a prelude to the second reform act, was defeated in March 1859, and the Conservative Government was dissolved. Bright attacked the House of Lords and aristocratic influence everywhere, and pledged to fight for a fair distribution of the nation's wealth in order to provide the working man with a fair wage. Palmerston began his new administration on the 17 June, joined by Gladstone after an absence of four and a half years. On the 12 July 1859 an Armistice was reached between French and Austria. There had been a real fear that the French were about to invade England. The Crown was violently opposed to Russell and Palmerston's sympathy towards Italian independence which had implications for England's relations with Austria. In 1858 Princess Royal had

Batts Row Bishop Auckland strike meeting 1850 (free pages.genealogy)

Batts Row Bishop Auckland evictions 1858 (free pages.genealogy)

married into the house of Prussia. Gladstone renounced Palmerston's assertive style in his dealings with other countries. This was the time when the issue of free trade, social stability and class reconciliation turned Gladstone towards the Liberal Party. There was a great wave of religious emotion in 1859, known as the 'Ulster Revival', which affected denominations of every variety but especially Presbyterianism. This led to the sectarian rivalry within the province which inevitably overflowed into the politics of Home Rule.

One year after the Government Press Prosecutions of 1858, in his book, Essay on Liberty, JS Mill made a plea for freedom of thought and against the tyranny of conventional public opinion, for example 'self-help'. Perhaps this was the final encouragement that Darwin needed, since on the 24 November his 'Origin of Species' was published to a storm of protest, stirring up some Malthusian innuendos of the Irish. In Newcastle the first dog show in England was held. Breeds such as pointers, setters and spaniels gave reinforcement to the evolutionary process, when only twenty-five years before the savagery of bull-baiting was outlawed. The irresistible law of progress had a revolutionary effect on the Established Church. However, Cobden in 1859 was to confess his astonishment that the 'people at large' were so 'tacit in their submission to the perpetuation of the feudal system in this country'. Moderates had a fear of democracy equal to social revolution. When upright, teetotal and Methodist miners were sent to jail after a strike which they had opposed at Seaton Delaval, the mine manager explained his actions as 'no use in sending to jail those who cannot feel'.

Gladstone went to Holyhead to see the launch of the Great Eastern, but a month later Brunel was to die of a stroke after hearing of the explosion on board his (iron) sailing steam ship. Robert Stephenson, son of the famous 'self-made' railway engineer, also died in 1859, the end of another great engineer. At this time, the National Winding and General Engineers' Society was founded. On its union banner was shown a colliery pithead and winding gear, highlighting the importance of this equipment, on which the lives of miners and sinkers so depended.

CHAPTER 11

1860–1866 American Civil War, Fenians and Franchise

(Death of Isabella Mason)

'The Lower Classes are being so well informed – are so intelligent & earn their bread & and riches so deservedly that they cannot & ought not to be kept back – to be abused by the wretched ignorant Highborn beings, who live only to kill time.'

(Bright in response to Prince of Wales 1866)

'You may bury the Bill that we have introduced but .... (you) cannot fight against the future. Time is on our side. The great social forces which move onwards in their might and majesty .... those great social forces are against you.'

(Gladstone warning to Tories on Home Rule 1866)

This period was to be dominated by events in America, where a civil war raged from 1861 to 1865, and also saw the deaths of Prince Albert, Abraham Lincoln and Palmerston. Lincoln became President of the United States of America in 1861. From 1862 to 1870 Bismarck waged three successive wars. The Jews in Russia like the Irish in Great Britain still sought their freedom. Gladstone, Cobden and Bright used their strenuous efforts to avert conflict with France, despite Napoleon III ever planning for war. France was to shortly annex Savoy and Nice. With a healthy economy, Gladstone as Chancellor of the Exchequer was determined that something should be done for 'trade and the masses'. The Tsar Alexander II did something for 23 million peasants by emancipating the Russian serfs in 1861.

The 'Book of Household Management' was published in 1860 by Isabella Beeton, nee Mayson, who died of fever at 28 years and so did her two infant children. She had relations with the Ulster Unionist Party. In contrast to increasing tolerance to Catholics, the Marchioness of Londonderry held fast to her refusal to allow the Seaham Catholics build a chapel in their local area. In Bishop Auckland, the first meeting of the Co-operative Society was held in 1860, and a store was opened on the 28th May.

John Bright was champion of the north against the southern slave trades of America. During this period, emigration to America noticeably increased. With duties on iron and French coal just reduced in 1860 following Cobden's free trade agreement with France, the prosperity of the 1850s was beginning to subside; 1866 was to see the ultimate shrinkage of Britain's coal supply. New forms of energy such as electricity were beginning to emerge. The early 1860's famine threatened rural Ireland, with only linen manufacture prospering at the expense of children labouring 12 hours a day. The Catholic Church attacked Fenianism with the slogan 'no priests in politics', and the Pope's Syllabus of Errors of 1864 highlighted their view of the 'evil of Socialism, Liberalism and Freemasonry'.

Gladstone was looking for economies in the education budget. A Paper Tax, commonly known as a 'tax on knowledge', was thrown out by the Lords in May 1860. Free trade included cheap postage and printed matter. It was reported from the North East coalfields that 'time for school attendance is spared only with the view to its being preparation for work. Parents have no idea that there is any advantage in children spending so many years at school if the same amount of learning can be acquired in a shorter time. In short, they regard schooling, not as a course of discipline, but only as a means of acquiring reading, writing, arithmetic, sewing, and knitting, as a preparation for the main business of life – earning a living'. Scottish education with its parochial schools, based on a traditional sixteenth century system, was held up as superior in its practicality compared to the English way. For working-class girls, they were lucky if they were sent to the voluntary school.

Artisans and miners sometimes took in an orphan girl from the workhouse, at practically no cost, who would carry out the same chores as a domestic servant in a middle-class household. Up to 1880 there was no compulsion on working-class children to receive an education. There was to be a radical shift in society with the third Reform Act of 1884–5. Writer Mary Louisa Molesworth, commenting on the pioneer Rochdale co-operators in 1861, noted 'their object and ambition appears to be that the working class should be well fed, well clothed, well housed, well washed, well educated – in a word that they should be respectable and respected'. This led to campaigns against beer consumption and promiscuity. On the latter point the royal family did not set a good example.

Lydia's third son Alexander, born on the fourteenth of July 1860, was named after Lydia's father, Alexander Calvert. The birth certificate gave the place of birth as Jack's Row, Bishop Auckland. The baptismal record of St Andrews Anglican Church confirmed that James Shannon had changed faith from Catholicism to Anglicanism. As with her other children, Lydia was the informant. In this case her surname was given as Shannon, but by mistake her maiden name was recorded as Talbot instead of Calvert. Her husband's occupation was again recorded as colliery sinker. It is likely that Jack's Row was a row of cottages specially built for the sinkers, first workers to arrive at the colliery.

Briggs' Directory described the area having once been very pretty: 'Jack's Row has retrograded from its beautiful and former healthy condition. The sight of the overhanging gardens and pleasant cottages in Wear Chare, on which throve and dwelt several local industries, has been covered with low and badly built dwellings, the sewerage and drainage from which oozes through the walls into the public road and perfumes the atmosphere with odours suggestive of dirt and disease.'

After only 5 weeks, baby Alexander Shannon died of 'convulsions' at home on the twenty-first August. Dick Sullivan noted in his book 'Navvyman', that in March 1860 near the Borders, the air was damp followed by a summer of cold and wet weather. This inclement weather may have also contributed to Alexander's death. Lydia's father, Alexander Calvert, who had died at Ferryhill in 1849, fortunately missed this sad occasion.

The death of children was commonplace in Victorian times, and it was normal for children to see dead relations laid out. In the Old Curiosity Shop, the death of Little Dorrit struck chords with the Victorian audience: 'When death strikes down the innocent and young, for every fragile form from which he lets the panting spirit flee, a hundred virtues rise, in shapes of mercy, charity and love, to walk the world, and bless it.'

On the 16 September 1860, Edward Shannon, (James Shannon's uncle), at the late age of 35, married Jane Donaldson at the parish church of St James Benwell, Newcastle upon Tyne. Edward's father was given as Philip Shannon, (deceased), a gardener; and Jane's father as David Donaldson, a cooper (deceased). Unusually for a female, but as the daughter of an artisan, Jane was able to sign the register; the 1851 census had given her occupation at the age of 17 as 'Out Door Teacher'. Edward also signed the register as expected of a printer, a well-paid occupation, but with the high risk of lead poisoning. Like his brother Richard in 1837, he had accepted his bride's religion. (One year earlier at Aghalurcher in Fermanagh, an Edward Shannon was baptised to parents Peter Shannon and Rose Monaghan).

In October 1860, there was a Shannon family marriage at St Mary's Catholic Church in Clayton Street at Newcastle. Thomas Shannon a coal miner of 23, married a spinster Bridget Loftus of 21. They both marked the marriage certificate. St Mary's was the mother church or Catholic Cathedral for Hexham and Newcastle, built between 1842 and 1844. It was designed by Augustus Welby Pugin who had just converted to Catholicism and who had been the architect for the Houses of Parliament.

At this time, Gladstone visited the new Britannia Bridge followed by some invigorating woodcutting at Harwarden, his home in Flintshire. He was advised by Cobden that free trade was a corrective to the mounting fear of war with France. Gladstone was starting to consider fiscal ways of alleviating poverty. He felt it was 'a mistake to suppose that the best mode of giving benefit to the labouring classes was simply to operate on consumables. If you want to do them the maximum of good, you should rather operate on the articles which give them the maximum of employment'. He would have been aware that traditional urban skilled craftsmen – printers, tailors, braziers, pewterers, cabinet-makers and saddlers fared better than other workers during the Industrial Revolution.

Alexander and Ellen were baptised under the name of Shannon at Bishop Auckland on the 17 August and 24 September 1860 respectively. However the census of 1861 recorded the James Shannon family for the first time living under the name of Mason at Adelaide's Colliery near Coppy Crooks. His wife Lydia, and children John, James and Ellen were all recorded correctly with their birth dates and places. The only other irregularity was that James's occupation was given as coal miner rather than as sinker, but it is likely that he just gave a general description of his work. At this time a Henry Armstrong was master sinker at West Auckland.

James, Lydia and their children will now be referred to as Mason, their public name henceforth. Also recorded living near St Andrew's Auckland, were Clement and Isabella Mason, with their children Ann Jane and John Lawrence. It gave Clement's birth place as New Lompton [Lambton] in Durham, and Isabella's as Scotland, in contrast to the 1851 Census record giving Longbenton for Clement and Ireland for Isabella. Both children were given as 'Scholars' with interestingly John Lawrence still at school at the age of fifteen, perhaps the reason that afterwards he did not work down the pit.

Richard Shannon aged 46 was still residing in the Westgate district of Newcastle with his wife Ann, but now working as a mason's labourer, a job taken up by many Irish expatriates. Also working nearby as a mason's labourer was a Thomas Shannon aged 38. It was not clear whether Richard was still working on the railways. At this time Catherine Reed was recorded as a widow and border in St Andrews Newcastle, born in Scotland and working as a Servant. Her husband Ralph had died in 1850.

In 1861, a Tory, Robert Lowe, stated that the 'lower classes ought to be educated to discharge the duties that are cast upon them'. Dickens had other views, when he commented on a Newcastle audience: 'A finer audience there is not in England, and I suppose them to be specifically earnest people; for while they can laugh till they shake the roof, they have a very unusual sympathy with what is pathetic or passionate'. After her mother's death in March 1861, Queen Victoria paid a visit to Killarney in Ireland, but this failed to lift her spirits. Former prime minister Lord Aberdeen had passed away a year earlier. William Jenner took over as the appointed physician for the Royal Family. Although Dr Jenner had recently identified the germs of typhus and typhoid, he was unable to prevent an already sickly Prince Albert dying of typhoid on the 14 December 1861. His widow went into deep mourning which was to last many years. Scottish gillie John Brown became her personal servant.

In January 1862, Britain as a nation became aware of the sacrifices that miners were making every working day. The disaster at New Hartley Colliery in Northumberland took the lives of 204 men and boys when the main beam of the shaft pumping engine broke, and fell down the shaft. Master Sinker, William Coulson, and his team of sinkers worked tirelessly in their attempt to rescue the entrapped miners but in vain. Brothers John and Duncan Gallagher died in this disaster.

By 1861, Edward, son of Philip Shannon, had moved from Newcastle, and was now living at Sunderland in the district of South Bishopwearmouth. On the thirteenth of November a son Richard, was born to Edward and his wife Jane, at 12 Smyrna Place. Edward's occupation was given as Letter Press Printer Journeyman (the first artisan of the Shannon family!). Their son was no doubt named after his uncle, Richard Shannon. Richard and Edward were names used for boys even of Catholic birth! About a year after Edward's son was born, James Shannon's third son, also called Richard, was born on the fourth of October 1862 at Old Pit Eldon.

Andrew Reed and his son James were working as [colliery] firemen at Trimdon, where Clement and Isabella Mason had recently lived. (These firemen were responsible for firing up the winding engines mounted above the shafts). Andrew in 1855 had been imprisoned for 6 months in Northumberland, having committed a misdemeanour for obtaining goods by false pretences. His son, James Storey Reed, was about to be guilty of a similar crime!

James Reed, now an engine smith, married Mary Ann Bulmer in 1862 at Hartlepool. He signed the wedding register and Mary Ann made her mark. He left for America some years later. During 1862, almost all the immigrants entering the United States who listed their occupation as 'miner' were from Britain. Coal miners in Britain were relatively well paid, therefore could easily pay £5 for the steamer taking ten days to cross the Atlantic.

After tireless work, agitator Martin Jude died just before the passing of the Coal Mines Regulation Act 1860. This improved the safety rules and raised the minimum age for boys starting work in mines from 10 to 12 years. At this time Old Eldon colliery was opened, having been first sunk in 1829. It can be assumed that further sinking work was required to repair or maintain the original shaft, or to provide an additional shaft. In response to the miners' outcry at the death-toll after the New Hartley Hester Colliery in 1862, a Miners Delegates' meeting took place to discuss the number of shafts at collieries. This led to public demand for improvements, and a Bill was passed requiring two shafts in all mines. The development of furnace ventilation also reduced the risk of an explosion, and this was to be the principal method of ventilation during the nineteenth century. A few months later at Walker Colliery, an explosion killed seventeen men; in 1863, Coxlodge was the next colliery to suffer an explosion, and three years later at Pelton Fell.

At Auckland Park Colliery where James Shannon was sinking, most of the coal was converted into coke for Bolckow, Vaughan & Co ironworks at Middlesborough. Seven sinkers were also working, and four paid the ultimate price. In 1863 Henry Davison, brothers George and John Elwen, and Richard Waggett were killed by falling down a shaft owing to the upsetting of the cradle upon which they were working. Master sinker William Coulson had been carrying out boring operations in 1862 at Etherley, three miles west of Bishop Auckland, and in 1864, a long-established Ferryhill boring company was working at Cassop A Pit.

The civil war that broke out in America during April 1861 arose from economic, social and political consequences flowing from slavery. Meagher, now a captain with the Union forces, was to play a prominent part in this war, although some of his countrymen joined the opposition, the Confederates. Meagher and a Tyrone general, James Shields, formed an Irish Brigade in recognition of those 'Wildgeese' brigades. Relations between the US and Britain became strained when the Americans attacked British ships, reversing the situation during the 1812 War. An American James Murray Mason, commissioner for the Confederates, failed to persuade the British Government to recognise their case for independence from the Union.

Many British politicians like most of their countrymen did not fully appreciate the roots of the American conflict. Terence Bellew McManus, born at Tempo, Fermanagh in 1811, worked as a shipping agent in Liverpool. He returned home as a Radical and became involved in the Young Irelander Rebellion of 1848. He was sent to Van Dieman's Land, but three years later escaped to the United States. MacManus was brought back to Ireland from San Francisco to be buried in 1861. This tradition was to take place many times – a coffin ship took them to America and they returned home in a coffin. With the destruction of most of Ireland's industries, it was said that all that was left was the making of coffins!

In early 1862, the Anti-Corn Law spokesman, John Bright, normally a man of peace, was urging Abraham Lincoln's government that the most bloody contest of modern times should not be brought to an end unless and until slavery was abolished. To use the phrase of Carlyle, Bright had 'swallowed formulas' – even those of peace. This was a time of strained relations between the US and Britain. In July by a bitterly repented error of Russell's, the British ship, Alabama, was allowed to sail from Liverpool docks to America,

Abraham Lincoln 1863
(en.wikipedia.org)

where it was used to assist the southern states. These states with the slogan, 'Cotton is King', were hoping that England and France would intervene to assure their supplies of cotton. Up till then the civil war had been fought on the issue of the 'union'. After the war Britain was forced to pay compensation to America, said to be the price to buy off American intervention in Ireland. Harriet Beecher Stowe in her book 'Uncle Tom's Cabin', noted how easily statesmen 'trod on Ireland … quietly and systematically', aware of the condition of the peasants' cabins in Ireland. She was also aware of evils of capitalism with starving English labourers, but still considered them better off compared to the slave sold, whipped and parted from his family.

In America, a sixteen year old Philip Martin Shannon born at Shannondale Pennsylvania, and inspired by Present Lincoln's call for troops to put down the rebellion, enlisted, deceiving the enrolling officer as to his age. He was injured during the battle of Gaines's Mills. Another Irish-American, Thomas McManus, was not 'forced to list up', although many destitute Irish newcomers were tempted by the bounty to join the Union armies. At this time a secret organization of Irish immigrant coal miners started up in Eastern Pennslvania, called the Molly Maguires (as in north-west Ireland) in revolt against the intolerable conditions.

The English working classes were generally in favour of the Yankees (northerners) since in the 'Hungry 40s' there had been a large emigration to the North of the United States. Also during the war, the cotton mills of south Lancashire were cut off from their supply, but the workers continued to support the blockade of the American southern ports despite their own starving condition. The 'common folk' of England at that time might have been hard pressed to agree with Lincoln's comment that 'God must have been fond of the common folk, since he made so many of them'. In his 'Autobiography', J S Mill expressed his strong feelings in support for the northern struggle. General Gordon despatched to the public subscription for the Lancashire famine, his Chinese medal as an anonymous gift. During the summer of 1862, Gladstone took an active part in schemes for finding employment at Harwarden in North Wales for Lancashire operatives thrown out of work by the cotton famine.

The Northern liberals devised the triumphal visit to the Tyne by Gladstone on the 7 October 1862, with Joseph Cowen prospective MP for Newcastle, as impresario. Before the visit, Palmerston had indicated that the cabinet was moving towards acknowledging the independence of the southern states. Similar receptions were awaiting Gladstone at Gateshead, Sunderland and Middlesborough. Morley gave a description of the scene: 'Newcastle gave Gladstone a tumultuous welcome with bells ringing and guns thundering. A great procession of steamers followed him to the mouth of the river, ships flew their gayest bunting, the banks were thronged with hosts of the black-handed toilers of the forges, the furnaces, the coal-staiths, chemical works, glass factories, shipyards, eager to catch a glimpse of the great man; and all this, not because he had tripled the exports to France, but because a sure instinct had revealed an accent in his eloquence that spoke of feeling for the common people'.

However, at a banquet hall in Newcastle in October, Gladstone let slip a sentence which gave recognition that the southern states would soon be a separate nation. In Bright's words, Gladstone made 'a vile speech full of insulting pity' for the North [of the American states], and of praise and support for the South. This produced an immediate sensation with Bright and Cobden naturally feeling that they had been let down. It was said that Bright referred to Gladstone's family connections with slavery that had affected Gladstone's judgment. In November 1862, Gladstone disclaimed that his Newcastle speech meant he supported the south in the American civil war. In 1896 he was to admit his error of judgement. It was said that Prince Consort's last task before dying was to tone down a draft letter from Palmerston to President Lincoln, which may have helped to avert bringing Britain into the war.

In November 1863, 'The Irish People' was first published in Dublin. This was to mark a turning point in the history of Fenianism, with the development of the underground organisation. The 'Fenian Conspiracy' lasted from 1864 to 1867. In 1865 the British Government suppressed the publication of The Irish People and Fenians were arrested throughout Britain. Also, the International Working Men's Association was founded in 1864; a year later the National Reform League largely inspired by the International, commenced its agitation for an extension of the franchise. Karl Marx, the theoretical and political leader of the International, was foremost in demanding Ireland's claims. He and his friend Engels had been interested in Ireland since the days when, as supporters of the

Chartists, they had supported the demand for Repeal. Gladstone's speech on enfranchisement in May 1864 electrified Parliament and the country, after which he became known as the 'People's William'. The sensation was caused by the words supporting general franchise:

> 'I call upon the adversary to show cause, and I venture to say that every man who is not presumably incapacitated by some consideration of personal unfitness or of political danger, is morally entitled to come within the pale of the constitution.'

The Griffiths Valuation, a boundary and land valuation, was carried out between 1862 and 1864 for the Derryvullan parish of Enniskillen, in the barony of Tirkennedy. It recorded a Philip Shannon who rented out a home and office (no land) from William Wilson at the townland of Lissan. Another Philip Shannon (a popular name) had lived at Templeport in Cavan in 1857.

1864 signalled a real demand by the people for the vote. The 1832 Reform had only resulted in the franchise of 1 out of 6 adult males, with no serious inroads in the positions of power and influence. Much to Palmerston's alarm, who considered that workmen were indifferent to enfranchisement, Gladstone was now an advocate of universal suffrage. Disraeli accused him of resurrecting the doctrine of Tom Paine. At that time, Gladstone found the visit of Garibaldi to England an annoying diversion, especially when Garibaldi became the 'idol of the nation'; Gladstone was glad when the visit was cut short. Gladstone's support for Italian independence at the expense of Papal dominance, was to cost him the 'friendship of those children of the Holy Father who came from Ireland'. However he could not be indifferent towards Ireland, and the tormenting question was to haunt him for the rest of his life: 'They could not look at Ireland and say that the state of feeling there was for the honour and the advantage of the united kingdom'.

The Irish felt that Lancashire had been hogging the limelight. Gladstone reflected on the energy that he had recently given to Mersey and the Tyne areas, and decided that the great national task for him was the eventual 'proposal of religious equality for Ireland in 1868'. There were annual outbursts of Orange-Day aggression, and in 1864 anti-Irish incidents took place in Barrow where contractor Thomas Brassey employed 1,500 navvies. The Barrow Herald did not hold back in highlighting the 'disgrace' of the English 'roughs'. There had been an argument between a Scottish worker from Dumfries and an Irishman called McManus accusing the Irish of undercutting wages.

During the building of the Caledonian Railway nearly Lockerby in 1865, there had been riots involving fighting between mainly Scots and English against the Irish. As the Scottish Herald reported, "there was a third of each: easy-going Roman Catholic Irish, Presbyterian Scots and impartially belligerent English; the Irish did not look for a fight: they camped with their women and children in some of the more secluded glades, and although most of the huts showed an amazing disregard of comfort, 'the hereditary glee of their occupants seemed not a whit impaired'. This glee enraged the Scots, who then added to their one genuine grievance – the fact that the Irish would work for less pay, and their sanctified outrage that the Irish should regard the Sabbath as a holiday, a day of recreation on which they sang and lazed around. As for the Scots, all they did on a Sunday was to drink often and pray occasionally, and it needed only an odd quart of whisky and a small prayer to make them half daft with Presbyterian fervour. They then beat up the godless Irish'.

On the 27 September 1864, James Shannon's mother, Isabella died at the age of 57 years, at Fyland Bridge, St Andrew Auckland. The occupation of her widower, Clement Mason, was given as 'Deputy Overman at the colliery'. His marriage to Isabella had provided him the opportunity to get promoted to his new position. As an overman, he was responsible for safety, and deciding the allocation of underground work areas.

Isabella's death certificate gave the cause of death as 'Paralysis, 1week, Not Certified', and the informant in attendance was John Mason, who was probably Clement's eldest son. Often paralysis followed a stroke. One year after Isabella's death, Clement Mason married Susannah Armitage at St Andrews Auckland, his fourth wife!

A second daughter, named Isabella after James's mother, was born on the eleventh of December 1864 at Deanery Colliery, St Andrew Auckland. Naturally, there would have been a period of bereavement after the loss of their previous child. James was still a colliery sinker and had not moved far to start work on sinking at Deanery Colliery, also known as Auckland Park. Widower Clement Mason and his step children were not living far away.

Robert Mason, a chargeman sinker at Wooley Colliery near Crook, in 1864 was killed during firing shot at shaft bottom. He was working for his brother (William Mason) a contractor responsible for sinking the pit. William Mason in 1861 had been a mining engineer at Whitburn, and must have worked at Crook before moving to Lancashire as a master sinker.

Master sinker William Coulson (who had been closely involved in the early training of James Mason) was buried in Durham City on 16 June 1865. His health had been seriously affected by his rescue at New Hartley colliery in 1862.

At Coxhoe Colliery in 1866, a hewer named John Shannon died at the age of 26 years, whilst ascending a shaft. This illustrated the fact that when a colliery was in production, many miners were killed during their journey up and down the shaft to their work station. Four years later at Coxoe four sinkers were killed falling down the shaft.

William Coulson, master sinker 1864
(NEIMME)

Colliery deaths continued unknown to the general public despite the catastrophe of New Hartley. The mining industry had always accepted a high number of fatalities.

At this time a staple shaft (between different underground levels) was being sunk at Monkwearmouth, the deepest pit in Durham. Sinking was also taking place at Rainton, Seaham, Harraton, Whitwell, Tudhoe and South Medomsley. As Seaton and Seaham collieries amalgamated, a number of underground explosions took place. Thomas Hepburn was to die in abject poverty after having been forced to give up trade union activity and brought to the brink of starvation by Lord Londonderry.

John Bright was the most eloquent spokesman of the Reform League which had formed in 1865, with its aims of manhood suffrage and the ballot. In contrast Disraeli considered that the Relief Bill gave too many working people the vote. The press reported that Queen Victoria was about to come out of mourning, but this proved to be untrue. In the General Election of July 1865, there was under-representation of industrial areas, but individual victory for John Stuart Mills and Tom Hughes. Russell became once more prime minister; Gladstone prepared a new Reform Bill during the Christmas of 1865 and the New Year 1866, after pressure from Bright's campaign. It was a period of 'political mixes' and uncertainty with the same ferment of outdoor Radical meetings as during the first Reform Bill. The Queen soon was to urge the Tories to accept reform which she now regarded as sensible and just. A demand from the pleasure-seeking Prince of Wales for sterner measures against 'rebels' among the 'lower orders' was dismissed by Bright.

Victoria went on to further castigate the 'Highborn beings' as responsible for persecuting her manservant John Brown and for condemning her seclusion. Of Disraeli's 'two nations', rich and poor, she declared that she was the 'Queen of the poor' who cheered her most, sympathized most with her grief, and were loyal. She most admired, like Prince Albert, the people who succeeded in a practical way to improve man's lot. For that reason one of her favourite books was Samuel Smiles 'Lives of the Engineers' published in 1865, and indicator of growing prosperity. Men from the 'lower orders' were beginning to succeed, such as Robert Applegarth the first working man to be appointed to a Royal Commission (on contagious diseases). Edwin Chadwick, the pioneer of sanitation was created [with some reluctance] a Commander of the Bath in 1854, and a Knight in 1884 'to distinguish me', as he said 'from the great unwashed'. The Union Chargeability Act 1865 brought an end to 'closed' parishes which were responsible for supporting only its own paupers. This was particularly relevant to the heavily settled areas. For the solitary of the Northumberland uplands where families were dependent on travelling hawkers, there was little distinction between open and closed parishes.

In 1865 Joseph Lister started using antiseptic methods in his operations but too late for some, as death was to visit both politicians and royalty. In April Cobden died and Palmerston in October, followed by King Leopold of Belgium in December. During 1865–66, cholera from Hamburg was to strike South Shields. The town of Boyle in Ireland was suffering from typhus and typhoid, and its local paper noted that back in 1818 a quarter of the town had been affected by a cholera outbreak. Cobden had hoped that Palmerston's death would mark the start of a new era in foreign policy, but the 'Crimean' approach was to continue for a few more decades. The 'Manchester School' renounced active diplomatic participation in a concert of powers.

The Locomotive 'Red Flag' Act 1865 made it compulsory for any mechanically propelled vehicle on the roads to have a person walking in front carrying a red flag to warn pedestrians and horsemen. For horseless carriages it introduced a speed limit of 4 mph, under pressure from the railway companies to stop any competition from steam carriages. By 1867 the railways had eclipsed the canals as goods carriers; more coal was being carried by rail than by sea. Self-Help by Smiles was published in 1865. Durham colliery managers were searching for miners from other counties especially from Cornwall.

The issue of the Jamaican Governor Eyre caused great public controversy, and divided opinion into two camps, with the scientists Darwin, Huxley, Mill, Stephen and Lyell on side of law and humanity, and Carlyle, Ruskin, Kingsley, Tennyson and Bright on the side of the 'strong man' fearing extension of the franchise. However Carlyle in later years when referring to Abraham Lincoln's heroic fight against slavery, said with tears: 'I doubt I have been mistaken'. The American Civil War ended in April 1865, as did the life of

Abraham Lincoln. In the USA, John Mitchel was released from prison in the 'fall' and joined the American Fenians. In March James Stephens, leader of the IRB, escaped to France with the help of Fenian port officials. There were rumours of an uprising taking place during 1866. From the USA there were Fenian raids on Canada, causing divided loyalties amongst the Irish-Canadians between those loyal to their new home and those with sympathies for the Irish back home. During 1865, a Fenian trial was held in County Cork with a population of 500,000 Catholics and 50,000 Protestants. A jury panel was called, composed of 360 Protestants and 40 Catholics. The Irish People warned that Catholic priests were calling on the people to be informers.

George Eliot's novel, Felix Holt, the Radical, was published in 1866. The hero was an educated man who chose to lead the life of an artisan. This was the dilemma that faced William Morris some years later. To Gladstone's disgust Parliament had forced through the twentieth Irish coercion bill since the Union. Gladstone, as a member of Russell's ministry, introduced in March a bill designed to enfranchise 400,000 men, about half of them working class, by lowering the 1832 £10 rental level to £7 and various other concessions.

The Tories were utterly opposed to the extension of franchise, and were assisted by Robert Lowe, the Times leader-writer and MP for Calne (Wilshire), who had fought doggedly against any advance in democracy. The defecting Liberals led by Lowe were against further enfranchisement on the grounds of its probable consequences rather than on the grounds of 'natural right' or 'social justice'. Gladstone only lost by four votes. This halt to the Government's reform bill caused such public fury, that a crowd of protesters stormed Hyde Park on the 6 May 1866, when an application to hold a reform demonstration was refused, resulting in a collision between demonstrators and the police. The irresolution of the Government contrasted sharply with their stern measures in 1848.

Bright was beginning to dominate the heart and mind of the Liberals on reform and Ireland; this was the era of Fenian outrage and conspiracy. Early in 1866 when he was urging remedial legislation on the Irish Church and land, a Bill suspending Habeas Corpus was passed. It was said that Gladstone did not admire the Irish, when he told the Queen they were an 'unstable' people and it was necessary to 'tranquallize' them, for their condition was a 'standing reproach' to Britain abroad. Perhaps Gladstone did not appreciate the Irish wit. Peabody, the philanthropist, and John Bright, often visited Ireland together to fish the Shannon. On one occasion the millionaire paid the boatman the correct price of three half-crowns. The boatman dissatisfied that it did not include a tip commented: "An' they call ye Paybody, don't they? Well, I call ye Paynobody."

As autumn approached in the main British cities, there were riots and street processions. During 1866–7, home-made bombs were exploded by Sheffield strikers in the homes of some non-union workers. Bright made maximum use of the wave of popular opinion by giving speeches in England, Scotland and Ireland. Since the Crimean War, wages had been high and food dear, but on the 11 May 1866, Black Friday, there was a major financial panic. Railway contractor Peto went bankrupt, with Brassey barely surviving. However, Lord Kelvin was successful in laying the Atlantic cable for telegraph messages.

The first Labour Party Prime Minister, James Ramsey MacDonald, was born at the Scottish town of Lossiemouth in 1866. As a youth, he worked as a pupil teacher. In the same year Queen Victoria visited the Windsor Union Workhouse and commented that although the poor old couples were kept clean, it was hard on them to be separated. Even John Bright came to her defence when she was attacked in a public meeting by a Radical for her secluded habits (This was also the period of the 'Mrs Brown' slander):

> '... I venture to say this, that a woman – be she the Queen of a great realm, or be she
> the wife of one of your labouring men – who can keep alive in her heart a great sorrow
> for the lost object of her life and affection is not at all likely to be wanting in a great
> and generous sympathy for you.'

Jane Carlyle died in April 1866. During her last days she was attended by two Irish sick nurses. The first from Brampton in Cumberland was a good-natured young nun with a good deal of brogue, and a tolerable share of blarney. She was replaced by an earnest French lady, who although well intentioned, became over-bearing in her efforts to draw her patient's thoughts to religious matters. Thomas Carlyle apparently had some pity for the Frenchwoman whom he suspected 'was under the foul tutelage and guidance, probably, of some dirty muddy-minded semi-felonious Proselytising Irish Priest'.

During a trip to Rome in autumn and early winter of 1866/67, Gladstone had an audience with the Pope, discussing amongst others the subject of Fenianism, apparently a favourite subject with British politicians when talking to Supreme Pontiffs. At this time, hundreds of Fenians died as the English Government suspended Habeas Corpus. Despite a £1000 reward, Stephens remained in Ireland until March 1866 when he left for America, not able to live up to his assertion that the year 'would not pass without a blow struck in Ireland'.

CHAPTER 12

1867–1873 New Reform and Trade Unions

(James Mason – Master Sinker)

'It was not benevolence but justice which can deal with great evils.'

(Bright 1867)

'...the English bourgeoisie has not only exploited the Irish poverty to keep down the working class in England by forced immigration of poor Irishmen, but has divided the proletariat into two hostile camps.'

(Die Neue Zeit Marx 1870)

The legislation of the early 1870s provided the foundations of modern trade unionism following the second major reform bill. Marx's Das Kapital was published in 1867, but it was the 'New Model Unionism' with its leaders, Robert Applegarth, Alexander MacDonald, George Odger and George Howell, which was influencing working class attitudes. These unions spread from the engineers to the ironfounders and the building trades, but were not taken up in mining, cotton and metals manufactures. It was trade union pressure that led to the Master and Servant Act and the introduction of Courts of Conciliation and Arbitration.

Following Gladstone's failure to bring in a new reform bill in 1866, Disraeli carried through a more comprehensive reform bill in 1867, despite the fact that the Conservatives were hostile to any bill that would give the working class the vote. Robert Lowe belittled the reform as the 'principle of numbers as against wealth and intellect'. This was to be a volte-face for Disraeli, similar to Peel's change of mind on the Corn Laws in 1846. Since the collapse of the Chartists, John Bright had been largely responsible for re-constructing the democratic movement. Throughout late 1866, Bright had attended large demonstrations in the major towns, and with a monster meeting at Newcastle. Three years later the Home Rule movement started in Ireland stirring interest by their expatriates and clergy, with less hostility to the Irish in England. In 1872 a mass meeting was held at Newcastle's Town Moor supporting an amnesty for Fenians.

While the Russians were selling Alaska to America, and the first Dominion was being created in Canada by the uniting of the provinces of Quebec, Ontario, New Brunswick

Benjamin Disraeli 1878 (Lord Beaconsfield)
(theguardian.com)

and Novia Scotia, Carlyle was highlighting the political watershed at home when he likened the passing of the Reform Bill to 'shooting of Niagara'. The Bill for Canada established as part of the constitution, the principle that 'one man is as good as another'. In 1867 a separate Reform Bill for Scotland and Ireland was passed, but there were external worries for the Government; Gladstone was to have commented that the 'Empire is in danger from Ireland, United States and Canada'. The Fenians in USA had tried to launch an armed invasion of Canada. For the post-Chartist class of ambitious skilled and semi-skilled workers, prosperity was the basis of the new unionism exhausting maximum benefit from the existing order. Wages in mining had doubled between 1851 and 1871.

Another indication of prosperity was the growing popularity of music halls and other forms of entertainment, and consumption of alcohol. Charles Dickens was touring the towns, including lectures in Ireland and America. He commented on the intelligence of the Tyneside people: 'The readings have made an immense effect on this place, and it is remarkable that although the people are individually rough, collectively they are an unusually tender and sympathetic audience; while their comic perception is quite up to the London standard'. In 1867, the Parliamentary Commission on the Employment of Women and Children reported on Northumberland: 'The people value education very much, and many of the children come several miles to school .... A few shepherds on the hills keep a schoolmaster among them; Virgil, Horace, and Caesar are not strange to them ...... children of agricultural labourers remain at school until fourteen or fifteen years of age'. Obviously the spotlight on children over the previous thirty years had made its mark at last.

Gladstone ensured that the 1867 Reform Bill included a vote for lodgers. Lodgers were considered a dangerous voting group which would have included many navvies and pit sinkers. On the 17 June 1867 at New Winnings Boldon, Alexander Shannon (author's grandfather) was born some seven years after James and Lydia's first Alexander had died as a baby. In Victorian times it was not unusual for the same

Christian name to be used as a mark of respect and affection for a child in the same family who had died earlier.

The father was still identified on the birth certificate as a 'Sinker', so it was clear that he had moved on to the next new mine since the birth of his previous child at Auckland. The shaft for New Winnings Colliery was sunk starting in 1866. The sinking of deep shafts involved very large financial expenditure for the colliery proprietors.

At Eppleton Colliery, a tragedy occurred in 1867 when a wooden cabin erected on the heapstead at the top of shaft caught fire, and the smoke was drawn into the downcast shaft and through the intake roadways of the mine. A deputy named Thompson was overcome by the fumes. In the same year, a nitroglycerine fire broken out on Newcastle Quay.

The mining term 'to win a material', meant to gain the material or ore by means of hand digging or mechanical excavation, but in colliery terms, a "winning" was a certain length of excavation along a coal seam on either side of a 'headway' which was the main working into the seam. In the North East, the typical length of a winning was about seven yards. However the general use of the term for a colliery was for a new working area or shaft. The publication 'the Compleat Collier', described the coal-stone or 'whin' as the 'hardest sort of stone met with in the Earth'. A 'head-sincker' had to understand the 'Nature of Stone and Styth and Surfet' since an inexperienced labourer could be severely wounded on whin or hard stone.

A master sinker had sole care of the framing a shaft during sinking. After the successful sinking of a shaft, it was customary for the sinkers to pay the labourers they had employed a 'Piece or Guinea, to Drink the good success of the Colliery, which is called their Coaling Money, and then lye Idle till you have occasion to break, or begin to sink another Pit, which I hope will not be long' During the winter season lower wages were paid. For shafts deeper than 30 fathoms (checked by 'Plumet line'), the sinkers were in charge of the 'Horse Engin' (shortened to 'gin' by miners) used to raise and lower their equipment. The control of the water entering the mine workings was critical, not only for the working of the coal but also because the water caused the coal to be 'black and heavy'. Springs or 'feeders' were the great enemy at depths greater than 40 fathoms, and could cost the owners thousands of pounds. Collieries could be flooded by careless boring. 'Oaken Spars, Firr bawks and deal Boards' were used down to the 'Stone Head' (Rock Head).

At Castle Eden in 1868, sinker William Dower aged 28 died when a plank fell on top of him; one year later sinker Joseph Anderson aged 50, fell down a shaft to his death when the kibble rope broke. James Mason was sinking there before heading to Hetton.

Despite the ban on Fenianism by the Catholic clergy, the International Republican Brigade (I.R.B.) in Ireland issued the word for a rising in February 1867, later delayed by one month. The insurrection broke out in Ireland during a terrific snowstorm. The North of England IRB failed to receive notice of this change, and an attempt to capture a stock of arms from Chester Castle was aborted. In September there was an attempted Fenian coup in Manchester. Five Irishmen had attempted to rescue two Fenian prisoners from a police van and a British policeman, Sergeant Brett, was killed. This was shortly followed by rumours of plots to assassinate the Queen. On the 23 November, the captured Fenians, O'Brien, Larkin and Allen, were hanged. The other prisoners O'Meagher Condon and Maguire were transported.

The 'Manchester Martyrs' were to bring the question of Irish reform within the sphere of practical politics; Gladstone's strategy for dealing with the Irish Church problem became known as the 'cutting down the Irish Upas tree'. His speech on the 19 December was almost entirely devoted to Irish issues, and was considered more courageous coming as it did immediately after a wave of Fenian attacks. Henceforth his mind was never to be free of the Irish. During the following spring in Australia, there was a Fenian reprisal when Prince Alfred was shot but survived. The attacker, James O'Farrell, was hung shortly after. Also an attempt to release a Fenian prisoner from Clerkenwell prison in London, resulted in twelve neighbouring residents being killed. Daniel Barrett a young Fenian from Fermanagh, sentenced to death for his part in this bomb attack, was the last man to be hanged in public in May 1868.

Gladstone standing in south west Lancashire, in a series of resounding election speeches, lashed out at the Protestant ascendancy in Ireland. He compared it to 'some tall tree of noxious growth ….. but now at last the day has come when, as we hope, the axe has been laid to root'. Gladstone was in his shirt-sleeves at Hawarden, North Wales, cutting down a tree, when he received the royal message requesting him to form a ministry. He recorded later that he said 'my mission is to pacify Ireland', and that fate had ordained him for a special task. John Maguire, MP for Cork, brought forward a motion on the state of Ireland, and after many days of debate, Gladstone declared for reform. The Irish Reform Act 1868 was not to have much effect on a so thinly urbanised country as Ireland. In contrast, the Liberals planned a great programme of reforms between 1869 and 1873.

The trade unions were refused legal protection of their funds in 1867, but this was reversed the following year. Then an embryonic Trades Union Congress took place in Manchester. Trades unions were now accepted (at the lower rungs of the capitalist ladder), and although Marx and Engels lived in England during the formative years of the trade union movement, they appeared to have had no influence on its development. Marx did not succeed in getting the International Working Men's Association to launch an agitation for Repeal – his efforts were cut across by Gladstone's accession to power, and his decision at once to introduce the Disestablishment Bill (1869). In this, Gladstone had the full support of Cardinal Manning, since he feared a threat to Roman authority if the Irish prelates and priests became pensioners of the London government. However, Marx did work strenuously through the International in support of the Amnesty Movement which secured the release of most of the leading Fenian prisoners on the 1st January 1871.

The Irish socialist, James Connolly, noted that Fenanism, though unquestionably a national movement and not a class movement, appealed successfully to the wage-worker class, especially the exile communities in England, Scotland, the USA and Australia. The future Home Rule Party, led by Charles Stewart Parnell, was a response to the need for an Irish political voice after the armed failures of previous years. Initially, it found expression in the demand for an amnesty led by Karl Marx and the I.W.M.A's campaign for a union of English workers and the Irish National movement. Gladstone averted this 'calamity' by conceding an amnesty for about a hundred of the Fenians first convicted. This had been prompted by the election of O'Donovan Rossa at Tipperary in 1869.

In 1869 there was a strike at Monkwearmouth Colliery in response to a 33% reduction in wages; in contrast overseas mining was really taking off. In Kimberley, South African diamonds were discovered. Many of the working classes had sympathetic feelings towards the colonies and imperialism, since they had relations who had been forced to emigrate, and if trade worsened it might be their lot as well. 1869 was to see the opening of the Suez Canal. Charles Kingsley in his book, 'At Last', described his travels around the West Indies on the 'good steamship Shannon'. He referred to the 'cities of the Old World, and the short and stunted figures, the mesquin and scrofulous visages, which crowd our alleys, and back wynds'. Comparing the inhabitants of these areas with the West Indies, he added that 'we have at home tens of thousands of paupers, rouges, whatnot, who are not a whit more civilised, intellectual, virtuous, or spiritual than the Negroes'.

The central preoccupation of writers like Matthew Arnold, John Stuart Mill, William Morris and Henry James was the 'Condition of England', and Arnold's Culture and Anarchy, a biting indictment of materialism, reflected on the social revolution up to 1869. Mill had abandoned the subsistence wage theory. In that year State inspection of schools had discovered that about two million children were not receiving any schooling. One year before, the National Education League had been set up, mainly at the instigation of Joseph Chamberlain, a Birmingham Unitarian screw manufacturer, dedicated to converting the Liberal Party to the idea of a free, secular and compulsory elementary education based on the American 'common school' model. The Education League and the Non-conformists were to be grievously disappointed by the Liberal Government; Gladstone never supposed that the 'products' of elementary education would ever become 'masters'. He reluctantly conceded legal status to trade unions on moral grounds, but considered the aggressive picketing as contrary to the classical doctrines of political economy and free market forces.

On the 2 April 1869 aged 65 years, Clement Mason died of 'Anasarca', a form of dropsy (3 weeks certified), at New Winnings Boldon. (Ann Shannon had died of the same illness). James Mason was to die at the same colliery seventeen years later. Clement's death certificate recorded the informant as Joseph Coates, present at death. Isabella Mason may have stayed for a short time with her son James who had just started sinking at Boldon. Two years later Isabella's son, John Lawrence, was recorded as a draper living in Boldon Colliery – he had escaped a life down the pit, but perhaps earning less than a miner. John was lodging with Joseph Coates. His sister Anne Jane was to marry Joseph Coates.

Bewicke Main Colliery was sunk in 1868, and Wheatley Hill in 1869. This was the year of the formation of the Durham Miners Association, a watershed in the relationship between the men and masters. In the preceding three years there had been down-turn in the coal-trade causing the owners to make savage cuts in the miners' piece-rate earnings. A series of strikes and disturbances swept the country, re-kindling the spirit of trade unionism. Old Tommy Ramsey, a hero of the 1844 strike who had trudged from village to village keeping the flame of unionism alight, shunned by miners fearful of the consequences of being seen in his company, was now given a job as full-time union agent and a salary to go with it. The Franco-Prussian war in 1870 reduced the capacity of the continental coalfields, and created a shortage of coal which the coal barons of Durham were only too eager to exploit. A period of peace in the coalfields was required if full advantage was to be taken of the new opportunities in trade. Alexander MacDonald, like other miners' leader at this time, was a Liberal, and favoured a conciliatory approach with employers.

In the company of a number of eminent people such as scientist Sir C Lyell and poet Robert Browning, Thomas Carlyle paid a visit to Buckingham Palace on the 4 March 1869. Queen Victoria recorded in her diary:'Mr Carlyle, the historian, a strange looking eccentric Scotchman, who holds forth in a drawling voice, with a loud Scotch accent, upon Scotland and upon the utter degeneration of everything'. John Stuart Mill disowned the rigid market rate of wages. Aristocracy (private property) and Radicals (private capital) were agreed on the fear of social revolution and the dread of an attack on the existing economic order. Public execution and flogging were abolished in 1868, but as late as 1871, army commissions could still be purchased. 'The Subjection of Women' by JS Mill was published, and in 1870 the Married Women's Property Act gave a wife the right to keep her own earnings; a later Act in 1882 extended women's rights after marriage.

The 22 July 1869 saw the dis-establishment of the Irish Church. Victoria's patience with the Irish had also worn thin. She noted that the Catholic Irish, even the upper classes, were 'totally unreliable, & utterly untrue .... grievances they really have none', and only 'a new infusion of race' would solve the Irish problem. These views had been passed on by

Prince Albert who had considered the Scottish superior due to their mix of Scandinavian blood. (He did realise that this was just as true for the Irish!) The First Land Act 1869 was in Gladstone's view, an embodiment of the custom of Ulster Tenant Right in law for all Ireland. In rural Ulster generally, the establishment of the 'Ulster Right' was another negation of the principle of laissez faire. In August Gladstone stayed four nights at Raby Castle in Durham, as the guest of the Duke of Cleveland.

One month later Engels paid his second and last visit to Ireland; he noted its depopulated appearance. The relative prosperity of Belfast and Ulster was a crushing condemnation of the English economic policy enforced on the rest of Ireland. Gladstone's Act failed because it contained restrictions that prevented tenants taking full advantage of it, but chiefly because its operation was sabotaged by the landlords. Ireland was to remain a feeder for England and crippled by parasitic landlordism. Revolutionary Irish writer, James Finton Lalor, was to explain the heart of the 'land question' which was later taken up by Henry George in Poverty and Progress:

> 'To any plain understanding the right of private property is very simple. It is
> the right of man to possess, enjoy, and transfer the substance and use of whatever
> he himself has created. This title is good against the world; and it is the sole and only
> title by which a valid right of absolute private property can possibly rest. But no man
> can plead any such title to a right of property in the substance of the soil.'

The essence of Lalor's doctrine was to provide a stimulus for Michael Davtt (of Land League fame) in his cell in Portland Gaol, and later for James Connolly. During this period, Disraeli laid low and did not resist the Irish Land Bill. Bright was convinced that the root of Irish misery lay in the land question. Gladstone was well aware that the path to achieving the land bill was threatened by the huge and bottomless ignorance of those in which the power laid. Bright and Gladstone differed in the best means of giving the widest benefit to the Irish people; Bright argued for tenants to become owners whereas Gladstone wanted to treat the tenant as a tenant. Lowe was against compensation on eviction, and took some convincing that unlike previous administrations, it was planned to consult with the Irish and not just 'make Irish law out of their own heads'. Gladstone was confident that Queen Victoria was in the same frame of mind as the cabinet.

Public opinion was ripening, with the Times for the first time bringing the facts of the land question before its readers, and Mill producing a pamphlet advocating the buying out of the landlords. In making life more tolerable for the Irish tenancy, there were fears that this would feed back to undermine the much less oppressive landlord system in England and Scotland. In Britain generally, the landlord made capital improvements whereas in Ireland with its multiplicity of holdings, it was mostly the tenants who carried out drainage, fencing, making farm roads and construction of farm buildings. The minimum approach involved tenant compensation, whereas a more comprehensive policy would include the 3 Fs – fixity of tenure, fair rent and freedom of sale.

MacDonagh in his book 'Irish Life and Character' relates the following incident: During the Land League agitation a tenant farmer, who occupied a conspicuous part in the movement in his own locality, returning from market one evening, not very steady in his walk, fell into a bog-hole by the side of the road, where he stuck fast. His landlord, chancing to pass on horseback shortly afterwards saw the tenant's dilemma, and laughingly cried, "Well, James, you've got fixity of tenure now". "Yes begor, yer honner," ejaculated James; "and shure 'tis I would be moightly obliged to yer honner if you'd be after evictin' me".

In September 1869, Thomas Shannon died of Supra Penal Capiraly [Capillary] at the age of 52. His occupation was given as a labourer like his brother Richard. His wife Elizabeth was the informant at Westgate, Newcastle.

The Home Rule Movement was founded by Isaac Butt at the beginning of the 1870s. During that decade, agrarian conspiracy led to many attempted murders of landlords; the very few informants were treated with intense hatred and abhorrence by their communities. No more opprobrious term than 'informer' was contained in the Irish peasants' ample vocabulary of abuse. He was subjected to the severest ostracism – harder to bear than death in a rural district. They were considered as traitors. Following the Land Act 1870, the years up to 1877 were relatively prosperous in Ireland, although the landlord's right to raise rents was not curtailed.

Gladstone was willing to admit that continuing Fenian outrages was very effective in concentrating the otherwise complacent English mind on the Irish problem. In September 1870 he failed to persuade his cabinet on the immediate release of Fenian prisoners. There were American-Fenian plots for an invasion of Ireland resulting in British pressure on the Pope to issue a decree outlawing the IRB. Jenny Marx initiated an international scandal by revealing in The French newspaper, The Marseillaise, the callous treatment of Fenian O'Donovan Rossa at Portland prison.

In 1870, Dr Barnardo, born in Dublin, founded his first home for orphan children in London. Perhaps his experiences in Ireland left him a deep conscience. In that year Britain's literary genius, Charles Dickens died, an untiring advocate for working class education. The most important education act of the nineteenth century was passed in 1870. This was the foundation of modern primary education, creating State schools to fill the gap left by voluntary societies. State grants to voluntary educational societies had begun in 1833 and had steadily increased. This Education Act required school attendance to the age of 13, and included the remittance of fees for poor parents. Only 1 in 8 Englishmen could read and write in 1800; Huxley suggested that 'Ragged Schools' or 'Free Schools' be named

'Substrata Schools' – perhaps because it had a scientific ring about it. Some progress had been made since 1839, when at that date twice as much was spent on Buckingham Palace stables as compared to state education. Up to then, the Mechanics' Institutes had provided instruction in English, arithmetic, elementary science and other subjects for thousands of workers; these were mainly skilled craftsmen since 1800, but after the Act their numbers declined.

Friedrich Engels seemed to understand the distinction between Fenian sympathy and action better than the Fenians were advocating. His mistress was an Irishwoman, and his home in Manchester was the centre of Fenian activity, and even decorated in Fenian colours of green and black. Though critical of the activities of the IRB, both Marx and he had great sympathy for the Manchester Martyrs. Marx wrote, 'I sought in every way to provoke this manifestation of the English workers in support of Fenianism'. But in the end he decided it was hopeless: 'England possesses a working class divided into two hostile camps, English proletarians and Irish proletarians. The ordinary English worker hates the Irish worker as a competitor'.

This was highlighted in the Murphy riots during 1867–1871 in Lancashire which followed the anti-Catholic ugly eruptions of 1850. William Murphy was the son of a Catholic born in Limerick who secretly turned Protestant. Murphy moved to England to offer his services to the Protestant Electoral Union. His lectures immediately attracted protest. William Murphy, habitually whipped up working-class anti-Catholicism and anti-Irish-ness during his lecture tours, causing considerable unrest in communities from Plymouth to Tynemouth, and Wolverhampton to Whitehaven. If casual drink-related violence and commonplace Orange riots were added to these specific examples of anti-Irish behaviour, then violence could be seen as a central feature of the life of Irish migrants. Thirteen years later the Cumbrian Orangemen tried to hold a demonstration, but the Carlisle Express noted that there were real dangers for them in the capital of the mining district, with 'little spirit of tolerance by the Catholic population of Cleator Moor'.

In 1871 about 200–300 miners at Cleator Moor trapped Murphy and threw him down some stairs. An Irishman named Doyle and six other assailants were jailed. Murphy died a year later from injuries sustained at Whitehaven, where a large Irish labour force worked in the local ironstone mines. The Irish there numbered 4,175 in 1851. Between 1851 and 1881 the population of Cumbria shifted markedly towards its coastal regions and the area around Carlisle, and the Irish-born portion of the county, steady at around 5%, was exceeded only in places like Lancashire and Tyneside. The new homes of the migrant Irish constituted the model 'urban proletariat'. The Orange-versus-Green division was overwhelmingly urban.

Hetton Colliery 1844
(t.h.hair)

Catholic churches were beginning to be built at Willington Quay, Boldon Colliery and Hebburn; Orange and Ribbon organisations from the 1830s were still maintained in most communities of northern England. Religious tensions were raised when after lengthy internal debates, the Roman Catholic Church pronounced on the Infallibility of the Roman Pontiff. Gladstone was to respond with a pamphlet entitled 'Vaticanism' which discussed the 'awful' implications of conflicting civil allegiances of Roman Catholics. However on the political front there was harmony between Irish Catholicism and English Liberalism. The Home Rule Federation of Great Britain was formed for the Irish in Britain. The 1870s was to see the Temperance Movement growing in strength, so much so that most working men's clubs before 1900 were teetotal.

A Report on the Inspection of Coal Mines, in the South Durham and Northumberland District in 1865, explained why young boys were particularly vulnerable underground: 'The great number of Shetland ponies now employed in this district to convey coal from the working places to the horse railway .... appears to add, in some degree, to the previous loss of life from accidents by crushes of tubs, as only young boys are employed in this work, and the lowness and narrowness of the galleries, often further contracted by the timber required for the support of the roof, renders the employment one of considerable danger, particularly where the dip of the seam renders it necessary to use drags ... The extensive use of engine and inclined planes for the conveyance of coals in mines in this district has already been noticed as tending to increase accidents from crushes by trains of tubs travelling at considerable velocities on underground railways ... Care ought to be taken to provide as much side room as possible for persons to get out of the way of trains.' Mrs Lowry living at Downs Lane who had lost two sons in the pit, one by a fall of stone, and the other when he fell down the shaft. The family had received little sympathy from officialdom.

Little progress had been made on workers' compensation since the 1830s when Isabella Shannon first became a widow. Young miners were to continue to face many dangers well into the next century, as recorded on the death certificate of a David Belshaw aged 20 years, killed at Eppleton Colliery in 1917, 'crushed between a plank and a tub'. The efforts of his mother to dissuade him from joining the young men in foreign trenches had been in vain. His cousin, Arthur Ford at the age of 17 years in 1883, had died running to work, by tripping and falling in front of a locomotive engine drawing waggons up Downs Bank at Hetton-le-Hole. James Mason would have heard of the latter death having known sinker Francis Ford at Hetton in 1871, a relation of Arthur.

Sinker, Francis Ford, was living very close by at 5 Downs Lane. In the census it gave his age as 25 years, and his birth place as Writhlington in Somerset. (Many years later author's father William Mason, the grandson of James Mason was to marry Annie Ford, the great-niece of Francis Ford). It was likely that Francis worked for James Mason. Francis Ford some years later moved to Australia to work in the mines there.

According to Elizabeth's Statute of Artificers, no man could set up as master or as workman till he had served his seven years apprenticeship. In those days, masters were expected to beat their apprentices and often laid angry hands on their journeymen. In sinking, the relationship between master and his sinkers had to depend on trust, firmness and not strictly on traditional rules.

This was a time of high coal prices and demand, and sinkers were working all over Durham. Coxhoe Colliery was also being sunk in 1871. Young sinkers Walter and Luke Mason born in Fatfield may have been twin brothers. At Ryhope Colliery near Sunderland there was a thirteen year-old compass boy who was assisting a mining engineer.

In July 1870, Prussia declared war on France despite Queen Victoria's efforts to avoid a conflict within her royal family, who were now scattered around the royal households of Europe. Although her sympathies were with Prussia, Britain was declared neutral. At this time Disraeli grabbed the opportunity to mobilise 'national' public opinion against the Prussians. On the 1st September Napoleon III was defeated, followed by his surrender and the declaration of a Republic. His son, the Prince Imperial fled to England. On the 28 January 1871 an armistice was signed. England in February recognised the new republic of France. The Emperor William I presided over a united Germany, and republicanism was in the air. The continental conflicts meant an expansion of the British coalfields with more Irish miners.

During October 1870, smallpox which was ravaging the north of England, broke out in South Shields. There many Irish, such as Henry Shannon, were working as labourers at the Alkali Works. Henry's wife died of exhaustion after a triple birth. At this time, William Mason, a master sinker, was employed on a waterworks at Aughton in Lancashire. The skills of sinking shafts and boring were being exported from north-east England to other parts of Britain. Ten years later he was still working at Aughton, and then in 1891 he was appointed master sinker at Ferryhill in Durham.

In 1870 the formation of the Labour Representative League took place. This organisation was composed of Radicals, Socialists and trade unionists in London. The Trades Union Act 1871, gave protection to trade union funds, but modifications by the Criminal Law Amendment Act made strike action dangerous. This Act passed by the Liberals, made picketing and intimidation in strikes illegal. It followed a number of cases in which blacklegs, who had refused to join the strike, had been injured or killed by fellow workers. Outside mining areas during the 1870s, Irish and English navvies still fought violently, as in the early confrontations of the 1840s.

The Universities Test Act 1871 allowed Roman Catholics to hold office at the universities of Oxford, Cambridge and Durham. Fenians, John Devoy and hard-liner O'Donovan Rossa were released as well as other Fenians John McClure, Harry Mulleda and Charles Underwood O'Connell. An American Fenian, O'Reilly, was to become a strong advocate for black and Indian rights. Fenians had expected great things from an insurrection, but only saw the fiasco of 1867, and the enforcement of the neutrality laws by the United States which deprived them of the hope of striking at England on American soil. However in January, the Irish State Church was abolished after having impoverished and enslaved Irish people for so long. On the 28 January Paris surrendered, but this did not give Marx any satisfaction as the necessary revolutionary transformation between a capitalist and a communist society, 'from each according to his ability to each according to his needs', did not take place.

In the 1871 Census, James continued to use the name Mason, and his family was shown to be living at 135 Downs New Houses in Hetton le Hole. Unlike the previous census, it gave his occupation as Pit Sinker, in line with more recent documents. His second son, James, was shown to be a Pony Driver at the colliery, but there was no entry for the occupation of his eldest son John (probably working as a sinker with his

father). In Iceland, William Morris was enjoying the exhilaration of pony riding near the sea in contrast to the son of James Mason who was driving his pony down in the depths of the earth.

From the age of around nine, a trapper could expect promotion to the position of driver with responsibility for a pony. The pit ponies were known as 'gallowas', derived from the dale ponies from Galloway. This job allowed the boy a certain mobility in the mine (compared with the restrictions of a trapper), and an increase in wages – from 10d to perhaps 1s. 3d a day in 1840. The next run in the ladder of promotion would be the putter. The putter was recruited from among the older stronger lads and his work was to heave the coal tubs from the coal-face to the gathering point called a landing, or 'flatts'. Putters were a race apart and took pride in their strength. A 'headsman' was a lad not strong enough to 'put' alone, who was helped in his task by a younger boy known as a 'foal'. Where two boys of equal strength were putting, they were known as half-marrows. Other jobs performed by pit lads included that of 'craneman' whose task was to transfer corves and tubs to the outgoing tracks of the mine. There was also the 'flatman' who linked the tubs together for the journey to the shaft. The 'Collier's Rant' described well the tremendous physical punishment borne by the putters:

> 'There is me horse, an' there is me tram;
> 'Twe horns of greese will mek her gan;
> There is me hoggers likewise me half shoon,
> An' smash me heart marra, maw puttin's a' done!'

In the 1871 census, Ellen daughter of James and Lydia, aged twelve, was shown as a scholar, but Richard aged eight and Isabella aged six were not shown as scholars, presumably because they were not attending school. The law now required her to remain in school until the age of thirteen. Their youngest son was recorded but misspelt as Alexandra. Their recorded non-attendance at school may have been an omission, since in a neighbouring household there was a girl recorded as a scholar at an age of four years. More likely it was due to sinkers and their families always on the move.

James (sinker) was due to move south to the Hamsteels area of west Durham. In this area the census gave a Peter Gallagher born in Fermanagh, who was recorded as a Coal Miner working at Esh in Durham. Peter could have been a relation of Isabella Mason, formerly Gallagher. Two brothers, John and Thomas Shannon, born in Monaghan, were also at Esh, working as Cinder Drawers.

On the twenty-sixth of May 1871, the third daughter and last child of James and Lydia, was born in High Row East Terraces at Downs, Hetton le Hole. She was named Dorothy Lydia after her aunt and mother, and her father's name was recorded as James Mason. It would seem at long last he had decided to rationalise his name to Mason. The birth certificate of Lydia (the name she was known by) gave her father's occupation as 'Master Sinker at a Coal Mine'.

James now had the main responsibility for the sinking of the new mine shaft at Hetton Downs (Eppleton New Winnings). Two sinkers died at Eppleton. Reported skylarking, sinker John Robinson aged 25 fell off a cradle (working platform). Two years later Isaac Burrowman aged 26 was killed from his injuries after being drawn up against pulley in a staple shaft.

By 1871 James Storey Reed was an Engine Driver at Shotton Colliery with wife Mary Ann and a step-daughter Ann Bulmer aged 9 years born in Hartlepool and daughter Sarah J Reed born in Castle Eden aged 7 years.

There were further births in the Shannon/Mason extended family during 1871. Ten years after the birth of their first child, Edward and Jane Shannon gave birth to another son named Edward Reed Shannon. Their first child born in 1861 had died at an early age. In 1871 the family were living at 215 Back Bonner's Field, Monkwearmouth. (Thomas Bonner was a former mayor of Newcastle). Back in 1839, Edward's sister Catherine had married Ralph Reed. Edward and Jane's last child born in 1873 was given the name Richard, after their second son Richard who had died in 1869 at the age of 7 years.

The first 'Durham Big Meeting' or 'Gala', a summer festival and meeting of all coal mining communities of Durham and Northumberland, took place at Wharton Park on the 12 August 1871, and republicanism was no doubt discussed between pints. Each colliery village was represented by its banner, and their brass band gave added emphasis to the occasion. Sometimes the weather-beaten old banners which had fluttered at many a miners' march in by-gone days, were brought out and borne behind the band in great style. Bands and banners were associated with the early trade union demonstrations as mentioned in Disraeli's Sybil. The banner was a symbol of pride and sacrifice. George Tutill, with a background in fairs, started in 1837 to make banners, and was to provide most of the banners for the Durham collieries, depicting mainly religious and political themes. On that first occasion, Thornley Colliery were proud to have their banner on the platform, but sadly in that same year five men were drowned in their mine. In the Big Meeting's second year it was held on the Durham racecourse, but by 1875 it had become so large that the North Eastern Railways withdrew all its trains between Bishop Auckland, Newcastle and Lanchester, claiming that the railway could not cope with so many people on a Saturday. Consequently, in the following two years the Gala was held on a Monday, but thereafter, once again on a Saturday. For most miners, the Gala Day was one of the few days in the year when he and his family could enjoy a holiday atmosphere.

The North East had always had gained a reputation for reform and radicalism; it was not surprising that MP Charles Dilke, a well-known Radical, should give a public speech at Newcastle in 1871. It caused a furore when he called for a British 'commonwealth', that is a republic. He was joined by George Julian Harney a veteran of the Chartist movement. Since the early 1800s, pitmen from Northumberland and Durham had gathered at various venues to discuss their grievances and to adopt resolutions. For instance in 1831 the meeting place chosen was Boldon Fell, between Gateshead and Sunderland. From the beginning, the state authorities had viewed these gatherings with suspicion, and for many years Durham shop-keepers boarded up their shops against the 'invading hoards'. Scottish miners' leader Smillie, remembered miners 'demonstrations' when questions like the abolition of the Truck system and the Eight-Hour Day for miners were put before the miners.

The less well-off had little opportunity for holidays, and for a miner, a day off work meant no pay for that day. They had to wait until the next century before paid holidays came into being. For the lucky few, the railway provided an escape to previously unknown resorts. A proposed rail connection to Scarborough, the 'Fair Mistress of the North East', was opposed on the basis that there was 'no wish for a greater influx of vagrants, and those having no money to spend'. However, Tynemouth was being developed for the less wealthy classes from Newcastle. Back in the 1820s there had been cheap steamer trips between Newcastle and Tynemouth, and Newcastle coal factors or agents had lived at Hexham or Tynemouth.

The North East Engineers' Strikes of 1871 had a substantial impact on the local community. During 1871–75, political agitation through direct action strikes increased. Taking part in these strikes were miners, engineers, shipbuilders, builders, agricultural workers, who took advantage of the boom of the early 1870's to press for better wages and hours of work. The railway workers had been campaigning for shorter working hours since 1867, but the railway companies refused to allow trade union recognition, considering it incompatible with 'public service'. In spite of this the National Union of Railwaymen was formed in 1871, stimulated by the Engineer's strikes for a 9-hour day. Even Queen Victoria expressed doubt about the match tax which would affect the livelihood of the poorest section of the population. She had few good words for the Irish or the French, and was wholly opposed to any release of Fenian prisoners. In July, Gladstone spoke on Irish home rule in Aberdeen, and this was the year of Gladstone's last anti-home rule speech. Unrest was also affecting the mining industry, with the Ryhope Colliery Strike in 1872 relating to the bond. At this time Cowen who campaigned against coercion laws saw Thomas Burt MP pandering to Gladstone.

One year later in America, railroad and mining employers in 1873 were fearful of trade union activities reducing their profits. They arranged for private detective agencies to spy on the activities of the Workingmen's Benevolent Association and the Shenandoah branch of the Ancient Order of Hibernians, an organisation for Irish immigrants run by the Roman Catholic clergy. He discovered that the latter body were active in the secret society, the Molly Maguires, with a local agenda to kill managers of coal mines. The struggle for the hearts and minds of the Irish at home and abroad continued in earnest.

Engels in many of his writings was deploring the mainly industrial preoccupation of trade unions. Republicanism was in the air as the Queen's expenses were criticised in Parliament. To ameliorate public opinion, Victoria opened up Parliament after a long absence. She would have to put up with five years of Reform and more! In November, at Newcastle, she was verbally attacked by Radical Sir Charles Dilke on her 'dereliction of duty', and he advocated a republic. In December, Bertie, Prince of Wales, contracted typhoid probably from bad drains, which produced a wave of sympathy for the Queen and lanced Dilke's campaign. Victoria had earlier refused permission for Bertie to take up a position in Ireland. In March 1872 a sixth attempt on the Queen's life was thwarted by her man servant John Brown. The gloom was raised for a while as the public rejoiced when Henry H Stanley discovered the whereabouts of Livingstone.

For the railways, a revolution took place on the first day of March 1872, when the Midland board decided to run third-class carriages by all trains. Up till then the speed of third class trains had been very slow since neither through tickets nor through journeys could be taken, and travellers had to get forward as best they could by a series of fragmentary journeys over the lines of different, rival and often conflicting companies. The public pressure for changes did not affect certain private lines such as the railway from Sunderland to Seaham Harbour, the property of the Londonderry family. Blackpool attracted 850,000 visitors to taste the delight of variety shows and fish and chips, perhaps allowed mining families to forget about their ordinary troubles. The first Football Cup Final took place at the Oval in 1872.

Other pastimes were to play a large part in the lives of working people, with the modern form of boxing starting in 1863. Football clubs were formed, Sunderland in 1877 and Newcastle United in 1895. The football association rules specifically banned the handling of the ball for this new 'dribbling' game. The development of ball games was due largely to urbanisation and it was in towns that the first main football teams were formed. The street life of children included a football played with a pig's bladder, or distinctly local games like 'knurr and spell' traditional in northern mining villages, a kind of incipient rounders played with a pick-shaft.

Master Sinker and Pit Sinkers 1878
(British Library)

1872 also heralded the formation of Patrick Kenney's General Labourers' Amalgamated Union, primarily for builder's workers, and Joseph Arch's National Agricultural Labourers' Union. This was a time of great activity in the coalfields all over Britain. Engineers were planning to restart work at the Arigna mines in Leitrim. In Durham, many shafts were being sunk, including No1 shaft at Chilton Colliery on the 29 February. Boring operations were being carried out on the Winston estate, and commencement of sinking of the New Pit at Trimdon Grange Colliery, and at the East Howle Colliery. Forced at last to recognise the legitimacy of the miners' union, the mineowners formed themselves into the North of England United Coal Trades Association. After negotiations in February 1872, the employers agreed to pay the miners an increase of 20%. After much pressure from the workers, legislation was finally passed in 1872 that every coal mine was to be provided with a second shaft for escape purposes.

The Durham Miners Association met the Coal Trades Association to demand the end of the yearly bond, and in April of the same year this was achieved. Also a bonus for the miner's wife was the Licensing Act 1872 which restricted the hours public houses could open, due much to the pressure from temperance societies. In 1861 a duty was placed on gin sales, and in 1869 all beerhouses had to get a license from the magistrates. Back in 1830 any householder could take out a license to sell beer in the hope that this would restrict the drinking of gin. In 1886 it was made illegal for children under thirteen to drink in pubs.

The 1872 Ballot Act pushed through by Bright giving secret voting at elections, enabled Irish peasants to return 'extreme' Nationalists to Parliament, and there followed the 'Clare election of Home Rule'. This was the first secret ballot by-election. For the first time a joint Irish and English workers demonstration took place at Hyde Park. In 1872 boys' working hours were restricted to ten hours. However there was still resistance to 'going too far' with social measures. Even Dr William Jenner believed that high mortality among the workers' children was not a bad thing – it kept the strain hardy! However in 1872 the Adulteration of Food, Drinks and Drugs Act was the first food law making it illegal to add other ingredients to foodstuffs to increase the weight (as was the practice at many truck shops). Previously dishonest traders had added sand to pepper and water to beer. Many towns including Newcastle had been reluctant to institute boards of health responsible for road and drainage improvements until compelled to by Gladstone's 1872 Act.

Despite the experience of Crimea, Queen Victoria and Gladstone both agreed that women should be kept out of the medical profession; it was thought an awful idea to allow young men and women together in the dissecting room. In Manchester, Disraeli appealing to public jingoism, denounced Gladstone's foreign policy. Later at Crystal Palace he proposed elevating the condition of the people without violating the principles of economic truth.

Drawing on 'national' issues, Disraeli was endeavouring to regain touch with 'the people'. Only four months earlier, the Albert Memorial in Kensington, had been opened to the public; the Queen liked Disraeli since he showed great sympathy with her grief.

In April 1873, a Manhood Suffrage demonstration was held at Newcastle. Support for the Irish nationalist movement continued to be strong in the North East. This was reflected by the first Home Rule Conference of Great Britain being held at Newcastle in August 1873. There was the cutting of the first sod at Shire Moor Colliery, the completion of the sinking of Silksworth Colliery after four years work, and the sinking of two shafts, the East and the West, at Mainsforth Colliery.

Hamsteels Taylor Pit (Quebec) near Esh Winning, was sunk in 1873. Previously, Esh had been a location of drift mining. James Mason was the master sinker, and would have moved there after the completion of sinking at Hetton Downs and Windlestone. Two years later Jessie Main was born at Esh; she was to marry James's youngest son, Alexander Mason (author's grandfather).

Joseph Cowen was to be a dominant figure in Newcastle in the second half of the nineteenth century. He represented the town in Parliament from 1873 to 1886, and was proprietor of the Newcastle Chronicle. He campaigned to build the Tyne Theatre in Westgate Road, which was where his monument was erected.

However, in 1873 an event at Durham was to capture the attention of the public in the North East. Mary Ann Cotton of West Auckland (daughter of a pit sinker) was suspected of poisoning fifteen people, and committed to trial in Durham; later she was hanged. Local children were to be reminded of her ill deeds for generations after:

> 'Sing! Sing! What shall I sing?
> Mary Ann Cotton tied up on a string
> Who? Where? Up in the air,
> Selling black puddings a penny a pair!'

Thirty years earlier, her father had fallen 150 feet to his death down a mine shaft at Murton Colliery. Mary Ann's widowed mother later married George Stott, a well-known colliery boring contractor.

CHAPTER 13

1874–1879 The Great Depression and Irish Land War

(Death of Lydia Lawrence/Mason)

'...the fighting Irish and the demonstrations of the English workers [are] the "motive forces" of English political development.'

(The English Elections by Engels 1874)

'The land is the source of all wealth. It is a mine from which must be drawn the ore that labour fashions.'

(Poverty and Progress by Henry George 1879)

Early in 1874 at a private meeting of the Irish Party, Mr Ronayne MP for Cork, proposed that Irish members should interfere more in English and Imperial questions, especially those questions which affected the working classes. He found little sympathy from Isaac Butt, then Irish Nationalist Leader and lawyer. Queen Victoria took revenge on all those she considered were undermining the Anglian Church by driving through a Public Worship Bill to purge 'Romish' practices. This measure was not supported by the Archbishop of Canterbury or Gladstone. Disraeli's 1875 Bill was designed to 'put down ritualism and mass in masquerade'. Victoria had no regrets when to her 'surprise' at the General Election of 1874, Gladstone was defeated – 'swept away ... by a torrent of beer and gin', and 'Education'. Parnell took over as Nationalist Leader from Butt.

Gladstone's successor, Disraeli, knew how to win the heart of his 'Faery' Queen, and as he was to admit in later life that 'everyone likes flattery, and when it comes to royalty, you should lay it on with a trowel'. This was to be the end of the period of unpopularity for Victoria. The Queen was to become increasingly suspicious of Gladstone, as it became public knowledge that he had associations with prostitutes, even though this was of a Samaritan nature.

At this time Queen Victoria was astounded to hear that one of the transported 'New Irishmen', Charles Duffy, had been appointed Premier of Victoria in Australia. On demanding a report on the rest of the transported Fenian convicts, their new status must have given her food for thought:

Thomas Francis Meagher – Brigadier General US Army & Governor of Montana

Terence Bellow MacManus – Brigadier General US Army (b. Tempo, Fermamagh)

Patrick Donahue – Brigadier US Army

Richard O'Gorman – Governor General of Newfoundland

Morris Lyene – Attorney General of Australia

Michel Ireland – succeeded Morris Lyene

Thomas D'Arcy McGee – MP Montreal, Minister of Agriculture, President of Council, Canada

John Mitchel – prominent New York politician (son became mayor of New York in 1914)

James Shannon – South Australian politician (1840-1891)

The General Election gave an overwhelming vote for Home Rule with sixty of its Irish candidates elected, a gain of fifty seats, and in the following spring Charles Stewart Parnell was elected for Co. Meath. Of the 13 working class / labour candidates who stood, only two who were miners were elected. Alexander MacDonald was elected for Stafford, and Thomas Burt for Morpeth in Northumberland. Burt who had started work at the age of ten at Haswell Colliery, became the 'first working-man Member of Parliament'. Joseph Chamberlain, with a reputation as Lord Mayor of Birmingham for 'municipal socialism', now entered Parliament on a Radical programme fuelled by the Non-conformist moral steam of the Education League. He considered Gladstone's lack of mission as the reason for the Liberal's heavy defeat. It was also to be the end of Liberalism as a major force in Ireland.

The relative short period of 'good money' working in coal mines during the Franco-Prussian War had come to an end. The period 1874 to 1896 was to be known as the 'Great Depression', heavily affecting coal, iron, cotton and cereal farming. This was caused by the great fall in prices, undoubtedly aggravated by the international competition of the new, rising industrial powers. One of the main causes was cheap wheat from the United States and Canada. In 1879 unemployment rose sharply causing widespread vocal protest. Britain was ceasing to be the only workshop of the world. Also in iron and steel production, Germany and America were now overtaking Britain. This was to release the stranglehold of the railways on transport, and probably encouraged the building of the Manchester Ship Canal in 1894, the first major canal to be constructed since the 1820s.

Social progress continued with the 1874 Artisan's Dwelling Act, containing measures to abolish slums, provide decent housing for poor, and various health measures. The artisans at this time still formed the rank and file of the unions. Their aims were for greater prosperity rather than intervention. For them the most familiar institution of State intervention was the hated workhouse. In the days before the unionization of unskilled labour, the lower orders lacked any effective constitutional means of translating social demands into effective pressure on the political process. Religion was considered an overwhelmingly middle class and artisan preoccupation. Occasionally, as with particular homogeneous working class groups such as agricultural labourers and miners, Primitive Methodism became an agency for a significant degree of political radicalism. Both for those workers with a vote or not, politics was often more to do with personalities and pageant rather than issues and policies. During the 1870s there was no popular demand for social reform in contrast to the 1860s.

David Livingstone's body reached England for burial in April 1874. Eight months later, after many days of thick snow, on the thirtieth of December, James Mason's wife Lydia, only 40 years old, died of 'Bronchitis, 16 days, certified by H. Clark MD' at Windlestone Colliery near Chilton. Again, very strangely, the deceased was certified as Lydia Lawrence and her widower and informant, as James Lawrence, the names in which they had married. However in the church burial registers she was given as Lydia Mason. Fortunately some light can be thrown on this event. In 1970, the author paid a visit to Lydia's niece, Dorothy, who lived in Kirk Merrington where Lydia was married. Dorothy was the daughter of Lydia's sister Dorothy (who had married John Brown). Dorothy recalled that at the time of her aunt's funeral there was thick snow lying in drifts on the road between Kirk Merrington and Ferryhill. The weather was so bad that the burial had to be delayed for more than a week because it was impossible for the hearse to make the journey between Merrington where the body was at rest and St Luke's grave-yard at Ferryhill. Apparently at the wake, certain 'mourners' became drunk and were unable to nail back the lid on the coffin!

On reflection, perhaps the use of the name Lawrence on the death certificate was not so surprising since the burial was to take place in the next village to where Lydia and James had married. Even if a different clergyman was conducting the burial ceremony, the church probably came under the same diocese, and this may have led to complications. By a strange coincidence at this time, a civil engineer called Francis Fox was designing miners' cottages in Yorkshire, and sought advice from a miner's wife who had previously lived in Durham. She pointed out that one problem they had suffered was that a coffin could not be removed from the bedroom owing to the sharp turn on the staircase, and it had to be taken out of the window!

It is not clear what arrangements were made for looking after the youngest children; Lydia was only three years, Alexander seven and Isabella ten. More than likely, they and their father went to live with the eldest son John, or at first a neighbour may have been paid to mind them when their father was at work. Two years later children at Medomsley pit village were singing 'Oh Happy English Children', but not for the Mason family. It was said that authorities were making the children pay for the sins of their fathers and grandfathers who had been involved in socially disturbing activities such as trade unionism.

The death certificate of Lydia gave the occupation of her husband as 'Changer and Grather'. At Lauderdale, Ballinamore in Ireland, William Watson carrying out pump repairs, fell to his death down a well shaft. Ten years later a similar fate was to befall James Mason.

A Changer and Grather, as defined in Greenwell's Glossary of Coal Trade Terms, was a man whose responsibility was to keep the buckets and clacks in order and to change them when necessary (a clack was the low valve of a pump used to support the column of water when the bucket is descending). This work was obviously related to keeping the seepage of water into the shaft under control, and was associated with the shaft works. The sinking of Chilton Pit took place between 1872 and 1874. Other pits sunk shortly afterwards were Langley Park and New Herrington in 1874, and Bearpark in 1876.

James might well have been carrying out sinking work on a part-time basis due to his recent bereavement, since in later documents, his normal occupation of sinker was given. It is possible that with James involved with the 'sinking' for Windlestone Colliery, his eldest son, John Mason, was given the opportunity to remain at that pit when it went into full production. James Reed was working at Castle Eden during this period, where sinker Samuel Spears aged 41 died when an iron beam fell on top of him. At Hedley Hill near Tow Law there was an influx of miners from Ireland and Cornwall.

In 1875 the great consolidating Public Health Act and Artisan's Dwelling Act was passed, but by the end of the century death rates in towns were twice as high as in the suburbs and countryside. In 1875 there were a number of Acts; Queen Victoria ensured that a Vivisection Bill required the 'humane' control of research on animals; Disraeli's Conspiracy and Protection of Property Act restored peaceful picketing; but the Enclosure of Commons Act made it possible for landowners to absorb public land into their estates. The Employers and Workmen Act allowed breaches in contract on both sides to be treated on the same basis. In 1876 education was made compulsory to the age of ten. The Trade Union Amendment Act, provided concessions which destroyed the impetus of the Labour Representative League. About this time Durham place names were influenced by America, for example Quebec near Tow Law. Philadelphia Row used to be pitman's cottages, three miles from Washington, the original home of George Washington's family.

It took five years up to 1875 for the Roman Catholic Cathedral in Enniskillen to be built, and the local Protestants were surprised at the opening to see so many people entering on the first day. In February, Disraeli, as prime minister, prevented Fenian John Michel, (who had returned from the United States), standing for election in Tipperary, and in March, Michel died of exhaustion during the following election. There was a 'Bismarck war scare' in 1875, which resulted from the French recovery after 1871. Disraeli felt saddled with the 'Crimean System' on foreign policy from previous administrations, and resented the Russian deal.

On the African continent, the Crown annexed Transvaal, and Napoleon IV serving there was killed in a skirmish. These foreign problems had Irish implications for Home Rule and tenants' rights. Disraeli tried to deflect public feelings by fan-faring the purchase of the Suez Canal in November for £4 million, but the massacre of 12–15,000 Bulgarians caused a public outcry resulting in hundreds of meetings – a throwback to anti-slavery and anti-corn laws days. Gladstone's late intervention was prompted by the people's passion over these issues. Victoria became Empress of India and Disraeli, the Earl of Beaconsfield in the same year. The Earl vetoed the initiative of the Three Emperors' League, and brought about the 'Berlin Memo'. Lord Derby advocated the breaking up of the Ottoman Empire. The Prince of Wales society divorce case in 1876 diverted the public to more trivial matters closer to home.

The period 1876 to 1880, culminating in the Midlothian meetings, was played out both in parliament and in the country separating the 'North from the South and the masses from the classes'. In September 1876 Gladstone addressed a rally in Blackheath against Disraeli's war-mongering, and in December Gladstone attended a peace conference with convenors including Darwin, Browning, Froude, Ruskin, Trollope, and W T Stead once editor of the Northern Echo published in Darlington. Gladstone also made three major tours around Britain, including a visit to Northumberland and Durham, again staying at Raby Castle as well as the Deanery in Durham Close and Ford Castle at Coldstream. He was greeted by welcoming crowds at railway junctions and at castle gates such as Alnwick, which would not have pleased his Tory host. The Duke of Northumberland was to record in May 1877, at an Eastern Question Association meeting held in the House of Commons, that he was impressed by Thomas Burt, the trade unionist and Liberal MP for Morpeth, who addressed the meeting eloquently 'with a strong Northumberland tongue'. By coincidence a Society for the Preservation of the Irish Language recently formed, was replaced by the Gaelic Union in 1879.

During the period 1866 to 1876, the Newcastle Swing Bridge was built by local contractor, Sir W.G. Armstrong, to replace the existing low stone bridge. The bridge was turned by hydraulic steam power. This was one of the first large opening bridges in the world, and was situated close to the High Level Bridge. With the growth of Armstrong's works at Elswick, it was essential to allow large boats up the river. The 1870 to 1875 harvests had been good, but from 1876 to 1879 there were four bad harvests. Half the wheat

Irish evictions 1870 (irishcentral.com) and below (freepages.genealogy)

consumed in Britain was imported, mainly from America where railways had revolution-ised grain production. In 1876 there were executions of Molly Maguires in America. The railroad and coal companies were determined to destroy the emerging trade union move-ment in America. During the years 1877 to 1879, the Irish potato crop was also poor; bankrupt and starving men could not pay the rent. The landlords caring nothing for the people insisted to the full on their legal rights. Evictions commenced again with 1323 in 1877, 1749 in 1878, and in 1879 there were 2667. In Ireland, 1876 to 1877 were famine years, and the agrarian tempest assumed formidable proportions, so that Fenians and Ribbonmen were forced to adapt extreme policies or else lose their following.

In 1877, there was further inter-marrying between the Shannon/Mason and Reed families. James's eldest son, John Mason, married Sarah Reed (true name Sarah Hall) at a 'Register Office' on the ninth of July at Windlestone Colliery. Sarah's step-father James Reed, a breaksman, was recorded as deceased. A breaksman's work related to the control of the winding of colliery engines. John's occupation was given as Colliery Engineman, a trade which was likely he learned from his father-in-law. Of course in the North East, the enginemen had a proud tradition going back to George Stephenson. James Mason was recorded as Pit Sinker, but had been working as master sinker since 1871. Another Mason (Thomas Mason) was recorded as an engine driver also at Windlestone.

James Reed turned out not to be deceased, returning from America a few years later very much alive! James Reed had emigrated to America during the period 1874 to 1877 when gold was discovered in the Black Hills of Dakota, but presumably he did not find his 'pot of gold'. There was a family rumour that he ran off to America with a school mistress, and had two sons there. Back in England, he became known by the nickname of 'Old Touch', not for good luck, but because of the tobacco (touchwood) he smoked, a habit he had taken up in America. Touchwood was also the material used to light a fire, and he certainly ignited a controversy when he returned home.

Miners' leader Robert Smillie mentioned that many old miners liked to 'season' a soft clay pipe giving an earthen flavour which blended well with the strong black tobacco miners smoked. MacDonagh noted that smoking was also prevalent among old women in Ireland. They took the habit as a solace in their declining years. On asking an old woman at what time of her life she began to indulge in tobacco, she replied, "I tuk to it as a bit of a divar-sion after me poor old man was tucked under the daisies."

A Durham miner, John Watson, formerly of Wrekenton, who had emigrated to Jefferson County, Ohio for eight years wrote to the Durham Chronicle, and his unhappy tale was published on 31 March 1865:

'Employers and capitalists, and others interested in getting cheap labour, have sent agents and commissioners among you, who, by advertisements and publications would make the English miner and English working man believe that America is at the present time little short of a terrestrial paradise, that here, if the millennium has not already arrived, it certainly is close at hand. No, the motive of employers and capitalists in sending agents among you is plain. It is to overstock the labour market, and thereby reduce wages. They may tell you we are making very high wages, which some of us may do but they don't tell you that all things we have to buy are high also. I worked over 20 years in the coal mines of Durham and Northumberland; therefore I am well acquainted with all the evils you have to contend with. I have worked eight years in the coal mines of this country so I think I may claim to be able to judge of a miner's life here and in England. In England you have a house and fuel for next to nothing – about 13s a year; you have medical attendance gratis in case of accidents, and at some places 5s per week; you have besides, what no amount of money can buy, your friends and your relations living about you, and very likely a snug little reading room where you can spend your leisure hours pleasantly and profitably. On the other hand here I have paid the last year over 90 dollars for the house-rent, and about 40 dollars for coal; here there is no medical attendance, except you pay for it; here is no smart money, here are no reading rooms where you may pass away an hour if you had it to spare, which you might not after you have worked 12 or 14 hours a day, if you are so lucky as to get work.'

Long after the Great Famine, many Irishmen were still leaving Liverpool seeking a better life in America. Especially in the winter time, the journey was often a nightmare contending with the cold and gales in the 'rolling forties'. However in contrast to the Durham miner's letter, there were emigrants who were rewarded as confirmed by the Irishman who was asked whether America was a good place for a working man to go to, replied, "Faith, it is : when I first went I hadn't a rag to my back, and now I'm just kiivered with 'em".

James Mason, in charge of a sinking contractor, worked independently of the main production miners, such as the hewers. He would have had a direct relationship with the colliery manager and owner, since he was the key to the search for the rich coal seams and a potential fortune. As master sinker, he would have been in control of his gang of sinkers as well directing the engineman with regard to the winding and pumping engines. Master sinkers were considered mining engineers and held in high respect by mining communities.

Family relations have passed down the information that in 1877, James Mason, his son James and perhaps James Reed, were sinking shafts in Staffordshire. Four years earlier at Talk O' Th' Hill colliery in Staffordshire, a John Shannon was one of the eighteen miners who died when firedamp exploded in 1873. Safety standards were worse in Staffordshire (compared to the North East) since the rescuers went down the

shaft in baskets. At this time master sinkers were being sought from the North East to all parts of Britain and overseas. During 1878, Cornsay Colliery was sunk; apparently its nickname at that time was Mason's Pit, after James Mason its master sinker.

All the workmen's associations in the Durham colliery districts joined into a single federation. Cokemen, enginemen, mechanics and miners were in future to work together in a desperate fight for their members' existence. Despite the large difference in wages between the hewers and the surface workers, the coalmining community remained close-knit. Hewers earned 40 to 50% more than underground hauliers. The special skills associated with hewing were not learned through a traditional apprenticeship but picked up by a distinct age group, early twenties to forties, that had the physical strength and had the experience of the local geological conditions and working customs, and where to cut the coal seam to produce a controlled fall.

The North East was distinctive in developing a double-shift system of hewers, who by the 1870s, worked shifts of six or seven hours, while the haulage workers kept the colliery running with a working day of ten to eleven hours. The effect of the double-shift system was that each hewer chose a mate or 'marra', and the pair shared the working of a stall shift and shift about. The method of working created stalls and 'bords' at the coal face, each worked by a single hewer and separated from adjoining stalls by pillars of coal that were left to support the roof; when an entire section had been worked in this fashion the coal pillars were removed in a retreating operation, leaving the roof to collapse behind them.

The industrial north praised Gladstone in his stance against war with Turkey in support of Bulgarian peasants in 1877. Russia declared war on Turkey, and in March 1878 forced on Turkey the secret Treaty of San Stefano; later Russia had to retract under Anglo-Hungarian pressure. The 'Eastern Question' and the connivance of the trade union leaders with the capitalist politicians were to persuade William Morris to agitate against Disraeli by giving a lecture on 'Socialism seen through Artist eyes'. On 11 May 1877, Morris issued a manifesto 'To the working-men of England' warning them of 'the bitterness of hatred against freedom and progress that lies in the hearts of a certain part of the richer classes'. Gladstone was accused of being a traitor by Queen Victoria, as he tried to calm a 'jingoistic' country. Victoria harboured contempt for the Liberals, especially for Gladstone, and went as far to invoke Gladstone's family background in slavery to suggest that 'sordid gain' was his sole inspiration for his conduct during the war. It was known that Queen Victoria held a dislike of Stanley (of Livingstone fame) who was reported keeping female slaves for his own use.

In November 1877, Parnell was elected President of the Home Rule Federation replacing Isaac Butt, both Protestants. At this time Gladstone and Morris were to pay their first visits to Ireland. On the road south of Dublin, Morris noticed the extreme poverty of the villages he passed through: "the cottiers' houses in outside appearance the very poorest habitations of man I have yet seen, Iceland by no means excepted". During 1878–80 Ireland was full of unrest – plainly the 1870 Land Act had not solved the land tenure hardships; the country was laid waste by another terrible famine; the failure of the crops meant the tenant could not pay his rent leading to eviction or workhouse or death through cold and hunger. This assisted the rising tide of militancy of the Land League waged by Michael Davitt with Parnell's powerful co-operation. 2,500 agrarian outrages were reported. Despite these uncertain times, a Patrick Gallagher opened a small mine at Ballinameeltoge in Leitrim which provided much needed income where farming had always been poor. Lord Leitrim was murdered at Milford, Donegal, by his agent and driver in April 1878. The 'New Departure' of working by open agitation with the underground organisation drew support even from non-Fenian Irish-Americans who readily took up the slogan 'Irish land for the Irish people'.

In 1873 Van Gogh was greatly affected by the poverty-stricken coal mining areas of south Belgium. In Scotland, dire poverty prevailed for many years (1878–85), however some good came out, in that it broke Keir Hardie's Lanarkshire bonds, and set him free for important tasks further afield. During the seventies, miners paid into a fund for medical attendance both for themselves and their families. In 1878 the Salvation Army was founded by William Booth, a former Methodist preacher, who broke away to set up an evangelical mission in the East End of London. The weather was particularly cold during the following Christmas and into the New Year. During the sixteen weeks of severe frost, navvies walked miles to get a bowl of soup and half a loaf. The corn crop was destroyed that summer. Global conflicts continued with Britain involved in the Afghan and Zulu Wars.

Embarking on his Midlothian pilgrimages of passion during the period 1879–80, Gladstone (nicknamed Grand Old Man) affirmed that it was his duty to destroy the whole fabric of Tory policy. He spoke to a crowd of 500 at Carlisle, and 4000 at Hawick in November 1879. The other parties' political positions were drawn with Parnell now the leader of the Irish; Disraeli considered Home Rule contrary to his imperialist policy. The famine of 1879 did not reproduce all the horrors of 1847. The resident landlords as a class were much less sympathetic than in 1847, when scores of them had been ruined in their efforts to alleviate distress. The Land League was at least able to avert the worst effects by preventing at source, the creation of distress by means of fundraising, both in America and Britain.

On the seventeenth anniversary of Prince Albert's death, the 14 December 1878, Princess Alice died of diphtheria. At this time, Engels married Lydia Burns of Irish roots. In Ireland it appeared that the horrors of the Great Famine were to be re-visited; there was a partial failure of potato crop and bad weather affected hay and oats leading to shortage of animal food. However, now the response by the Irish was more militant. There were reports from the west of Ireland that the people were suffering more than at any time since the Famine. Rain and cold weather had diminished the grain crop, producing a shortage of food for cattle and pigs, and encouraged that old black rot of potatoes. The exponent of the new gospel of defiance and self-help was Michael Davitt. At a meeting in May, in Irishtown Co Mayo, the renewal of the fight against eviction, rack-renting and landlordism began. In Davitt's Mayo, tenants were resisting eviction by fighting police with stones whilst the main body of the Catholic Church united behind the landlords. The Dublin Daily Mail denounced 'Communism in Connaught'.

The Irish Land War began with a rally at Irishtown on the 20 April 1879. Parnell at first was reluctant to be associated with this movement, but in June changed his mind and attended a meeting in Westport. The desperate poverty in Ireland forced Parnell to see that there was no longer any possibility of conciliation between landlord and tenant, and on the 8 June in Westport, he was to famously rally his people with the words, 'Keep a firm grip on your homesteads'. After disillusionment with the EQA (Eastern Question Association – league against British imperialism), Morris became treasurer of the National Liberal League, largely a working-class association founded in the late summer.

Two striking miners during April 1879 were collecting scrap coal on coal heaps near Bishop Auckland. There was a collapse of the coal heap and both miners died. In the same year a catastrophe hit the tunnel works for the Great Western Railway. Massive Cornish engines were brought in to cope with the inrush of water. In addition divers were required to carry out underwater repairs. The decade ended in gloom on the 28 December with the Tay Bridge Disaster. The end of the 1870s brought in the 'Great Depression' with mass unemployment and a painful reminder that great inequalities still existed. The newer trade unions collapsed.

T P O'Connor MP noted 'With Ireland starving, and at the same time exasperatingly loud in menace and complaint, with England angry, ignorant, and misinformed, the time was ripe for an anti-Irish cry; and Lord Beaconsfield determined to play that villainous card'. The demand in Ireland for self-government was described by Disraeli as 'a danger in its ultimate result scarcely less disastrous than pestilence and famine'. But that was exactly the condition of the people in Ireland.

CHAPTER 14

1880–1886 Socialism, Irish Agitation and Home Rule

(Re-marriage and death of James Mason)

'Three Shafts of Death' – reflections on death and the conduct of human life
(Geoffrey Keating, Celtic Poet 1631)

'Perhaps you will be killed suddenly by a fall of earth, by the blasting of a rock, by the crushing blow of an engine, by a bruise which may fester, and mortify, and poison the life blood, by a fall, by the slow torture of disease, or by the burning heat of fever ....But however it may be, or where it may happen, let me ask you, are you ready now? Shall you be ready to meet death then?'
(Quarterly Christmas Message letter to Navvies 1878)

'Nowhere had he found the exiles from Ireland more warm-hearted or more determined to do the best that in them lay for the welfare of their native land ..... He had also to thank the people of Newcastle for the core that they took of the interests of Ireland during the last general election.'
(Parnell at Newcastle Town Hall 1880)

'Ireland stands at your bar, expectant, hopeful, almost suppliant .... think,
I beseech you, think well, think wisely, think, not for the moment but for
the years ahead that are to come, before you reject this Bill'.
(Gladstone's closing speech 8 June 1886)

The 1880s was to see the revival of socialism, with the Fabian Socialists expounding their 'socialism by instalments'. For most working people, co-operative shopping was the only form of socialism they appreciated. Morley had said that in no country had socialism been discussed so little. The first forty years of the century had seen small examples of socialism, and for the next forty years it had been virtually extinct. Thomas Spence had been considered the first British socialist, a schoolmaster living in Newcastle in 1817. This was followed by Robert Owen's experiments in industrial co-operation, but afterwards little progress. The first Labourer's Acts were passed in 1883 and 1885. Following the lead by Marx, Parnell advocated the joining of the English masses and Irish nationalists.

The Webbs asserted that Henry George's book Progress and Poverty published in 1879 had stimulated the revival in socialism. George, an American, came over to Ireland to give a lecture in 1881, where the land question had reached an acute stage. He was arrested by the Government, and with this free publicity, returned to lecture in England. Unrest in Ireland was at its height in 1880 with 2000 evictions and 2590 outrages. When the Lords threw out a measure for compensating evicted tenants, fury blazed up in Ireland, persuading Gladstone to consider an Irish Land Bill. Arthur James Balfour, future chief secretary of Ireland and Prime Minister, objected to Gladstone's land legislation largely based on his anxiety that it would encourage socialism in England. Balfour considered that the 'north-east of Ireland had a closer affinity through religion and blood to the Scotch', a marker for the future split in Ireland.

The 1880s were dramatic years for Ireland; also for the Shannons and Masons. At Seaham Colliery, an explosion took 164 lives including a twenty-one year old hewer called John Mason. Two weeks after the death of Gladstone's sister Helen in January 1880, James Shannon's uncle Edward Shannon, died at the age of fifty-five of typhoid fever, after three days illness. Bad sewerage and the handling of dead bodies after the colliery disaster was said to have been the cause of this typhoid which was highly contagious. The death certificate gave Edward's address as 8 Bonner's Field Monkwearmouth (close to St Peter's Monastery), and his occupation, still a printer.

Two months later, as recorded by the 1881 Census, Edward Shannon's family were living at the same address, with his widow Jane Shannon now head of the household and working as a seamstress. Jane's second eldest son, Frederick, aged seventeen years, had followed in his father's footsteps with his occupation given as a Printer's Apprentice. The other children included Mary Ann, Edward Reed and Richard. The two younger children were given as scholars, but Mary Ann was probably helping her mother at home.

It is interesting that the name Reed had been used as a Christian name for one of the children, again indicating the close ties to the Reed family. In September 1885, Edward Reed Shannon was to die at the age of 14 years of meningitis at 6 Rendlesham Street, Monkwearmouth. (October often marked the start of the 'meningitis season'). Fortunately, printer chapels provided funds for sickness and burials.

Joseph Chamberlain arrived on the political scene when he carried through an Employers' Liability Act to provide workers with insurance for accidents arising during the course of their employment. A Bill allowing Dissenters to bury their dead in parish graveyards, was much approved by Queen Victoria. Colliery accidents during 1856–86 were 1000 annually. This was to be a disastrous decade for colliery explosions costing 74 lives at Trimdon Grange in 1880, 41 lives were lost at Usworth Colliery in 1885, and also explosions at

Tudhoe and West Stanley. Surprisingly, one gain secured by the miners' union was a reduction to seven hours, 'bank to bank', for hewers. There was an economic depression in the 1880s, which like the 1840s caused social unrest among the working classes, and heightened social consciousness among the middle classes. More Irish were working in mines and on Tyneside shipbuilding.

In 1880 Gladstone repealed the malt tax (which had started in 1697) to fund the national debt. In Scotland, the 'Tattie Strike' of 1881, was one of the hardest-fought battles in the history of Scottish mining. The name was derived from the potatoes doled out in proportion to the size of the miner's family, organised by the strike leaders. Increasingly, Irish tenants were unable to pay their rent, and evictions mounted. Durham colliers condemned the recent coercion laws for Ireland; Cowen in 1881 told of the Irish predicament:

> '.. the Irish immigrant carries with him bitter memories; and with honourable devotion and commendable liberality he aids his countrymen to free themselves from laws that overmastered him and drove him into exile'.

Three quarters of the potato crop failed, and starvation and coercion took a grip on Ireland. At Enniskillen in 1881, Shannon families like many others suffered fatalities. Ellen wife of John Shannon died at the age of 38, and also Catherine wife of Patrick Shannon, at the age of 28, and her three infant children.

In March, Gladstone was back on the election trail greeted by massive crowds at Newcastle. The surprise dissolution of Parliament by Lord Beaconsfield resulted in the 1880 General Election, causing Parnell to rush back from America to a disorganised party without candidates or funds. This was overcome by Davitt using the Land League's funds. Parnell's sister paid a visit to the pressure group 'Newcastle Irish Women' on behalf of the Land league. General Gordon arrived back in England after failing to eliminate the slave trade in Sudan, and before long was off on more foreign assignments eventually leading him to his last journey to Sudan.

The news of the British election was welcomed by the Afrikaners, in the hope that a different government would be sympathetic to their cause. In December 1880, South Africa proclaimed itself a republic, and in the following February, a small British force was annihilated by the Afrikaners. After the Transvaal War in 1881, Gladstone fulfilled his election promise and gave independence to the Transvaal. Queen Victoria disapproved of the withdrawals, since she loathed the idea of handing over the African natives to the Boers – 'a most merciless and cruel neighbour, and in fact oppressor'. The claim of Home Rule was being demanded by both South Africa and Ireland, as well as by Afghanistan and Egypt.

The Irish vote in England and Scotland came out solidly against Disraeli and the Tory ('landlords') Party. In Ireland Parnell fought the 'Moderate' Home Rulers, as well as Liberals and Tories. There was a sweeping victory for Liberalism – 347 Liberals, 140 Conservatives, and 65 Irish Nationalists. At least four of the sixty-five Nationalists were not Home Rulers. One wing of the Liberal Party relied on blue-blooded Whigs and the other wing on Radicals, Socialists, Republicans, Irish and atheists. Beaconsfield gave the reason for his defeat as six bad harvests running and the Zulu loss in 1879. Irish issues were to dominate the new government of 1880, more than that of 1868.

The industrial downswing was accompanied by the onset of agricultural depression caused largely by the recovery in America after its civil war. This was even more so in Ireland, especially in the western provinces of Connaught and Munster, with conditions worse than any time since the Great Famine. There was a mounting wave of agrarian crime (outrages), particularly in Connaught. Agitators John Dillon and Thomas Brennan urged that those responsible for the evictions of tenants should be treated as lepers, and to be 'boycotted', thus carrying on the tradition of the Land League set up by Parnell and Davitt in 1877. Parnell had other things on his mind as he started his relationship with Kitty O'Shea.

The ostracism of Captain Boycott in Mayo was extended into Parliament by Parnell, proving an effective weapon. Parnell introduced a Bill to give compensation to all tenants disturbed by eviction. Gladstone countered this with a Bill of his own. The resulting struggle ended with the Bill being thrown out by the Lords. Gladstone also had to face a famine-stricken Ireland. General Gordon described the peasantry during a visit there in 1880 as 'worse than that of any other people in the world, let alone Europe'. They were patient beyond belief, but broken-spirited and desperate. This desperation led to murder and violence. Parnell's eloquence at various meetings around Ireland stirred up emotions to boiling point. As Toynbee noted in 1881, the landed gentry 'were led by the strongest motives of political zeal and personal interest combined, to widen and tighten their hold upon the land'. In 1881 the Royal Inniskilling Fusilliers, an infantry regiment of the British Army, was founded at Enniskillen.

In 1881 there were ice-floes up to ten feet thick in the Solway. The years of depression and poverty following 1879 were to bite deeply, especially during the winter periods, and above ground workers were suffering as well as miners. This period of Irish political ferment was to see the death of Richard Shannon on the 23 of January 1881, one year after his brother Edward's death in Sunderland. Richard at the age of 65 years was to die in the Union Workhouse at Westgate in Newcastle upon Tyne. The cause of death was given as diarrhoea, which suggested a similar illness as his brother's.

By strange co-incidence in 1881, the Westgate workhouse records revealed an Ann Fenwick aged sixty-six – could this have been Richard's wife?

Perhaps they had been forced to enter the workhouse over a period mainly affected by unemployment. Injuries of railway workers were nearly as frequent as those of miners. At this time a James Shannon from Dumfries, of the same age as Richard, was working as a bookkeeper on railway works at Everton (Lancashire). Another Shannon named John, aged 45, who had worked as clerk at Westgate, died one year later. The fact that Richard ended up in the workhouse indicated that he was unable to continue working and support himself and that he was isolated from his family. During 1881, at Westgate Workhouse, residents included George [Mc]Rae, aged 36, an agricultural labourer from Ecclefechan, Dumfriesshire, Margaret O'Reilly, aged 29, a housekeeper from Tyrone, and Michael McDermot, aged 60, a builder's labourer from Roscommon.

The workhouses obviously did not wish to publicise the fact that their sanitary conditions were not up to standard. It was generally considered the ultimate disgrace in Victorian times to be buried a pauper, and many on the bread-line would starve themselves in order to continue their payments to a friendly society. Dickens' Mutual Friend was to describe the disgrace of the workhouse.

Tsar Alexander II, ruler of Russia since 1855, was assassinated by a Nihilist group in March 1881. Another death which was to attract a little more attention was that of the Earl of Beaconsfield, who died in April. His death was grieved by the Queen, but not by Gladstone, who considered that Disraeli had had a corrupting influence on the Queen, and that 'Dizzy is of course looking for the weak side of the English people on which he has thriven so long'. In February, Carlyle's wishes were observed when he was buried at his birth-place, Ecclefechen in Dumfriesshire, on a cold wintry day, rather than at Westminster Abbey. It is significant that at his graveside were Lecky and Tyndall, two of the foremost men of Ireland, the land that he had rebuked but pitied so much.

In the 1881 Census, James Mason and his children Richard, Alexander and Lydia were shown to be living at 199 Corner House, Whitburn. Also living with James was his eldest son's mother-in-law, Mary A. Reid [Reed] and her children, Ann, William and John. She was recorded as a lodger and widow aged 41 years. James's occupation was now given as 'Stone Sinker' and his son Alexander aged 14, a 'Stone Labourer'. John Hann was recorded as master sinker at Whitburn Colliery. It was likely that Alexander was working for his father in sinking shafts. In August 1882, Whitburn had a shaft tragedy; an engineman, aged only 26, fell out of a kibble to his death.

When cutting through to a coal seam, in some areas like Marsden or Whitburn Colliery, the sinkers had to break through stone overlying the coal. This stone (perhaps whinstone) was 'waste' material; in hewing work miners had to separate this from the coal, since tubs found to have stone in them were rejected without payment. Sinkers used blasting techniques when excavating through solid rock, which was hard but straightforward, since there would be little ingress of water in stone areas. Frederick Williams recorded that during the blasting for the Greenock Railway, 314 tons of gunpowder was used to pass through 2,300 yards of whinstone. More Irishmen were rising through the ranks of the coal industry with a Patrick McGarrity born in Ireland a master sinker at West Auckland during 1881.

In April 1881, James's eldest son John aged 26 and family including wife Sarah (Sally) and son James, were also living in Whitburn, at 116 Peintic Cottage. John's occupation was given as 'Onsetter at Coal Mine', whose job was to transfer the coal tubs at bottom of shaft to the cage to be raised to bank. James's son Richard, aged 19, was a Banksman, at the top of shaft unloading the kibbles. So the whole Mason family were involved in the sinking operation at Whitburn other than James Mason's second son James, aged 24, who was a boarder lodging with a family in Holmside, Lanchester.

James(son) was working as a coal miner and on the 21 May married Jane Clough at the Burnhope register office in the district of Lanchester. His father was recorded as a Sinker, and Jane's father, a coal miner. Jane was 20 years old, and yet even by this date she was not able to write, since she had signed her marriage certificate with a mark. In the 1881 census before their marriage, Jane Clough had been shown as a general domestic servant, lodging and working for an innkeeper at Hamsteels, Lanchester, giving her birth place as Earsdon. The Clough family were well-known boxers, and James (son) was to gain a reputation as a fighter.

In 1881, Clement, son of James's step-father Clement Mason, was a coal miner living close-by at Medomsley. Also at Medomsley, James's daughter Ellen, was living with her husband William Kirsopp, a coal miner. William was born in Eston Yorkshire. Their four-year old daughter, Lydia, was named after Ellen's mother. Twenty years later, the 1901 census showed Ellen, as a widow, living with the family of her brother Alexander. She later re-married to Richard Gorst, a deputy overman.

James Reed had now returned from America, and on the 19 March 1881 he had married Emma Wilson at a Newcastle register office (His father Andrew was now a Gas Man). However two weeks later the 1881 census revealed that he was already married to Anna, (born in Askam Yorkshire) and living at Castle Eden! Two of Anna's children to her previous husband and a child to James Reed were living with them. James was employed as Engine Driver at the colliery. However the law later caught up with James Reed; in the Criminal Registers of 31 October 1883, he was before the court accused of bigamy; his case was postponed until the next assizes.

John Mason 1890 at Esh, Durham
(author's collection)

James Mason (son) 1900 at Hanley, Staffs
(author's collection)

Mary Ann Bulmer/Reed/Mason 1895
at Esh, Durham
(author's collection)

Sarah Mason [left] and James Storey Reed
[centre]1895 at Esh, Durham
(author's collection)

Isabella Dunn and Ellen Kirsopp 1935
at Murton, Durham
(author's collection)

Jessie Main and Alexander Mason 1900
at Ferryhill, Durham
(author's collection)

Lydia Taylor 1920
at Usworth, Durham
(author's collection)

By autumn William Morris was writing that 'it was good to feel the air laden with the coming storm'. The Democratic Federation (DF) had just formed, and Morris was to join it one year later. At this time the DF had not totally declared for Socialism, and had not yet established its political manifesto. The politics of protest were a confused amalgam of the London working-men's and Radical clubs, the remnants of the Chartists and the more recent influx of foreign refugees from Austria and France after the Commune, from Bismarck's Germany and from the repressive Russian regime. Morris explained giving up on the Radicals and his joining of the DF, as the one body that could offer, even 'hazily', the hope of a society of real equality, without masters and men, without rich and poor. From 1874 to 1880, working class leaders had backed the Liberal opposition. This was to change.

The winter of 1881 caused soup kitchens to be set up in Ireland; the period 1881 to 1891 saw the fastest rate of decrease in population since the Great Famine. On the 22 August 1881, the greatest Land Act of the nineteenth century was passed, with Parnell and one of his followers, Captain O'Shea, negotiating with Joseph Chamberlain on the basis of the 3 'F's. This Land Act helped to make it worthwhile for tenants to improve their tenancy. The Government were deeply suspicious of the motives of Parnell's Land League, and put into effect the suspension of Habeas Corpus. There was much public hostility between Gladstone and Parnell; Parnell was blamed for encouraging sheer lawlessness, and Gladstone was accused of masquerading as the champion of Irish rights. Gladstone did admit long after that 'without the Land League, the Act of 1881 would not now be on the Statute Book'.

Seven years after his wife Lydia died in 1874, James Mason, master sinker at Hamsteels Colliery, re-married on the seventeenth of January 1882. His second wife was Mary Ann Reed who had been living in and probably acting as housekeeper and mother to his younger children for at least three years. They married in the parish church of Hamsteels. It would seem that Mary Ann had learned that James Reed had returned from America just before her marriage to James Mason, when she decided it was more appropriate to revert to her earlier married name of Mary Ann Bulmer, as recorded on her third marriage certificate.

Only a few weeks later James would have learned of the disaster at Trimdon Grange Colliery when seventy-three men died after an explosion. He was bound to have remembered the death of his first step-father, John Lawrence, who had died at Trimdon in 1849.

On the marriage certificate, James's father was given as James Mason, a 'Moulder'. It might have been expected that in 1882, James could have either registered his father as Peter Mason, (that is using the Christian name of his father Peter Shannon), or John Mason, (the name after his first step-father), or perhaps Clement Mason (the

William Morris 1887
(Bridgeman Images)

full name of his second step-father). In everyday life, James had continued to present himself as James Mason; the names Shannon and Lawrence had slipped into history.

When James's father, Peter Shannon, first arrived in Newcastle, he may have found work at the ironworks near Walker, and then after a few years progressed to the work of iron moulding. It is not inconceivable that James on being told the true name of his father, had learned of his father's work before he died. (A century later Michael Shannon, a blacksmith, living at Derrylin in Fermanagh, was distinguished as a maker and player of fiddles. He was born in 1930, and his family for many generations had been blacksmiths, perhaps connected to Philip Shannon of Kesh.) Ironwork was a vital skill of the pit sinker.

During the period 1882–3, there were many Fenian outrages with evictions in Ireland still widespread even though the recently passed Land Act allowed tenants to buy an allotment of bog. However it was too late to stop inflamed passions spilling over, leading to the arrest of Parnell in October under the Coercion Act. At the time of his incarceration, in the Catholic Whiteboy tradition, 'Moonlighters' were plunging Ireland into chaos. From May to August 1882, Irish agitator Dillon had also been in prison. In March there had been a seventh attempt on Queen's life. Gladstone made a supreme effort to solve the Irish problem, finally negotiating a deal with Parnell. Parnell was released in May under

what was called the Kilmainham Treaty. This Treaty was an agreement with Parnell to quell land agitation in return for Gladstone's promise to suspend coercion. On release he campaigned for the Land Act based on the '3 Fs', first started by the Tenant Right League.

There were great hopes all over Ireland that the dark days were over. However, the work of assassins was to intervene. The Government was to regret the release of Parnell since two days later on the 4 May in Dublin's Phoenix Park, Lord Frederick Cavendish and his Under-Secretary were knifed to death. A statement was issued by Parnell, Davitt and Dillon deploring the murder as the worst that had stained the annals of Ireland for fifty years. Five of the conspirators were hanged, and Patrick O'Donnell from Donegal was taken to England, and executed by firing. Despite Gladstone's efforts, public opinion in England was outraged, and in some places Irishmen were assailed simply because they were Irish; in many places they were dismissed from their employment. On the 11 May, the Crimes Bill was introduced, the most drastic coercion bill for half a century. The Act was to run for three years. The only relief for the Irish, as part of the Kilmainham Treaty, was the Arrears Bill which assisted in the payment of outstanding rents. In October, the illegal Land League was revived by Parnell as the Irish National League began to build huts for hundreds of evicted tenants at Glenfarne/Kiltyclogher.

The attack on Alexandria, with British forces occupying Egypt, resulted in Bright's resignation in July 1882. Bright had become disillusioned with Home Rule. Nevertheless in

Newcastle, Cowen's powerful assault on behalf of Home Rule, coupled with the city's long radical traditions, created a powerful regional centre of sympathy in which there were Irish successes. Bernard M'Anulty, Newcastle's most celebrated Irishman, became the first nationalist city councillor. Also the 'Cowen' branch of the Land League started up in Barrow – a real tribute to Newcastle radicalism. The 1880s and 1890s were to see the re-birth of three working class movements. These political movements included the Social Democratic Federation founded in 1881 by Henry Mayers Hyndman and William Morris, followed by the Fabian Society in 1884, and Keir Hardie's Independent Labour Party in 1893. Sidney Webb helped the passage of the 1882 Municipal Corporation Act, which gave local boroughs greater power. Trade union membership was one million in the 1880s, increasing to nearly two million by 1900.

After 1882, Michael Davitt, a leading active Irish nationalist, was to give much of his time and energy to the labour movement in Britain. He identified the struggle of the British working men for political emancipation and social justice with the peasant revolt in Ireland that he had inspired and led. This was the theme of his 'Leaves from a prison diary' completed in Portland prison in 1884 and published 1885. During these years he carried out a vigorous campaign for land nationalisation and labour alliance working in the areas where the Irish element was strongest – Lancashire, Yorkshire, Tyneside, the Clyde and the London area. Davitt clashed with Parnell on strategy, and reacted strongly against Parnell's decision to instruct the Irish to vote for the Conservatives in the 1885 general election. Gladstone's conversion to Home Rule in early 1886 was to bring Davitt and Parnell together again, but not in the 1888 Lanark by-election when Davitt supported Keir Hardie's independent labour party, with Parnell supporting the Liberal candidate.

On the 5th January 1883, Clement Attlee, a future Labour Prime Minister, was born into a well-off family. From a similar background, William Morris was beginning to feel the need to participate in the new political organisation, the SDF. At this time he gave a speech at Oxford on the ruination of his beloved cities and beloved country landscapes, and the regimented chaos of commerce – unwelcome music to many in the audience. Morris had always to contend with the criticism that as one of the middle class himself, his own position was indefensible. He freely admitted the difficulty he faced in his religious zeal for Socialism:

> ' ....to be consistent we should at once cast aside our position as capitalists, and take rank with the proletariat; but he must excuse my saying that he knows very well we are not able to do so; that the most we can do is to palliate as far as we can the evils of the unjust system which we are forced to sustain; that we are but minute links in the immense chain of the terrible organisation of competitive commerce, and that only the complete unrivetting of that chain will really free us'.

In 1883 there was a massive volcanic explosion in Summakia, Java, a reminder of the natural disaster in 1817. However the political explosion that Marx had predicted never happened. Marx and Engel's attempts to rescue the English working class from its state of political castration failed, perhaps due to their avoidance of direct involvement with working class organisations: 'the reform movement in England, which we had created, nearly killed us'. Frustrated by the slow realisation of his hopes for a new revolutionary society, Karl Marx died on the 14 March 1883. Morris's socialist education had developed by reading Das Capital in French after Mill's 'Chapters on Socialism'.

In 1883 it was the turn of James's next son to wed; on the 24 November Richard Mason married Mary Askew at the parish church of Hendon near Sunderland. Again as with his brother's wives, Mary gave her mark on her marriage certificate. The occupation of Richard's father was given as a miner rather than sinker. It is possible that James Mason was no longer an active sinker, and had taken up less strenuous work.

Two amendments to the Land Act of 1881 were passed in 1883, accompanied by a ferocious Crimes Act. Parnell's response to all measures was based on maintaining the legislative independence of Ireland. He thus supported Gladstone's Franchise Reform since it widened the electorate in Ireland, and therefore of his own party. Gladstone considered that a working class party would destroy the Liberal Party. Well before the 1885 General Election, Gladstone was politically astute to know that he needed to do something about Ireland, since Ireland had been on a tight-rope between subversion and coercion during the period 1883 to 1884. O'Brien in his newspaper, United Ireland, was able to expose every illegality committed by Government agents during their enforcement of coercion, and several prominent officials were convicted of hideous and unnatural crimes. Parnell's power and influence were increasing as the 'Liberal Coercion Government' was growing weaker.

Following the Monaghan by-election, Landlord Ascendency and Orange bigotry were weakened. Parnell was gaining the support of the priests and of English Liberals, like Mr Cowen and Mr Labouchere, who cast their party allegiance aside to show their disgust at the treatment of Ireland. In 1884, an Orange Day riot took place in Cleator Moor where Irish miners were unwilling to accept an open insult to their religion. The newspaper image of the Irishman was a uniformly violent and dangerous specimen called 'Paddy'. The Irish suffered from what G S Goschen, the Liberal Unionist, described in 1886 as 'a double dose of original sin', damned as they were by their class and their race.

During late 1883, the newspapers were full of articles on Sudan and Egypt, with letters from colonels and clergymen demanding vengeance. On the 7th January 1884 the Egyptian Government resigned, and by the 18th January General Gordon was sent out to relieve the situation, already acclaimed a hero by the British public. On the 25th March,

General Gordon, killed
in Sudan, 1885
(Bridgeman Images)

Queen Victoria was expressing her fears for his safety. Two days later Prince Leopold died – a haemorrhage of the brain. In 1884 distress of the poor was at a peak; on the 9 July the Lords threw out the Reform Bill – 'Peers versus People'. The Queen feared a burst of reform applied to the House of Lords – where would it stop? However Lord Salisbury held fast to Churchill's speeches of alarm; Gladstone hit the campaigning trail speaking to packed audiences. William Morris was also making speeches around Britain's main cities including Newcastle. On the 5th August, the Government passed a grant for the relief of General Gordon.

The 1884 Reform Bill extended the limited town democracy of 1867 to the countryside, and was magnified by the Bill's running mate, Redistribution of the Seats Bill, giving the counties for the first time more seats than the boroughs. The coal miners, who mostly lived in the industrially scarred countryside rather than in towns, were also brought within the franchise, opening the way to much the largest group of working men representatives in Parliament. Whigs and Conservatives making use of the obstructive powers of the House of Lords, extracted from the Liberal Government a pledge that equitable distribution would follow in the next session; the Liberals wanted a Reform Act more than they wanted a conflict with the Lords.

In late November a compromise was reached. The Reform Bill passed through the Lords while an agreed Redistribution Bill simultaneously came before the Commons. Queen Victoria was well pleased with this unconstitutional agreement 'to avert serious dangers so much desired by Radicals and Republicans'. Two Gladstonian reform bills were passed in 1884 /1885, including a vote for country households' redistribution of seats to the larger towns and a national system of compulsory education.

Queen Victoria recorded as early as February 1884, her concern and that of the general public for the safety of General Gordon. Her fears were realised on the 26 January 1885 when England received the news that he had been speared to death in Sudan. He had been a sapper during the Crimean War. Gordon was the same age as James Shannon – both sustained injuries that were to prove fatal at about the same date, but James had to suffer another 12 months before his death.

Gladstone had to bear the brunt of public vilification, but still refused to seek revenge in Sudan, and fortunately for him, very soon public attention was diverted by a Russian/ Afghan crisis. It is said that during Gladstone's visit in 1885 to Norway, he was impressed by the democratic way of life there inherited from the Vikings, as in Ireland.

Chamberlain in January 1885 was attempting to split the Radical programme from Home Rule. He resigned on 20 May at the introduction of further coercion. John Burns who was to take a leading role in the Independent Labour Party, was a journeyman engineer in 1881, when he drove the first electric tramcar in the British Isles. Later in 1885 he and John Ward were to share the same platform demanding 'We must have work or bread'. In July 1885, the Agricultural Labourers Union was formed. Three months later, Lord Shaftesbury, campaigner for improved conditions for children down mines, died and was buried in Westminster Abbey, attended by the famous, and not so famous such as former colliers and chimney sweep boys.

Germinal, the novel by Emile Zola, first published in 1885, gave a story of the hardships and brutality of a mining community in the Belgian coalfields. It depicted a 'nightmare' vision of the proletarian coalminers undetected underground menacing the bourgeoisie. In 1889, a bookseller, Vizetelly was imprisoned for three months for selling translations of Zola. The 'realism' of Zola was considered too contaminating for British morality. Another author whose realism in print was thought too indecent for British consumption was D H Lawrence, born on the 11 September 1885 in a Nottingham coal-mining area.

On the tenth of October 1885, James Mason's daughter Isabella married William Dunn, a coal miner, at the register office in Sunderland. (Isabella later married James Dunn – she was 'Dunn' again!) Both Isabella and William signed the register. They lived at 66 Chilton Street, in Monkwearmouth. The marriage certificate again contained an anomaly. Isabella's father was given as James Mason (deceased), a coalminer, yet James's death certificate was to be issued some four months later?

A witness to the marriage was recorded as M. Sword, a name originating in Ireland. When the Shannons were living in Dumfriesshire, baptismal records in 1823 and 1827 included sponsors called Swords. It appeared that the Shannons were part of an Irish community in Sunderland. Sally Mason's son, Arthur, revealed many years later that his father used to play the button accordion in the local pubs. Apparently, when his father was in a merry mood he would call himself Jacky Shannon. It seems that James Shannon's children had been told or had found out by other means their true surname. Roker Park the local football ground had opened in 1880. Arthur was to play for Leeds United during 1922/24.

In 1884–1886 there were serious riots in the West End of London, particularly in February 1886. William Walker a teenager in Belfast remembered the riots during the Home Rule debates of 1886 when twenty-nine lives were lost. An Irish labour candidate fought the North Belfast seat as early as 1885. English trades unions comprised of the working class elite tended to be particularly militant compared to the inert mass of disorganised labour. Socialism remained essentially the doctrine of the small bourgeois and artisan intelligentsia, and working class development from traditional chapel elite. Socialist pamphleting and journalism started to flourish in the 1880s, and saw the introduction of the sixpenny telegram. Cheap mass press became economically possible by technological advances like linotype and monotype. Practical Christianity and social justice eventually coalesced into the Labour Party, campaigning for eradication of poverty. The Socialist paper Justice carried an article by John Burns MP on 'Our Mining Population':

> 'Their individual is completely crowded out, and they have become as Shelley says but 'mechanised automata', supply profit making machine, to build up large fortunes for the mine owner, who whilst his men are working under brutal conditions, is luxuriating on the shores of the Mediterranean or gliding up the Bosphorus in a steam yacht purchased out of the unpaid labour of the miners'.

A year later the same SDF paper published 'Chants for Socialists' and 'All for the Cause'. William Morris had described in a Socialist League pamphlet the miseries existing in 1885: 'The misery and squalor which we people of civilisation bear with so much complacency as a necessary part of the manufacturing system, is just as necessary to the community at large as a proportionate amount of filth would be in the house of a private rich man. If such a man were to allow the cinders to be raked all over his drawing room, and a privy to be established in each corner of his dining room, if he habitually made a dust and refuse heap of his once beautiful garden, never washed his sheets or changed his table-cloth, and made his family sleep five in a bed, he would surely find himself in the claws of a commissio de lunatico. But such acts of miserly folly are just what our present society is doing daily under the compulsion of a supposed necessity, which is nothing short of madness.'

The Ballot Act and the franchise gave the Irish great influence in England during the 1885 election. Gladstone was forced to admit to Queen Victoria that his cabinet was split on Irish policy. He had proposed for Ireland a 'central Board of Local Government on something of an elective basis', but it was not accepted by all of his cabinet and was dropped. A defeat on beer duty by a combination of Conservatives and Irish Nationalists on the 9 June brought to an end Gladstone's third ministry. Parnell was mistaken in thinking he could get Home Rule from the Conservatives when Lord Salisbury's ministry took over. Parnell saw that Chamberlain would never agree to Home Rule, and therefore had reckoned that a Tory Government was more likely to pass a Bill since it would not be opposed on Party grounds.

During the summer of 1885 Chamberlain's efforts to satisfy Ireland with local, self-governing councils earned him the violent hostility of Parnell's extremist followers. If he had visited Ireland they had threatened to duck him in a horse-pond or bog hole. From that moment Chamberlain was through with Parnell. It became public knowledge that Opposition Leader Gladstone was intent on Home Rule (revealed by his son), and became known as the Gladstone's 'Hawarden Kite' on his adoption of the Home Rule policy as recorded in the Pall Mall Gazette on 17 December. It was said that the Irish voting with the Tories in 1885 had forced the Liberals into Home Rule.

When Gladstone under pressure from his Right Wing announced that he intended to re-introduce the expiring Crimes Act, Parnell used the Nationalist balancing vote to defeat the Government, thus precipitating the 1885 General Election during November and December.

The Ballot Act and the franchise gave the Irish great influence in England during this election. Parnell cast the Irish vote in England with 85 'Home Rulers'. Gladstone asked the Liberals to take the Irishmen to their hearts, and they did. A Liberal and Parnellite combination defeated the Conservatives, and Gladstone returned to office.

The Tories numbered 247, Liberals 335, and Home Rulers 86. Neither of the two main parties was satisfied. The Irish alone had done well, literally sweeping the board in Munster, Leinster and Connaught. In South Mayo the numbers were 4900 to 75, in West Mayo 4790 to 131; in East Kerry 3169 to 30. Even in Ulster the Home Rulers had a majority of its 33 members, 17 out of 33 were pledges from supporters of Parnell. Mr Healy was returned for South Derry and Mr William O'Brien for South Tyrone. There were 85 out of 103 Irish members followers of Parnell; but not one Liberal was elected in Ireland.

At this time of great interest in Ireland was the election of Dr Walsh as the Catholic Archbishop of Dublin, a pronounced advocate of Home rule, having defeated Dr Moran a nephew of Cardinal Cullen. In August it was evident that the Tories could not continue in office, but with only 250 MPs they were not strong enough to discard the Orangemen. Their attitude changed with Lord Caernarvon being replaced by the new Lord Londonderry, a descendent of Castlereagh, and Mr W H. Smith, one of the most anti-Irish of the Tories appointed as Chief Secretary.

Writer MacDonagh recalled whilst walking in Hyde Park, one Sunday afternoon, being attracted by a crowd round a man attacking the movement for Home Rule. The speaker had only one leg; and his maimed condition was made the subject of chaff by some hostile Irishmen who were in a group. "Arrah, how did yez lose your leg, me ould bhoy?" said one. "Well, I'll tell you," said the man, interrupting the discourse. "On examining my pedigree, I found there was some Irish blood in me; and, being convinced that it had settled in my left leg, I had it cut off at once." "Wisha, thin," said the Irishman, "I'm sorry it wasn't in your head it settled."

With changes in franchise legislation, there were now a significant number of Irish among the electorate in England, Scotland and Wales. Parnell opened up the election campaign in January 1886 by making it quite clear to the Tories and Liberals on what terms the Irish votes depended, that was an Irish Parliament with an independent Irish executive. Unlike Lord Hartington, Chamberlain favoured giving Ireland a generous measure of self-government. Both Lord Randolph Churchill and Lord Salisbury kept a low profile, unwilling to concede Home Rule, but at the same time not wanting to offend Irish friends. (Later Lord Randolph Churchill was not so quiet with 'Ulster will fight, Ulster will be right' which was to be the catchphrase for the Orange Order).

Towards the end of 1885 there was a severe winter with snowdrifts twenty feet high at Springwell Colliery, about three miles south-east of Newcastle. This weather would not have helped James Mason during his last days. Twelve days before James Mason's death, London was in a state of siege and riot over unemployment, which became known as Black Monday. The death certificate was registered on the 22 February 1886, with his son James, the informant, giving the date of death as the 20 February, as Gladstone became Prime Minister for the third time. The place of residence was given as Church Street, Boldon Colliery, and James's occupation a Colliery Sinker.

It was appropriate that James Shannon ended his days at Boldon Colliery (first sunk in 1866, and then in 1885), since this colliery had a 'Rose, Shamrock & Thistle' banner. An explanation for James Mason's death at the age of 52 years has been passed down the family, from generation to generation. Apparently, James fell down a shaft and his fall was arrested by a grappling hook which caught into his back. He was held by the hook for one day, and survived a further four days. This 'story' holds some truth in that he certainly suffered a body injury which was confirmed on the death certificate, but the period he survived is still in doubt. Since he died sometime after the injury at work, therefore his death would not have been officially recorded.

Also, it was a serious injury, in that death resulted from the 'abscess of hip joint and thigh accidently received' which had developed in the affected area over the period since the accident. The surgeon, J Grant, certified the nature of the injuries. (At that time, a remedy for an abscess was sometimes treated with 'meat and porter'. Professor Lister had lanced an abscess on Queen Victoria in 1872). The death may have occurred during an operation to remove the abscess, or due to septicaemia caused by blood poisoning. The nature of the injury may explain the implication of the entry on his daughter's marriage certificate in October 1885 which recorded him as deceased. It is possible that Isabella informed the registrar that her father was dying, and he in error translated his notes later to record 'deceased'. The words, 'accidently received', no doubt were included to protect the colliery owner from a compensation claim.

James Mason was buried at Boldon cemetery on the 23 February, three days after his death. It is recorded that he was laid to rest in a 'pauper's grave', which suggested that his last days were spent in the workhouse – as suffered by his uncle Richard. Also an interesting record of the South Shields Union Workhouse on the 31 December 1884 gave a resident James Mason aged 50. Could he have been taken to the workhouse after his accident?

In February 1886, Chamberlain subscribed to Gladstone's Irish policy – vaguely defined as an examination of Home Rule; it was in the private belief that 'he might soon be looking for a bog hole in which to dump it'. On the 26 March Chamberlain resigned and the Liberal Party split in two. The critical figures deciding the fate of Home Rule were Gladstone, Chamberlain and Parnell. Gladstone introduced the Home Rule Bill on the 8 April 1886; the Irish Land Purchase Bill followed on the 16 April. A month later the Scottish Home Rule Association was founded with the support of Keir Hardie.

Bright throughout his life, a strong advocate for freedom and a special friend of Ireland, was to dessert Ireland at this critical point; he stated that he was against these policies since they would lead to the dissolution of the Union. Nevertheless, Tim Healy spoke positively of John Bright on the latter's death in 1888 despite his late opposition to Home Rule: "..

William Gladstone 1886
(Bridgeman Images)

when Ireland had fewest friends....your voice was loudest on her side". When Chamberlain in 1886 joined the Conservatives on the issue of Ireland remaining part of the United Kingdom, they became known as the Conservative and Unionist Party. Chamberlain later was known as 'Judas' and prompted the start of the Labour Party.

Only one day after Gladstone's closing speech, William Morris was in Dublin. The bill that had been defeated would have provided an Irish Parliament and executive in Dublin with its own powers of legislation, except over certain reserved areas such as foreign policy and defence. Morris and the Socialist League had supported the policy of decentralisation, seeing 'a gross form of exploitation in progress in Ireland'. The League was to continue to take part in demonstrations organised by Irish nationalist supporters.

On the 7 June the Home Rule Bill was defeated by 341 to 311. This sent the Liberal Party into the wilderness for 20 years. Gladstone resigned on the 20 July 1886. The new Prime Minister, Lord Salisbury, soon let the Irish know what to expect. He said he would sooner spend public money to secure the emigration of a million Irishmen than in buying-out one single landlord – a foretaste of the 1887 coercion measures.

In November 1887, Bloody Sunday was to gain notoriety as a SDF demonstration took place against O'Brien's imprisonment on incitement charges (This had followed demonstrations in County Cork against 'Bloody Balfour' for the Chief Secretary's draconian policies). Six months earlier, when the Queen opened the People's Palace in the East End of London, she was assailed by what were described as 'only Socialists and the worst Irish', a reminder that the 'Irish Question' was not going to go away!

Irish luck ran out in 1886 with the dreams of the Irish people at home and abroad of an independent Ireland. Perhaps the two-faced stone idols on Boa Island in Fermanagh, looking opposite ways, symbolised the Irish struggle between Catholics and Protestants, unable to reconcile their differences.

Janus Figure Boa Island Fermanagh, 400–800AD (pdphoto.org)

CONCLUSION

Starvation and Slavery to Social Justice

'England is guilty towards Ireland; and reaps at last, in full, measure, the fruit of fifteen generations of wrong-doing ….. Crowds of miserable Irish darken our towns …. The uncivilised Irishman , not by his strength, but by the opposite of strength, drives out the Saxon native, takes possession in his room. There he abides in his squalor and unreason, in his falsity and drunken violence, as the ready-made nucleus of degradation and disorder'.

(Carlyle 1840 Chartism)

' ...... what I mean by Socialism is a condition of society in which there should be neither rich nor poor, neither master nor master's man, neither idle or overworked, neither brain-sick brain workers, nor heart-sick hand workers, in a word, in which all men would be living in equality of condition, and would manage their affairs unwastefully, and with full consciousness that harm to no one would mean harm to all – the realisation at last of the meaning of the word commonwealth.'

(William Morris 1893)

'Life springs from death and from the graves of patriot men and women spring nations. They have left us our Fenian dead, and while Ireland holds these graves, Ireland, unfree, shall never be at peace!'

(Patrick Pearse warned the oppressors that
Nationalist feelings would not die: 1916)

ORIGINS

Shakespeare wrote:'Some men are born to greatness, others achieve greatness, and others have greatness thrust upon them'. James Shannon lived through a period of great changes and like his fellow workers, most of his life and theirs were never recorded. This book aims to address this by celebrating his and his family's achievements, as they responded to the circumstances thrust upon them by their origins, work and by the cruel hand of fate.

With Viking connections, the Shannons were an old Irish family from County Fermanagh. They left Ireland in 1815 due to a combination of reasons – unemployment, famine, disease and eviction. They probably had no intention of leaving on a permanent basis. Over the years in Scotland they would have learned that the situation in Ireland had not improved, and after their move to England, inevitably ties of marriage and work in their new home would have made a return to Ireland less likely. However, as with most exiled Irish families, their emotional links to their homeland would have remained strong.

James Shannon was born in revolutionary times, and his life was to span the period between the first and third Reform Bills. Thirteen years after the Declaration of Independence by America, in 1789 France had struck the decisive blow for 'Liberty, Equality and Fraternity', and had intervened in the War of Independence, costing England her American colonies. The French Revolution was to have a profound effect on many countries. In England, following the 1832 Reform Act and the people's expectations of better times, the New Poor Laws were to 'pauperise the poor' and provoke Chartism; this was still the age of masters and servants as the Tolpuddle Martyrs found to their cost, when they were transported to the other side of the world. This time saw the first attempt at organising a national trade union rather than under separate trades. In Ireland, a bloody war was being waged against the forced payment of tithes to an alien Church.

James Shannon entered a violent and disease-ridden world in 1834; Newcastle upon Tyne was at the centre of technology and political reform. The slave trade was dying, helped on its way by the new Irish votes in Parliament, and the iniquitous chimney-sweep trade was all but over. The Irish Brotherhood was born, but the Irish masses hung on to their Catholic religion, their proof of nationality. Thomas Telford was soon to depart this world having made his mark at the start of the Industrial Revolution. His life had begun in poverty, at Glendinning in Dumfriesshire, apprenticed to a stone mason at Lochmaben.

Even those born in better circumstances were often to die young, like engineer Brunel aged 53, due to overwork and sometimes sharing the same arduous working conditions as his miners, navvies, shipwrights and mechanics. (Shakespeare and Napoleon also died around the age of 52 years). Some working men were 'self-made', in that the harsh conditions of the time required strength of character and an element of luck to gain advancement. During the nineteenth century, there were two figures in the public eye who were to have a continuing influence on the progress of Irish people: Thomas Carlyle, a historian and philosopher, and William Gladstone, a politician and three times Prime Minister.

THOMAS CARLYLE and WILLIAM GLADSTONE

Thomas Carlyle appeared as a benevolent spirit watching over the trials and tribulations of the Shannons. He saw the 'Age of Machinery' as spelling the doom of laissez-faire in politics and economics, and called for a 'Dynamic' spirit to oppose the purely mechanistic conception of existence. Although an advocate of extreme authoritarian rule based on his Scottish Calvinism roots, Carlyle had sympathy for the oppressed and hatred for the oppressors. His foremost principle was that 'injustice ... is unsupportable to all men'.

Carlyle understood the importance of the opening of the first Mechanic's Institute, and that the 'rights of men were not gracefully asked for and granted, but are obtained by one section of society at the expense of another'. He considered the 'great dumb toiling class' was unable to speak for itself, other than through physical violence, for example Captain Swing with his tinder-box and Chartism with its pikes. His many writings on the 'Condition of England', were designed and largely succeeded to shake the Government's conscience regarding the plight of the People, and their 'Human Condition'.

In a letter to his wife in 1845, Gladstone wrote, 'Ireland, Ireland! That cloud in the west, that coming storm, the vehicle of God's retribution ...'. Over the next forty years his views on Ireland were to change dramatically. By the end of 1885, he had decided to risk the survival of his party for the national interest of an Irish settlement, but this was doomed to failure. During his third short-lived ministry of 1886, he introduced his first Irish Home Rule Bill. Conservative forces hung on to their grip on Ireland. As James Shannon suffered the last twelve months of his life, like many expatriate Irishmen he must have hoped that at last, Ireland was to gain some independence and respect.

SLAVERY

Alexander the Great's father, Philip of Macedonia 'dragged home slaves by the 10,000 to work his mines ...'; Alexander also had a keen eye for mineral resources. Worldwide, throughout the centuries, miners in particular were forced into slave-like existence. The Industrial Revolution would also create a social revolution. The north-east of England became a leading region in support of anti-slavery campaigns and Chartist activities.

Chartist John Frost, as he contemplated life from his confinement in Australia, commented on slavery throughout the world and the negligible interest by the British government to suppress it at home. In the wider world the campaign for rejection of slavery of black people had grown, initiated by the Quakers. Britain abolished its slave trade in 1807, and the Slavery Abolition Act was passed in 1833. Spain was one of the last European countries to formally abolish slavery in 1886. Ireland had to wait nearly forty more years, but only to win partial independence from its slave-master, England.

The idea of one man holding another in servile bondage was completely alien to Celtic culture. Ginnell noted that Irish Brehon law 'was distinctly and uniformly adverse to slavery'. This ancient law based on discussion and arbitration also gave women an important place in Celtic society; it provided everyone with 'full sick maintenance' and promoted a 'healthy hunger for knowledge'.

From the time of William the Conqueror, England considered Ireland as a vassal land with its slave-market so overstocked that the slave was worth nothing as a matter of commerce. Engels described Ireland as England's first colony. The Shannon family came from the part of Ireland that had suffered most from Oliver Cromwell's ruling for the Catholic Irish, 'To Hell or Connaught', and the area of Ireland that had resisted the English forces most fiercely. This was followed by theft of Irish land by the imposition of the 'plantation', starting in the early sixteenth century, involving the 'transplant' of all Irish into the region west of the River Shannon, there to be penned up like men infested with the plague, while all the rest of the territory was allotted to English and Scottish families.

From the beginning of the next century under the Penal Laws, the native population was laid under the lash of absolute oppression. The penal code was used by the English Government to bribe or terrify the Irish into giving up their Catholic religion. Burke castigated the architects of this deliberate act of control: 'Never did the ingenious perversity of man put forth a machine more perfect, more thoroughly elaborate, more calculated to oppress, to impoverish, to degrade a people, to lower in them human nature itself'. A 1790 decree in France for toleration of every religion, was to have little influence on Britain. A French writer was equally barbed in his summary of the English Government:

> 'One feels a sort of shame for the human kind in having to record such consistent acts of systematic cruelty. The violence of military retaliation, the sacking of towns or the massacre of vanquished foes, may be explained by the heat of combat, and are found in the annals of other countries. An economical compression exercised during ten or twelve generations on one nation by another nation of Shylocks is, happily, a fact without parallel. From the beginning of the 18th century all industrial enterprise had thus been unmercifully forbidden in Ireland. All the factories were closed, the working population reduced to field labour, emigration or street-begging. This population therefore weighed even more heavily on the soil, still exaggerating its tendencies to subdivision; which tendencies, already a curse for Ireland, were to cause in the future new ferments of hatred and misery'.

Historians from other countries have asked why in Britain during the industrial revolution, men were willing to inflict such miseries on their fellow beings. General Gordon once wrote to his sister: 'For some wise design, God turns events one way or another, whether man likes it or not, as a man driving a horse turns it to right or left without consideration as to whether the horse likes that way or not. To be happy, a man must be well-broken, willing horse, ready for anything. Events will go as God likes'. The concept of the need for people to be 'broken in' like a horse was used as a justification for the grind of work that many of the poor had to suffer in the factories, on the farms and down the mines.

After the Shannons escaped the slavery of Ireland, and then the serfdom in Scotland, they arrived in the coalfields of Tyneside still gripped by the brutal conditions imposed by the colliery owners. However the miners were beginning to wrestle with the binding chains which they had suffered for centuries. The wage-earning workers started to learn that the large numbers drawn to the urban areas gave them industrial and political muscle, and the Irish newcomers after a difficult transition labelled as blacklegs, willingly joined the growing radical movement.

EMIGRATION & SETTLEMENT

Rev Malthus wrote on Ireland, a country he had never visited: 'The land in Ireland is infinitely more peopled than anywhere else; and to give full effect to the natural resources of the country, a great part of the population should be swept from the soil'. The work-houses brought in by the New Poor Laws were to stigmatise the poor. As soon as the Irish migrants had done their work and began to be a burden on the parish, they became 'paupers' to be packed off back to Ireland with all possible speed.

The Irish arriving in Britain, or America and Canada, were required for physically demanding and dangerous work. British urban areas were able to offer work unlike the few urban centres in Ulster such as Belfast and Londonderry, where work was mainly available to non-Catholics. Agricultural specialisation placed ever greater emphasis on the need for intensive short-term labour. Farmers on the British mainland began to realise the good value of Irish labour as manufacturers and miner owners were to find out later. Canal construction attracted a large labour force, but most canals had been constructed by the end of the Napoleonic Wars. The railways in their infancy during the 1820s, later gave an escape for surplus labour.

1817 was a panic year for the British authorities with suspected revolutionary plots and maximum unrest leading to the Treason Act of that year against secret oaths and the Combination Laws. The Shannons escaped the start of Ribbonism in the western counties and the famines that followed. It was not surprising that the Shannons like many other Irish families sought to leave Ireland. The English Government saw this as necessary 'blood-letting', and in particular that this would help to quell revolutionary passions. In contrast, the Elgin Marbles arrived in England during 1816 to great acclaim.

FAMINE, DISEASE & SANITATION

The exact date that the Shannon family left Ireland is unknown, but Robbins recorded that 1816 and 1817 were cold wet years, and the peat on which people depended for fire and warmth could not be cut and dried because of excessive rain; a poor harvest led to crop failure and famine, and an outbreak of typhus, which lasted until 1819. During the first four months of 1817 typhus fever spread extensively in the provinces of Ulster, Munster and Connaught. Throughout Ireland, families shut up their cabins in time of scarcity and took to the roads, the whole family, 'fearful and wretched, united in their misery'.

When James's father, Peter Shannon, became ill in 1837, probably due to poor sanitation affecting tenement houses in Newcastle, there would have been no money to cover the cost of a doctor's visit. The lessons for survival in a brutal age would have been learned quickly, and no doubt helped workers to cope with the dangerous conditions down the mine, especially in the art of sinking which required skill, courage and stamina. The Ancient Egyptians saw the 'pit' as the entrance to death, and for too many miners this turned out to be true. However, the dangers from epidemics were just as lethal as those below ground.

Chadwick an advocate for improved sanitation following the epidemics of the 1830s, met great resistance from across the political spectrum. The introduction of pressurised piped water was essential for clean water becoming available to working people, especially in urban areas. When the better off in London became affected by the stench from the River Thames, then action was demanded, and this spread across the country. Charles Darwin followed by Herbert Spencer introduced the phrase 'survival of the fittest', which well described the early life of James Shannon living in Newcastle. Victorian slum conditions still persisted as reported by the Royal Commission on the Housing of the Working Classes in 1885. The carnage of miners continued, especially those working in mines vulnerable to explosive gases.

STEAM POWER & MINING

In Ireland the name of 'Shannon' is synonymous with its major watercourse. Water as a means of power was to have a tremendous bearing on the nineteenth century, and in particular its effect on the Shannons' life after leaving Ireland. In the 'Age of Steam', firstly, agricultural drainage was improved by steam pumping which created the demand for more workers to harvest the crops; it also powered the steam-packets, a cheap means of transport.

The coal trade was beginning to expand which was to hasten the complete redistribution of the population and the growth of towns; the importance of the close proximity of coal and iron ore was to see the transfer of heavy industry to the north. Steam powered pumps enabled the deep coal mines to become financially viable, and accelerated the industrial revolution in the North East coalfields. Engines developed by James Watt and George Stephenson provided the motive force for the railways, opening up the country to all kinds of social and political influence.

RELIGION & SCIENCE

The Shannon's period in Scotland coincided with O'Connell's campaign for Catholic Emancipation. Grattan's final petition on Emancipation had been defeated in 1819, but ten years later the Catholic Emancipation Act was passed. The Liberator's following campaign for Repeal of the Union was to end in failure at the time of the devastation caused by the Great Famine. As Daniel O'Connell's embalmed body returned home in the summer of 1847, it was to pass ships full of famine refugees.

The artisans and middle-class saw religion as part of their status of achievement and respectability. The lower classes considered the established church on the same side as the employers and the law, screwing the last drop of blood from their workmen. The Church of England retained its hold over the respectable classes until the 1880s when church-going started to decline. Methodism played a vital role in giving the working man the ambition that he was capable of bettering himself. It gave him the confidence to take a leading role in the work-place and later in negotiations and strikes for improved conditions and basic education. In their new countries, the dislocation of the Irish people, and inter-marrying with the natives, were the factors which caused some Shannons to lose their faith. Marx considered religion as 'the opium of the people', but 'No-Popery was' still to be an emotive issue for many decades.

Both Samuel Butler the author of 'The Way of all Flesh' and Carlyle were to comment critically on the struggle between Church and Science. JS Mill, although considering the Catholic Church as the most intolerant of churches, quoted his age as being described as 'destitute of faith, but terrified at scepticism' – in which people feel sure, not so much that their opinions are true, as that they should not know what to do without them. Even then Mill recognised the power of public opinion. The Catholic Church allowed its priests to hear the arguments of its opponents, but the laity had to accept this on trust. Even by 1874, restrictions on 'Romish' practices were still being enacted by the British Government. It was only by 1885 that Cardinal Manning gave open support to the Irish Nationalist party. Charles Kingsley saw the dominating influence of the Catholic religion as being the main flaw to social progress for the Irish people (but ignoring the fact that their faith had often been their only means of survival):

'The Irishman, to his honour, has passed, centuries since, beyond the stage at which he requires to be educated by a priesthood in the primary laws of religion and morality. His morality is – on certain important points – superior to that of almost any people. What he needs to be trained to loyalty and order; to be brought more in contact with the secular science and civilisation of the rest of Europe : and that must be done by a secular, and not by an ecclesiastical system of education'.

WORKERS AND WOMENS RIGHTS & EDUCATION

Following the English Levellers, Thomas Paine excited the working classes by his Rights of Man published in 1791, which was read in great numbers. The philosophy that peoples' rights should be derived from labour and not land or property had been taken up by William Godwin, Thomas Spence, William Thompson, James Fintan Lalor, Henry George, Marx and Engels. The evolution towards granting rights to English working people goes back to the Magna Carta of 1215, the Statute of Labourers in 1349 and 1351, then the civil war of 1455–1485, followed by the 'Glorious Revolution' of 1688. However Irish natives were excluded from these benefits.

Following the American War of Independence and the French Revolution, the 'Rights of Man' championed the merits of a democratic and republican system of government, and was enthusiastically received by the lower classes, including those in Ireland, despite Government attempts to suppress its publication. Paine highlighted the lack of humanity in England which later Carlyle was also to question: 'When in countries that are civilized, we see age that is going to the workhouse and youth to the gallows, something must be wrong in the system of government'. Irish expatriates were to feature prominently in agitating for workers' rights during the nineteenth century.

The advancement of peoples' own talents, the essence of education, was the kindling touch which inspired workers at the beginning of the century to seek a better life for their children. Corresponding societies provided the means for radical artisans to further their ambitions, stimulated by the actions of the United Irishmen. By 1815, the argument in education was not whether but by how much for the lower orders. By the mid-century, Bishop Douglas of Carlisle suggested that permanent schools offered a means 'to strike at the root of that ignorant and brutal ferocity, which daily prompts so many unhappy wretches, the pests of society, to acts of horrible outrage, reproachable to good government, and disgraceful to humanity itself'. The trade unions, especially in the coalfields, maintained a continuous struggle for educational opportunities, resisted tooth and nail by the Conservative Party.

The death of his father at an early age must have had an enormous impact on James Shannon's formative years. The influence of his uncle Edward, a printer and perhaps also a Chartist, could have been important. Most of the Shannon children from Dumfriesshire were able to write; generally Durham colliers were only able to use a mark. State schools started for the poor in 1833, with the "Outline of a System of National Education" published in 1834, and this may have helped James to gain the basics of reading and writing, but it was to take up to 1886 before state secondary schools began. The small parish school of the 1830s, small, accessible even if dirty and inefficient, by the 1880s had been replaced by the Board school, large, remote and forbidding, though clean and efficient. Lord Shaftesbury, foremost in the fight for improved working conditions died in 1885. The miners' demand for basic rights continued the pressure on Government to progress education including mechanics institutes. Charles Dickens who died in 1870 had strongly promoted the 'liberal' education of working people, rather than left to 'self-help'. In his Hard Times he foretold James Shannon's death by arranging for the main character of his novel to end his life by falling down the Old Hell shaft.

In ancient Ireland, Brehon Law gave both men and women equal rights. However, in Britian before and during the nineteenth century women had no political rights. John Stuart Mill was the first to recognise that women deserved rights as well as men. Josephine Elizabeth Butler, daughter of Northumbrian John Grey, also advanced women's position during the nineteenth century. She led the campaign against the White Slave Traffic, by which young girls were bought for a few pounds from their parents and shipped abroad to become prostitutes. This trade was abolished by law in 1886, forty-four years after the abolition of women and young children working down mines.

History has mainly focused on men's lives, however in mining communities women traditionally held control of the family finance, since the pub was often a dangerous drain on their men's wages. The prominent women in the Shannon family must start with Ann (Kellegher), Philip's wife, who set off to a strange country and was required to work long hours in the fields while looking after her young family. Isabella (Gallagher) suffered the loss of many of her children at an early age whilst struggling to live in the appalling conditions of the Newcastle's tenements. Then she had to bear the early deaths of her first and second husband by working as a labourer. Her son James Shannon was to benefit from her resilience. Lastly, Lydia (Calvert), wife of pit sinker James Shannon, would have had to accept the uncertainty of being constantly moving from one colliery to another, and knowing that her husband's life was 'always on the line'.

CHARTISM, TRADE UNIONS & FRANCHISE

One of the Charter's six objectives as far back as 1838 was to obtain voting rights for all people. In England and Scotland the workers were exploited as a class; the Irish workers in addition were exploited as a subject nation. This led to agitation on the mainland in the form of working men's trade unions and Chartism, whereas in Ireland it generated national agitation for Repeal of the Union and for the setting up of an Irish republic. The massive fervour of the Irishmen who joined the early trade unions and Chartist movement was to shape the pattern of English politics. However, the breach between O'Connell and O'Connor was to rob Chartism of one of its strongest possible instruments of action

– Irish discontent. Irish strike-breakers in the 1840s delayed the acceptance by trade unions of Irish workers.

In 1867, lodgers obtained the right to vote which affected navvies and sinkers, considered a dangerous group of workers by Government. Gladstone, starting in the 1870s, was the first leader to consult with the Irish. The 1872 Act permitted secret balloting, which encouraged Irish Nationalists to vote for their own candidates. It took three reform acts, in 1832, 1867 and 1884, to overturn the landowners' majority in the House of Commons. In 1866, Gladstone at the defeat of the Franchise Bill (eventually passed in 1885), warned of the inevitable social forces:

> 'You cannot fight against the future. Time is on our side. The great social forces which move onwards in their might and majesty, and which the tumult of our debates does not for a moment impede or disturb – those great social forces are against you; they are marshalled on our side; the banner which we now carry in this fight, though perhaps at some moment it may droop over our sinking heads, yet it soon again will float in the eye of heaven, and it will be borne by the firm hands of the united people of the three kingdoms, perhaps not to an easy, but to a certain and to a not distant victory'.

FENIANISM, MARXISM & SOCIALISM

After the Great Famine, a growing number of emigrants, especially in America and Australia, were to keep the memory alive of the injustice suffered by their families and fellow Irish, and this was where Fenianism was born – the desire for retribution. From their ranks came the conspirators who were to terrorize England and Ireland with their periodic 'outrages'. A considerable fund was raised during the years 1848 to 1887 to fuel agitation.

The Irish clung onto the principles of Celtic common ownership for a surprisingly long time, partly from the inheritance and instinct of the clan life of their forefathers, and partly because these customs were their only barrier to poverty. The people were only conscious of socialism as an open objective for a relatively short time. The main contributors to British 'socialism' were Paine, Owen, Marx, Engels, Mills, Morris and Hardie; socialists Lalor and Connolly had great influence in Ireland. The Chartist, John Frost, believed Jesus to be the first socialist – protector of the disadvantaged.

Another Chartist, Feargus O'Connor, wanted to mobilise the combined strength of the English operatives and Irish peasants for social and political reform. His visits to the industrial North showed that the Irish in England and Scotland remained deeply interested in the plight of agricultural Ireland which they had left, and yet they were also very involved in the problems of the new industrial Britain where most were employed. Marx and Engels were convinced at first that this union would eventually lead to a political revolution by the working-class in Britain.

Marx admitted that communal socialism grew out of and was the 'child of capitalism'. However, he considered that the 'red blood of revolution flowed through Celtic veins'. During the 1860s, Marx endeavoured to create a union between the English working class and the Fenian movement, but failed to obtain any significant collaboration, although a release of Fenian prisoners was gained in 1871. This failure was mainly due to counter-initiatives by Gladstone leading to his later campaigns for Irish Home Rule. It is said that the Methodist's influence had earlier blunted revolution by the masses.

Marx noted with great disappointment that the English workers were unable to put on one side their anti-Catholic prejudice which was always under the surface and easily ignited when the Conservatives wished to stir the populace. Later, James Connolly, an Irish socialist and union leader, appealed to the working communities of England, Scotland, USA and Australia to come together but it was not to be, and the Irish was left to fight for themselves. Karl Marx wrote that Ireland got its vengeance on England 'by bestowing an Irish quarter on every English industrial maritime or commercial town of any size'.

SEEKING SOCIAL JUSTICE AND INDEPENDENCE

It was said that the publication by Matthew Arnold of Burke's 'Letters Speeches and Tracts on Irish Affairs' in 1881 'set Gladstone thinking,' and was to result in the Home Rule Bill of 1886. The influence of the Irish across Britain would eventually bear fruit, by their increased political representation in parliament. William Mason's 'Ode to Independence' echoes the Irish aspirations:

> 'In awful poverty, his honest Muse,
> Walks forth vindictive through a venal land;
> In vain Corruption sheds her golden dews,
> In vain Oppression lifts her iron hand:
> He scorns them both, and arm'd with Truth alone,
> Bids Vice and Folly tremble on the throne'

The year of James Shannon's death was a watershed in the nineteenth century, signalling the start of the modern revolution. Tennyson's pessimism was based on the reality of the festering slums, 'city children soaking in city slime', sweated labour, and enforced prostitution. However, Gladstone, in considering this period, was keen to cite a list of good works such as abolition of slavery, savings banks, cheap communications and holidays, – a general improvement in the conditions of the masses. Certainly there had been sanitation improvements with decreased mortality rates, and cholera and typhus ceasing to be epidemic threats, and workhouses humanised. The large loss of life and injury down the mines showed little improvement as technology advances increased physical and health risks.

For someone of Irish working class origins who died about 130 years ago, it is not surprising that very little information about James Shannon has survived the passage of time. In those days, to have risen from the hovels of Newcastle and advance to the position of master sinker at the age of 37 years was a considerable achievement, and gives some indication of the determination and physical strength that was needed to have overcome all the hardships of coal-mining in Britain during the Industrial Revolution.

Statue of Liberty
(face) 1885
(en.wikipedia.org)

Statue of Liberty
1886
(wallorg.com)

On the 28 October 1886, the erection of the Statue of Liberty in New York Harbour was completed. The Statue of Libertas, the Roman goddess of freedom, was a gift to the United States of America from the people of France, and commemorated America's Independence from Britain in 1776 when oppressed people around the world were given the expectation that they too could win freedom. In 1886 the Irish were given hope that the Home Rule Bill would at last give them independence from Britain. Ironically, the Irish helped the English to form a socialist party, but not for Ireland, where nationalism dominated. The Irish with their enormous resilience had to wait another 36 years before they broke free. In the meantime, the Statue of Liberty with sombre face looked across the Atlantic brandishing her torch at Britain!

H V Morton in his book 'In Search of Ireland', described his visit to Connemara during 1930, and summarised the state of Ireland:

> 'The burning peat, one may fancy, is the Gael; the ashes are the centuries of suppression under a foreign power; the darkness needs no comment, and the morning is the Ireland of the future. When these ashes are raked off in the morning there is a faint pinkish heart of fire in the turf, and the peasants blow upon it until a flame bursts out and new fuel is added on the hearth'.

APPENDIX A

Change from Shannon to Mason

The bare facts give a straight-forward explanation of the twice widowed family adopting the name of the second step-father. However, what reasons made them take that decision? Initially James Shannon married in 1854 under the name of his first step-father, Lawrence, and registered the birth of his first child under that name. The first evidence of the adoption of the surname Mason was recorded in the 1861 Census, that is, eleven years after his mother married Clement Mason.

In 1856 James started to register the birth of his children under the name of Shannon. It seems that this was a 'defining moment, when he moved from Leasingthorne, where he had married, to Thornley in the district of Easington. His job also changed from pitman to sinker. It is likely that at this time he also changed his public name to Mason. It was known that miners changed their name to avoid the bond or other employment laws.

Clement Mason was later to become a deputy overman, and therefore was in a position of influence in terms of obtaining a better job for his step-son. Clement appears to have had a close relationship with the Coulson family of sinkers. In Durham collieries there was a reluctance to employ Catholics as late as the mid-twentieth century!

Thus with strong prejudice against the Irish, especially someone with a Catholic name like Shannon, James probably decided to use the more 'respectable' English name of Mason. (Respectability then was just as important to the working class as for the middle class.) His loss of faith may have been caused by the refusal of the Catholic Church to baptise his children for his previous involvement with Chartists and trade unionists, or because of the name change. Working in a new district, the use of a new name would not have presented a problem, especially if he was living in same the house as his step-father. Being respectable also meant abiding by the law, and therefore it probably seemed right that he should register his children by their blood name, Shannon.

His mother's other children did not adopt the name of Mason; the children of his uncle Edward Shannon in Sunderland continued with Shannon, and the children of John Lawrence with the name of Lawrence. It was rumoured in the family that James Mason was involved in the death of a blackleg during his time at Thornley, a colliery which had a strong reputation for agitation. This may have forced him to change his name?

Although Clement Mason may have been a Quaker, he was charged with larceny in 1847, so the colliery managers probably had him marked as future trouble-maker. There was evidence of name changing carried out in Scotland to avoid financial penalties. Changing names to avoid prosecution was not new in the story of the Shannons.

APPENDIX B

Connection between James Storey Reed, Mary Ann Hall and James Mason

James Storey Reed was born in 1840 to Andrew Reed and Sarah Storey, and Mary Ann Hall was born in 1841 to Robert Hall and Sarah Gregg, both on Tyneside.

Mary Ann married John Bulmer in 1859 at Hartlepool; John died a few years later. However, Mary Ann's daughter Sarah, was born in 1858; John Bulmer may have been the father. In 1862 Mary Ann then married James Storey Reed, an enginesmith, also at Hartlepool.

Nine years later, James Storey Reed was an engine driver at Shotton Colliery with wife Mary Ann, a step-daughter Ann Bulmer aged 9 born in Hartlepool, and daughter Sarah J Reed born in Castle Eden aged 7.

During the early 1870s, James Reed was lured abroad by the prospect of gold in the 'black hills of Dakota' leaving his family behind, and nothing was heard of him for some years. Therefore in 1877, he was recorded as deceased when Mary Ann's daughter married under the name of Sarah Reed to James Mason's eldest son John at Windlestone.

Then without warning he returned from America, and on the 19 March 1881 he married Emma Wilson at a Newcastle register office. However two weeks later the 1881 census revealed that he was married to Anna, (born in Askam Yorkshire) and living at Castle Eden! Two of Anna's children to her previous husband and a child to James Reed were living with them. James was employed as engine driver at the colliery. Thus he had married illegally at least twice since leaving for America!

In 1881 James Mason may not have known that James Reed had returned, and had married again. Reed's legal wife Mary Ann, was still using his name and living with James's family as a housekeeper. However, at Mary Ann's marriage to James Mason in 1882, she had used her previous married name of Bulmer indicating that she had probably learned that James Reed was back and re-married.

In the criminal registers of 1883, James Reed was before the court accused of bigamy; his case was postponed until the next assizes but there was no record of the outcome. There is no record of James Reed, Anna Reed or Mary Ann Reed in the 1891 census – perhaps James Reed had 'disappeared' looking for gold again! By a strange coincidence in the 1891 census there is a record in Newcastle of a William Storey Reed married to an Anna? Perhaps James Reed was convicted and spent some time in prison.

In 1901 James Reed re-appeared working as a colliery engineman, and living with Sarah and her husband John Mason at Esh in Durham. What would James Mason have thought!

[It is interesting to compare the real Reed/Mason connection with the fictional characters of Jane Eyre by Charlotte Bronte. James Storey Reed was born near Gateshead; he left for America and abandoned his wife, who later re-married to become Mrs Mason. Jame Eyre began her life under the cruel Mrs Reed at Gateshead Hall; her first marriage plans were upset by a Mrs Mason from America]

Bibliography

Georgius Agricola, De Re Metallica c1556

E Allen, J F Clarke, N McCord, D J Rowe, The North–East Engineers' Strikes of 1871 (Frank Graham Newcastle 1971)

Keith Armstrong (Ed), The Big Meeting, A people's view of the Durham miners' Gala (Trade Union Printing Services 1994)

T S Ashton, The Industrial Revolution 1760–1830 (Oxford University Press 1976)

Frank Atikinson, North-East England, People at Work 1860–1950 (Moorland Publishing 1980)

Barker & Cheyne's Report, Fever in Ireland 1817–19 (published 1821)

C J Bates, History of Northumberland (Elliot Stock London 1895)

Georgina Battiscombe, Shaftesbury, A biography of the Seventh Earl 1801–1885 (Purnell Book Services Ltd 1974)

The Venerable Bede, The Ecclesiastical History of the English People c 731

David Bell, The Fire Doon on the Kee (D Bell South Shields 2009)

Bell's 'Description of the Condition and Manners of the Peasantry of Ireland between 1780 to 1890'

Lionel Birch (Ed), The History of the TUC 1868–1968 (General Council of the trades Union Congress 1968)

Brian Blake, The Solway Firth (Robert Hale Ltd 1966)

W S Boulton, Practical Coal Mining (The Gresham Publishing Company 1909)

Edward Boyle, Modern Britain, a Social History 1750–1997 (Arnold 1997)

Edith Bradley, The Story of the English Abbeys (Robert Hale Ltd 1938)

Brian de Breffny (Ed), The Irish World [including article 'The Irish in America' by William V Shannon] (Thames & Hudson 1977)

Asa Briggs, Victorian Cities (Penquin 1968)

Angus Buchanan, The Life and Times of Isambard Kingdom Brunel (Hambledon Continuum 2001)

Edmund Burke, Reflections on the Revolution in France 1791 (Walter Scott Publishing 1920)

Anthony Burton, The Canal Builders (David & Charles Ltd 1981)

Anthony Burton, The Railway Builders (John Murray Publishers Ltd 1992)

J. C., The Compleat Collier: Or, The Whole Art of Sinking, Getting, and Working, Coal-Mines, &c. (G Conyers 1708)

John C Cairns, The Nineteenth Century 1815–1914 (The Free Press 1965)

Thomas Carlyle. The Latter Day Pamphlets (Chapman and Hall, London 1850)

Thomas Carlyle, Chartism (James Fraser 1840)

Thomas Carlyle, Sartor Resartus (Frazer's Magazine 1833/4)

Thomas Carlyle, Past and Present 1843 (Chapman & Hall 1870)

Thomas Carlyle, The Nigger Question (Frazer's Magazine 1849)

Thomas Carlyle, Reminiscences of my Irish Journey 1849 (Harper & Bros New York 1849)

Catholic Tablet XII (Catholic publication 1851)

Bruce Catton, The American Civil War (Penquin Books 1960)

Paul Cavil, Stephen Harding & Judith Jesh, Wirral and its Viking Heritage (English Place-Name Society 2000)

Raymond Challinor, Radical Lawyer in Victorian England: W P Roberts and the struggle for Worker's Rights (I B Tauris London 1990)

James Christie, Northumberland its history, its features, and its people (Mawson, Swan and Morgan 1893)

Marcus Clarke, For the term of his Natural Life (Australian Journal 1871)

John Clarke, The Price of Progress Cobbett's England 1780–1835 (Granada Publishing 1977)

William Cobbett, Journal of a Year's Residence in the United States of America (Alan Sutton 1983)

G D H Cole, The People's Front (Victor Gollancz 1937)

G D H Cole, Chartist Portraits (Macmillan 1941)

Terry Coleman, The Railway Navvies (Penquin 1981)

Donald S Connery, The Irish (Eyre & Spottiswoode 1969)

James Connolly, Labour in Irish History (New Book Publications, Dublin 1973)

James Connolly, the Re-Conquest of Ireland (New Books Publications, Dublin & Belfast 1983)

James Connolly, Labour in Ireland, Introduction by Cathal O'Shannon (At the Sign of the Three Candles 2009)

Roger Cooter, The Irish in County Durham and Newcastle (Durham University Theses 1972)

Roger Cooter, When Paddy met Geordie (The University of Sunderland Press 2005)

A J Cronin, The Stars Look Down (Victor Gollancz Ltd 1935)

W Copeland Trimble, The History of Enniskillen (William Trimble, Enniskillen 1919)

W Cunningham and Ellen A McArthur, Outlines of English Industrial History (University Press Cambridge 1920)

Mary Frances Cusack, An Illustrated History of Ireland, from AD400 to 1800 (Bracken Books 1868)

Charles Dickens, Pickwick Papers (Chapman & Hall 1836/7)

Charles Dickens, Oliver Twist (Richard Bentley 1838)

Charles Dickens, Barnaby Rudge (published in installments 1841)

Charles Dickens, The Old Curiosity Shop (Chapman & Hall 1841)

Charles Dickens, Bleak House (Bradbury & Evans 1852/3)

Charles Dickens, Hard Times (Bradbury & Evans 1854)

Charles Dickens, Great Expectations (Chapman & Hall 1861)

Charles Dickens, Our Mutual Friend (Chapman & Hall 1865)

Myles Dillon, Early Irish Society (Colm O Lochlainn Dublin 1954)

Benjamin Disraeli, Crisis Examined (Sanders and Otley, Conduit Street 1834)

Disraeli Benjamin, Sybil (Henry Colburn 1845)

Disraeli Benjamin, Conningsby (Henry Colburn 1844)

Rev E A D'Alton. The History of Ireland (The Gresham Publishing Co Ltd no date)

David Dougan and Frank Graham, Northumberland and Durham, A Social Miscellany
    (Frank Graham 1969)

David D Douglas, The Age of the Normans (Thomas Nelson and Sons Ltd 1929)

Dublin Chronicle 1875

Godfrey Duffy (and Terry Arthur) Dissertation The Irish Ancestry in North-East England
    Group (Durham University 1996)

Patrick Duffy, The Skilled Compositor, 1850–1941, An Aristocrat among Working Men
    (Ashgate 2000)

A S G Edwards, The manuscript and Texts of the Second Version of John Hardyng's
    Chronicle (1987) – ref Newcastle Norman origins

Peter Berresford Ellis, The History of the Irish Working Class (Pluto Press London 1972)

Eric J Evans, The Forging of The Modern State 1783–1870 (Longman London and New
    York 1983)

Nial Fallon, The Armada in Ireland (Stanford Maritime Ltd 1978)

H J Fleure and M Davies, A Natural History of Man in Britain (Bloomsbury Books 1951)

Henry Fielding, Tom Jones (Andrew Miller London 1749)

H A L Fisher, A History of Europe Vol II (Fontana/Collins 1977)

Francis Fox, River, Road, and Rail some Engineering Reminiscences (John Murray, London
    1904)

W J Fox, Lectures to the Working Classes (Charles Fox 1846)

Richard Fynes, The Miners of Northumberland and Durham (Thos Summerbell 1873)

Robert L Galloway, A History of Coal Mining in Great Britain (Macmillan and Co 1882)

John Galt, Annals of the Parish: The Ayrshire Legatees Vols I & II (William Blackwood &
    Sons Edinburgh 1821)

Henry George, Progress and Poverty (Doubleday, Page & Co New York 1879)

Henry George, The Science of Political Economy (The Henry George Foundation 1932)

'Oxford Man', Anecdotes of Gladstone (Joseph Toulson 1912)

J M Golby, Culture & Society in Britain 1850–1890 (Oxford University Press 1988)

Frank Graham, Newcastle, A Short History and Guide (Frank Graham 1978)

J R Green, A Short History of the English People (Macmillan and Co London 1913)

Frederick Grice, The Bonny Pit Laddie (Oxford University Press London 1960)

Charles Hadfield, British Canals, an illustrated History (David & Charles 1979)

J L and Barbara Hammond, The Town Labourer 1760–1832 (Longmans, Green, and Co
    1918)

J L and Barbara Hammond, The Village Labourer 1760–1832 (Alan Sutton Publishing
    1987)

J L and Barbara Hammond, The Skilled Labourer 1760–1832 (Longmans, Green & Co 1919)

J L & Barbara Hammond, The Bleak Age (Penguin Books 1947)

James E Handley, Irish in Scotland 1789 – 1845 (John S Burns 1964)

Thomas F Henderson, Lockerbie, A narrative of village life in bygone days (Herald Press, Lockerbie 1937)

Christopher Hibbert, The English, A Social History 1066 – 1945 (Paladin Books, Collins Publishing Group 1988)

Eric Hobsbawn, The Age of Revolution 1789–1848 (Weidenfeld & Nicolson 1962)

Eric Hobsbawn, Industry and Empire (Weidenfeld & Nicolson 1968)

E J Hobsbawn, The Age of Capital 1848–1975 (Weidenfeld and Nicolson Ltd 1975)

Eric Hobsbawn, How to change the world, Tales of Marx and Marxism 1840–2011 (Little, Brown 2011)

George B Hodgson, The History of South Shields (Andrew Reid & Co Ltd Newcastle 1924)

Thomas Hood, The Song of the Shirt [unemployment] (Punch 1843)

Pamela Horn, Labouring Life in the Victorian Countryside (Alan Sutton Publishing Ltd 1976)

P M Horsley, Eighteenth-Century Newcastle (Oriel Press 1971)

Brian Inglis, Poverty and the Industrial Revolution (Hodder & Stoughton Ltd 1971)

Henry D Inglis, A journey through Ireland during spring, summer and autumn of 1834 (Whittaker & Co London 1835)

Tim Jeal, Livingstone (Heinemann London 1973)

Paul Johnson, Ireland : Land of Troubles (Book Club Associates 1980)

Geoffrey Keating, History of Ireland (Irish Texts Society 1908)

Paul Kerr, The Crimean War (Boxtree 1997)

Thomas Kineally, The Great Shame (Sutton Publishing Random House Australia 1998)

Charles Kingsley, Alton Locke (Walter Scott Ltd 1850)

Walker Carol Kyros, Walking North with Keats, (Yale University Press 1992)

Barbara Laurie, Bishop Auckland in the 1850s (Barbara Laurie, Bishop Auckland 1996)

Alexander Leighton, Wilson's Tales of the Borders and of Scotland (Brook & Chrystal 1857)

Pedar Livingstone, History of Fermanagh (Clogher Historical Society 1969)

Peadar Livingstone, The Fermanagh Story (Cuman Seanchais Chlochair 1969)

Elizabeth Longford, The Years of the Sword Wellington (Granada Publishing Ltd 1969)

F S L Lyons, Charles Stewart Parnell (Fontana/Collins 1978)

Rev G F Maclear, The Celts (Society for promoting Christian Knowledge 1893)

Seumas MacManus, The Story of the Irish Race (The Devin-Adair Company, Connecticut 1966)

Donald M MacRaild, The Irish in Britain 1800–1914 (The Economic and Social History Society of Ireland 2006)

Michael MacDonagh, Irish Life and Character (Hodder & Stoughton 1899)

James Mackay, A Biography of Robert Burns (Mainstream Publishing Co 1992)

Edward MacLysaght, Surnames of Ireland (Dublin, Irish Academic Press 1958)

Thomas Robert Malthus, An Essay on the Principle of Population 1798 (Pelican Books 1970)

Joyce Marlow, The Tolpuddle Martyrs (Panther Books Ltd 1974)

Edward A Martin RGS, The Story of A Piece of Coal (George Newnes Ltd 1898)

Marx. Engels, Ireland and the Irish Question (Lawrence & Wishart 1971)

Peter Ford Mason. The Pit Sinkers of Northumberland and Durham (The History Press 2012)

F C Mather, Chartism (Historical Association London 1965)

Peter Mathias, The First Industrial Nation An Economic History of Britain 1700–1914 (Methuen & Co Ltd 1969)

Ian Maxwell, Irish Ancestors – a guide for family historians (Pen & Sword Family History 2008)

Henry Mayhew, London Labour and the London Poor (Morning Chronicle 1851)

Mina na Mianadoiri, Threads of Gold through Seams of Coal, Arigna Mining Memories (Arigna Mining Experience 2003)

Kerby A Miller, Emigrants and Exiles: Ireland and the Irish Exodus to North America (Oxford University Press 1985)

John S Mill, Principle of Political Economy (Longmans, Green & Co 1848)

Kerby A Miller, Emigrants and Exiles, Ireland and the Irish Exodus to north America (Oxford University Press 1985)

G E Mingay, Rural Life in Victorian England (Alan Sutton Publishing Ltd 1990)

James Mitchell Esq, Children's Employment Commission South Durham (Picks Publishing 1842)

William Molyneux, The case of Ireland's being Bound by Acts of Parliament (1698

John Morley, Oliver Cromwell (Macmillan and Co Ltd 1900)

John Morley, Life of Gladstone (Edward Lloyd Ltd 1908)

A L Morton, The life and ideas of Robert Owen (Lawrence & Wishart 1962)

A E Musson, British Trade Unions 1800–1875 (Macmillan 1972)

W P Nimmo, Wallace the Hero of Scotland (William P Nimmo 1873)

Report of the Whig Club on 'The State of the Labouring Poor 1796 (Life of Henry Grattan)

Daniel O'Connell, An Historical Memoir of Ireland and the Irish (James Duffy & Co 1843)

T P O'Connor MP, The Life of Lord Beaconsfield (T Fisher Unwin 1905)

T A O'Donahue, Colliery Surveying (Macmillan and Co Ltd 1896)

Anne O'Dowd, Spalpeen and Tatie Hokers (Irish Academic Press 1991)

Sean O'Faolain and Paul Henry, An Irish Journey (Readers Union with Longmans Green 1941)

L T O'Shea, Elementary Chemistry for Coal Mining Students (Longmans, Green and Co 1911)

Old Statistical Account of Kirkoswald Scotland 1792

Thomas Pakenham, The year of Liberty, The Great Irish Rebellion of 1798 (Weidenfeld & Nicolson 1997)

Charles Stuart Parker, Life and Letters of Sir James Graham 1792–1861 (John Murray London 1907)

Joseph Parker DD, Tyne Folk, Masks, Faces and Shadows (H E Allenson 1896)

Robert Peel, Coal Mining (Blackie and Son Ltd 1918)

Henry Pelling, A History of British Trade Unionism (Penguin Books Ltd 1963)

Harold Perkin, The Age of the Railway (Routledge & Kegan Paul Ltd 1970)

John Prebble, Glencoe (Penguin 1968)

E G Power, Modern Ireland (Longman London and New York 1989)

Susan Price, Twopence a Tub (Faber and Faber Ltd 1975)

A Seth Pringle-Pattison, Treatise On Liberty by John Stuart Mill (George Routledge & Sons Ltd 1910)

Charles Read, It's never too late to mend (Australian Gold) 1850s (Chatto & Windus London 1901)

Charles Read, Put yourself in his place [trades union] (British Library 1870)

William Reitzel (Ed), The Autobiography of William Cobbett (Faber and Faber Ltd 1967)

Julian Richards, Blood of the Vikings (Hodder and Stoughton 2001)

Moses Aaron Richardson, Borderer's Table Book (Henry G Bohn 1846)

Ruth Richardson, Death, Dissection and the Destitute (Routledge & Kegan Paul 1988)

Joseph Robbins, The Miasma, Epidemic and Panic in Nineteenth Century Ireland (Institute of Public Administration Dublin 1995)

George Robinson, Inquiry in Newcastle Poor (M & MW Lambert 1850)

Dennis Carolan Rushe, Monaghan in the Eighteenth Century (Dublin & Dundalk 1916)

Select Committee on Poor Rewards 1854 (Gold Rush NSW)

Caroline L Scott, A comparative re-examination of Anglo-Irish relations in nineteenth century Manchester, Liverpool and Newcastle upon Tyne (Durham E-Thesis 1998)

Walter Scott, Minstrelsy of the Scottish Border (James Ballantyne 1802)

Walter Scott, Guy Mannering (Longman, Hurst, Orme and Brown London 1815)

Stephen Desmond Shannon, Irish Nationalist Organisation on the North East of England 1890–1925 (PhD Thesis Newcastle Dept history 2013)

Richard Shannon, The Crisis of Imperialism 1865–1915 (Paladin 1976)

Speeches from the Dock or Protests of Irish Patriotism (A M Sullivan Dublin 1868)

Samuel Smiles, Lives of Engineers (John Murray 1857)

Adam Smith, The Wealth of Nations (Methuen & Co Ltd 1776)

Alexander Somerville, The Autobiography of a Working Man (MacGibbon & Kee 1967)

Alexander Somerville, The Whistler at the Plough (The Merlin Press London 1852)

David R Sorensen and Rodger L Tarr, The Carlyles at Home Abroad (Ashgate 2004)

Thomas Southwood Smith, Treatise on Fever (Carey, Lea and Blanchard 1830)

P F Speed, British Social and Economic History from 1760 (Pergamon Press 1977)

Stephen Spender, Forward from Liberalism (Victor Gollancz 1937)

Dirk J Struik, Birth of the Commmunist Manifesto (International Publishers 1971)

A M Sullivan MP and T D Sullivan MP, Irish Readings (M H Gill & Son 1895)

Dick Sullivan, Navvyman (Coracle Books 1983)

Roger Swift & Sheridan Gilley [Editors], Irish Migrants in Britain, 1815–1914 (Cork University Press 2002)

R H Tawney, Religion and the Rise of Capitalism (Pelican Books 1972)

A J P Taylor, From Napoleon to the Second International (Hamish Hamilton 1993)

Alexis de Tocqueville, Democracy in America (Wordsworth Editions Ltd 1998)

Stephen Tomkins, William Wilberforce a biography (Lion Hudson plc 2007)

Hugh Thomas, The History of the Atlantic Slave Trade 1440–1870 (Simon & Schuster 1997)

E P Thompson, The making of the working class (Vintage 1966)

David Thomson, England in the Nineteenth Century (Penquin Books 1950)

G M Trevelyan, The Life of John Bright (Constable and Company Ltd 1913)

G M Trevelyan, English Social History (Longman Group Ltd 1978)

Anthony Trollope, The MacDermots of Ballycloran (Thomas Cautley Newby 1947)

Ian Sutton [Editor], The Irish World, The History and Cultural Achievements of the Irish People (Thames & Hudson Ltd 2000)

Rev P White, History of Clare and the Dalcassians clans of Tipperary, Limerick and Galway (M H Gill & Sons 1893)

William Wilde, Table of Irish famines 900 – 150 ref M E Crawford (John Donald Edinburgh 1989)

Francis Williams, The Rise of the Trade Unions (Oldams Press Ltd 1954)

Frederick S Williams, Our Iron Roads, Their History, Construction and Administration (Bemrose & Sons 1885)

Angus Wilson, The World of Charles Dickens (Viking Press 1972)

John Wilson, A History of the Durham Miners' Association 1870–1904 (J H Veitch & Sons 1908)

Anthony Wood, Nineteenth Century Britain 1815–1914 (Longmans 1960)

Emile Zola, Germinal (Penguin Books 1954)

Index

American Acts
    Kansas-Nebraska1854 176, 189

American Independence 1776 28, 29, 44
    Washington, George 28, 243

American Civil War 206, 211–213, 217, 218

American mining
    Ancient Order of Hiberians, Shenandoah
        branch 235
    Black Hills of (South) Dakota 246
    Californian & Nevada goldfields 191
    Philadelphia 101, 161, 212
    Duffy's Cut (cholera) 101
    Ohio Coal Mining 246

American Cotton 159, 212

Anglo-Saxons
    AEthelstan 11
    Alfred the Great 11
    Queen AEthelflaed 11
    Harold and Tostig 12

Architects
    Clayton, John 90
    Dobson, John 90, 176
    Grainger, Richard 90, 139
    Paxton, Joseph 171, 183, 184, 202
    Pugin, Augustus Welby 208

Australia
    South Australian Association 108
    Coal mines 34, 35
    Goldfields, Ballarat 119, 178, 190
    Transportation of Convicts to Australia
        42, 44, 72, 99, 109, 112, 129, 136, 168,
        184, 198, 212, 240

Convicts Boats Edward and Parmelia 52
Select Committee 126

Battles
    Battle of Athboy, Meath 33
    Battle of Ballinafad, Sligo 33
    Battle of Boswell Field 1435 14
    Battle of the Boyne 1690 24
    Battle of Bunker's Hill 1775 23
    Battle of the Diamonds 1795 33
    Battle Dryfe Sands 1593 64
    Bosworth Field 1485 14
    Battle of Fontenoy 1745 23
    Battle of Gaine's Mills 1862 212
    Battle of Lexington 1775 23
    Battle of Magheracloon 1843 149
    Battle of Stirling Bridge 1297 13
    Battle of Vinegar Hill 1798 34, 37
    Battle of Yellow Ford 1598 18
    Battle of Waterloo 1815 128

Bridges
    Britannia 1826 181, 209
    Menai Bridge 1822 69
    High Level Bridge Newcastle 1849 176,
        244
    Newcastle Bridge 1781 88, 121, 122
    Newcastle Swing Bridge 1876 244
    Tay Bridge 1879 250

Bronte
    Branwell 160
    Charlotte 175, 191
    Patrick 28, 113, 175

Bronte books
    Shirley 67
    Wuthering Heights 160

Burke and Hare 77, 101

Calverts 207
    Alexander 173, 194, 206, 208
    Dorothy 194, 242
    Hannah 173
    Lydia 173, 192–194, 196

Canal Mania 35, 50, 195
    Ballinamore-Ballyconnell 161
    Bridgewater 26
    Caledonian 1822 35
    Manchester Ship Canal 241
    Newry Navigation 26
    Pontcysyllte 36
    Royal Canal 35
    Sankey 26
    Shannon Navigation Improvement Works
        161, 196
    Tyrone & Coalisland Navigation 26
    Ulster 36
    Union 50, 77

Carlyle
    Alexander 76
    James 73
    Jane 144, 219
    John 123
    Thomas 58, 59, 70, 75, 83, 84, 106, 107,
        118, 120, 123, 130, 142, 149, 150, 152,
        160, 169, 217, 221, 225

Carlyle Books
    Chartism 120, 130
    French Revolution 69, 118, 130, 150
    Latter Days Pamphlets 176, 196
    Past and Present 65, 148, 175
    Sartor Resartus 98, 106, 159
    The Nigger Question 176

Catholic Association, Society and Rent 69

Catholic Confederacy 18

Catholic Defence Association 177

Catholic Emancipation 30, 38, 39, 67, 69, 78,
    79, 92, 95, 167

Catholic Churches, Chapels & Schools 229
    Bishop Auckland, St Wilfrid's Church
        1846 186
    Boldon and Hebburn 1870 229
    Broom, St Cuthberts Chapel 1802 158
    Catholic Cathedral St Marys Hexham &
        Newcastle 1842-44 150, 209
    Catholic Chapel Dumfries 1813 64, 76
    Enniskillen Cathedral 1875 243
    Newcastle St Andrews Catholic Church
        1798 107
    South Shields School 1849 177
    Swinburne private chapel 167
    Ushaw College 126
    Willington Quay 1870 229
    Dumfries School 1838 75

Cattle trade 13, 27, 39, 44, 45, 48, 55, 72, 76,
    83, 87

Celtic Records
    Annals of Ulster 5
    Book of Kells 6
    Historia of de Sancto Cuthberto 11
    Linisfarne Gospels 8

Chartism 31, 118, 120, 121, 130-133, 135,
    136, 141-145, 148, 149, 151, 152, 159,
    168, 177, 220

Chartists 31, 148, 175
    Attwood, Thomas 102, 132
    Bates, John 141
    Burdett, Francis 100
    Cowen, Joseph 197, 213, 234, 239, 253,
        263
    Duncombe 130
    Frost, John 133, 191
    Hall, John 148
    Harney, George Julian 177, 234
    Jones, Ernest 177
    Jones, William 135, 191
    Jude, Martin 97, 148, 210
    Lovett, William 130
    Mason, John 141
    McNulty, Bernard 168, 263
    O'Brien Brontere 121, 143

O'Connor, Feargus 100, 104, 119, 121, 130, 143, 149, 151
Place, Francis 69
Penderyn, Dic (Richard Lewis) 100
Stephens, J R 118, 131, 167
Williams, Zephaniah 135, 191

Child Labour 137, 139, 142, 146, 147, 151

Civil Engineering Contractors
    Peto, Betts & Brassey Corps 109, 196, 219

Civil & Mechanical Engineers & Institution 78
    Armstrong, William 161, 200, 243, 244
    Bazalgette, Joseph 203
    Blackett, William 80
    Brassey, Thomas 194, 214, 219
    Brunel, Isambard Kingdom 86, 109, 126, 149, 161, 167, 168, 189, 203
    Chapman, William 29
    Fox, Charles 183
    Fox, Francis 242
    Hackworth, Timothy 194
    Hedley, William 80
    Jessop, William 35, 36
    Rennie, John 47
    Smeaton, John 47, 88
    Stephenson, George 80-82, 84, 87, 93, 109, 139, 149, 167, 176, 180, 181, 246
    Stephenson, Robert 74, 82, 87, 98, 167, 176, 181, 183, 196, 203, 204, 205
    Stott, George 197, 239
    Telford, Thomas 47, 63, 64
    Watt, James 80, 91, 278

Cokeworks, Brandon & Esh 193, 232, 248

Colliery/Coal Owners/Magistrates
    Bell Stobard & Fenwick 168, 197
    Braddyll & Partners (Murton) 151
    Grand Allies 94
    Fairless, Nicholas 102
    Lord Durham (Lambton) 99
    H T Liddle of Walker & Ravensworth 65, 77
    Maria Liddle, Ravensworth 134

Londonderry, Lord & Marquis 64, 94, 99, 111, 147, 166, 216, 235, 269
Lowther, Christopher and James 46
Ridley, Sir Matthew 94
Stobart, Henry 197
Vane Tempest, Sir Henry 93

Colliery trades
    Breaksman 109, 246
    Craneman 232
    Changer & Graither 243
    Enginesmith 211
    Fireman 210
    Flatman 232
    Half-marrow 232
    Poney driver 142, 231, 232
    Putter/hurrier 116, 146, 187, 199, 229, 231, 232
    Trapper 116, 127, 138, 142, 146, 186, 199, 232

Communist League 1847 & Manifesto 167, 169, 250

Cornish Engineers and Inventors 82
    Bickford, William 98
    Newcomen, Thomas 80
    Trevithick, Richard 80, 82
    Savery, Thomas 80

Corn Law Repeal 54, 93, 113, 130, 131, 141, 144, 145, 148, 157, 162, 179, 185, 212
    Speenhamland 113

Crimean War 189, 192–198
    Alma 192
    Battle of Alma 1854 192
    Battle of Balaclava 193, 196, 198
    Balaclava 193, 198
    Sebastopol 194
    Lord Cardigan 109
    Lord Raglan 198
    Florence Nightingale 173, 197, 198
    Mary Seacole 197

Cromwell, Oliver 3, 21, 22, 23

Cumberland 55
  Brampton 83, 219
  Carlisle 49, 84, 85, 183
  Cleator Moor 183, 228, 264
  Patterdale 6
  Preston 144
  Whitehaven 46, 183
  Workington 51

Darling, Grace & William 129

Dickens books
  Barnaby Rudge 141
  Bleak House 183
  Christmas Carol 143
  Great Expectations 112
  Hard Times 127, 189
  Mutual Friend 1862 255
  Oliver Twist 101, 189
  Pickwick Papers 118
  Old Curiosity Shop 208

Diseases & Sanitary Pioneers
  Anasarca 191
  Asthma 123, 174
  Barnardo Dr 227
  Black Death Pandemic 1348–50 14
  Blackwell, Elizabeth Dr 131
  Chadwick, Edwin - Report 1842 112, 122,
    123, 132, 168, 181, 197, 217, 278
  Cholera, Great Epidemic 100, 101, 109,
    121, 123, 164, 165, 172-175, 187, 188,
    189, 191-193, 197, 198, 217
  Consumption (tuberculosis) 191
  Diptheria 249
  Dropsy 78, 163, 174
  Epidemic diseases 116
  Hospitals 52, 125, 127, 128, 191
  Jenner, Edward, William 69, 188
  Kay, James 122
  Rammell, Thomas 174
  Simpson James Dr 128, 188
  Smallpox 68, 69, 161, 188, 231
  Smith, Thomas Southwood 122
  Snow John Dr 101, 174
  Typhoid 39, 77, 116, 117, 121, 129, 165,
    175, 210, 217, 252

Typhus Fever 40, 77, 121-123, 125, 127,
  129, 161, 164, 165, 173, 175, 190, 191

Disraeli Books
  Conningsby 151, 159
  Sybil 87, 126, 135, 137, 159, 161, 180

Durham Big Meeting & Banners 233

Durham Towns/Villages
  Berry Edge (Consett) 166
  Bishop Auckland 7, 186, 192, 203
  Eldon 210
  Esh/Quebec 232, 257, 258
  Ferryhill 173, 231, 242, 259
  Gateshead 133
  Hartlepool 99, 211
  Murton 259
  Penshaw 156
  Shadons Hill 149
  Shildon 81, 192, 194
  South Shields 133
  Stockton 192
  Sunderland 32, 157, 192, 267

Durham collieries
  Adelaide's (Copy Crooks) 209
  Bearpark 243
  Berwicke Main 225
  Black Boy 186, 192
  Boldon 221, 225, 229, 269, 270, 271
  Bowden Close 192
  Brancepeth 203
  Burnhopefield 142, 174, 192
  Castle Eden 178, 222, 233, 243, 256
  Cornsay 119, 248
  Coxhoe 215, 216
  Coxlodge 211
  Chester-le-Street 93, 98
  Chilton 238, 243
  Crookhall 98
  East Hetton (Kello) 115
  East Howle 238
  Edmondstey 142
  Eldon 98, 210
  Elvet 142
  Eppleton 115, 154, 222, 230, 232, 233

Fatfield 94, 230
Felling 142
Friar's Goose 135
Hamsteels Taylor Pit 239, 260
Harton 196
Harraton 216
Harrington Mill Pit 94
Haswell 115, 154, 241
Hebburn 94, 229
Hedley Hill 243
Hetton 98, 115, 231, 239
Holmside 256
Houghton 98
Hunworth 192
Kibblesworth 138
Lambton Pit 93, 99
Langley Park 243
Leasingthorne 188, 191, 192
Littleburn 142
Longbenton 180
Mainsforth 211, 239
Medomsley 216, 242
Monkwearmouth 8, 98, 139, 142, 151,
    168, 216, 224
Murton 151, 168, 239
New Hartley 210, 211
New Herrington 243
Ouston (Birtley) 98
Page Bank 203
Philadelphia Row 243
Rainton 216
Ryhope 234, 230
St Helens 192
St Hilda 142, 147
Seaham 98, 216, 252
Seaton Deleval 205
Shincliffe 173
Shire Moor 239
Shotton 233
Silksworth 239
Snipper's Gate 110
South Medomsley 216, 242
Tanfield Lea 98
Thornley 115, 133, 187, 188, 199, 233
Trimdon Grange 173, 178, 238, 252, 260
Tudhoe 216, 253
Urpeth 115

Usworth 168, 252
Wardley 192
West Auckland 192
West Stanley 253
Westerton 142, 192
Wheatley Hill 225
Whitburn 142, 255
Whitwell 216
Whitworth 192
Willington 142, 192
Windlestone 239, 242, 246
Wingate 142
Woodhouse 192, 197
Wooley 215

Economists/Philosophers
    Bentham, Jeremy 31, 112, 113, 122
    Smith, Adam 27, 59, 60, 70, 74, 87, 91,
        201
    Ricardo, David 72

English MPs
    Bennett, John 85
    Bright, John 82, 110, 175, 185, 206, 212,
        213, 216, 217, 220, 226, 270
    Burns, Thomas 244, 266
    Chamberlain, Joseph 241, 252, 260, 266,
        268, 271
    Cobbett, William 77, 78, 84-86, 102, 103,
        113, 136
    Cobden, Richard 130, 144, 145, 160, 205,
        206, 209, 217
    Disraeli, Benjamin 114, 125, 132, 137,
        153, 160, 216, 217, 221, 230, 238, 253,
        255
    Forster, John 118
    Gladstone 77, 95, 104, 125, 131, 157, 174,
        178, 189, 198, 202, 203, 206, 209, 214,
        221, 223, 224, 226, 234, 251
    Goschen, G S 264
    Graham, James Sir 86, 98
    Lambton, William 92
    Lowe, Robert 210, 218, 220
    Palmerston 184, 189, 190, 217
    Peel, Robert 163, 164
    Rolley, Denys 35
    Wakefield, Edward Gibbon 108

Wellesley, Arthur 64

Explorers
    Columbus, Christopher 42
    Livingstone, David 136, 158, 235, 242
    Maguire, Patrick 42

Famine
    1317 14
    1817 39-41
    1822 68
    1845-49 (Great) 36, 157, 158, 160–165,
        170, 172, 247, 254, 260
    Hungry Forties 148, 161

Famine Ships
    Montezuma 172
    Rosa-linda 171
    W M Vail 171
    Yorkshire 171

Fenians & Fenianism 202, 207, 213, 221-224,
    228 [Manchester Martyrs*]
    Allen, William Philip* 223
    Barrett, Daniel 223
    Brennan, Thomas 254
    Davis, Thomas Osborne 159
    Davitt, Michael 183, 190, 225, 226, 249,
        250, 254, 262, 263
    Devoy, John 231
    Dillon, John 254, 261, 262
    Donahue, Patrick 241
    Duffy, Charles Gavan 185, 199, 240
    Healy, Timothy 271
    Ireland, Michel 241
    Larkin, Michael* 223
    Lyene, Morris 241
    Meagher, Thomas 150, 168, 169, 191, 211,
        241
    McClure, John 231
    Maguire, John Francis 185
    Maguire, Thomas 223
    Martin, John 191
    McGee, Thomas D'Arcy 241
    McManus, Terence Bellew 212, 241
    Mitchel, John 150, 168, 184, 189, 190,
        191, 218, 241, 243

Mulleda, Harry 231
O'Brien James Brontere 121, 143
O'Brien, Michael* 223
O'Brien, William Smith 168, 191, 199,
    223
O'Connell, Charles Underwood 231
O'Doherty, Kevin 191
O'Donovan Rossa, Jeremiah 224, 227, 231
O'Farrell, James 223
O'Gorman, Richard 241
O'Meagher Condon, Edward 223
O'Reilly, John Boyle 231
Rossa O'Donovan 224
Shannon, James 241
Stephens, James 168, 202, 218

Fenwicks
    Ann 118, 121, 254
    James 121
    Rosanna 118, 139
    William 118, 139

Ford
    Arthur 230
    Francis 230
    John 85

Gallagher family 8, 33, 103, 105
    Anthony 158
    Duncan 210
    Isabella 65, 96, 103, 105, 157
    John 96, 210
    Michael 159, 172
    Patrick 249
    Peter 96, 167, 232
    Rozanne 96

O'Gallagher, Manus 21

Gallowglasses (Redshanks, mercenaries) 13,
    16, 17

General Gordon 108, 212, 213, 253, 254,
    264-266

Great Exhibition 171, 181, 183, 184

Hanlon
    Ann 117
    John 76
    Owen 117
    Rose 117

Hiring Fairs 44, 48, 49

Home Rule 29, 206, 220, 224, 227, 234, 244,
    248, 249, 253, 254, 262, 263, 266-271

Ireland (Ancient)
    Erin 4, 5, 135
    Hibernia 4

Irish Ancestors 1
    Brigantes 5
    Firbolgs 4
    Milesians 4
    Phoenicians 3
    Scoti 4, 8, 15
    Scythians (Iranians) 3, 5
    Tuatha Danann 4

Ireland, Deputies/Governors/ Chief
    Secretaries
    Bayly, Nicholas 52
    Bingham, Richard 18, 190
    Cavendish, Frederick 262
    Chichester, Arthur 20
    Castlereagh, Robert Stewart 34, 38, 64,
        68, 75
    Cunningham, Peter 52
    Drummond, Thomas 117, 118
    Fitzwilliam, William 18
    Grey, Leonard 15
    Peel, Robert 38, 79
    Skeffington, William 15
    Smith, W H 269
    Sydney, Henry 17, 18, 19
    Wesllesley, Arthur 31, 37, 58

Irish/Anglo Monasteries/ Islands
    Boa 25
    Clonmacnoise 11
    Devenish 11, 19
    Iona 6, 7, 8, 25

Jarrow 7, 8
Lindisfarne 6-8, 12
Lisgoole 19
Monkwearmouth 7, 8
St Mogue's Island 25

Irish Chieftains / High Kings
    Buro, Brian 4, 12
    King of Leinster 12
    Maguire of Fermanagh 13, 15
    Maguire, Thomas Og 14
    Maguire, Philip of the Battle Axe 14
    Maguire, Hugh (Tyrone) 17, 18
    Niall Glundubh 11
    Niall of the Nine Hostages 6
    O'Brien Turlogh 12
    O'Connor, Rory 12
    O'Connor, Turlogh 12
    O'Donnell, Hugh 18, 20
    O'Donnell, Garv 13
    O'Donnell, Red Hugh 21
    O'Neill of Clannaboy 15
    O'Neill, Conn 26
    O'Neill, Hugh (Earl of Tyrone) 13, 15,
        19, 20
    O'Neill, Owen Roe 21
    O'Neill, Shane 13, 16, 17, 20
    O'Rourke, Tieran 13

Irish Clans
    Clanrickard 15, 18
    Bohill 18
    Burke 14, 16
    Butler 20
    Gallagher 18
    MacDermot 14, 15
    Maguire 16-18, 20
    MacDonnell, McDonnell 16, 18
    MacMahon 14, 20
    MacSweeney, Sweeny 15, 18
    MacRannell 14
    O'Boyle 15
    O'Connor 15
    O'Doherty 15, 18
    O'Donnell 14-16, 19
    O'Farrell 14
    O'Gallagher, Gallagher 15, 16, 18, 21

O'Kelly 16
O'Neill, 13, 16, 17, 19, 20
O'Reilly 14, 17 21
O'Rorke 13, 14, 16, 18, 19, 21
Preston 20

Irish Counties
Antrim 17
Armagh 21, 44
Belfast 4
Cavan 20-22, 25, 27
Clare 4, 78, 79
Derry 44, 101
Donegal (Tyrconnell) 4, 6, 22, 96, 101, 249
Down 43
Fermanagh 4, 18, 22, 27, 103, 129
Galway 33
Kerry 21, 43
King's County (Offaly)17
Leitrim 4, 17, 18, 21, 33, 36, 43, 86, 149, 159, 164
Mayo 22, 36, 41, 52, 53, 68, 250
Meath 7, 14, 24, 31
Monaghan 4, 21, 27, 34, 36, 149
Roscommon 21, 36, 78, 86, 100, 255
Sligo 11, 18, 22, 36, 86, 100
Tyrone 4, 15, 21, 22, 27, 44, 101, 168, 255
Westmeath 17, 190
Wicklow 21

Irish Emigration 25, 109, 113, 129, 134, 160, 170, 172, 184, 198, 211
Hiring Fairs 48
Spalpeens 43, 45, 56
Vagrants 42-50, 54, 72, 97, 103, 172, 277
Ultachs 33

Irish Industries
Aghacashel Ironworks 33
Arigna Ironworks 21, 30, 69
Creevela Ironworks 21
Flax growing & Linen Spinning 20, 27, 30, 34, 36, 40, 44, 67
O'Reilly Bros Ironworks 30

Irish Landowners, Middlemen and Squireens 27, 38

Boycott, Captain 253
Cole, William Sir 19
Coote, Charles 19, 21, 30
Edgeworth, Richard 27
Jardine, Sir William 49
Marquis of Sligo 169
Seymour, Robert 169

Irish Laws
Brehon 275, 281
Law of the Innocents 6

Irish Loughs
Lough Allen 30, 151, 177
Lough Erne 19, 25, 34
Lough Neagh 17, 26
Lough Ree 8, 11

Irish MPs
Brophy, P M 153
Butt, Isaac 227, 248
Grattan, Henry 29, 31, 59
MacFarlane, Donald H 68
Maguire, John Francis 223
O'Brien, William 223
O'Connell, Daniel 28, 36, 37, 58, 61, 93, 96, 99, 102, 136, 141, 143, 152, 167, 279
O'Connor, T P 250
O'Shea, Captain William 260
Parnell, Charles Stewart 190, 224, 240, 248, 251, 253, 260, 261, 262
Ronayne, Joseph 240
Sydney, Henry 17, 19
Wellesley, Arthur 31, 37

Irish Mines
Aghacashel 31, 33
Arigna 21, 30, 151, 192, 238
Ballinameeltoge Leitrim 249
Blackville 26
Coalisland 26, 109
Creevela 21
Lough Allen Mines 151
Tipperary 203
Tullyniskan 21

Irish Newspapers/publications
    Dublin Daily Mail 250
    Fermamagh Main (Herald) 177
    Irish People 218
    Roscommon & Leitrim Gazette 100, 177
    The Nation 145, 175, 177

Irish Settlements & Farming 67
    Conacre 48, 52, 143
    Crannoge 25, 63
    Enclosure 26, 43, 243
    Rath 71
    Rundale 143
    Sweathouse 114
    Tuatha 13

Irish Saints/Bishops
    Adamnan 6, 8
    Aidan 7, 8
    Columba 6
    Finian the Wise (Clonard) 6
    Ninian 5
    Palladius 5
    Patrick 5, 6, 45

Irish Towns/Villages
    Aghalurcher 209
    Athlone 13, 172
    Ballycloran 33
    Ballyhaise Killougher 29
    Bawnboy 25
    Belcoo 170
    Belfast 4, 24, 26, 40, 51, 137, 267
    Belturbet 14, 21, 24
    Birr 13
    Carrick-on-Shannon 164
    Castlecoote 21
    Cavan 24
    Clanaboy 15
    Cleenish 26
    Clogher 25, 26, 29
    Clones 4, 11, 13, 21, 25, 27, 34, 49
    Clontarf 12, 151
    Cork 39, 52, 150
    Croagh Patrick 6
    Derry 24

Derrygonnelly 170
Derrylin 261
Derryvullan 26, 67, 214
Donaghmore 25
Donaghadee 41, 43, 46, 57
Downpatrick 34
Drogheda 21, 43
Dromore 34
Drumahaire 43
Drumohaire 43
Drumshambo 33, 69, 159, 193
Drunmurrish 110
Dungarvan 185
Dublin 11, 17, 21, 35, 40, 150
Ederney 170
Enniskillen 4, 11, 14, 18, 19, 21, 24, 41, 86,
    104, 129, 135, 143, 243, 253, 254
Eshnanumera 49
Galway 68
Grisson 170
Irvinestown 49
Kesh 34, 170, 261
Kilfaoughna 72
Killeshandra 20
Kinawley 29, 49
Kinsale 19, 20
Lack 170
Limerick 4
Lisnaskea 24, 29, 164
Londonderry 24, 98, 129, 216
Longford 172
Magheraboy 170
Maguiresbridge 29
Manor Hamilton 21
Magherculmony 20, 129
Monaghan 20, 27, 172
Mullinaherb 29
Omagh 49
Portadown 33
Skibbereen 163
Stokestown 34
Swanlinbar 14, 49
Templeport 214
Tempo 170, 211
Trim 14
Tyrconnell 15

Ireland - Visitors
    John Bright 1834, 1849, 1866 110, 176,
        218
    Thomas Carlyle 1845, 1849 150, 175
    Christopher Columbus 1490 42
    Charles Dickens 1867 221
    Charles Gavan Duffey 1849 175
    William Gladstone 1845, 1877 160, 248
    General Gordon 1880 254
    Henry George 1881 252
    Morris, William 1877 160, 248, 254
    George Peabody 1866 218
    Sydney Smith 1833 106
    Walter Scott 1825, 71
    William Thackeray 1843 150
    Queen Victoria & Prince Albert 1849,
        1861 174, 210

Ironworks & Steelworks, North East
    Armstrong's Works, Elswick 244
    Berry Edge Ironworks 167
    Cleator Iron Ore 183, 228
    Consett Steelworks 120, 166
    Felling Chemical Works 134, 213
    Friars Goose Works 134
    Hawks, Crawshaw & Co 167
    Middlesborough Bolckow & Vaughan 90,
        181, 211
    South Shields Cooksons Chemical Works
        134
    South Shields James Hartley Glass Works
        183
    Walker Losh, Wilson & Bell 115, 134,
        145, 167, 261
    Westoe Alkali Works 193, 231
    Whitehaven Ironworks 46, 183

Islands
    Enniskillen (Island) 14
    Isle of Man 6
    Isle of Mull 6
    Isle of Rathlin 8, 16, 18
    Scattery Island 4

Kellegher family
    Anne (Agnes) 76
    Catherine 76, 77

Helen 76, 117
Patrick 175
Peter 76
Thomas 77

Kilmainham Treaty 260, 262

Land League 249, 254
    Evictions 17, 162, 164, 165, 245, 246, 250,
        252, 261
    3 Fs 176, 227, 260, 262
    Tenant Right League 1850 249, 254, 262

Lawrence
    Isabella 160, 165, 173, 178
    James 166, 168, 173, 186, 191, 192, 196,
        197, 199, 242
    Ann Jane 161, 173, 209
    John 153, 168, 173, 178, 192, 196, 209,
        225
    Lydia 196, 242

Little Irelands 80, 86, 96, 97, 151, 152

Lords & Earls
    Ashley 146, 147, 150
    Beaconsfield 121, 221, 244, 250, 253, 254,
        255
    Belmore 30
    Bentinck 160, 163
    Brougham 46, 64, 93, 94, 95, 109
    Brudenell (Cardigan) 109
    Burleigh 20
    Caernavon 269
    Clarendon 169
    Clements 149
    Derby 244
    Duncannon 98
    Durham (Lambton, Radical Jack) 67, 92,
        93-95, 98, 100, 105, 110, 117, 119,
        137, 150, 154
    Eldon 98
    Enniskillen 159
    Granville 117
    Grey Charles 64, 86, 87, 92, 93, 95, 100,
        114,
    Howick 77, 141, 149

Kelvin 219
Leitrim 248
Lewis, George Cornewall 42
Liverpool 67
Lucan 190
Londonderry 98
Lonsdale 153
Melbourne 108, 111, 112, 162
Morpeth 118, 141
Mountcashel 24
Russell, John 95, 98, 99, 109, 110, 131,
    160, 189, 203
Salisbury 171, 269
Shaftesbury 74, 147, 266
Shannon (Henry Boyle) 27
Sidmouth 55, 69
Spencer 114
Stanley, Edward (Earl of Derby) 106, 141
Stewart, Charles 64
Stowell 98

Magna Carta 13

Mason-Dixon Line 29

Mason Family
    Alexander 232, 239, 256, 259
    Annie 105
    Charles 29
    Clement 127, 166, 178, 180, 186, 209,
        210, 215, 225
    Clement (son) 127, 256, 260
    Dorothy Lydia 232, 256, 259
    Elizabeth 105
    Ellen 255, 259
    Isabella 180, 209, 210, 215, 259, 267
    James 222, 225, 230-232, 239, 256, 260
    James (son) 231, 255, 257, 264
    John 215, 231, 252, 256, 257, 260
    Luke 116, 230
    Mary 105
    Mary Ann (Reed) 258, 260
    Peter 116, 260
    Richard 232, 255, 256
    Robert 116
    Thomas 39, 116
    Walter 230

William 116

Massacre of Glencoe 17, 25

Massacre of Peterloo 65

Massacre, Manchester 223, 228

Massacre of Rathlin Island 1575 18

Master & Chargeman Sinkers 247
    Armstrong, Henry 209
    Coulson, Matthew 178
    Coulson, William 197, 202, 210, 211, 215,
        216
    Coxon, James 202
    Green, Joseph 186
    Hann, John 255
    Kellet, Thomas 203
    Longstaff, John 203
    Mason, James 220, 222, 230-233, 239,
        243, 246-248, 255, 260, 264, 269, 270,
        271
    Mason, Robert 215
    Mason, William 215, 231
    McGarrity, Patrick 256

Mechanics Institutes 197, 228

Methodism 102, 106, 117, 131, 140, 150, 185,
    186, 193, 194, 242, 279, 204, 205
    Wesley, John 27, 88
    Methodist Chapels 194, 199

Midlothian pilgrimages 214, 244, 249, 253

Miners Sports, Music & Amusements
    Bull-baiting 69, 90
    Cock-fighting 69, 194
    Dog-fighting 194
    Football & clubs 235
    Gardening (allotments) 85
    Greyhound racing 85
    Hare-coursing 90
    Drinking 85, 90, 194, 238
    Accordion, Bag-pipes and Brass bands 90

Mine Acts & Regulations
    Abolition of Yearly Bond 1872 238
    Scottish Miners & Salters 1606 61
    Truck Acts 1820 and 1831 97
    Child Labour Act 1842 147
    Coal Mines Regulation 1860 211
    Shafts Act 1872 211

Mines Inspectors
    Leifchild, John Roby 139, 140, 142
    Tremehere, Seymour 138, 179

Miners' Bond 63, 97, 122, 154, 155, 198, 199

Mineralogists
    Agricola, Georgius 183, 201
    Frederick Augustus of Poland 201

Miners' Leaders & Lawyers
    Hepburn, Thomas 98, 121, 216
    Roberts, W. P. 148, 199

Mining Engineers & Viewers
    Buddle, John 84, 122, 137
    Mulvaney, William Thomas - Erin Colliery
        Westphalia 194
    Peile, John 84
    Seymour, Francis 26
    Sutcliffe, Richard 203

Navvies 50, 99, 157, 167, 168, 172, 176, 184,
    195, 196, 198, 208, 214, 231, 251

Newcastle
    Coal Whippers 133, 169
    Colliers 91, 96
    Keelmen 63, 133, 201
    Rookeries 97, 108, 117, 129
    Staithes 63, 81, 133, 213

Newcastle areas/streets
    Ballast Hills 109, 128
    Blyth's Nook 132
    Butcher's Bank 122
    Cross Keys 191
    Dogger's Entry 124
    Head of Side 122, 140
    Quayside 96, 97, 222

Queen's Street 122
Pudding Chare 181
Rosemary Lane 127, 140, 156, 174, 175
St Peter's Quay 107, 109
Sandgate 125
Skinner Burn 129
Westgate 17, 137, 161, 179 210, 227,
    255

Newspapers
    Barrow Herald 214
    Durham Chronicle 246
    Dumfries Courier 56
    Edinburgh Observer 123
    Fraser's Magazine 175
    Glasgow Chronicle 53
    Illustrated London News 195
    Leeds Mercury 94
    Miners' Advocate 140, 149
    Newcastle Daily Chronicle 197 239
    Northern Liberator 121
    Northern Star 121, 143, 148
    Pitman's Happy Times 138
    Scottish Herald 214
    The Economist 175
    The Voice of the People 121
    The Times 65, 84, 178, 192, 196
    Tyne Mercury 98
    Voice from the Coal Mines 141

Normans (Anglo) 6, 11, 12, 19, 111
    Earl of Pembroke (Strongbow) 13
    John de Courcy 12
    William the Conqueror 12, 87

Northumbria (ancient)
    Bernia & Deira 6, 7, 8

Northumbrian Bondagers 21, 72, 74

Northumberland Border Families
    Douglas 14, 86
    Elliott 20
    Johnstone 20, 64
    Maxwell 64
    Percy 14, 15, 20, 86

Northumberland Towns/Villages
    Benwell 107
    Bamburgh 6, 7, 139
    Earsden 256
    Elswick 107, 244
    Hexham 83
    Morpeth 180
    Newcastle Quay 222
    Whitfield 79

Northumberland collieries
    Blaydon Main 83, 144
    Cowpen 142
    Killingworth 80, 92, 105
    Longbenton 115, 180
    New Hartley 210, 211, 215, 216
    Percy Main 142
    St Anthony 32
    Seaton Deleval 205
    Seaton Union Pit 161
    Seghill 199
    Walker 26, 108, 115, 211
    Wallsend 115, 116
    Willington Bigges 138
    Willington Quay 229

Northumbrian (Anglo-Saxon) Kings
    Ada the Flameblower 6
    AEthelfrith 7
    Aldfrith 7
    Eanfrith 7
    Ecgfrith 7
    Edwin 7
    Oswald 7
    Oswiu 7

North-East Saints and Priests
    Bishop Eadfrith 8
    Monk Simeon 8
    St Cuthbert 7, 8, 12, 15
    Venerable Bede 3, 5, 7, 8

Orange Order 33, 34, 38, 44, 68, 69, 86, 114, 118, 123, 164, 177, 199, 214, 228, 229, 264, 269, 271

Outrages 27, 44, 69, 72, 158, 159, 199, 252

Catholic Defenders 30, 33, 143
Dragooning of Ulster 34
Molly Maguires 143, 159, 212, 235, 246
Peep-o' Day Boys 30, 33, 34
Raparees (Tories) 23, 24, 26, 27
Ribbonmen 39, 52, 86, 143, 176, 203, 229, 261, 277
Shanavests 39
Trashers 39
Ultachs 33
Volunteer Corps 29
Whiteboys 27, 30, 110, 176, 261

Parliamentary Bills, Acts & Laws
    Abolition of Slavery Act 1833 102
    Act of Good Affection 1653 22
    Act of Supremacy 1536 15
    Act of Union, England/Scotland 1707 26
    Act of Union, England/Ireland 27, 59
    Anatomy Act 1832 102
    Public Health and Artisans' Dwelling Act 1874 241, 243
    Ballot Act 1872 238
    Catholic Toleration Act 1791
    Catholic Relief Act 1778 29
    Catholic Relief Act 1813 59
    Catholic Relief Bill 1827 39, 67, 77, 78
    Catholic Emancipation Act 1829
    Coercion Bills, 1833
    Combination Laws 1799, 1800 58, 76
    Corn Laws 179
    Disestablishment bill 1869 223
    Dissenters' Bill 1828 126
    Ecclesiastical Titles Act 1852 185
    Emancipation Bill 1829 79
    Factory Act (Althorps) 1833 139
    Fancy Franchise Bill 1859 203
    Gauge Act 1846 161
    Great Reform Act 1832 102, 107
    Gregory Clause (Poor law Ext Act 1847)
    Health of Town Act 1848 197
    Home Rule Bill 1886 271
    Insurrection Act 1798 34
    Irish Coercion Bill 1833 105
    Irish Coercion Bill 1846 162
    Irish Land Purchase Bill 1885 271
    Irish Reform Bill 1832 101

Jamicia Bill 1839 131
Land Act 1869 & 1870 226, 249
Land League Act 1881 260
Law of Settlement 1579, 1662, 1772,
    1782, 1795, 1796 50, 131
Licencing Act 1872 238
Limited Liability Acts 1855 & 1862 199
Married Women's Property Act 1870 225
Master & Servant Act 1867 220
Maynooth Bill 1845 159
Municipal Reform Act 1835 117
Municipal Corporation Act 1882 263
National Winding & General Engineers
    Society 1859 205
Oath of Allegiance 1757 27
Oxford University Reform Bill 1854
Pains and Penalties Bill 1820 67
Penal Laws 1695 25, 26, 31
Poachers Act 1816 52
Poor Law, 1579 Act (workhouse unions,
    overseers) 112
Poor Law 1722, 1782, 1795 51, 112
Poor Law Amendment Act 1834 112
Poor Law Ireland 1838 131
Poyning's Law 1495 15
Treasonable Practices & Seditions
    Meetings 1795 55
Public Worship Regulation Bill 1874 240
Railway Act 1844 149, 151
Red Flag Act 1865 217
Reform Bill 1832 100, 102, 274
Reform Bill 1885 265, 266
Reform Bill 1867 220, 221
Repeal of Combination Act 1824 77
Sabbatarian Bill 1855 197
Settling of Ireland 1652 & 1662 22, 51
Six Acts 1819 55
Speenhamland 1795 113
Statute of Kilkenny 1367 14
Statute of Labourers 1351 14
Test Act 1673 23
Test Act 1727 26
Third Class Midland Railways 1872 235
Tithe Bill 1835 109
Toleration Act 1689 24
Trade Union Amendment Act 1876 243

Treason Practices and Seditious Meetings
    Acts 1796 55, 58
Universities Test Act 1871
Vagrancy 1548 51
Vagrancy 1824 50, 76

Penal Code/Laws 25, 26, 28, 30, 31, 33, 34,
    36, 58

Pitman Poets
    Hornsby, William 155
    Skipsey, Joseph 103
    Werth, George 155

Pit Ponies 92
    Galloway 87, 90-92, 232
    Shetland 229

Pit Sinkers 200
    Anderson, Joseph 222
    Barker, F 173
    Burrowman, Isaac 233
    Cowey, Nicholas 154
    Dower, William 222
    Elwin, George 211
    Elwin John 211
    Ford, Francis 230
    Mason, James (son) 257
    Mason (Shannon), James 199, 202, 203,
        207, 209, 211, 215
    Mason, Joseph 161
    Mason, Luke 230
    Mason, Thomas 138
    Mason, Walter 230
    Oliver, Matthew 173
    Robinson, John 233
    Spears, Samuel 243
    Waggett, Richard 211
    Wandlas, Anthony 103
    Wilson, William 173
    Wind, Henry 173

Plantation/Settlement 13, 21
    Antrim 1572 17
    Crossing of Shannon 41
    Fermanagh 1612 19
    Ulster 1629 17

Plantation Adventurers/Undertakers/
    Discoverers 17, 21, 24, 29
    Carew, George Sir 19
    Cole, William 19
    Coote, Major Charles 19, 21, 30
    Courcy, John de 13
    Drake, Francis 18
    Huguenots 24
    Smith, Sir Thomas 17
    Raleigh, Walter 18, 20
    Spence, Edmund 18

Poaching 25, 52, 97, 138

Poets
    Bronte, Branwell 160
    Browning, Robert 225
    Burns, Robert 20, 46, 55, 58-62, 70, 71
    Colleridge 80
    Crabbe 113
    Goldsmith 75
    Keating, Geoffrey 251
    Keats 46
    Mason, William 283
    Rossetti, William Michael 42
    Shelley 39
    Southey, Robert 84
    Tennyson, Lord Alfred 217
    Werth, George 155

Poor Laws 49, 85, 108, 119, 120, 123, 128,
    131, 132, 162, 277
    Settlement Paupers/Convicts 50, 52, 109
    Workhouses 51, 102, 107, 108, 112-114,
        120, 122, 123, 125, 131, 132, 143, 148,
        162, 164, 165, 172, 207, 219, 241, 254,
        255, 271

Popes
    Adrian IV 12
    Augustine 8
    Celestine 5
    Gregory 8
    Pius IX 178

Potatoes 20, 37, 39, 40, 42, 49, 68, 71, 73, 111,
    126, 160, 175, 186, 250, 253

Prime Ministers
    Aberdeen, Lord 210
    Balfour, Arthur James 252, 272
    Canning, George 39, 68, 78
    Disraeli, Benjamin 140, 243, 280
    Gladstone, William 238, 240, 252, 253,
        270, 249, 273
    Grey, Charles (Earl) 92
    Huskisson, William 93
    Liverpool, Lord 67, 78
    Melbourne, Lord 108, 111, 112, 130, 141,
        162
    Palmerston 162, 202, 203, 204, 213
    Peel 144, 149, 161, 162
    Perceval, Spencer 38
    Pitt, William 36, 58
    Russell, John 164, 185, 198, 216
    Wellington 95, 111, 118

Protestant schools & churches
    Escombe Co Durham 7
    St Andrew's Bishop Auckland 1860 207
    St James' Benwell 208
    St John Baptist Church Newcastle 1287
        107

Quakers 55, 186
    Blackhouse 80
    Bright, John 110, 131, 144
    Mason, Clement 178
    Pease, Edward 80, 201
    Pease, Joseph 201
    Priestman, Elizabeth 131
    Richardson 80
    Society of Friends 131, 163

Radicals 66, 79, 95, 100, 114
    Attwood, Thomas 79
    Cartwright, Captain 64, 84
    Duncombe, T S 145
    Fielden, John 132
    Hume, Joseph 69, 77, 114, 131
    Dilke, Charles 233, 235

Railways, Structures and Investors
    Balaclava to Sebastopol 1854 196
    Caledonian Railway 1865 157, 161, 214
    Causey Arch, Railway Bridge 1726 80
    Greenwich Railway 256
    Great Northern Railway 183
    Great Western Railway 181
    Hudson, George 157, 158, 167, 183
    Irish Railways 164
    Newcastle & Carlisle 82
    Newcastle High Level Railway Bridge 167
    Newcastle & Darlington 1844 151
    Ouseburn Railway Viaduct 121
    Redpath, Leopold 183
    Stockton/Darlington Railway 1825 176
    Tanfield Tramway 1671 80
    Wylam Waggonway 80

Reed family
    Agnes 68
    Andrew 133, 143, 210, 256
    Catherine 140, 143, 156, 158, 179, 210
    James 68
    James Storey 133, 143, 210, 233, 243, 246,
        247, 256, 258, 260
    Mary Ann 210, 233
    Margaret Armstrong 178
    Ralph 133, 140, 156, 175, 179, 210, 233
    Sarah 246

Religions
    Catholic Recusants 92
    Covenanters 53
    Papists & Popery 24, 86
    Popish Plot 1678 23
    Pope's Brass Band 177
    Papal Aggression 1850 177
    Protestant Ascendency 24, 25, 32
    Scotch Presbyterians 19, 29
    Ulster Revival 1859
    Ulster Prebyterians 17
    Unitarianism 131

Religious leaders
    Booth, William (Salvation Army) 90, 249
    Boulter, Primate 22

Chalmers, Frederick - Rector of
    Beckenham 192
Cullen, Cardinal 269
Douglas, Bishop of Carlisle 280
Keble, John 106, 109
Knox 19, 76
Luther, Martin 15
Malthus, Thomas Robert 36, 43, 67, 113,
    119, 204
Manning, John Henry 177, 223, 224
More, Thomas 15
Newman 106, 174, 177, 278
Nulty Dr, Bishop 190
Plunkett, Oliver 23
Pusey, Philip 109, 160, 198
Riddell, Bishop 122
Walsh, Dr 269

Repeal of the Union, Ireland 111, 145, 148,
    149, 150, 153, 159, 160, 183, 279
    O'Connell, Daniel 79, 104, 111, 114, 118,
        141, 150

Reports
    Conditions of the Poorer Classes in
        Ireland 1833 105
    Condition of Poor in Ireland 1837 126
    Chadwick Report 1842 146
    Child Labour 1842 138, 146
    Mendicity Report 1815 51
    Poor Law 1817 49
    Poor Law Commission 1847 164
    Royal Commission 1834 113
    Santitary Condition of Labouring
        Population of Great Britain 1842
    Sanitary Condition of Dumfries 146
    South Shields Committee investigation of
        Accidents in Coal Mines 1839 147
    State of Popery 1731 26
    State of Labouring (Bells) 56
    Statistical Account of Kirkoswald 1792 48

Revolutionaries
    Younge, Richard, Poores Advocate 23
    Tyler, Wat 14
    Sarsfield, Patrick (Flight of Earls) 19, 24

Thomas Paine, Rights of Man 31, 32, 34,
    45, 46, 55, 213, 214, 280, 282
Wild Geese 24, 169, 211

Riots 85, 148, 214
    1641 Irish Rebellion 20, 21
    1823 Catholic/Orange Riots 69
    1826 Poor Law Riots 1826 77
    Anti-Poor Law 132
    Berry Edge 166, 167
    Gordon 1770 31, 141, 178
    London Riot 269
    Luddites 63, 86
    Murphy Riots 228
    Newcastle 1850 177
    Nottingham Castle 1831 100
    Plug 144
    Sandgate 177
    Scottish Clearances 65
    Swing 86, 94, 111, 112
    Tinder-box 275
    Tyne Keelmen 26, 63

Rising Revolutions, Revolts & Rebellions
    1381 English Rising 14
    French Revolution 31, 58, 118, 130, 150
    Orange Rising 68
    Peasants Revolt 1381 14
    1399 Revolution 14
    1637 Scottish Covenanters Uprising 21
    1641 Irish Rebellion 20, 23
    1688 Glorious Revolution 24
    1776 Agarian Rebellion 29
    1783 Volunteers Agitation 31
    1798 Rising 34, 44, 45, 46
    1831 Merthyr Rising 100, 101
    1839 Chartist Rising 143
    1841 Irish Rebellion 21, 22
    1842 Chartist Rising 65, 168
    1848 Irish Rising 169, 190, 191

Rivers
    Boyne 24
    Shannon 3, 4, 11, 12, 218
    Tyne 87–89, 138, 139, 201
    Wear 98, 139, 196, 201

Romans 61
    Agricola 5, 63
    Hadrian and Wall 5
    Ptolemy 4

Royalty/Rulers
    Adelaide 100, 174
    Albert, Prince 171, 173, 174, 183, 184,
        191, 199, 210, 217, 249
    Anne, Queen 25
    Bertie, Prince of Wales 206, 235
    Caroline 66, 67
    Catherine of Aragon 18
    Charles Stuart (Prince) 26
    Charles I 21
    Charles II 23
    Charles X 94
    Charlotte 65
    Duke of Cleveland 226
    Duke of Kent 67
    Duke of Newcastle 95
    Duke of Wellington 160
    Edward I 64
    Edward IV 15
    Elizabeth I 17, 18, 19, 20
    George III 31, 46, 55, 67, 80, 92
    George IV 67, 93
    Henry II 12
    Henry VIII 15, 16
    James II 22, 23
    James IV 19
    James VI 19
    King of Naples 185
    Leopold of Belgium 217
    Louis XIV (Louis Napoleon) 24, 184, 230
    Louis Phillipe 168
    Mary Queen of Scots 16, 18
    Napoleon & Wars 27, 34, 37-39, 68, 70,
        168
    Napoleon III 168, 192, 206, 230
    Napoleon IV 244
    Philip of Macedonia 275
    Philip II Spain 16, 19, 29
    Prince Leopold 188
    Prince Regent 68
    Richard II 14
    Richard III 14

Tzar Alexander II 206
Tzar Nicholas 198
Victoria, Queen 108, 115, 117, 122, 123,
        131, 133, 141, 148, 159, 164, 165, 174,
        176, 184, 190, 191, 198, 199, 210, 217,
        219, 225, 234, 235, 238, 240, 243, 244,
        248, 253, 266, 268, 270
William I Emperor 231
William III 24, 29, 33
William IV 99, 101, 119, 120, 123, 174

Schools/Colleges 280
    Annan Academy 75
    Free schools 1570
    Hedge 74
    Maynooth 131, 144, 159
    Methodist Sunday School 138
    Protestant Free Schools 17, 227
    Ragged 74, 227
    RC School Dumfries 1838 75
    Scottish education 74
    State 227, 228
    Ushaw College 186
    Walker Day School 146

Scientists/Philosophers
    Airy, George Biddell 195
    Aiton, William 49
    Darwin, Charles 107, 126, 132, 204, 217,
        244
    Darwin, Erasmus 131
    Faraday, Michael 154
    Huxley, Thomas Henry 217, 227
    Lyell, Charles Sir 217, 225
    Tyndall, John 255
    Philosophical Society, Newcastle 32

Scotland (ancient)
    Alba 5, 6, 11
    Dal Riata 6-8

Scottish Clans
    Caledonii 5
    Dalarida Scots 4, 8
    Campbells 21, 25
    Donald 5
    McDonnell of the Isles 16

Macdonald 16, 21, 25, 26
Picts 5–8

Scottish Counties 48, 58
    Annandale 14, 26, 58, 59, 62, 64, 117
    Argyll & Bute 6
    Ayrshire 59
    Dumfriesshire 45, 48, 60, 61, 74, 76, 83,
        267
    Dunbartonshire 59
    Galloway 5, 45, 48
    Hebrides (and Islay) 4, 8, 14
    Kintyre 5, 14
    Lanarkshire 59, 179
    Renfrewshire 59
    Western Isles 5, 16
    Wigtonshire 48, 56, 57

Scotland Visitors
    Keats, John 1818 46
    O'Connell, Daniel 1835
    Victoria & Albert 148

Scottish Kings/Chiefs
    Alpin, Kenneth 8
    Bruce, Edward 14, 63, 64
    Bruce, Robert 13, 14
    John of the Heather 25
    MacGabrain, Aidan 7
    MacDonnells of the Isles 16
    Stuarts 4
    Wallace, William, 13, 76

Scottish Mines
    Ayrshire Sinking 26
    Goldilea 60
    Sanquhar 61, 62, 118
    Thornhill 61, 118
    Wanlockhead 60, 61

Scottish Towns/Villages
    Annan 45, 55, 64, 74, 76, 118, 144
    Coldstream 244
    Ecclefecken 58, 70, 255
    Edinburgh 61, 175
    Dumbarton 6

Dumfries 48, 55, 58, 64, 71, 72, 77, 100, 118, 214
Glasgow 56
Glendinning 274
Glenuce 56
Gretna Green 45, 64
Lockerbie 56-58, 63-65, 70, 76, 82, 83, 96, 181, 214
Lochmaben 58, 62-66
Melrose 7
Newton Stewart 57
Portpatrick 43–48, 54, 56, 57, 83
Shenannton 57
Stranraer 47, 56
Torwood Muir 63
Whithorn, Wigtownshire 5
Wigton 54, 69

Shanachie - story-teller 1

Shannon/Shennan family, O'Seanains, O'Shannon,O'Sheanan, O'Sionain 4

MacGulshenan, Gilshenan Gilsenan 4, 5, 13, 72

MacShenoig, MacShannon 4, 5,14

Tuaim-da-ghulann 5

Mac an tSionaigh (Shenanigan) 5

O'Shanaghan O'Seanain 4, 12, 13

Seannan, Saint 14

Morogh & Hugh O'Shewman 20

O'Sheerin, O'Sheanan 20

Shannon/Shenan/Sheanon/O'Shannan
    Agnes/Ann 48, 65, 68, 96
    Alexander 191, 206, 208, 209, 221
    Barney 110
    Bridget 158, 171
    Bryan 110
    Cathal 202
    Catherine 65, 66, 121, 133, 253

Charles 25
Daniel 29, 68, 117, 127, 139
Edward 25, 94, 140, 143, 197, 208, 252, 254
Edward Reed 233, 252
Ellen 203, 209, 253
Francis (Sheane, Priest) 25
Helen 117, 137, 203
Henry 231
Hugh 110
Isabella 107, 117, 127, 215
James 25, 48, 80, 107-109, 122, 127, 134, 137, 145, 171, 191, 199, 202, 206
James (son) 199
Jane 180, 208, 210, 252
John 92, 215, 232, 247, 215, 253, 255
Lakall 25
Lydia 199
Margaret 158, 159, 171
Mary 25, 158, 167
Mary Ann 103, 105, 108, 109
Michael 159, 261
Patrick 29, 158, 167, 253
Peter 29, 34, 82, 96, 103, 107, 109, 117, 121, 122, 127, 171, 172, 181, 208, 261
Philex 29
Philip 25, 29, 34, 48, 61, 63, 66, 68, 82, 96, 110, 118, 121, 139, 140, 167, 171, 174, 213, 214, 261
Philip Martin 212
Richard 48, 117, 118, 121, 139, 156, 180, 181, 210, 254, 255
Rosannah 48, 65, 118, 139, 156
Stephen (Gilsenan) 72
Stephen 114
Susan 34, 129
Thomas 20, 48, 49, 66, 77, 107, 110, 134, 135, 139, 158, 171, 191, 208, 227, 232
William 66

Shipbuilding 133, 140, 156, 179, 213, 253
    Belfast Harland 196
    Great Britain 1843 161
    Great Eastern 1859 205
    Palmers (Hebburn) 133
    Spanish Armada 18
    Tyneside 140, 179

Sinking contractors 126
   Coulson, William 186
   Coxon, James, Joseph 202
   Mason, William 215, 231

Slavery & Slave Trade 8, 29, 38, 53, 59, 62, 95,
   102, 104–106, 120, 121, 131, 136, 144,
   150, 190, 206
   Alexander the Great 275
   Black Slaves of Monserrat 23
   Clarkson, Thomas 38
   Equiano, Olaudah 31
   Female Slaves 12, 248
   French Slave Trade 38
   Gladstone, John sale of slaves 95
   Lincoln, Abraham 189, 206, 212, 213, 217,
     218
   Oastler, Richard 94
   Quaker Society 55
   Slave Ship Creole 144
   Slave children 12
   South Africa (Boers) 114
   Turner JMW 29
   Wilberforce, William 58, 77, 106
   Duke of Wellington 95

Socialists/Communists/Labour Party 169,
   175, 207, 273
   Atlee, Clement 263
   Burt, Thomas 234, 241, 244, 267
   Connolly, James 224, 226, 282, 283
   Engels, Frederick 83, 84, 122, 149, 151,
     174, 223, 225, 228, 240, 249, 264, 282
   Godwin, William 32
   Hardie, James Keir 199, 249, 263, 271,
     282
   Hyndman, Henry Mayers 263
   Kingsley, Charles (Christian Socialist) 175,
     279
   Lalor, James Fintan 69, 169, 170, 191, 226,
     282
   MacDonald, James Ramsey 219
   Marx, Karl 60, 87, 149, 169, 179, 213, 220,
     223, 228, 231, 251, 264, 282
   Morris, William 87, 107, 108, 169, 183,
     189, 218, 224, 232, 248, 260–265,
     264, 265, 267, 273, 282

Owen, Robert 67, 77, 106, 107, 112, 113,
   251, 264
Smillie, Robert 196, 234, 246
Spence, Thomas 32, 251
Thompson. William 36
Webb, Sidney 93, 252, 263

Socialist movements 24, 189, 248
   Amnesty Movement 1869 220
   Christian Socialism 169, 175
   Co-operative Movement 151, 169, 177,
     206, 207, 251
   Combinations 77, 97
   Fabian Society 1884 251, 263
   Independent Labour Party 266, 271
   International Republican Brigade 1868
     202, 222, 228
   Irish Brigade 24
   Labour Party 271
   Social Democratic Federation (SDF) 260,
     263, 267, 271, 282
   Society of Friends of the People (Earl
     Grey) 92
   Young Irelanders 165, 202

Staffordshire Collieries 148
   Hanley Deep 257
   Talk o' Th' Hill 247

Strikes
   Batts Row (B Aukland) 1850 204
   Bloody Sunday 1887 271
   Keelmen 1815 63
   Great Strike 1832 102
   General Strike 1842 148
   Great Strike 1844 151, 156
   North East Strike 1830 93
   Thornley 1843
   Monkwearmouth Strike 1869 224
   North East Engineers 1871 234
   Northumberland & Durham 1810
   N&D Bond Strike 1810 63
     Preston 1854 189
   Ryhope Colliery 1872 234
   Tattie Strike 1881 253
   Walker Strike 1765 26

Strike-breakers (Blacklegs/candyman) 59, 94, 98, 153, 154, 156, 166, 199, 231, 277
  Cornish 140
  Irish 136
  Welsh 140

Temperance Movement 229, 236

Tithe Laws 38, 104, 109, 110, 131, 132, 274

Trade Unionists/Strikers
  Applegarth, Robert 217, 220
  Arch, Joseph 235
  Doherty, John 69, 99. 190
  Howell, George 220
  Kenny, Patrick 235
  Loveless, George 120
  Odger, George 220
  Ramsey, Tommy 225
  MacDonald, Alexander 220, 225, 241
  Tolpuddle Martyrs 112, 114, 120, 274

Trades Union/Friendly Societies &
  Combinations 58, 97, 110, 120
  Agricultural Labourers Union 1885 266
  Amalgamated Society of Engineers (ASE)
    1851
  Birmingham Union 100,102
  Colliers of the United Association 93, 122
  Cotton Spinners Union 1829 69
  Durham Miners Association 225
  Grand National Consolidated Union 1834
    106, 112
  General Labourers' Amalgamated Union
    1872 235
  International Working Mens Association
    223
  Irish Universal Suffrage Union 153
  Lambton Colliers Association 99
  Miners' Union 1831 110
  National Union of Working Classes 1831
    100
  Female Political Union of Newcastle 1839
    132
  London Working Men's Association 130
  Miners' Association of Great Britain 1842
    147

Miners' Trade Union Association 148
Municipal Corporation Act 1882
National Agricultural Labourers' Union
  1872 235
National Association of Trades 1845 179
National Winding and General Engineers'
  Society 205
National Union of Railwaymen 1871 234
Navvies Union, 1891
Northern Political Union 1830 94, 141
Northern Typographical Union 1830 94
Pitmen's Union of the Tyne and Wear,
  1831, 1869 93, 139
Scottish Ironmoulders Friendly Society
  1829 78
Scottish Miners Union 196
Thornley Colliery Union 144
United Colliers 1831 94, 99
Working Man's Association 1837 121, 130

Truck & Tommy Shops 97, 109, 145, 196,
  234, 238

United Irishmen 27, 32, 33, 34
  Emmett, Robert 34, 37
  Fitzgerald, Edward 34, 68
  Muir, Thomas 46
  O'Connor, Arthur 37
  Tone, Theobald Wolfe 31, 32, 34, 46

Vikings 1, 8, 10, 11, 16, 266
  Erik Bloodaxe 12
  Cnut, King 12
  Danes 8, 11
  Dubh-galls (black strnagers) 11
  Fin-galls (white strangers) 11
  Magnus Barelegs 12
  Olaf the White 11, 12
  Sigtrygg Silkbeard 11
  Raegnald 11
  Turgesius 11

Volcanoes/Earthquakes
  Summalia 264
  Tambora 39

Wars
    Afghan and Zulu Wars 1878 249, 254
    Franco-Prussian 225, 230, 241
    Kaffir War 1834 111
    Peninsular War 38
    Spanish Armarda 18
    Transvaal War 1881 253

Welsh Towns/Villages
    Harwarden 208
    Llangollen 31, 194
    Newport 136

Welsh Collieries
    East Lothian 121
    Merthyr Tydfil 99

Women's Rights 62, 105, 181, 253, 225, 281

Writers, Historians, Artist, Poets & Journalists
    Aiton, William 50
    Arnold, Matthew 224, 283
    Bayley, Nicholas 52
    Borrow, George 91
    Butler, Elizabeth 281
    Burke, Edmund 3, 25, 26, 29, 30-32, 58,
        191
    Challinor, Raymond 148
    Cole, G D H 118
    Colum, Padraic 105
    D'alton Rev E A 15
    Defoe, Daniel 88
    De Latocnage 30
    Dickens, Charles 69, 74, 87, 197, 210, 220,
        221, 227
    Elliot, George 218
    Engels, Frederick 84, 151
    Gaskell, Elizabeth 87, 159
    George, Henry 36, 225, 252
    Grousset, Paschal 17, 162
    Guizot, Francois 158
    James, Henry 224
    Hammond, JL 75
    Handley 62, 115
    Hobsbawn, John Ernest 192

Inglis, Henry David 45
Johnson, Dr Samuel 7
Kingsley, Charles 175, 224
Lawrence D H 194, 266
Le Blanc, Abe 90
Lecky, William Edward Hartpole 56
Lewis, George Cornewall 42, 84
Locke 31
Macaulay, Thomas Babington 99
MacDonagh 135, 193, 227, 246, 269
Marttineau, Harriett 67, 118, 144
Mill, John Stuart 30, 101, 118, 130, 160,
    165, 185, 204, 212, 216, 224, 225, 264,
    282
Molesworth, Mary Louisa 207
Molesworth, William 132
Molyneux, William 25
Morley, John 251
Morton, H.V. 285
O'Dowd, Anne 48
Price, Susan 138
Rousseau, Jean-Jacques 22
Ruskin, John 144, 183, 184, 217, 244
Russell, William Howard 196
Scott, Walter 59, 71, 87, 123
Shakespeare, William 273
Smiles, Samuel 3, 109, 183, 217
Smith, Sydney 106
Sommerville, Alexander 73, 75, 89, 90,
    102, 103
Southey, Robert 83
Stowe, Harriet Beecher 212
Swift, Jonathan 27, 36, 160
Thackeray, William Makepeace 184
Thompson, Flora 53
Thompson, E P 86, 103
Toynbee, Arnold 254
Trevelyan, George Macaulay 3, 200
Trollope, Anthony 33, 180, 244
Web, Sidney 93, 252
Williams, Frederick S 82
Young, Arthur 27, 79, 82, 84, 85, 91, 160
Zola, Emile 266